These United States

These United States

Original Essays by Leading
American Writers on Their
State Within the Union

EDITED BY JOHN LEONARD

Thunder's Mouth Press · Nation Books
New York

THESE UNITED STATES

Published by
Thunder's Mouth Press/Nation Books
245 West 17th St., 11th Floor
New York, NY 10011

Nation Books is a co-publishing venture of the Nation Institute and
Avalon Publishing Group Incorporated.

Library of Congress Cataloging-in-Publication Data is available.

ISBN 1-56025-285-5

9 8 7 6 5 4 3 2 1

Book design by Paul Paddock
Printed in the United States of America
Distributed by Publishers Group West

With a salute to the exemplars:
Grace Paley, Pete Seeger, and Studs Terkel.

CONTENTS

xiii INTRODUCTION
John Leonard

1 ALABAMA
Diane McWhorter

11 ALASKA
John Straley

21 ARIZONA
Charles Bowden

29 ARKANSAS
Gene Lyons

41 CALIFORNIA (NORTH)
Rebecca Solnit

50 CALIFORNIA (SOUTH)
Mike Davis

58 COLORADO
Thomas J. Noel

66 CONNECTICUT
Maureen Howard

75 DELAWARE
Eric Zencey

86 FLORIDA
T. D. Allman

96 GEORGIA
Jim Grimsley

102 HAWAII
Lee Siegel

112 IDAHO
Judith Freeman

122 ILLINOIS
Ana Castillo

133 INDIANA
Richard Lingeman

142 IOWA
Frank Conroy

148 KANSAS
Antonya Nelson

158 KENTUCKY
Dwight Allen

167 LOUISIANA
James Lee Burke

175 MAINE
Janwillem van de Wetering

183 MARYLAND
Wayne Karlin

190 MASSACHUSETTS
Elizabeth Benedict

198 MICHIGAN
Jim Harrison

206 MINNESOTA
David Mura

221 MISSISSIPPI
Steven Barthelme

231 MISSOURI
Gerald Early

241 MONTANA
Walter Kirn

249 NEBRASKA
Ron Hansen

257 NEVADA
Marc Cooper

266 NEW HAMPSHIRE
Donald Hall

271 NEW JERSEY
Luc Sante

277 NEW MEXICO
Tony Hillerman

287 NEW YORK (NEW YORK CITY)
Marshall Berman

307 NEW YORK (LONG ISLAND)
Tom Gogola

317 NEW YORK (UPSTATE)
JoAnn Wypijewski

331 NORTH CAROLINA
Jill McCorkle

338 NORTH DAKOTA
Larry Watson

345 OHIO
Kiki DeLancey

351 OKLAHOMA
Elizabeth Seay

362 OREGON
Joanne B. Mulcahy

371 PENNSYLVANIA
Kathryn Davis

379 PUERTO RICO
Rosario Ferré

391 RHODE ISLAND
Scott MacKay

400 SOUTH CAROLINA
MariJo Moore

408 SOUTH DAKOTA
Kathleen Norris

418 TENNESSEE
Nikki Giovanni

421 TEXAS
Molly Ivins

430 UTAH
Terry Tempest Williams

441 VERMONT
Jay Parini

447 VIRGINIA
David Berman

454 WASHINGTON
Sherman Alexie

464 WASHINGTON, D.C.
William Greider

475 WEST VIRGINIA
Michael Tomasky

485 WISCONSIN
John Nichols

495 WYOMING
Annie Proulx

509 ABOUT THE CONTRIBUTORS

521 ACKNOWLEDGMENTS

522 PERMISSIONS

IN THESE
UNITED STATES

John Leonard

Jean-Paul Sartre said somewhere that thought has its own geography. Since J.P., before sitting down to write books of philosophy, used to gun his mental motor on a peppy compound of aspirin and amphetamines, he might very well have been hallucinating. But suppose he wasn't? Suppose some thinking resembles the grandest of canyons, some a metropolis, some an igloo, a bunker, or a Love Canal? And then suppose, not altogether whimsically, that the formulation is reversible, that geography has its own thought: hither-and-thithering rivers, volcanic eruptions, deep ecology, desert solitaire, nuclear winter, mother earth, and weatherbirds— our childhood is speaking, or our political economy, or our vanished community, or our difficult exile, or the kindness of strangers and the idea of sanctuary.

Eighty-one years ago, on April 19, 1922, *The Nation* launched a series of forty-nine articles by a distinguished, skeptical, and contentious group of writers—novelists, journalists, educators, social workers, lawyers, unionists, maverick intellectuals— each of whom had been asked to contemplate his or her state of the union. Their essays, short but not at all sweet, were collected and published in two volumes, in

1923 and 1925, as *These United States: Portrait of America from the 1920s*, less a symposium than a remarkably evocative crazy quilt of styles and apprehensions, moods and meditations, art and anthropology, reportage and polemic. Local was to politics what location was to real estate.

We have invited a similar group of maverick minds to pick up in the new century where the likes of Edmund Wilson (New Jersey), H. L. Mencken (Maryland), W. E. B. DuBois (Georgia), Willa Cather (Nebraska), Theodore Dreiser (Indiana), and Sinclair Lewis (Minnesota) left off back in the jazz age. (As it happens, Indiana will receive its second look from the biographer of Dreiser and Lewis both, Richard Lingeman.) Ours is less of a jazz than a buzz age, so full of yak cable, white noise, advert/agit-prop videos, disinformation, and hypnotherapy, that sorting out the signals to arrive at scruple, gravity, or grace gets harder every day. It is also practically impossible to see the handmade for the homogenized anymore. While many Americans may be too nomadic to stay put and sink roots, most of us are also chained to the wheel of the nation-state mobile home, with network television as our windshield and the World Wide Web our weather. Still, seeing and sorting is what we asked these writers to do, as well as tell us something we didn't know, because New York editors are often the last to know what the rest of the country is really thinking. Nor did the editors particularly care about the form such thinking took. If we hoped for essays of 2,500 words or so, we were prepared to accept interior monologues, one-act plays, heroic couplets, even haiku.

We got—from Mike Davis and Rebecca Solnit on Southern and Northern California, and Kathryn Davis on Pennsylvania, and Michael Tomasky on West Virginia, and Molly Ivins on Texas, and Charles Bowden on Arizona, and Nikki Giovanni on Tennessee— everything from songs to sermons, including X-rays, autopsies, valentines, legal briefs, love letters, and arrest warrants. Maureen

Howard notices that not all the Native Americans in Connecticut were slaughtered by pious colonists ("We had sufficient light from the Word of God for our proceedings") in the Pequot War of 1637; witness their moneymaking resort complex of spas, pools, and casinos, not to mention their website, in a small state nevertheless big enough to accommodate Harriet Beecher Stowe and P. T. Barnum. Dwight Allen, on his way to a clogging contest at the World Chicken Festival, surprises us with the information that marijuana is one of Kentucky's major cash crops. Jill McCorkle takes us to Bald Head Island off the Atlantic coast of North Carolina, where Aaron Burr's daughter Theodosia disappeared on her way north to New York, probably abducted by pirates. Marshall Berman looks at a vulnerable New York City not only through his own eyes, but through those of Willy Loman, Allen Ginsberg, and Grandmaster Flash and the Furious Five:

> They pushed a girl in front of a train,
> Took her to a doctor, sewed her arm on again.
> Stabbed a man right through the heart,
> Gave him a transplant and a brand new start.

Sherman Alexie can't really expect us to believe that "Indian" is short for "indigenous," nor that the Kalispel Indians of what would later be called Washington State actually said to the Canadian explorer David Thompson on the Pend Oreille River: "Smelly white man, we give you our most sacred food, the salmon, who always returns to us, and we will accept your tobacco, and the many generations of tumors that will come with it." But there's no arguing with the fact that there were at least 5 and as many as 15 million Native Americans in 1492, and only 250,000 in 1900, which still doesn't explain why, besides Microsoft and Boeing, Washington is also the home state of so many serial killers.

MariJo Moore, who is part Cherokee, part Irish, and part Dutch, graduates from a moving account of the evolution of the Gullah language among West African slaves in the plantation fields of South Carolina to the chilling observation that there were Native American as well as African slaves, and Native American as well as white owners of those slaves; that Chickasaws sold Choctaws to the best bidder in Charleston in 1702; that 1,600 Cherokee slaves made the trip on the Trail of Tears to the Oklahoma territory in 1838.

Thinking about Missouri, Gerald Early mentions native-born writers like Mark Twain, T. S. Eliot, Kate Chopin, and Tennessee Williams, and seems distressed to note that Kansas City is now more populous than St. Louis. But what really seems to bother him most is that the same state that gave us Chuck Berry, Scott Joplin, Count Basie, and such Kansas City Monarchs as Buck O'Neill should wind up also producing Clarence Thomas. (And John Ashcroft!)

Whereas Alabama, according to Diane McWhorter, has decided to forgive and forget its racist past the better to cash in on the tourism opportunities afforded by the dramatic history of the civil rights movement, from Montgomery to Birmingham to Selma. McWhorter herself can't remember registering that four little girls had died in the bombing of Birmingham's Sixteenth Street Church in September 1963, "even though we all vividly recall our fellow white schoolchildren cheering the assassination that took place only two months later in Dallas." Perhaps, however, "the reason some of us have been able to confront the sins of the fathers is that we did not feel guilty. . . . We now have a generation of southerners who are laying down the burden of southern history, not in penitence but simply because they don't recognize it as something they owned."

Jim Harrison wonders where else, outside of Michigan, "can I live where I can see a large timber wolf on the two-track leading to my cabin?" Montana's real problem, says Walter Kirn, isn't Unabombers or militias, but the fact that the state is "close to last in per capita income" and "close to first in percentage of families living in poverty." Ron Hansen describes Nebraska thunderstorms that "are the stuff of horror movies: lashing rain and a far-off flash of light in the heavens, then the scratchy sound of sailcloth tearing until the fifty-megaton bomb goes off and children scream all over the neighborhood." Elizabeth Seay advises us from Oklahoma: "Always bring your own lawn chair to a powwow." Frank Conroy observes of Iowans after 9/11: "They are pissed, but they are calm." Annie Proulx notes that "Wyoming is full of contradictions and anomalies. The state thinks small and likes its elbow room." Janwillem van de Wetering, who has lived Down East for only thirty years, is reliably informed by a Zen native: "In Maine, if you don't care, it don't matter."

Rosario Ferré submits a history of Puerto Rico not to be found in any stateside textbook, from the unillusioned point of view of the people being stepped on. Marc Cooper, crossing the line into Nevada's outlaw state of mind, suddenly understands slot machines and ATMs as related totems, yin and yang. Luc Sante paints a pretty picture: "The predominant look of New Jersey these days is pale if not pastel, ostensibly cheerful, ornamented with gratuitous knobs and fanlights, manufactured in such a way that clapboard is indistinguishable from fiberglass—the happy meeting of postmodernism and heritage-themed zoning codes." While Judith Freeman is worried about what she can't see in Idaho: "The truth is no one really knows who's out there in the woods of the Northwest—harmless nature lovers? Or more dangerous types—people [Bo] Gritz has called 'Spikes'—Specially Prepared Individuals for Key Events." And David Berman, who has left Virginia five times and returned five times, considers it "the least 'rock and roll' of all the states I've lived in. Virginia may be for lovers, but it is not for hell-raisers."

This from someone whose father, wearing knee breeches, buckled shoes, and a tricorne hat, was a waiter at the King's Arms Tavern in

Colonial Williamsburg; someone who was born in Williamsburg in 1967, "exactly 360 years after the first British colony in North America was founded, down the road, at Jamestown. In mathematics 360 degrees is regarded as a return to zero. A flipping of the odometer"; someone who, as an undergraduate at the University of Virginia and a part-time orderly in a hospital morgue, "liked to stop in at an ancient drugstore where they sold the products of the Caswell-Massey company. George Washington and Thomas Jefferson wore their men's cologne and I loved to sniff a bottle with my eyes closed and pretend I had quietly snuck up behind Jefferson at Monticello, sleeping head-down at his roll-top desk, and inhaled the odor coming off his neck. Amazing, One could actually smell the founding fathers!"

In all, *These United States* has turned into a sort of rescue project, as if each of these writers sought to save another part of America from greed or banality or stereotyping—and, in the process, take the flag, and the Statue of Liberty, and "The Battle Hymn of the Republic" back from hate radio, Fox News, and the blogosphere; from the bullyboys, the pickleheads, and the wogstompers. Thinking about more than Louisiana, James Lee Burke speaks of a place each of us has in our hearts, like "a stained-glass cathedral visited by the people who are emblematic of our lives. . . .The special place where I live is full of Americans who to me are heroic: Dorothy Day, the Maryknolls who were martyred in El Salvador, Molly Brown, Joe Hill, Thomas Jefferson, Woody Guthrie, the women and children in the Ludlow Massacre of 1914, Audie Murphy, and Flannery O'Connor. And once again, the great irony is that the bravest people I've ever known are people who are so humble and nondescript you cannot remember what they look like ten minutes after they leave a room. But in the final say each of them is a descendant of Natty Bumppo."

We are reminded again and again in these essays not only of our monumental beauty, from the Grand Canyon to the Lincoln Memorial to the Golden Gate Bridge to the Chrysler Building. And of our shrewd investments, from public schools to land-grant universities to lending libraries to Planned Parenthood. And of our brilliant inventions, from baseball to jazz to blue jeans. And of our exemplary citizens, from Eugene Debs to Margaret Sanger to Rosa Parks to Cesar Chavez to Allen Ginsberg. And of our talking heads, from Nathaniel Hawthorne's Goodman Brown (shouting "'Faith' in a voice of agony and desperation") to Herman Melville's Ishmael and Mark Twain's Huck and J. D. Salinger's Holden and Saul Bellow's Augie and Toni Morrison's Beloved. But also of our sacred texts—the Bill of Rights, Henry David Thoreau's essay on civil disobedience, Abe Lincoln's Second Inaugural, Walt Whitman's "Democratic Vistas" and Dr. Martin Luther King, Jr.'s "Letter from a Birmingham Jail."

Consider this our very own reality programming.

As Molly Ivins observed for the ages, "Given all the horseshit, there's bound to be a pony in here somewhere."

ALABAMA

THE PAST IS STILL NOT PAST

Diane McWhorter

Sometimes it seems as if Alabama has turned into a giant historical marker. That's the way we've always liked it, of course. Typically our cherished history has taken on the form of fusty bric-a-brac, like Indian mounds, Civil War forges, white columns. The real landmarks—latter-day battlegrounds for freedom that more than offset the paucity of actual Civil War engagements on local soil—were obscured for a generation under a mist of collective amnesia.

But 'Bama has slowly been waking up to its chloroformed past—the mid-twentieth-century turning point still known as "the modern civil rights era." The "it's all coming back to me" eye-fluttering started in the mid 1980s, as scholars and graying players gathered in symposia to pool primary sources and memory. Next came formal authentication: plaques on bridges and bus stations to commemorate the blood spilled there for justice; museums to preserve the past (and put it to rest under glass). And finally we are in the redemption stage. It began with calls for "closure"—cheap grace for the white folk—but now seems to be moving toward a richer, integrated hybrid of spirituality and Chamber of Commerce-ness: reconciliation.

The history so long repressed inside Alabama is ironically the state's claim to fame throughout the rest of the world. It is the bracing American past to which the present seems compelled—far more than to that other formative mid-century conflict, the Vietnam War. The civil rights epoch opened with the Montgomery Bus Boycott of 1955–56, which moved the struggle out of the courtroom and onto the streets—and catapulted into history the green young Reverend Dr. Martin Luther King, Jr. Birmingham, 1963, was the movement's masterstroke, toppling the institution of segregation and producing the era's indelible icons—King's nonviolent school-age demonstrators facing down the city's police dogs and fire hoses, and four girls killed by Klan dynamite a few months later at the Sixteenth Street Baptist Church. In 1965, the Selma to Montgomery march provided the thrilling valedictory of the movement's integrationist season, prompting the federal voting rights act that enfranchised African-Americans. And the Montgomery-Birmingham-Selma trifecta doesn't even take into account only slightly lesser doozies, such as the mob attacks against the Freedom Rides of 1961, and Governor George Wallace's 1963 "Stand in the Schoolhouse Door" to fulfill his vow of "Segregation forever!" at the University of Alabama.

Why, of all the Deep South options, was Alabama destined to be the country's ultimate racial destination: Armageddon? "Thank God for Mississippi" next door had the benightedness title sewn up, as the Heart of Darkness to our Heart of Dixie. But that was its problem. Mississippi could not muster enough of an opposition to give the segregationists a media-worthy fight. Georgia, though its politics were often more heinous than Alabama's, had finessed a benign glow of Babbittry from Atlanta's distinction as the world headquarters for Coca-Cola. Somehow, Alabama had matched good versus evil in a real contest—and in Technicolor vivid enough for instant mass perception.

The best theater of the civil rights era was provided by Birmingham's kamikaze of a movement reverend, Fred Shuttlesworth, double-dog-daring the city's redneck dictator, Bull Connor, the keeper of the police dogs and fire hoses. (Commissioner Connor left the heavy lifting to his protégé inside the Ku Klux Klan, "Dynamite Bob" Chambliss, who dealt with Shuttlesworth's temerity by blowing up his church.) Before that there was Alabama's hormone-rich behemoth of a liberal governor, "Big Jim" (aka "Kissin Jim") Folsom, ridiculing the well-heeled Dixiecrats, who had railed against "pool-mixin" at their founding in Birmingham in 1948. Seven years later, Big Jim pushed his integrationist views too far when he invited the Harlem congressman Adam Clayton Powell over to the mansion for a politically fatal Scotch and soda. And even earlier, Hugo Black, the Birmingham ambulance-chaser (and Klansman, but that's another story) turned New Deal architect, lashed Alabama's powerful anti-Roosevelt reactionaries from the U.S. Senate before taking his harsh progressivism to the Supreme Court. The three-ring morality circus that was twentieth-century Alabama also featured a wonderful supporting cast running the gamut from the boozy mountebank of a Methodist minister who revived the Ku Klux Klan in 1915, to the Depression sharecroppers who mounted a Communist-inspired uprising in the plantation-studded Black Belt, all the way back to the equivocal Booker T. Washington, practicing the black magic of accommodation as the "Wizard of Tuskegee Institute."

The genius of Alabama is that, for all the Dixie idiosyncrasies, it held up a mirror to the entire nation. As the heavy-manufacturing anomaly of the Deep South, Birmingham brought segregation to a modern industrial setting and exposed with X-ray clarity its skeleton of economic interest: racial strife was fomented by the tough industrialists known as "Big Mules" in order to keep the biracial work force divided, labor unions meek, and wages depressed. Because the local steel industry was dominated by absentee owners from up north, Birmingham spread the shame of the South around the country. U.S. Steel, for example, was the force behind a local fake-grassroots organization called the League to Maintain White Supremacy, seeing that its southern fiefdom was not only "the Pittsburgh of the South" but also "the Johannesburg of America."

Then there was the state's most popular political export: George Wallace. In 1963, Governor Wallace seemed to be a national pariah, accused by President Kennedy among other eminent Americans of fostering the context of violent defiance that led to the bombing of the Sixteenth Street Baptist Church that September. The following year, however, the first of Wallace's surprisingly strong runs for president confirmed that racial demagoguery played well on the other side of the Mason-Dixon. He turned out to be the John the Baptist of the conservative gospel that has since pervaded the civic conversation—about affirmative action, states' rights, welfare.

We as a nation have always looked south to track our progress in expiating the country's original sin of slavery. It is a no-lose proposition. If those racists down there have repented, that's good news for America. And if they haven't, even better! The white man's burden—the modern version of which is the pressure *not* to be considered racist—stays isolated in the lower right-hand corner of the map.

The new twist on this is the transformation of Alabama's own role in the redemption process: from resistance to acceptance. Even during our heyday of infamy, white southerners had been adamant that there wasn't anything peculiarly noteworthy about Our Way of Life. The year after Selma, when I toured Europe with a group of students from Denver, Colorado, I couldn't understand why our local guides insisted on meeting "the girl from Alabama." I figured they were interested in my cute accent and Scarlett O'Hara head toss, but instead they wanted to know about Selma, George Wallace, and "Martin Lutterking." I wasn't sure what appalled me more: that they would think I might be acquainted with a Negro "agitator" like King or that they would place me in the same social class as George Wallace, whom I considered the worst politician imaginable next to a

Kennedy. The southern stereotype of tacky rednecks disturbed me more than the disgrace of my hometown as the host of a church bombing that took the lives of four black Sunday-school girls.

And yet, when the white people did acknowledge Birmingham's reputation as what King had called "the most segregated city in America," it was with a certain vanity. There was an old joke about a black man in Chicago who wakes up one morning and tells his wife that Jesus came to him in a dream and told him to go to Birmingham.

"Did Jesus say he'd go with you?" asks the horrified wife.

"He said he'd go as far as Memphis."

Memphis's mystique as the home of Elvis remained relatively uncompromised by the King assassination. But an Alabama dateline in the national press invariably announced racial controversy. Like clockwork, northern journalists tromped down to some old civil rights battlefield on every multiple-of-five anniversary. White Alabama rigidly averted its gaze.

The state began to blink in 1986, the year a national holiday was dedicated to Martin Luther King. The ordinary folks of Selma, Montgomery, and Birmingham began staking their claim on the extraordinary historical moment solely owned, as far as much of the public was concerned, by Dr. King. Like competing Freudian sects, movement partisans combed through the King dreamscape and caviled over a seemingly boundless supply of key participants and what-really-happeneds. Rosa Parks—phooey! The unsung hero of the Montgomery Bus Boycott was E. D. Nixon, the sleeping-car porter unionist who had instigated the "refuse-to-ride" movement and tapped a reluctant King as its leader. (Or "spokesman," as some of the indigenous activists invidiously referred to King, who hailed, after all, from Atlanta.) But wait. Historians were soon on to a *new* real unsung heroine of the boycott—the mystery woman who had already written, mimeographed, and distributed leaflets announcing the boycott *before* Nixon had solidified any plans. Jo Ann Robinson, an English professor at a black college in Montgomery, kept her contribution hidden for decades: the college president had been so apoplectic about her using the school's mimeograph machine (thus putting him in jeopardy with the all-white legislature he answered to) that he swore her to nearly eternal secrecy. Oohs of gratification greeted the unveiling of Robinson's role at a symposium held at the Alabama Department of Archives and History on the boycott's thirtieth anniversary. That event—in 1986—was said to be the first state-sponsored observance of a civil rights milestone.

A correction was taking place. What had up till now been a story of "bad" (white) Alabama was turning into a story of moral triumph: the black folks' narrative. Alabama's perennial governor, George Wallace, had himself made a dramatic transition to redemption, going beyond the obligatory apologies to confessions of wrongdoing. His retirement in decent standing as an integrationist earned the state the most goodwill it had received in years. That was also in 1986.

The Establishment began to adjust its attitude toward the historic struggle that had once been synonymous with "unfavorable business climate." In the spring of 1986, the Birmingham Chamber of Commerce pledged unprecedented support for a civil rights museum. The mayor at the time, David Vann (who as a liberal young lawyer back in 1963 had engineered the ouster of Bull Connor from city hall) recognized that "what had been 'bad publicity' made Birmingham an attraction to a lot of people": when the United Negro College Fund chose the city for its annual meeting, it was the first time there had ever been 100 percent attendance. Still, the civil rights museum remained a paper entity for nearly seven years. The white business leaders had been hard-pressed to part with their mantra of "Why can't we forget about all that?" Finally they began to understand, as Vann wryly observed, that the best way to put the past behind them was to label it history and place it in the museum. That seemed to be the effect, if not the intention, on a national scale, of the federal holiday for Martin Luther King: confine his work and memory to one calendar day a year.

Over and over, history has borne out a corollary to Frederick Douglass' famous observation that "power concedes nothing without a demand." Power also tends to concede only as much as it must in order to preserve itself. White Alabama's burgeoning civil rights self-consciousness sometimes seemed like the minimum concession the haves made to the have-nots in order to serve the economic imperatives of inequity once enforced by segregation. Absent from the efforts to acknowledge the ugly past was any notion that somebody was responsible for it. One might have gotten the impression that this terrible system of state-sponsored racism had spontaneously generated and then converted just as spontaneously into the sterile typeface of history textbooks. There was no admission of guilt or exposure of the guilty, no reparations or even apologies to the sufferers (except from Wallace). This strategy of denial might have worked, the past might have simply faded away, if it hadn't been for one thing: children had been murdered in the name of that now alien civilization, and the killers still lived among us, free and unpunished.

The bombing of Birmingham's Sixteenth Street Baptist Church was the spot Alabama could not expunge. The four girls—Denise McNair, Carole Robertson, Addie Mae Collins, Cynthia Wesley—were, in death, segregation's deathless victims, incapable of accepting Wallace's regrets. Perhaps they—and their dead counterparts around the South—were the reason that there were so few repentant segregationists. To confess to past sins might entail responsibility for murdering the young. The social consensus about the church bombers was that they were lunatic demons who had nothing to do with the rest of the city's law-abiding bigots.

Hannah Arendt wrote, in *Eichmann in Jerusalem*, of the apathy of postwar Germans toward the Nazi war criminals in their midst:

"They did not much care one way or the other, and did not particularly mind the presence of murderers at large in the country, since none of them were likely to commit murder of their own free will; however, if world opinion . . . became obstinate and demanded that these people be punished, they were perfectly willing to oblige, at least up to a point." Likewise, various law-enforcement bodies—the FBI, the state and city police—periodically reopened the Sixteenth Street case, satisfying the "up to a point."[1] Other dormant civil rights cases around the South were perfunctorily revived when there was some indignation from the national news media. Then suddenly, after thirty years, as if waiting for some biblical generation to elapse: justice. In 1994, the conviction of Byron de la Beckwith for the 1963 murder of the NAACP leader Medgar Evers led off a series of belated prosecutions of old civil rights crimes in Mississippi. Then, in May 2000, Alabama trumped its neighbor state with incredible news: two men, the last living suspects in the Sixteenth Street Baptist Church bombing, had been indicted for the murders of Denise, Addie, Carole, and Cynthia.

I am working on a theory about why these cases are finally, now, being unearthed from their shallow graves of oblivion. It runs counter to the conventional one of, you know, "closure." That had been the angle of the international media covering the trial of the first suspect, Tommy Blanton, in the spring of 2001. Everyone had been expecting a redemption drama: Birmingham expiates its signature sin. But instead of confessing collective civic guilt, the public reacted to the trial with yawning apathy, resulting from nearly forty years of mass denial that the community had anything to atone for.

1. In 1977, a liberal young state attorney general, Bill Baxley, won a conviction against "Dynamite Bob" Chambliss for his role in the church bombing, but Baxley claimed to have suffered politically because of his pursuit of the case.

History works in mysterious ways. It may be that the prosecutions themselves were an unintended, affirmative consequence of the city's failure of moral imagination. Most of the people involved in bringing these "reconciliation cases" back to life—the journalists, scholars, and public servants—were children at the time of the crimes, the last generation to grow up under segregation. The prosecutors of the church bombers were white sons of Birmingham who, like me, have no memory of hearing that the Sixteenth Street church had been bombed in September 1963, even though we all vividly recall our fellow white schoolchildren cheering the assassination that took place only two months later in Dallas.

Perhaps the reason some of us have been able to confront the sins of the fathers is that we did *not* feel guilty. The repudiation of the past meant that we hadn't "dealt" with shame, but it also meant we hadn't masked it with phony ideals and rationales. All southerners have heard those arguments that the Civil War "wasn't really over slavery." But one rarely encountered apologies for segregation, beyond the insistence of the professional racists that what they had *really* been fighting against was the "federal government" and "Communism." And so, when we were exposed as adults to the most stomach-turning banalities of evil—church bombers at large in the community—the reaction was pure: those bastards can't get away with this.

Such is the convoluted course of progress, often requiring an aerial view to discern the bend toward justice. We now have a generation of southerners who are laying down the burden of southern history, not in penitence but because they simply don't recognize it as something they owned. Yet even as the skulls in the mirror recede, Alabama continues to provide the country a reflection of itself, all the more challenging for its obliqueness.

During the year between the 2001 conviction of Tommy Blanton and the trial of the final church-bombing suspect, in the spring of

2002, a landmark building, in another exceptional American city, had been turned to rubble by terrorists. I think 9/11 explains why the second trial, of Bobby Frank Cherry, was so different from Blanton's, with none of the first one's emotional hard sell of the "four little girls" or the rueful tsk-tsking about the bad old days. Suddenly, every juror, every American, could appreciate what it had been like to be an African-American living under a constant death threat in a segregated South before the word "terrorism" was in common parlance. The Cherry trial seemed to transcend the self-conscious regional rites of reconciliationism. Its very lack of melodrama elevated it into an American redemption drama, offsetting the terror of the past with ordinary protocols of a society that will keep trying to get it right, no matter how long it takes. Yet recognizing that we will never get it right: no one believed that our national innocence had been restored by a life sentence for Bobby Frank Cherry. The age of "closure" had come to a close on September 11.

New whirlwinds inevitably loom on the Alabama horizon, and they will be embarrassing, yes. But also perversely reassuring: reminders that we do, after all, live in a country that is capable of shame.

ALASKA

WOBBLIES IN ALASKA: WHO OWNS AN UNCAUGHT FISH

John Straley

O n stormy days Bill Hills and I used to sit under the nursing home's covered porch. There are so many storms in Sitka, Alaska, some months we met there every day. Fishing boats running in from the storm passed each other in the channel, the wind in their rigging sending a clatter up the seawall to where we sat in our rocking chairs. I asked questions mostly and the old man would stare out across the lawn, lost in memory as if he could see beyond the harbor to the Gulf of Alaska where the storm swells lined up like vast regiments into the distance. I asked him to tell me one more time about his experiences as a union man in the Industrial Workers of the World. I asked him to tell me about what happened in Centralia, and he'd start by saying, "Goddamn bastards hung a Wobbly."

On November 11, 1919, some members of the Centralia, Washington, Industrial Workers of the World opened fire on a group of American Legionnaires who were either thinking about or were actually in the process of destroying the Wobbly Hall as their patriotic duty. What started the shooting remains mired in partisan debate, but the aftermath is clear: four Legionnaires were killed by Wobblies and a union member named Wesley Everest was taken from his jail cell and lynched. The international furor over the shootings (though not over the lynching) caused the Washington authorities to enforce the sedition laws making membership in the IWW a jailable offense. Wobblies began leaving Washington, some fading into the woods of Montana and Oregon. Some of them rode boats up the coast to southeastern Alaska. Bill Hills was one of those men.

Alaska was then, and remains, a good place for anarchists. There are 600,000 people in an area one-fifth the size of the lower 48 with three times the coastline. It is a place where the sun can disappear for months at a time, then return in the summer and refuse to leave. It is the territory of boom or bust, of fresh starts and few questions. The Wobblies who came north were able to make a home for themselves.

I met Bill before his days in the nursing home. It was 1978, and Bill was living in a cabin built in a snug cove called Greentop, north of Sitka. He was uncommonly strong back then, particularly for a seventy-eight-year-old man. He had a full white beard and just a slight tremor in his right hand. He wore wool pants with suspenders. His shirts smelled vaguely of diesel fuel and cooked cabbage. He fished a wooden hand troller, a small boat used for catching salmon by dragging hooks through the ocean. I was in Greentop working on a trail crew for the Forest Service. Bill started asking me about my wages. He wanted to know how much the crew boss made. He wanted to know how much the boss back in the office in Sitka was making. He suggested we ought to stick up for ourselves. Even then, Bill was an unrepentant Red.

Greentop sits out on the remote coast on the edge of a wilderness area. There were three cabins in the cove. Bill and his brother, Jim, lived in one, Joe Scott in another, and the third was owned by someone who was dead by the time I arrived, known to me only as "the old man." The men hunted deer and fished from their small boats. Humpback whales, once hunted to near extinction, fed on herring in the old men's fishing grounds. Bill sold a few fish for cash to a buyer who anchored in the cove during the summer. Joe was a remarkable gardener. A short growing season in a country with up to a hundred inches of rain makes for difficult gardening, but his garden was a wonder of hard-won productivity. He loved flowers, and thought of gaudy flowers the same way he thought of beautiful women.

Long before, Bill and Jim had tried to organize a Troller's Union. Trollers were, and still are, an independent lot, but Bill felt certain that if they stuck together they could force higher prices from the fish buyers. "Trying to organize fishermen," Bill told me, "was like trying to herd a bunch of goddamn cats."

Alaskans are known for being cranky and independent. Getting them to agree on any collective principle, such as the need for taxes, or even funding state government, has always seemed a little like cat-herding. In 1978, oil money was flowing through the pipe and stories of the boom times in the Kodiak king crab fishery abounded. A policeman from Dutch Harbor once told me about a couple of drunken deckhands sitting on the edge of a pier having a contest to see who could throw their Rolex watches farthest out in the bay. It hardly seemed the time or place to talk about the exploitation of the workers. We were awash in money. Even then, Alaskans knew it wouldn't last and we joked about it. There was a bumper sticker that read: PLEASE GOD, SEND US ANOTHER BOOM. WE PROMISE NOT TO PISS THIS ONE AWAY.

Sitting in Greentop on that warm summer day surrounded by bright flowers and fresh-caught salmon, I thought I had found an old seditionist's paradise. Here, the workers owned the fish, here they reaped the direct benefit of their labor. This romance I was experiencing is part of the dream still embedded in the lure of the north, but is Alaska by any stretch of the imagination a place where a radical philosophy could take root? Consider this letter from the February 2002 issue of *Alaska Fisherman's Journal*:

When the housewife pays for a can of salmon, the fisherman receives only three percent of the overall price. To whom does the remaining 97 percent go? . . . I feel that there are several things to look at when seeking answers to the recovery of our salmon industry. Most importantly is the ownership of the fish. When the fisherman sells his fish for $.40 per pound, he understands that he is relinquishing ownership of the fish. Similarly the housewife understands when she buys the fish that she accepts ownership of the fish. We need to understand the lines of ownership in between the fisherman and the housewife.

Here are the old machinations of class and exploitation. Here is a worker asserting his ownership of the resource and wanting control of the means of production. It could be Centralia, Washington, in 1919. Who owns the land? Who owns the fish?

For the most part, state biologists have wisely managed the fisheries, but today it's the fishermen themselves who feel threatened with extinction. Most fisheries are flush with fish. In many cases there are too many fish for the processors to keep up with, but the world markets have conspired against the industry, which, like family farming, works to preserve a sensible lifestyle. In that same *Alaska Fisherman's Journal* is an article entitled "Alaska Fisheries Outlook: Radical Surgery or Slow Death?" by an executive from a fish-processing company. It lays out the dangers in the modern fishing economy: the strong dollar, the threat of fish farming, the decline in Japanese buying power, the increased competition caused by globalized markets, and the reentry of the Russians into the fishing economy. These forces combine to drive down fish prices and make it harder for the independent "owners" of the fish to make a profit. The sidebar in the article brought the point home. There, set off from the fishing story, was a graph giving facts about the cost of raising chickens. In 1952, Americans ate 9 pounds of chicken per capita, it took 15 weeks to raise a chicken to maturity, and Tyson Foods made a million dollars from chicken sales. In 1995, Americans ate 72 pounds of chicken, it took 8 weeks to raise a marketable bird, and Tyson Chicken made 6.4 billion dollars.

When it comes to creating marketable protein, American agribusiness is efficient. Certainly more efficient than paying a bunch of hunter-gatherers to drag little hooks around in the ocean.

This is the nightmare of every fishing family in Alaska: that they will soon be selling their boats and going to a job walking a metal catwalk, throwing food pellets to a pen full of engineered salmon.

Bill's brother, Jim, died out at Greentop in 1975. He had been sick for a few weeks and had avoided calling a plane to take him into town to see the doctor. He was seventy-three, and he and Bill had lived together almost continuously their whole lives. Bill stayed on at Greentop a few years by himself, but life there on the coast was turning bitter. His health declined and so too did his relationship with Joe Scott. Some slight had festered there in the cove so that the two men barely spoke. Finally Bill decided to sell out and move to town. Unfortunately he didn't have much to sell. The brothers had leased their land from the Forest Service, so Bill got what he could for the old cabin and his few tools from a pair of young fishermen and moved into the Pioneers' Home. There he got nursing care, a room, a bed, and three hot meals a day, and although he was grateful for it, he missed his brother. He missed his old life. "I wish those young fellas good luck," he told me. "Fishing's a fine life, I guess, just not too much to show for it."

Who owns the land? Who owns the fish? These questions underlie the Alaskan economy. But when starting in on the question, it must be remembered that before written history, before deeds, economic theory, and just a few years before Greentop was a garden spot for the old Wobblies, this tight little anchorage on the northern coast belonged to the Tlingit people.

Greentop sits close to the site of the first landing of white men in this part of North America. In 1741, Vitus Bering was a Danish sea captain in the employ of the Russian czar. He had tried to find the "great land" to the east in 1728 but had failed to sight the mainland. In July 1741, the captain of the expedition's second ship, Aleksey Chirikov, sighted land that must have been close to Greentop. From there he traveled a short distance to the north and sent a boat ashore for fresh water. A heavy fog shrouded the coastline and the long boats rowed steadily into it. The boat containing the first Europeans onto the mainland of Alaska did not return to the ship. Chirikov sent another, and *that* boat did not return. Chirikov returned to Kamchatka without his lost crew members. But other ships soon followed the new route to Alaska.

The Russian era was marked by a kind of boozy capitalism that received little real state support. They were after sea-otter pelts and pressed the indigenous people of the Aleutian Islands into service. Yet even with slave labor, the Russians had problems making a profit. Moscow and St. Petersburg were almost half a world away and the czars had their own troubles: Napoleon, the Enlightenment, and the Crimean War. By the middle of the nineteenth century they decided to fold their North American enterprise.

In 1868, when the Russians sold the Alaska Territory to the United States, the official transfer ceremony took place in Sitka. Here, Europeans lived inside a walled settlement made up of a few log buildings. Tlingit Indians were let through the gates during daylight hours to trade. When the transfer ceremony took place, it's easy to imagine that the Tlingits assumed the Russians were deeding over the little plot of ground inside their compound. It would be hard for anyone to fathom the great expanse of land that was changing hands with the stroke of the pen.

This new world imposed a new economy on this place the Russians called the "great land." Not that there hadn't been booms and busts in the natural world of the Alaska natives. Populations of wild game periodically rose and fell and occasionally crashed, and human populations dependent on the game suffered greatly sometimes and then adjusted. But the booms and busts of the European era had more withering effects because they were intentional, created by one group of people in disregard for the welfare of others. In Russian times, the once abundant sea otter was hunted almost to extinction before fashions changed and the market collapsed. The Aleut people were enslaved in service of this market. By the late 1800s, commercial whalers had decimated bowhead whale and walrus populations, causing starvation in Eskimo villages along the Arctic coast. Then came the fish traps that blocked spawning streams, seriously deflating prodigious runs of salmon that had once seemed as plentiful as the water itself.

One of the smaller but surely the craziest economic booms occurred in 1958, when the Atomic Energy Commission proposed using a chain of five nuclear explosions to blow a huge hole in the Arctic coast that could serve as a harbor. This project, named "Project Chariot," had as its avid proponent the most noted physicist of the day, Edward Teller. Teller promised the people of the north that there would be no ill effects from the blast. He also promised that at least three-quarters of the five million dollars set aside for the project would be spent right here in Alaska, which helped to gain powerful support in the territorial legislature. It took a galvanizing effort from the people of bush Alaska to stop the explosions. Native people, worried about the effects of radiation on their food chain, railed against the nonsensical assurance of the experts. Eventually, Project Chariot was scrapped. It was the village councils' opposition to this incredible plan that helped to spur the movement for native self-government.

Today Alaska is an oil state. In March 1968, ARCO announced that their discovery well on the north slope was flowing at 1,152 barrels of oil a day. In June another well found oil, and it confirmed that

Prudoe Bay was a major discovery. But this time the newly awakened Native community, led by veterans of the Project Chariot resistance and a new generation of Native leaders experienced in litigation, demanded a settlement on their land claims before the oil could be moved to market. The resulting Alaska Native Land Claims Settlement Act of 1971 parceled out land to competing interests and established Native corporations that imbedded Alaska's indigenous people firmly into the capitalist model. The new Native corporations provided money and a cooperative business structure to their shareholders, though some argued that the corporations threatened the autonomy of their cultural existence. Traditional people found themselves caught between two worlds. The life they lived, once grounded in tradition and memory, was overlaid with new values and new loyalties. They are now both hunter-gatherers and corporate citizens with responsibilities to the corporate bottom line.

Today we live in an Alaska where everybody is in the oil business. Radio announcers read the price of West Coast Crude on the morning news right along with the weather, and where many of the Eskimo citizens of the north slope both treasure their heritage and support the drilling of oil in the Arctic National Wildlife Refuge. At the same time, the Gwich'in Indians point to the dangers oil development will pose to the caribou they count on for their subsistence.

More than 80 percent of Alaska's revenue comes from the taxes on oil. This is the money that builds our schools and paves our roads. Oil money supports the state-run retirement home where Bill Hills and Joe Scott spent the last years of their lives. As of today (March 2002) Alaskans have no state sales or income tax, and in 2001, each man, woman, and child received nearly two thousand dollars as our dividend from the Permanent Fund established as the people's share of the oil royalties. Some of my friends, queasy about getting oil money, give their yearly Permanent Fund checks to environmental groups or needy charities. Last year my family of three gave some of our dividend money to our son's school for field trips, some to an animal shelter, and some to a local arts group, but this year our income had dropped and we put our three dividend checks into our bank account to pay bills, and I was grateful for the money. We still gave to our charities, but less than before. The oil money is what made it possible for us to give any at all. For years now Sitka's public radio station has held a yearly fund-raiser timed for the month when the Permanent Fund checks are mailed out. Airlines offer special "Permanent Fund Getaway" tickets. In the last twenty-five years the Permanent Fund has become a part of Alaska's culture.

Among the spoiled people of the world, Alaskans may be some of the most spoiled. On one hand we think of ourselves as independent citizens of the frontier. On the other, we have become dependent on a pool of wealth that the majority of us did nothing to create. Not only do we depend on this wealth, we demand it as a right. Yet, even as rich as we are, unmet needs abound. Vast regions still need hospitals and septic systems. We need good schools with auditoriums and computers. Alcoholism and domestic violence are disproportionately prevalent here. Of the fifty states, Alaska ranks 1st in its per capita incidents of sexual assault. We are twentieth-century people, but too many of us still live in untenable conditions.

Bill Hills died in Sitka's Pioneers' Home in 1987. Several months before his death he asked his friends to make sure the FBI didn't send an agent to fingerprint his body before burial. "They'll be wanting to close out their files," he said. As far as I know, no one ever did bother to take his prints, and I never did find out why they would be so interested in him. Bill never told me of any crimes he and his brother might have committed, but then there were lots of things he didn't tell me. Bill Hills didn't have a lot to show for himself when he died. He didn't leave much behind, and he took his fingerprints with him.

I pass by the Pioneers' Home every day. The small boats still come and go from the harbor, and old faces still stare out the windows.

Many people choose to leave Alaska when they grow old. The climate is hard. Winters can be one long series of storms battering the window glass, and some summers slip past almost unnoticed. But the ones who stay, like Bill and Jim, grow to love the storms. They love the wild flailing of the spruce trees as the wind sizzles up the mountains. They love the sensation that rises in their chests when they look out at the ocean swells rolling in from the west. Here, they think, is the place beyond mortality. Here is the place where those myriad uncaught fish belong only to themselves.

ARIZONA

D.O.A.

Charles Bowden

They live on the edge of the nation and the edge of the state and the edge of life. And now they seem to be going over that final edge and spilling into the land of death. The rain failed last winter, the rains have been failing for half a decade here, and then the spring brought dust. The summer monsoon was late and feeble. Now there are perhaps thirty-three *Antilocapra americana sonoriensis*, Sonoran pronghorn, an all but extinct subspecies, wandering their last two-thousand-square-mile redoubt against the Mexican line. Hardly anyone in my state knows that they exist. They, and their cousins in Mexico (doomed bands totaling perhaps two or three hundred), have pioneered the driest ground of their species on this continent, land with one to three inches of rain per year. The pronghorn are living in the elemental Arizona and now as they brush against doom my species is bringing them help in the only way we seem to know: our denial that Arizona exists at all. We are proposing to plant four patches of irrigated ground of six acres each to give them a basis for life. Of course, for years beyond counting they flourished without our cares.

But then Interstate 5 denied them access to the bottomlands of the Gila River, and before that our agriculture largely murdered the

Gila River by damming the water far upstream, and after that our irrigation project, the notorious Wellton-Mohawk Project, renowned in federal circles as possibly the most uneconomic scheme ever floated in our conquest of the desert, fenced them out of what bottomlands had persisted.

They are beneath contempt in the Sunbelt hype that is the state's self-image. But they are the real bottom line of life here.

I was there in the early eighties when science first learned they could make sounds—a buck captured by a net dropped from a chopper suddenly cut loose with a bloodcurdling cry as we probed it for rectal temperature and for blood. Until late in the twentieth century, we did not even know if they drank water (they do) or persisted off the moisture in plant tissue. Now they are going and we are still coming. Arizona has over five million people, with no end in sight. The grizzly is gone, the wolf faint as a reintroduction program barely keeps up with the penchant of locals for killing them on sight. Homo sapiens are the new biology, one almost completely clustered in two metroplexes, Phoenix and Tucson, both based on a denial of the ground under their feet.

I have lived here most of my life and I have learned a few hard truths. There is no Arizona identity; the name conjures up no person or type. Once, in the brief settlement gore of the late nineteenth century, an Arizonan meant an outlaw, some border-jumping scum full of violence and theft. Now the state is faceless and has all the charm and charisma of tract housing. In part this is because hardly anyone here is committed to being here—migration is constantly gnawed at by out-migration as newcomers take a look around and then flee. For every ten people who settled in Arizona in the 1980s, seven left. There is another reason for the facelessness and this constitutes the core fact of the state. People came here to begin over, to correct the mistakes of life and have a new go at things. And by this act, they have created failure on a massive scale.

Here is what failure looks like: Arizona ranks 1st in the nation in crime, 46th in the ability of its citizens to find food. Arizona ranks 48th in the ability of its citizens to house themselves, 44th in the percentage of its citizens living below the poverty line. Like any right-to-work state, Arizona offers miserable wages—33 percent of the citizens of Tucson stagger along in what is gamely called the service industry. The medical system is collapsing as federal funds vanish and as new residents without money or insurance pour into the state. The educational system in its plucky way stays just ahead of Mississippi and other centers of learning. The sky is slowly dying from pollution, the water table declining from over-pumping (one town north of Tucson, Eloy, has dropped fourteen feet in a half century as the ground compacts from water withdrawal). The entire state is savagely overgrazed—a quirk that contributed to the giant forest fire last summer that consumed in one gulp five hundred square miles of pine. Mines, once a mainstay, are declining. But not from lack of effort—there are over a hundred thousand abandoned mine shafts and the state looks remarkably like Swiss cheese.

All this is managed by a comic government (in the last fifteen years, one governor was impeached, a second fell on her head and never seemed quite the same again, and a third had to resign to deal with some messy felony charges). Corruption here is a tradition: in the late 1870s when the Southern Pacific railroad tried to bribe the territorial legislature with $25,000, the governor returned $20,000 and noted the railroad had no sense of local prices. The state government is selected by people who have barely arrived here and seldom vote anyway. Over 70 percent of the ground is federal (large chunks of it reservations) and ruled by distant bureaucrats in Washington. Lately, the grinding poverty of the twenty-three tribes (Arizona hosts the largest Native American population in the country, with some reservations the size of eastern states) has been temporarily papered over with casino gambling, an unaudited income transference from retirees to tribal bureaucrats. The business class is at best third-rate since it has fed for generations off real estate speculations, a habit that hardly stimulates invention and rewards any player who can remain breathing while raw dirt rises in value. All the traditional economic activities (mining, farming, and ranching) are dying and of little consequence except for their frisky destruction of the land.

Given these facts I arrive at a passionate position: I love it here.

I love it here because the ground is dangerous and beautiful and smashes any human fantasies of ultimate control. I love it here because Mexico is near and the lies and fables of our nation's fabled heartland cannot be sustained here as the largest folk movement in the history of our planet—the flight of the Mexican poor north— streams across my ground. But mainly I love it here because I know I live in the future while people in other parts of the nation struggle to imagine the future.

I'll tell you about the future. As human numbers swell, resources will become pinched and Arizona has already staked out this ground. Water has always been rare here and now, thanks to the Central Arizona Project, a lifeline of federal largesse that sucks the flow of a dying river, the Colorado, and pumps it uphill to Phoenix and Tucson, Arizona must live with absolute water numbers that will never improve. There will be no future relief for us here. Overpopulation is the forbidden word in our culture. Here it will become the fact of life. Since 2000, 130,000 people have moved to Arizona and two-thirds of them, mainly illegal Mexicans, live in poverty. Most of the increase in population in Arizona is now illegals. Generally, they lack health insurance but need medical care, they lack decent wages but need government help, they lack education but need education in order to get decent jobs. And they lack a welcome—probably two hundred or more simply keeled over and died in the desert in the past summer trying to enter the United States. The rest are hunted like dogs along a militarized border. Recently, vigilantes have joined the fray (Arizona has a rich history of racism, with school segregation of blacks ending in the early fifties but with flickers of the faith lingering—William Rehnquist harassing black voters in Phoenix in the early sixties, the state's refusal to countenance Martin Luther King Day until the early nineties, and its continual embarrassment over the fact that Cesar Chavez was born near Yuma). Here the future will be murder.

The Mexican government in November 2001 projected an illegal migration into the United States of 300,000 to 500,000 people a year for thirty years regardless of the most optimistic performance of the Mexican economy. The major crossing point is Arizona. Some activists like to see this as the reclaiming of the Southwest by La Raza. This is nonsense. People are not coming north to expand Mexico, they are coming north to flee an economic and social ruin. Some see this as the destruction of American culture by aliens. This is nonsense. People are coming north to join another culture and shake off the dust of village life. Some see this as a godsend since the illegals do work that locals fail to desire. This is nonsense. Americans will do anything if the price is right, from being lawyers to contract killings. The illegals drive down wages and perpetuate poverty by this act.

The border is shattered, not just the border between the United States and Mexico but the border between American dreams of dominance and the land's hard facts of life. Here the future will show the wrath of the ground. The forests, mismanaged for almost a century, will burn in veritable firestorms for at least a decade or until the massive fuel load is consumed. The range, heroically overgrazed, will continue to decline. The irrigated districts, preposterous in their conception as federally subsidized schemes to grow crops in spots where the rain does not come, will continue to surrender their ground and water rights to the cities. The cities, located in a desert, will feel the hot winds slap them in the face as water declines and human numbers grow. And the economy, a mixture of federal subsidy, service industries, an unacknowledged but large drug industry, and second- and third-tier industrial plants, will continue to sputter out low wages as more and more people arrive at the trough. Arizona, long a welfare state that for its entire existence has gotten more money from the federal government than it pays in federal taxes, will increasingly become yet a larger burden on the federal treasury. As the United States enters a determined drive for empire, Arizona will host yet more military installations and intelligence centers (the Army intelligence center is near the Mexican border; the CIA runs an airbase outside Tucson). After all, the modern state of Arizona is simply an artifact of empire and only boomed with World War II and the endless permutations of American military adventures since that date. This is part of its tradition, since the territory was literally sustained in the nineteenth century by peddling things to the U.S. Army, which was busy slaughtering Apaches.

Politically, Arizona will continue with its traditional reactionary style and send various demented souls to Congress. How else can one characterize a state that is simply a public beggar yet constantly creates various versions of Barry Goldwater bleating about state's rights and limited government? Ranching would vanish here without federal subsidy, as would agriculture. The military is the spine of the state's economy. Mining survives only thanks to an 1872 mining law that decrees that no mine is liable for the pollution or destruction of federal land that it causes. The social services that many parts of the nation fret over maintaining have never existed here. Arizona is the future, where you work for little and when that proves to be not enough, you get to die in a ditch. It is the laboratory of the post-welfare state so many American dreamers seek.

I will never leave here because I love this ground. The mountains and deserts and forests and canyons own my soul. That is part of the draw. But there is more, this thing I mentioned earlier, the future.

The explosion of poverty that is a planetary fact as the new global economy uproots whole peoples is here a concrete reality. Just north of Tucson, for example, the new 192,000-acre Ironwood National Monument is being mowed down by visitation. There are only two BLM agents to patrol the place but last year, they seized more than a car a day from smugglers of either Mexicans or drugs. They also removed forty tons of trash dropped by illegals fleeing north. The monument is seventy miles from the border. Federal lands on the border are much more heavily trafficked. I retain an image from two summers ago: a living one-month-old baby was found in the desert clinging to the breast of a dead eighteen-year-old Mexican woman.

For me the problem is flesh and blood and love. I'll give you something burned into my brain. It is Sunday on a ranch fifty miles north of the border. I am on the porch sipping coffee in the gray light. Just to the south are abandoned homesteads once populated by the Buffalo soldiers, freedmen who came here after the Civil War to hunt Apaches as part of the U.S. Army. To the north lies an elaborate ruin of Native Americans who farmed the area in the thirteenth century. A short ways across the desert is the saloon where Billy the Kid murdered his first man. I see a man standing in the soft light of the ranch yard. He is in his late fifties, his skin dark and creased. He works like a beast tending stock, fencing, building water holes. He gets a house, and wages—wages legal Americans shun as too low. He is an illegal out of Chihuahua. He knows no English. And he is standing in the gray light in a white shirt, clean jeans, and polished boots to catch a ride to a nearby town where he can hear a mass in Spanish. He is the problem, he is the person bundled inside the lies on immigration and its consequences. And of course, he is the man I admire.

That is the value of Arizona. Here the abstractions are made flesh, whether they hail from the dull tomes of ecology or the dry statistics of economics or the various fables of pro- and anti-immigration groups. Here the collision of human life with limited resources is being played out. Mark Twain once wrote that when the world ended he hoped he was in Cincinnati because it will happen there ten years later. In Arizona, the future is likely to happen early. Long perceived as a backwater on the edge of the nation, Arizona today and in the years to come will be at the very center of the future. It is the brilliantly lit arena where the realities of overpopulation, declining resources, human migration, and a consumer economy played against miserable wages will be starkly revealed. My ground will devour the fables of both the left and the right and bring us home to the facts we normally bury in biology studies or other tombs. The Sonoran pronghorn, gamely browsing on the rim of extinction, is just one of many canaries in this new mine probing the future.

When I arrived here as a boy I was stunned by the smiling denial of the ground by the cities with their emerald smears of golf courses. I still am. I was stunned by the preposterous Marlboro Man stancing of politicians as they fought like dogs for federal handouts. I still am. And I was amazed at the pretense that Mexico did not exist except as some gardener working quietly outside the home. And here, too, I still am.

I bet my life on the hunch that in Arizona the real future will appear first. My bet is still on the table and I'm happy to let it ride. In the white light of this place, even the blind will eventually be able to see the true lay of the land.

ARKANSAS

LIFE AFTER CLINTON

Gene Lyons

For one who grew up around New York City, living in Arkansas is like inhabiting an endless Victorian novel. Not everybody knows everybody else, but it sometimes feels as if they do. Partly that's because my wife, Diane, grew up and went to college here, and used to work as an aide to Governor David Pryor. (These days, she's an administrator at Arkansas Children's Hospital.) Partly too because we live in the Hillcrest neighborhood of Little Rock, an older part of town between the state capitol and the University of Arkansas Medical School, that draws longtime residents. Although it's possible for us to go out to dinner in the city without seeing anybody we know, it doesn't happen very often. Within twenty-four hours of my taking her sister to the movies one time, somebody was sadly informing Diane that her husband was dating a cheap blonde. The gossip is fantastic. Paradoxically, that may be one reason Bill Clinton got away with whatever he got away with for so long. As an island of relative cosmopolitanism in a sea of sex-obsessed, small-town fundamentalists, Little Rock is perpetually awash with sexual rumors, mostly false.

Every bit as much as New York, the state of Arkansas is a world unto itself. For decades, schoolchildren here have been taught the

comforting myth that Arkansas alone among the states has the natural resources—plentiful water, timber, some oil, considerable
reserves of natural gas, and vast stretches of fertile alluvial soil—to
build a wall around itself and nevertheless thrive. True or false, it's
revelatory of the state's mindset. Prosperity eludes many, yet local
patriotism runs very strong. Lampooned for its backwardness since
territorial days—"Will We Always Be the Barefoot State?" a local
magazine once asked—Arkansas has long felt itself maligned and
misunderstood. Proud and touchy, bitterly self-critical yet resentful
of condescending outsiders, Arkansas constitutes "not quite a nation
within a nation," as the historian W. J. Cash wrote of the entire South
of sixty years ago, "but the next thing to it."

Many things divide Arkansans, often bitterly. Race, class, religion,
politics, the usual subjects. But they're as gregarious a bunch of small-
town storytellers as you're ever going to meet. Everything's personal.
When I stop by the feed store, it's necessary to allow at least fifteen
minutes for small talk. If I failed to chat about the weather, my family,
the proprietor's family—odd word for a man in bib overalls—the
Razorbacks, my little dog Buffy, and how my horses are getting
along on the new sweet feed, they'd wonder if they'd somehow
insulted me and start asking my veterinarian friend Randy if I'd been
feeling alright.

Granted, these are country folks, but my local supermarket's not
all that different. There, what we mostly talk about is that crazy
Texas sumbitch George W. Bush and how he's taking the country to
hell in a handbasket. That and the Razorbacks, of course. Texans are
something we got our fill of in the days of the old Southwestern
Conference, and the Arkansas–Texas game was the statewide equivalent of a Holy Day of Obligation. Somebody once dreamed up a
scheme to pump Arkansas River water through a nine-hundred-
mile pipeline to irrigate the high-plains cotton crop around Lubbock. It pretty much got laughed to death. Just give the Texans a

nine-hundred-mile straw, the joke went. There'd be no need to lay pipe if they could suck as hard as they blow.

Something else that's true of Arkansans is that they tend to make allowances. As the token non-right-wing political columnist in the *Arkansas Democrat-Gazette*, the statewide daily newspaper, I'm theoretically a somewhat controversial figure. Judging by the letters to the editor, you'd think I needed a bodyguard. Fact is, however, I don't even have an unlisted phone number. I have exactly one anonymous caller, whose identity I think I know. (Haven't heard from ol' Hubert in a couple of months, come to think of it.) Anyhow, in years of lampooning the madcap delusions of the Religious Right, racial bigots, gun nuts, homophobes, etc., I've never once felt personally threatened.

Geographically, Arkansas is the smallest state west of the Mississippi in land area, but comprises several distinct regions—from the Ozark and Ouachita mountains, thickly forested, sparsely populated, and running with white-water streams—to the cypress-filled bayous of the south and east, shallow, murky, and crawling with alligators. Although it was a part of the Confederacy, only the cotton-plantation country along the Mississippi River was fully settled at the time of the Civil War. Most of the rest was, and arguably remains, a frontier, albeit one amply provisioned with mobile homes and satellite TV receivers. It's a terribly beautiful place everywhere people don't live, and heartbreakingly bedraggled and trash-strewn in too many places where they do. A philanthropist who wanted to make a big impact on the state's quality of life could do worse than to haul off and recycle the astonishing number of abandoned house trailers littering the landscape. I do believe, however, that God resides near the hamlet of Gilbert, along the Buffalo River in Searcy County, Arkansas.

The great environmental enterprise of the contemporary era has been to preserve the remaining free-flowing highland streams—the Kings River, the Buffalo, the Mulberry, Crooked Creek, and Bear

Creek—from being dammed and converted to lakeside "resort communities" for retired midwesterners. Also to conserve what small portion remains of the primeval bottomlands of the Arkansas–Mississippi river delta from being drained, ditched, and turned to unprofitable soybean, cotton, and rice fields. Lest I be misunderstood about "gun nuts," allow me to stipulate that Arkansas duck and deer hunters have played a more effective role in preservation than anybody else. Before World War II, market hunting and habitat destruction had all but eliminated deer, bear, wild turkey, alligator, and other wildlife species whose prodigious numbers so astonished nineteenth-century European visitors to Arkansas (Native American populations having been decimated by smallpox and other diseases introduced by the sixteenth-century Spanish explorer Hernando de Soto). Their return has been largely financed by hunters' license fees and political pressure.

To understand Arkansas's unique politics, it's necessary to grasp both its cultural complexity and its history of (sometimes self-inflicted) humiliation. State pride notwithstanding, the novelist and essayist Bob Lancaster once half-humorously suggested that regardless of political boundaries, what most people think of as Arkansas actually consists of Little Rock and a half-dozen contiguous counties smack in the middle of the state. The rest, he said, were separate realms held together by a legal fiction. Culturally and ethnographically, the Ozarks resemble Missouri or West Virginia more than they do the adjacent cotton-growing, slave-holding, flatland plantation counties along the Mississippi.

Slavery, hell. Most of the Scotch-Irish highlanders who populated Arkansas's hill country didn't even believe in hired help, let alone buying and selling Africans. What little row-crop agriculture penetrated the hills and hollers of north Arkansas was mostly corn, and it was exported, if at all, in liquid form. (Today's No. 1 cash crop in most of those counties is either chickens or marijuana, depending upon whom you talk to.) Participation in the Civil War was about half Union and half Confederate, mostly guerrilla raids and banditry on both sides.

It's a good bet that *The Nation* has more Arkansas subscribers than *Southern Partisan* does. But even among Confederate nostalgists, one phrase you'll never hear is "Arkansas aristocracy," an oxymoron if ever one was. The Arkansas Delta, however, greatly resembles neighboring parts of Mississippi. From a journalistic standpoint, maybe the most accurate description of the antebellum Arkansas slaveholding country was Mark Twain's *Huckleberry Finn*, in which a pair of vagrant mountebanks styling themselves a king and a duke hoodwinked a ramshackle village full of Delta rednecks with insufficient energy to do much more than chew, spit, and cheer dogfights. For all his parody, Lancaster wrote, "Twain was a careful observer who truly hated inaccurate descriptions. His squalid picture of this wretched village had much truth in it. Life in frontier Arkansas was coarse and brutal, and the dregs of society—indolent, hanging about the wharves and blind pigs of the little river towns (practically the only kind of towns we had until a hundred years ago) and dulled either by inheritance or by the parasitic and nutrition-deficiency diseases that preyed on the lowland poor—were the Arkansas people that river travelers tended to see most and judge the state by."

Actually, it's a lot more complicated than highland-lowland. The piney woods of south Arkansas, Lancaster argued, are a whole lot like east Texas; Fort Smith, the jumping-off point for Indian Territory throughout much of the nineteenth century, is culturally linked to Oklahoma. Hot Springs, a spa city on the edge of the vast Ouachita National Forest, as several of Bill Clinton's biographers have noted, was always an anomaly: its streets lined with illegal casinos, whorehouses, and Baptist churches. The most persuasive depictions of Arkansas's separate realms may be found in its novelists, particularly Donald Harington's *The Architecture of the Arkansas Ozarks*, Charles

Portis's *True Grit*, and Maya Angelou's memoir *I Know Why the Caged Bird Sings*. Also in its music, because it was along the cultural fault line between the hills and the flatlands that country met the blues, and Arkansas musicians like Johnny Cash, Louis Jordan, Ronnie Hawkins, and Levon Helm helped invent rock and roll.

Exaggerated or not, mockery like Twain's was hard to live down. What's more, the tradition persisted. Writing in *The Smart Set* in 1921, H. L. Mencken wrote of "trackless, unexplored" Arkansas and sardonically asked: "Who indeed has ever been in it? I know New Yorkers who have been in Cochin China, Kafiristan, Paraguay, Somaliland and West Virginia, but not one who has ever penetrated the miasmatic jungles of Arkansas." Even though Mencken wrote in mock astonishment at the founding of a literary quarterly he respected in the college town of Fayetteville—located in far northwest Arkansas because the rest of the state wanted no part of the federal law creating land-grant universities in 1865—the insult stuck long after hookworm and malaria disappeared.

The Industrial Revolution, Arkansas's Pulitzer Prize–winning poet John Gould Fletcher suggested in his 1947 history of the state, finally arrived here with World War II. "The slow agricultural rhythm of Arkansas, progressing from wet spring to summer drought, from summer drought to smoky fall, from smoky fall to frost and back again via snow to wet spring, seemed definitely to change between 1942–1945," Fletcher wrote. If slightly exaggerated, statistics do bear him out. Not for nothing has the unofficial state motto long been "Thank God for Mississippi." Traditionally ranking near the bottom of the states in per capita income, in 1940 Arkansas's per capita income was just 43.7 percent of the nation's—virtually a Third World standard.

Patterns of land ownership and distribution of wealth in much of the Delta resembled those of Nicaragua or Guatemala. By 1945, however, wartime investment had pushed Arkansas's share of the national per capita income to 60 percent. (Out-migration of many thousands of poor blacks to Chicago, St. Louis, Detroit, and other northern cities during this period also improve the statistics. Altogether, it's estimated that upward of a third of Arkansas blacks and roughly a fifth of whites left Arkansas seeking work during the war.) Even so, when future Governor Orval Faubus returned home from World War II in 1945, his native Madison County, deep in the heart of the Ozarks, had exactly twelve miles of paved highway. Large parts of rural Arkansas still lacked electricity, telephones, and indoor plumbing.

Needless to say, the name of Orval Eugene Faubus is hardly associated with progressivism in the American political tradition. Faubus's shameful and futile resistance to President Dwight D. Eisenhower during the Little Rock Central High integration crisis of 1957 fixed Arkansas's image as a bigot's paradise for a generation. At least in part because what Lancaster has called "the most famous mob scene since the French Revolution" became America's first major nationally televised political "crisis," the stain seemed ineradicable. In vain did embarrassed Arkansans point to peaceful racial integration in other parts of the state, to far more violent confrontations elsewhere in the South—indeed, nobody was killed or even hospitalized in the Central High fracas—to the principled resistance of the *Arkansas Gazette*. "The received wisdom of the thinking classes," wrote Roy Reed in his brilliant biography, "is that Faubus inflicted permanent and irreparable harm on Arkansas. Such sweeping condemnation is hard to agree with. He certainly interrupted a centrist trend that the state had begun during the New Deal. But the most serious period of interruption lasted only a few years, and before the end of his administration the state was pottering along toward the American mainstream much as it had been before he entered the picture—and as it had been during the first two and a half years of his tenure. Business and urban interests, on the rise everywhere in Dixie, replaced the low-country planters as the dominant political force in the state. With black voters gaining new strength, the stage was set during Faubus's last years in office for a generation of progressive leadership in the state's Democratic party."

It was the strange and paradoxical election year of 1968 that permanently released Faubus's six-term, twelve-year stranglehold on Arkansas politics. Not only did Arkansans reelect liberal Republican Winthrop Rockefeller governor, defeating Faubus's comeback bid, but they returned anti–Vietnam War senator J. William Fulbright to the U.S. Senate and gave their presidential vote to the third-party racist candidacy of Alabama governor George C. Wallace. (Heretics are admired in Arkansas if they have grit; nor did it hurt that Fulbright and Wallace were both giving hell to Lyndon Baines Johnson, a noted Texan of the era.) Just beneath the surface, however, there was good news. Wallace took Arkansas's electoral votes with scarcely more than a third of the vote, with Richard M. Nixon and Hubert Humphrey finishing in a virtual dead heat. The sorehead white racist vote thus defined, in 1970, a previously unknown country lawyer from northwest Arkansas named Dale Bumpers was able to forge a centrist Democratic coalition that has endured ever since. As school-board chairman in the Franklin County town of Charleston, Bumpers had overseen peaceful school integration immediately following *Brown v. Board of Education*. By the time boy wonder Bill Clinton came along in 1978, he was the third in a tradition of moderate progressivism defined by Bumpers and David Pryor. Actually some would say that Clinton was the fifth, behind crusading World War II Marine veteran Sid McMath and Faubus himself, before the demiurge of race swallowed him.

Greeted by euphoric throngs in downtown Little Rock on November 7, 1992, Clinton's election as president of the United States seemed to many Arkansas's best chance to put past embarrassments behind them. At last we belong, was the collective feeling. Alas, that euphoria proved short-lived. Had Clinton and his immediate predecessors done a creditable job of moving the state into the national mainstream? The numbers were hard to deny. Arkansas still trailed most of the nation in statistical measures of well-being, but the gap had narrowed. By 1990, the state's share of the national per capita income had risen to 76 percent. Pockets of extreme poverty still persisted, mostly in the Delta, especially given that agriculture now accounts for a mere 3 percent of the state's total income. Particularly in the Fayetteville-Springdale corridor of northwest Arkansas, however, home to Wal-Mart and Tyson Foods, some began to worry that rapid growth and development had gotten out of hand. Jobs, highways, and education were the perennial big three issues of state politics; even coded racial appeals were a sure loser. One reason Arkansas was slow to join the rest of the South in shifting to the Republican party was that it took conservatives almost twenty-five years to do the arithmetic: if they conceded Arkansas's 16 to 18 percent African-American vote (depending on the election), roughly 64 percent of the white vote was required to win a statewide contest. It simply couldn't be done. Indeed, sheer frustration accounted for an awful lot of the negative energy among local Clinton-haters. Not every Arkansan who hated Clinton was a bigot, but all the old sheet-heads loathed him.

Alas, it was not to be. Clinton's extravagant folly in the Lewinsky affair notwithstanding, his presidency coincided with a near-total breakdown of the already shaky standards of evidence used by American news organizations. Driven by talk radio, by trash-for-cash tabloids, by hireling scribblers for journals like the *American Spectator*, by Internet conspiracy theorists, and not least by publishers competing for lucrative book-length "revelations" about the intimate lives of the famous, a puritanical credulousness appears to have replaced skepticism among many contemporary journalists. Arkansas found itself besieged by squadrons of would-be Menckens, portrayed as a dark and blighted land whose bankers are money-launderers and worse, whose judges and lawyers are whores, whose journalists are mostly deaf and blind, and where only courageous (albeit bribed) state troopers ever spoke the truth. (Whatever Clinton's real sins, a governor who sent troopers out to hustle babes for him couldn't get away with it for twelve days, much less twelve years.) Veteran Arkansas journalists found themselves patronized by Washington sophisticates who could scarcely write coherent sentences, couldn't get the simplest details of a $200,000 real estate transaction straight, but who acted as if efforts to set them straight had been dictated by arch-villainess Hillary Clinton.

"There is no party machine in predominantly Democratic Arkansas," then Senators Dale Bumpers and David Pryor pointed out in a 1994 letter to the *New York Times Magazine*. The two men wrote in response to a critical article by Michael Kelly portraying the Clinton years, as they put it, "as a kind of wasteland, during which a hollow man played it slick and safe to insure a certain path to the presidency." Kelly's article was a classic example of what I came to call "naïve cynicism," in which the reporter willfully blinds himself to basic political information—the strength of the Arkansas poultry lobby in the state legislature, for example—while cynically pretending that every compromise represents a corrupt bargain. Both former governors, the senators noted that "the political scientist V. O. Key long ago observed that a one-party state is a no-party state. The governor of Arkansas must forge a new coalition on each issue. The resulting bartering and negotiation may look slick to the unpracticed eye, but the novice should try it before judging. In his twelve years as governor, the president alienated every large interest group in the state at one time or another: utilities, timber, building contractors, the Chamber of Commerce, the Arkansas Medical Society, the Education Association, the poultry industry, the Farm Bureau, the National Rifle Association."

Maybe Clinton's Democratic colleagues laid it on a bit thick. Bill Clinton's idea of leadership was always a balancing act. Political allies as well as enemies who fell over the side often found themselves treading water as the good ship Bill and Hillary sailed for the horizon. While certainly possessing its share of rogues and opportunists, in terms of everyday political corruption Arkansas is like Denmark compared to New Jersey, where I grew up. Or to Louisiana, where many of my wife's relatives live. Correct the errors and fill in the blanks, and the famous Whitewater "scandal" basically disappeared. Reading about it in the *New York Times* and *Washington Post*, however, was like reading an account of a baseball game by a sportswriter who failed to comprehend the infield-fly rule.

Suffice it to say that by the time Kenneth Starr's heavy-handed prosecutors got around to trying Susan McDougal on criminal contempt and obstruction of justice charges in 1999, they couldn't have convicted a snake of crawling under the porch. Partisanship aside, word had gotten around. After five years of the Starr Captivity, almost everybody knew of somebody they trusted who'd been dragged through the mill. Susan's testimony that she feared Starr would prosecute her for perjury if she refused to confirm her late ex-husband Jim McDougal's tall tales persuaded a Little Rock jury to acquit her. The story's admirably told in her spunky, plainspoken book *The Woman Who Wouldn't Talk*. Starr's team wasn't investigating crimes, most Arkansans came to understand. It was investigating people.

Ironically, the most lasting impact of the Clinton presidency may be to free Arkansans from their traditional worry about what the Yankees think. The soreheads and the Bible-beaters never cared; now hardly anybody does. Nobody's ready to build that wall around the state, but we're not so quick to apologize for our shortcomings either.

Meanwhile, the single greatest beneficiary of Starr's partisan quest to destroy Clinton finds himself picking up pretty much where his Democratic predecessors left off. A Baptist preacher and a conservative Republican, Mike Huckabee succeeded to the governorship when Starr convicted his predecessor Jim Guy Tucker of filing a false loan application. (On dubious evidence, in my opinion; the case remains on appeal.) Given his background, many worried that Huckabee would attempt to enact the entire Religious Right agenda, guaranteeing strife and bad feelings all around. But it hasn't happened. Speaking at Little Rock Central High on the fortieth anniversary of the painful events of 1957, Huckabee delivered himself of an address that most observers thought surpassed President Clinton, who also spoke. He said that racial segregation and bigotry were terrible sins, and that while "forgiveable" in the religious sense, they were also not "excusable." He lamented that "in many parts of the South, it was the white churches that helped not only ignore the problems of racism, but in many cases actually fostered those feelings and sentiments." He even said a few words about African-American bigotry, and how he was against that too.

Like most of America, Arkansas is a fine place to live if you're well-born and fortunate, not so hot if you're poor, uneducated, mentally ill, or just plain unlucky. It's too damn hot in the summer, and too close to Texas. But all things considered, most people would tell you we're getting along just fine.

CALIFORNIA
(NORTH)

THE METAMORPHOSIS

Rebecca Solnit

San Francisco is bounded on three sides by water and on the fourth by the San Bruno Mountains, a small kingdom whose heights lift you up above the urban density to see the hills, the bay, the sea, whose grid of straight avenues becomes lines to the horizon, light shafts and axes: you always know that there's a beyond to this most densely urban American city after New York. I've been walking it for three decades, since I'd cut school to catch the bus in, and now the place is layered with ghosts, of my own life, of the events of my lifetime, and of the histories that unfolded here before me. Everything used to be something else. This mutation itself seems a definitive condition of the place. Where the Batman Gallery showed avant-garde art by the likes of Bruce Conner in the 1960s, a Starbucks now serves up Frappuccinos, and where the African Orthodox Church of St. John Coltrane survived into the twenty-first century, a boutique now showcases ironic denim creations and stretchy sweater items. That's gentrification's cultural degradation for you, but the longer stretches of metamorphosis get really interesting.

The particular stretch of South of Market where photographer Eadweard Muybridge lived in the 1870s while he was laying the foundations for motion-picture technology was, by Jack Kerouac's time, "the poor grime-bemarked Third Street of lost bums even Negros so hopeless and long left East and meanings of responsibility and *try* that now all they do is stand there spitting in the broken glass sometimes fifty in one afternoon against one wall at Third and Howard." Third and Howard, not far from downtown's shopping and financial districts, is now the location of the San Francisco Museum of Modern Art, across the street from Yerba Buena Center, whose strange mix of nonprofit arts and corporate entertainment was built where the residential hotels of Kerouac's time stood.

Those hotels were full of the old white guys who'd launched the great dockside strikes and union drives of the teens through the thirties, and when redevelopment came to their neighborhood they fought the toughest battle in the country against it and won a lot of concessions that, for example, the African-American community across town in the Fillmore didn't. When I was a young punk, this central place where the old men had lived out the ends of their lives or been evicted to die elsewhere was nothing but a vacant lot. Moscone Center, named after the progressive mayor assassinated in 1978 along with gay city supervisor Harvey Milk by ex-cop Dan White, opened in time to host the Democratic Convention of 1984, but what would become Yerba Buena Center to the north was just a huge expanse of gravel and dirt where we held demonstrations against the Democrats. I still remember watching MDC (whose initials initially stood for Millions of Dead Cops but, as their political education progressed, came to signify Multi-Death Corporations) play there, that summer of my brother David's War-Chest Tours of the downtown corporations backing the Democrats and building nukes.

Kerouac continued: ". . . and here's all those Millbrae and San Carlos neat-necktied producers and commuters of America and steel civilization rushing by" to catch the train. The commuter train still runs, but the huge Mission Bay railyard that was long the headquarters for

America's first spectacularly corrupt megacorporation, Southern Pacific, is no more. It was actually a bay, once, a fact preserved, after all the landfill dumping, only in its name, Mission Bay, and it was thus named because Mission Creek emptied into it for all those millennia when Ohlone Indians must've been paddling their reed boats after shellfish there. Mission Creek was long ago driven underground, but the mission that gave the creek and the bay their names still exists— Kim Novak visited its cemetery in Hitchcock's *Vertigo*—in the core of the hipster zone of the Mission District. As for Mission Bay: after being a rail hub it was a spacious, morose hobo jungle, and now it's halfway to being a huge biotech campus, for Southern Pacific money begat Leland Stanford's fortune, and that fortune begat Stanford University, which begat Silicon Valley and as a sort of by-blow a fair bit of biotechnology, come back as another form of colonization where the railroad Frank Norris described as "the Octopus" once sat.

The Bay Area has generated plenty of octopi: Bank of America, Wells Fargo, Chevron, and Bechtel, the last recently shut down for being such a war profiteer under the Bush administration, protested a year before for its attempt to privatize water supplies in Bolivia. It was *Santa Clara County v. Southern Pacific* that in the 1880s laid the legal basis for corporations to claim the privileges of individuals. If we generate octopi, we also generate their opposite as activism, and not all the trajectories are downward. In 1877, when all across the country the anti-railroad riots of the Great Strike were breaking out, San Francisco's working class, underpaid and unemployed, instead of joining that commune of anticorporate action, started the anti-Chinese riots. They blamed the Chinese for taking jobs and undercutting wages, though they eventually ended up on Stanford's doorstep atop Nob Hill anyway, facing off the real reasons they were being squeezed. And the riots were organized in the sandlots next to city hall, a sort of oratorical equivalent to Hyde Park, and where those sandlots stood, the new San Francisco Public Library stands, across the street from the old library, damaged in the earthquake of 1989 and reborn as the Asian Art Museum, one of the finest of its kind outside Asia, a victory over a past almost no one remembers. Everything metamorphoses; some things don't decline; much is reborn.

San Francisco was destroyed by fire six times in its first few years, destroyed on a far grander scale when it was a far grander city by the 1906 earthquake and fire, its buildings, populations, and continuities ravaged by redevelopment and gentrification since World War II and around the turn of the millennium raided by the dot-com kids come like Huns to sack Rome or maybe like Romans to sack our Barbary Coast before the recession fixed them. The image on the state flag is the California grizzly, which went extinct several decades ago, but the creature on San Francisco's flag never existed at all; it's the phoenix, the bird that rises from its ashes. San Francisco is forever being destroyed, forever reinvented, and some thread of continuity always runs through. The naked peaks of the highest hills are reminders of the bleak windswept expanse of dunes, the original terrain, that underlies much of the city.

In some ways the tip of the San Francisco peninsula seems like an island waiting for its fourth side to be sawed loose from the North American continent. The city has, since its gold rush birth, been an anomaly and a sanctuary from the American way of pretty much everything except the pursuit of happiness and profit, and even the happiness is likely to take the form of religious and sexual practices and self-expressions that might not be so available in Iowa. It is its own place. After all, the Pacific gave the whole Bay Area a Mediterranean climate and San Francisco a particular proneness to fog, and this has made the region to some extent and the city far more so an island ecology. San Francisco had two endemic species of butterfly go extinct as it developed, and has several species of plants that are imperiled. Some days I think our eclectic artists and activists demonstrate that the place's talent for developing unique species didn't stop when the place was paved over: we do have, for example, more AIDS educators cross-dressing as nuns, more deployment of giant puppets in antiglobalization demonstrations.

But some of this eclecticism has been evident throughout all Northern California: if you look at a map of Native California, you see that the tribes and language groups were incredibly diverse—more languages were spoken in indigenous California than throughout the rest of the continent, and this diversity reflected the diversity of bioregions, from desert to mountain to several kinds of forest to grassland, with countless variations in between. Among those languages were ones in which men and women spoke different dialects, in which there were no words for right or left because you specified your body's relation to the cardinal directions instead, or in which there were no cardinal directions because in the twisty terrain, upriver and downriver were more useful terms. There's more biotic change and biodiversity in a few miles uphill from the coast than in a thousand miles of prairie, and somehow this seems to have lived on even in the gold rush city full of Chileans and Chinese and Frenchmen and Missourians and New Englanders and in contemporary California, with its Hmong and Portuguese and Samoan communities. San Francisco became the nation's first white-minority city decades ago, complicatedly enough as it stopped being a blue-collar port city, and whites are due to achieve the same status statewide in the next decade. To say that Latinos will be the new majority is to flatten out the complexity of Colombians and Salvadoreans and Mexicans and those old southwesterners who can say, "We didn't cross the border; the border crossed us."

Speaking of that crossing, on a big grass-and-oak hillside facing San Pablo Bay, not far north of the town I grew up in thirty miles north of San Francisco, was Rancho Olompali. It had been a big Miwok village before the Spaniards came, then a Spanish-style rancho run by a Miwok guy named Camille Ysdero with a knack for adaptation. In a precursor of drive-by shootings, a bunch of Yankees rode by one day in 1846 and shot up the place while the ranchers were having breakfast. They were part of the Bear Flag Revolt that merged with the war that extracted Mexico's northern half for the United States, but Ysdero survived annexation so nicely that his daughter married a Harvard man. By the turn of the century the ranch belonged to a wealthy dentist who surrounded his house with exotic plantings—a pomegranate hedge and some palms live on— and by the late 1960s it was a hippie commune called The Family where Grateful Dead lead singer Jerry Garcia, speaking of assimilated Latinos, had an acid trip awful enough to make it his last. The rancho buildings and the surrounding hillside became a state park not long ago, where I still hike for its shaded groves, gracefully cascading native grasses, and wildflowers.

Its evolution from indigenous hamlet to battlefield to dental estate to bad trip sometimes seems like an encapsulation of Northern California to me, where things are always mutating, where erasure and replacement are the only constants. What's erased, though, tends to reappear. Maybe it's easier to imagine the place as a deck of cards constantly being reshuffled into royal flushes and losing hands, where we play poker with memory and identity and meaning and possibility, which are not quite four of a kind. When I was growing up, the Coast Miwoks of Olompali and elsewhere were supposed to have vanished. Now not only are they resurgent as the Federated Indians of Graton Rancheria, whose attempts to build a casino in the next county north are contested by environmentalists, but the tribe's chair is the brilliant novelist and screenplay writer Greg Sarris. Things are like that here: mixed-up, forever metamorphosing, but returning when you think they're gone. We thought the dot-com invasion had eviscerated radical San Francisco but during the first days of Gulf War II, activists by the thousands shut down downtown, the federal building, and traffic arteries in the most powerful demonstration of outrage in the country.

In some ways the tip of the San Francisco peninsula seems like an island. In other ways the whole Bay Area seems like a laboratory where America invents itself, because what comes out of here counts, because it spreads. Some of the stuff is pretty obvious: environmentalism from the Sierra Club founded in downtown San Francisco in 1892 and from Global Exchange and Rainforest Action Network more recently; the Black Panthers out of Oakland; California cuisine out of Berkeley's Chez Panisse and its vegetarian version out of San Francisco's Greens, itself an offshoot of San Francisco Zen Center, one of the major sites for the arrival of Buddhism in the West; mountain bikes from Marin County; the nation's major wine supply and culture from Sonoma and Napa; silicon stuff since Hewlett-Packard through Oracle and Netscape and Sun Microsystems and Apple from what used to be a big orchardland called the Valley of Heart's Delight; the Free Speech Movement from the students of San Francisco State and UC–Berkeley; inspiration for Native American activists nationwide from the late-sixties occupation of Alcatraz Island; beat poetry from the Fillmore and North Beach. (And if you go farther north, south, and east, you arrive at the vast factory farms—and more and more little organic ones—from which a huge percentage of the nation's produce comes—fruit and nut jokes are old stuff here.)

Some of it is not so obvious, not movements, but individuals— Jack London and Maxine Hong Kingston and Jello Biafra and Congresswoman Barbara Lee, ideas, scents on the wind, shifts in ideas about sexuality, about citizenship, about spectacle. Sometimes I think of the place as "amateur hour," because so many people are committed to creative expression as a pleasure rather than a discipline, and that involves more costumes and pop-culture ironies than, say, writing history. Consider, for example, the hundreds of thousands of revelers at Halloween in the queer Castro or Nevada's Burning Man festival, born in and organized from the city.

The important thing about San Francisco being a laboratory is that this is just an extension of its being a port city: we import people from Peru and Indiana and send them back educated or out of the closet, and our definitive figures are often, like Kerouac or Muybridge, people who are just passing through for a few years or decades, but who will be indelibly stamped and will stamp back. Or people like Gary Snyder, who came down from the Pacific Northwest to the Bay Area in the 1950s, studied and wrote poetry and hiked around the mountain on which mountain bikes would be invented, went to Japan, came back and moved into the Sierra Foothills. From there, with books like his Pulitzer-winning *Turtle Island*, he forecast the hybrid of Asian philosophy and indigenous place-sense and ecological ideas that would become how we think around these parts.

The factors that make it a good laboratory might include what another poet, Snyder's forebear Kenneth Rexroth, once snarled: "It is the only city in the United States which was not settled overland by the westward-spreading puritanism or by the Walter-Scott fake-cavalier tradition of the South. It had been settled mostly, in spite of all the romances of the overland migration, by gamblers, prostitutes, rascals, and fortune seekers who came across the Isthmus and around the Horn. They had their faults, but they were not influenced by Cotton Mather." Long the "Capital of the West" and the biggest city west of the Mississippi, San Francisco never faced Europe but was instead at the center of an unequal triangle of influences formed by the wild interior of the continent, Mexico, and Asia. These influences and the peculiar balance of the region between the provincial backstage in which experiments are safe, and coterie-culture encouraging such flowering, has made it peculiarly productive of ideas on all fronts.

The city achieved a European density that allowed it to function as a true city rather than the amorphous, suburban diffusion of almost every other Western city in the United States, and thus it has a lively street life, civic and cultural life, public institutions, and nightlife. I've always thought we were the most radical city in the nation not because of our inherent virtue but because of our good fortune: who would demonstrate in a Chicago winter or Houston summer; where would you march to in Los Angeles or Phoenix and who would notice? Whereas eternally room-temperature San Francisco is full of boulevards connecting parks and plazas, full of places where it's possible to be a member of the public acting in concert with your fellow citizens, an opportunity absent elsewhere. This is the anti-America America draws from in its eternal reinvention.

CALIFORNIA
(SOUTH)
THE INLAND EMPIRE

Mike Davis

C alifornia hangs upside down, close to Cipango, on the great world map in the Palazzo Ducale in Venice. Geographical intelligence was, of course, a foundation of Venetian wealth; so, unlike other contemporary maps in European courts, the ducal map correctly depicts the exotic land of Califa as a peninsula, not an island. There is an elegantly inscribed notation in the part that is today Southern California. It reads "Antropofagi— Eaters of Men." Perhaps the cartographer was predicting realtors.

A month after admiring the Doges' map rooms, I was buying mangos from an illegal street vendor on Base Line Street in San Bernardino. West San Bernardino is an older Mexican and black neighborhood at the foot of Cajon Pass. It sits uncomfortably on the San Jacinto Fault, which is almost as dangerous as its nearby big brother, the San Andreas. Coyotes still prowl in the washes, and the Santa Ana winds periodically blow out of the pass like dry hurricanes. Hard times have reigned here since the railroad repair shops closed a decade ago. On most upscale mental maps of Southern California, this is still *antropofagi* territory: the wild void that lies east of ethnic cuisine.

In fact, Base Line Street is the Euclidean progenitor, the Ur-line, from which all the glamorous movieland boulevards and drives—Wilshire, Rodeo, Sunset, and so on—were originally derived. It was plotted in November 1852 by Colonel Henry Washington, working under contract to Samuel King, the surveyor general of California. The summer before, a survey point had been established on the top of Mount Diablo, incorporating the Bay Area into the conquering Jeffersonian grid. Now it was Southern California's turn to submit to the geometry of Manifest Destiny. The colonel and his party of a dozen men first established a cadastral Initial Point on ten-thousand-foot-high Mount San Bernardino, then laid down the Base and Principal Meridian lines. They are the absolute coordinates from which Southern California has been subsequently subdivided.

When Washington first ascended his mountain, he could see the smoke from Indian villages as well as the adobe houses of the Mormon pioneers sent to stake a claim on the Pacific for Brigham Young's independent State of Deseret. Now the lucky hiker who reaches the Washington Monument Initial Point on a smog-free winter day can survey a megalopolis sprawling from distant beaches to the furnace hearts of the Mojave and Colorado deserts. More than 100,000 named streets have been cloned since 1852 from the platonic ideal of Washington's Base Line. Meanwhile, the surviving Indians own casinos, and local Mormons can drive to Salt Lake City in a day on high-speed Interstate 15.

From Santa Barbara to San Diego, what one local wag calls "Gross Angeles" is a bigger urban universe than many suppose. According to the 2000 census, 19.3 million people now reside within Washington's grid: a population equivalent to Mexico City's and not far shy of Greater New York's. Graying "Anglos" are a bare plurality, about 40 percent of the population, and will soon yield demographic leadership to younger Latinos (already 7.5 million in 2000). This Latin Americanization of Southern California has been accompanied by equally epochal shifts in residential and economic geography. The congested coastal zone, where three-fifths of the population lives, is divided between the poor black and Latino flatlands and the lush thickets of white affluence in the foothills and along the beaches. Here land inflation is the most powerful law of nature. There is no more room to build, and the rule of thumb says that if you can smell the Pacific, the land under your feet is worth a million dollars per acre. Even shotgun shacks in Watts can cost more than a palace in Dubuque. So for the past generation, growth has been centrifuged eastward, across the Chino and Puente hills, into western San Bernardino and Riverside counties. Although many Americans are hardly aware of its existence, this "Inland Empire" has a bigger population (3.2 million in 2000) than the city of Chicago or, for that matter, Detroit, Philadelphia, and Seattle combined. By 2025 it will swell to more than 6 million: the entire population of California in 1935.

Two sociologically distinct streams of intra-urban migration are responsible for the boom. First, white-collar and public-sector commuters are ceaselessly moving eastward in search of affordable mortgages. The Inland Empire is the new Promised Land, where "starter" homes, although still expensive by midwestern standards, are $100,000 to $200,000 cheaper than in older coastal-zone suburbs like Westchester, Pasadena, or Torrance. The punitive trade-off is the grim three-hour daily commute between new homes and coastal office parks and factories. As regional planners daintily put it, the Inland Empire suffers from a radical "jobs/housing imbalance." Long-suffering moms and dads routinely serve two or three years' aggregate hard time in traffic for each child raised in the sanctum of a spacious Moreno Valley or Temecula tract home. The long ride to work is even more of a burden for those who lack the compensation of a dream home. Soaring rents are relentlessly driving the families of low-wage workers toward the desert and far away from major job concentrations. The hard-core poor—senior citizens, the handicapped, parolees, and families cut from welfare—are also being expelled to the hinterlands. This is the second, more pathological source of the Inland Empire's demographic dynamism. As one local economist complained recently: "What you are seeing is the exporting [of] the coastal communities' problems to the inland region." Indeed, during the 1990s individual poverty increased 51 percent in San Bernardino County and 63 percent in Riverside County.

One result is a Darwinian competition for the region's limited supply of low-skill jobs in Ontario warehouses or Perris mobile-home factories. Another is the nomadic homelessness diffused throughout the interior counties. The structurally generated stress levels of long-distance commuting and poverty, not surprisingly, often redline in family breakdown or addiction. The San Bernardino area, with perhaps the nation's largest concentration of over-the-road truckers and outlaw bikers, has long been the methamphetamine Medellín. It is not surprising, therefore, that some long-distance commuters have taken to starting each day with a booster-rocket of speed or crank with their cappuccino. More alarming, according to the *San Bernardino Sun*, their kids also consume drugs at almost triple the national average.

But the Inland Empire, if gridlocked and addled by speed, also adds something positive to the balance sheet of civilization in Southern California. It may not have beaches, but it has the most democratic and racially mixed neighborhoods in the state. If you blended the 2000 California census in a Cuisinart, the result would resemble the multiethnic student bodies of Fontana or Perris high schools. Unlike much of Los Angeles, where diversity is often the transitional artifact of ethnic replacement, the blue-collar interior is a true rainbow. Affordable and, for once, racially unrestricted housing has attracted working-class whites following the eastward migration of warehouses and trucking companies, as well as African-American families trying to save their kids from the carnage of LA's gang wars. Chicanos, more than a third of the population, follow in the footsteps of their grandparents, who toiled in the Inland Empire's orchards and railroad shops.

Base Line Street, from San Bernardino to Ontario, provides a fascinating cross section of this new society. Unlike in the wealthy planned communities of the Ventura plain or southern Orange County, land use in western San Bernardino County has the capricious quality of a Chinese encyclopedia. Thus, pager-sales shops, Bible stores, and barbecue places alternate with long lines of storage sheds, the ruins of 1920s chicken ranches, and new subdivisions advertising "Still Low 100s." If some blocks now look like Levittown, others are still defiantly Appalachia. Enough debris, meanwhile, remains exposed—derelict cars, farms, and steel mills—to suggest a Noachian flood event sometime in the area's recent past.

Cruising Base Line, in fact, is rather like watching a Jim Jarmusch movie. The dull moments are always promptly relieved by some new enigma or unexpected absurdity. The landscape here is fractally strange. At first glance, for example, a corner mini-mall looks like any other until you notice the hand-chalked sign promising FRESH GATOR on its way from Lafayette, Louisiana. (Hard times along the Gulf Coast have propelled thousands of Louisianans to the Inland Empire, where Cajun accents and Creole cooking now spice local culture.) Likewise, the dusty bramble next to a Mexican Pentecostal church on closer inspection reveals itself to be a ghostly fragment of a famous vineyard, once the world's largest, first planted in the 1850s. Exiled "Rollin' 60s" Crips graffiti, meanwhile, brazenly tags the protective wall of a new tract development preposterously called "The Village of Heritage."

In other suburban belts, artificial reality eventually smothers all intelligent life. But the Inland Empire's new commuter lifestyles must contend with a formidable quotient of traditional grit. The old blue-collar culture of the region, forged in the great Henry Kaiser steel plant in Fontana and in the freight yards of Colton and

San Bernardino, has survived plant closure and deunionization. Harleys are still more common than Lexuses, and there are more gun shops than Merrill Lynch franchises. Although white-collar commuters during the week shelter inside their walled compounds in Rancho Cucamonga or Ontario, on Friday nights they mingle with the working classes at the local gridiron. High school football is the Inland Empire's ecumenical religion. The corridor of communities along Base Line compete in the famed Citrus Belt and Sunkist leagues. These are deceptively genteel names for some of the meanest prep football in the country. The pioneer generation of Kaiser steelworkers transplanted the gladiatorial football traditions of the Allegheny valleys to Fontana in the 1940s. Although the blast furnaces are long cold and dead, FoHi and its local rivals— A.B. Miller, Kaiser, Eisenhower, Rialto, and Colton—still play ball with milltown passion. These Homeric battles over town honor frequently continue after the final whistle. In 1999, for example, FoHi players avenged themselves on an arrogant opponent by beating up the visiting coaches. Adults on both sides were scandalized, but many kids relished the payback.

Indeed, there is a populist element in the Inland Empire that bitterly resents the partial gentrification of once-happy badlands. A few years ago, I visited the little house on Montgomery Street in Fontana, a half-block south of Base Line, where I was born in 1946. The current resident and his sons were in the backyard vigorously stripping down an automobile. I knocked on the door and was quickly confronted by big glaring men with socket wrenches in their hands. They became friendlier when I explained that I had stopped on sheer impulse to revisit my Fontana early childhood. As his sons returned to their demolition work, the dad shared his views about the population explosion in the Inland Empire.

"This used to be a good neighborhood." He gestured toward the sagging bungalow shaded by an elderly pepper tree across the street.

"There was bikers and truckers. Regular people. Now," he said fiercely, "there's goddamn yuppies everywhere." He was obviously referring to the new "Falcon Pointe" subdivision a few blocks away. Although the dental assistants, schoolteachers, and paralegals who live there are scarcely "yuppies" by West LA standards, I took his point. The new Fontanans do tend to be intolerant of the old-timers' penchant for junk cars and biscuits and grits. "What's to be done?" I asked.

"Move to Victorville. I'm movin' to Victorville," he responded with the certitude of a new convert. Victorville is the nearest edge of the high desert, half an hour up the steep ramp of Cajon Pass from San Bernardino. Once a town of tough cowboys and gandy dancers, it is picturesquely sited where the railroad tracks (and now I-15) cross the mysterious Mojave River. Hollywood screenwriters with a tight deadline or a drinking problem used to be exiled to Victorville to finish their scripts without urban distractions. Herman Mankiewicz wrote the first draft of *Citizen Kane* there, although only a handful of English eccentrics, like J. B. Priestley and Aldous Huxley, genuinely seemed to have liked the Mojave and its relentless, howling wind. Now Victorville is the suburb of a suburb, the overflow basin for a rapidly urbanizing Inland Empire.

Most of the homes in the desert have space between them, the Jeffersonian antidote to the claustrophobia of folks like my Fontana informant, who fear living cheek by jowl with "yuppies." For the moment, Victorville is still a sanctuary for loners and good old boys attached to a ramshackle sense of personal freedom and the right to squalor. For culture they have had the Roy Rogers–Dale Evans Museum and the Striptease Hall of Fame, not to mention gun shows and swap meets. But even the high desert—on the outer limits of LA commuter space—is rapidly growing strip malls and grassy subdivisions. Soon will come the day when the yuppies move in next door and a Starbucks replaces the Deadwood Saloon. Then it will again be time for the hard core to load up the family Peterbilt and move farther out, to Barstow, Baker, or even Death Valley.

Indeed, Victorville is just one of the many pseudopods that the amoebic megalopolis is currently extending into its far-flung hinterlands. At the base of Grapevine Canyon, ninety miles north of downtown LA, developers have already used Washington's ancestral Base Line to plat thousands of home footprints on the dusty San Joaquin floor. Likewise, the chronic housing shortage in San Diego is turning agricultural Imperial County, two hours away over rugged mountains, into a dormitory for its blue-collar families. Without the rail infrastructure that weaves Greater New York together, and lacking any regional coordination of housing and employment, the outward expansion of Southern California—as urbanists have warned for a generation—becomes intolerably destructive of family life, community health, and the natural environment.

Yet it also seems unstoppable. Opinion surveys consistently confirm that Southern Californians' hunger for affordable single-family homes remains insatiable, and that they are willing to endure truly purgatorial commutes to attain suburban heaven at the end of each workday. It matters, of course, that they have so few real alternatives to choose from. The celebrated "New Urban" vision of pedestrian-scale villages on light-rail lines has had negligible impact on local building culture. Regional planning, Southern California's eternal will-o'-the-wisp, remains little more than the desperate race to add more lanes to a rapidly petrifying freeway system. This side of the apocalypse, at least, the future belongs to the desert suburbs and their simmering discontents. Greater LA's deepest impulse is still infinity.

COLORADO

THE HIGHEST STATE

Thomas J. Noel

Colorado reigned as "The Highest State" until the war on drugs and alcohol wiped out such aspirations. Yet Colorado is the highest state, with an average elevation of about 6,800 feet. It is the eighth-largest state and twice the size of Old England or, for that matter, New England. If Colorado could be ironed out flat, locals brag, it would be the largest state.

Colorado is the Spanish word for red, as explorers from Mexico called the state's major river with its awesome red sandstone canyons. *Colorado*, as a Chicana student once reminded me, also means colorful, flushed, or embarrassed. Coloradans should be embarrassed, she added, because they have voted to make Colorado an English-only state—a slap at the Spanish who were the first Europeans to explore, map, write about, and settle in a colorful state of blue skies, red rocks, purple sage, and snowcapped gray granite mountains skirted with evergreen forests and golden aspen trees.

The Spanish, like the French and the Yankees, were slow to settle the state with its central maze of mountains, high and dry eastern plains and western canyonlands. Not until 1858, when prospectors found golden sands in the South Platte River at Cherry Creek, did a barrier become a goal. A hundred thousand fortune-seekers stampeded in, combing gulches and stony hillsides for gold, then for silver, coal, oil, molybdenum, natural gas, and other minerals. Mining booms have come and gone, leaving gravel and sand the state's most valuable mined resource today. Booms and busts as drastic as the state's fourteen-thousand-foot mountains and as deep as its whitewater canyons continued with the 1980s oil crash and the early-2000 collapse in high tech and cable TV, the growth stars of the 1990s.

Amid all the ups and downs, the scenery and the atmosphere have remained Colorado's greatest resources. The air is clear, dry, and invigorating—what my grandmother called "air that only the angels have breathed before." Blue skies, brilliant sunshine, and crystal clear air—if you will overlook a little smog here and there— generally treat anyone who will look up to snowcapped mountain ranges, even from a hundred miles away.

Indians called Colorado the "land of the long look" for its clear atmosphere, high points, and relative lack of vegetation. Now most Native Americans do look at Colorado from faraway places, as nearly all of them were expelled and put on reservations. Only 2.3 percent of the population is Native American. The Arapaho and Cheyenne were wiped out or chased away. Only the Utes are left, confined to two reservations in the southwestern corner of Colorado. They are next to Mesa Verde, the first national park devoted to a prehistoric race. The awesome cliff palaces and pit-house ruins were designated by the United Nations as the first U.S. World Cultural Heritage Site.

Coloradans slaughtered Indians at Sand Creek and striking immigrant coal miners at Ludlow. Indians got brief revenge at the Meeker Massacre. There the Utes massacred the agency staff and the cavalry galloping to the rescue. Indian Agent Nathan Meeker was found naked, tortured, and very dead in the field he wanted the Indians to plow, a field where they preferred to race their painted ponies. The Utes dragged his body around the way they complained they had been dragged around the state that they used to control. In his mouth, rescuers found a barrel stave, as in "white man speak with forked tongue."

Unlike the Utes, labor never got its revenge in a conservative state given to union-busting and shortchanging the working class. For instance, the Colorado legislature still refuses to require port-a-potties in the fields for migrant workers. Yet these itinerants raise much of the state's wheat, potatoes, lettuce, honeydew melons, and other crops, including barley for Coors beer and the state's 100-odd brewpubs.

Spectacular scenery and three-hundred days of sunshine a year make "The Highest State" a favorite with tourists. Colorado is famous for its skiing, including North America's largest ski area— Vail. Other ski areas have given new life to the former mining towns of Aspen, Breckenridge, Crested Butte, Keystone, and Telluride. Colorado's mountains also draw summer tourists, who can frolic among the wildflowers and have snowball fights in July. Late snowmelt feeds white-water rivers fancied with rafters, canoeists, and kayakers. Tourists and locals also fancy the dude ranches, which now tend to be far more expensive and elaborate, competing for four-star designations. Energetic folks can fish crystal cool trout streams and bike, hike, or climb the mountains. Lazybones can drive to the top of the two most famous peaks, Mount Evans and Pikes Peak. Colorado has 3,232 named mountains and hundreds of unnamed ones. Scattered among them are fifty-three peaks higher than 14,000 feet. Colorado's highest mountain is 14,433-foot-high Mount Elbert. At 14,110 feet, Pikes Peak is a solitary, splendid granite bulwark that inspired an English teacher, Katharine Lee Bates, to celebrate its purple mountain majesty in "America the Beautiful."

Mountain scenery and minerals brought in greenhorns who stayed, helping to make Colorado a territory in 1861 and a state in 1876. The most novel and important political change came in 1893, when Colorado became the first state where men voted to give women the vote, setting an example that inspired other states to do likewise and led to national women's suffrage in 1920. Women pushed successfully for political reforms, including Denver's national pace—setting juvenile court and a Scientific and Cultural Facilities District Tax. The latter is a 0.1 percent sales tax that has bailed out Denver metropolitan area cultural facilities shortchanged by state government.

Women championed better schools, libraries, hospitals, and treatment of Colorado's down and out. The promise of quick wealth has been irresistible from the initial gamble on gold to casinos constructed during the 1990s in three fading cities of gold: Black Hawk, Central City, and Cripple Creek. Golden expectations have long attracted the poor or those who became poor looking to get rich quick. Nineteenth-century ne'er-do-wells have evolved into thousands of homeless. Colorado has always been a go-for-broke, Pikes-Peak-or-Bust state.

After the mining boom fizzled around 1900, the majority of migrants were tuberculars. They arrived coughing and spitting up blood, although tourist agencies and chambers of commerce downplayed that. Health care became a big business, along with mining, agriculture, services, tourism, and in recent decades, computers and cable TV.

The state's oldest creatures have also become a new tourist marvel and economic boon. Dinosaur trackways and bones discoveries in Morrison—near Denver, Canon City, and the Grand Junction region—are reminders that eastern Colorado once contained an inland sea with sandy beaches now preserved as monumental rock formations such as Garden of the Gods, Red Rocks, and the Flatirons. Swampy highlands produced fossil fuels from decomposed plant and animal life. This oil, natural gas, and coal, remain major resources in Colorado. Coal that once fueled smelters and railroads now provides most of the state's energy, extracted from giant open-pit mines in northwestern Colorado.

Colorado, with 4.3 million residents as of 2000, is the most populous state in the Rocky Mountain region and twenty-sixth among the fifty states. Yet "The Highest State" is sparsely settled, particularly on the high, dry eastern plains. Heavily Hispanic southern Colorado and the Western Slope, which includes the mountains and plateaus west of the Continental Divide, are also filled with open, lonely spaces. Three-fourths of all Coloradans live along the eastern base of the Rockies in a sprawl of cities, suburbs, and ranchettes stretching from Fort Collins near the Wyoming border to Pueblo, the hub city of southeastern Colorado.

Colorado's largest, best-known museum is the Denver Museum of Nature and Science. It has elaborate dinosaur exhibits, life-size dioramas of many wild animals, a mineral hall, and a planetarium. One life-size diorama depicts a Cheyenne Indian village, once on the site of Denver International Airport: DIA's Teflon-coated fiberglass tent terminal mimics those Cheyenne Indian tepees.

Among many music events are summer festivals such as Aspen's Music, Vail's Dance, and Telluride's Bluegrass Festival. The largest and longest festival, however, remains the National Western Stock Show, held for two weeks every January. With hundreds of exhibits, sales, contests, rodeos, and dancing horses, this event keeps Coloradans in their cowboy and cowgirl boots, Western hats and snap-button Western shirts. Many of the state's wealthy families, along with such part-time residents as fashion designer Ralph Lauren, maintain vast ranches where Angus and Herefords graze with buffalo, llamas, emus, and the longhorns which first turned Colorado into a cowboy state.

Colorado's booms and busts have left the state littered with more dead towns than live ones. Not only most mining camps but some two-hundred farming and ranching communities have bitten the dust. Prowling their lonely, historic ruins is a favorite recreation, as well as an escape from urban traffic, crime, and pollution, the state's three largest headaches.

In an isolated state of high mountains, deep canyons, and long distances, transportation has always been a key issue. When the transcontinental railroad bypassed Colorado in the 1860s to build over the gentler mountains of Wyoming, Colorado almost shriveled away. A sort of inferiority complex, a "bypass phobia" leads Coloradans to fear being overlooked, outshined, bypassed. So Coloradans have focused on building railroads, then roads, and then on constructing "the world's largest airport" on a fifty-four-square-mile site northeast of Denver.

The first gold-rushers used oxen, mules, horses, wagons, and even wheelbarrows to get to Colorado. After railroads arrived in the 1870s, rail lines were built up the canyons through rock cuts and tunnels, and over trestles. Almost a hundred different railroads reached even small and remote farming and mining communities. Railroads gave birth to half the towns in Colorado and explain Denver's phenomenal rise from a dusty little hamlet in the middle of nowhere to the metropolis of the Rockies. Amtrak still provides year-round rail passenger service, as does the Denver & Rio Grande Ski Train, and old-time narrow-gauge steam trains operate as summer excursions, time trips such as the Cumbres & Toltec, Durango & Silverton, and Georgetown Loop.

As Colorado is far from any sizable body of water and has no navigable rivers, railroads, automobiles, and airplanes have been the way to travel. Coloradans have one of the nation's highest rates of motor-vehicle ownership—and the smog and traffic jams to prove it. Aviation has been important in this remote state with high mountain barriers. A dozen Colorado cities offer regularly scheduled commercial flights. Denver is the hub of Rocky Mountain and High Plains air travel, with the seventh-busiest airport in the world. Opened in 1995, Denver International Airport has inspired Colorado boosters to claim that the translucent tent terminal, which is brightly lit at night and shiny white by day, makes Denver the most obvious hub even for intergalactic travelers wondering where on earth to land.

Denver, the capital and largest (2.2 million) city, is a mile high. Numerous parks and parkways as well as fifty tightly zoned historic districts make it a healthy and attractive city, with little of America's usual urban blight. Denver's old skid row has been reborn as the Lower Downtown Historic District (LoDo), boasting brewpubs, the Tattered Cover Book Store, nightclubs, art galleries, Coors Field, Mile High Stadium, and Elitch Gardens, the state's oldest and largest amusement park. LoDo, since its 1989 designation as a historic district, has gone from dollar-a-night flophouses to million-dollar lofts.

Although Denver now has a decent urban scene, it is the great outdoors that makes Colorado special. About a fourth of Colorado's land has been set aside for national forests, grasslands, parks, monuments, and wilderness areas. Together with state and local parks, these make Colorado one of America's biggest playgrounds. Some of the finest sites include the Rocky Mountain National Park, which straddles the Continental Divide northwest of Denver, and the Mesa Verde National Park, which includes the Southwest's finest cliff dwellings. The Black Canyon of the Gunnison National Monument features Colorado's deepest and narrowest river gorge, while the Colorado National Monument, near Grand Junction, has fantastic rose-colored canyons and tall pillars sculptured by the wind and water. Colorado's prehistoric past is revealed at the Dinosaur National Monument, where a dinosaur-bone dig and reconstructed skeletons revive the monsters that roamed Colorado when it was a tropical swamp, and likewise at the Florissant Fossil Beds, where ancient fossilized insects, seeds, leaves, and petrified stumps of giant sequoia trees are perfectly preserved. The spectacular Great Sand Dunes National Park is located in the San Luis Valley and has dunes reaching six-hundred feet high, nestling against the snowcapped Sangre de Cristo (Blood of Christ) mountains.

Major Stephen H. Long, who explored the state in 1820, pronounced it "The Great American Desert." Since 2000, a series of droughts and wildfires have left many Coloradans wondering if maybe Long was correct. He argued the state was too dry for white folks and should have been left to the Arapaho, the Cheyenne, the Utes, and the buffalo.

Palefaces massacred buffalo and Indians to get at the land. They quarreled with the federal government over land use, spent money lavishly when they had it, then went broke digging holes into the ground or driving railroads up the mountains, and replacing cattle kingdoms with dry land or irrigated farming.

Today Coloradans fight over whether to preserve the state's natural beauty or to develop it, be that for extracting natural resources or building yet another of the residential subdivisions and shopping malls that accommodated the 1 million newcomers who arrived during the 1990s. Despite the problems, newcomers keep coming, lured by the state's natural beauty and economic opportunities, which continue to dazzle visitors and residents. And even though John Denver, Colorado's favorite troubadour, crashed into the Pacific Ocean a few years ago, the state remains, as he sang, a "Rocky Mountain High."

CONNECTICUT

IDEAS OF ORDER IN CONNECTICUT

Maureen Howard

D riving Interstate 95, which pretty much tracks the route of
the Old Post Road, you seldom connect with the natural
lay of the land in Connecticut. The interstate passes from
shopping plazas to malls to nests of condominiums, by the cityscapes
of Stamford and Hartford, occasionally opening to the surprising
vistas of the shore and broad rivers that sustained the Algonquin, the
Mohegan, the Pequot. Pure American Highway of the urban variety,
until you consider the idyllic marina at Greenwich, the working port
of Bridgeport, cross the Housatonic at Stratford with the Sikorsky air-
craft plant in view, then to the broad port of New Haven Harbor and
on to New London with the Coast Guard Academy and the Naval
submarine station on the banks of the mighty Thames.

It seems a pity that we must scout out these natural prospects, so
that when driving north to the University of Connecticut, the state
university in Storrs founded as an agricultural college, we discover
the upland farms as pleasant New England scenery. But they are
working farms, still producing dairy products, though the famous
tobacco fields with their haze of white gauze to protect the broad
leaves grown for wrappers are mostly gone thanks to the discovery

that cigars are not a healthy pleasure. Farming and fishing were the riches offered to the tribes native to this rocky soil and to the colonists who forced them aside, bought them off, or killed them— as in the Pequot War of 1637, where women and children were slaughtered, of which event Captain James Underhill had this to say: "We had sufficient light from the Word of God for our proceedings."

It is difficult for farmers to yield a profit from the soil now, though some properties in Fairfield and Litchfield counties may be considered gentlemen's farms that need not support a family. The main agricultural yield comes from nurseries, which furnish suburban gardens, our domestic Edens; thus the famous crop of daylilies and Japanese tree peonies in the commercial gardens of White Flower Farm and the profusion of herbs in Gilbertie's Garden in Westport. As for the gifts from the sea, the oyster crop, reputed to be the largest in the world, is as delicious as ever—and trustworthy, after an arduous cleanup of polluted waters still in progress. The lobster catch may still be problematic; same with the trout and the spring running of the shad once famous in Connecticut, but the rivers and shores, if not totally cleaned up, are on the mend.

The lowlands of the river valleys and the highlands (not so high: 2,380 feet at Mount Frissell) reach to the Taconic Range in the northeast corner of the state at Norfolk, but the land has been so heavily populated with industrial pursuits launched early in the nineteenth century that we have to look hard to appreciate Connecticut as it was given—not contrived as village greens, college campuses, landscaped as Olmsted's parks, which simulate the natural, or the formal rose garden of Hartford's Elizabeth Park.

It's true that the modern history of this state began with the Dutch, the first settlers coming for furs, and the Portuguese who arrived for the fishing, but the story of the Connecticut Plantation, the second coming, is that of the migration from Massachusetts: Puritans in search of fertile land, thus the Pequot Wars. The next sensational moment in a lurid colonial history would be the witch trials, the territory being second only to Salem in persecution of women (at times joined by their husbands), the "Goodys," not deserving of the title Goodwife, publicly hanged for a mole or a perceived misdemeanor. Only Samuel Sewell, a hanging judge, confessed that he might have erred. Morally, the state is a rough terrain. The Fundamental Orders drawn up in 1639 were the first constitution in America, an enlightened move toward self-government; so was the charter John Winthrop procured from England in 1662 granting Connecticut territory from the border at the Bay Colony to the Pacific. Despite all the progress in matters civic, we (this is my place though I have wandered) were to be spiritually improved by religious reformers during the Great Awakening, which came our way from Massachusetts—which had, to some rigid minds, gone slack in matters of Good and Evil. Jonathan Edwards, born and bred in Connecticut, preached his punishing sermon, "Sinners in the Hands of an Angry God," in Endfield (1742). *The wrath of God burns . . . the pit is prepared, the fire made ready.* The good citizens would be treated to yet another scolding, the Second Great Awakening, launched by Timothy Dwight, grandson of Edwards and president of Yale. Dwight found the students lax in matters religious after the Revolutionary War, but his revival of strict Calvinism reached far beyond the college to become a missionary spirit intended to convert the Indians and ward off Methodists, Baptists, even Papists, who were gaining spiritual ground.

Yet all the while the shopkeepers and traveling salesmen were becoming known as sharp Yankees. Commerce and faith, corruption and rectitude, hoodwinks and the heroic: a melodramatic state. Take, for instance, two Connecticut-born soldiers who fought side by side at Fort Ticonderoga during the Revolution—heroic Ethan Allen and traitorous Benedict Arnold, who sold out to the British, then pillaged and burned the homes of his neighbors in New London. "The Nutmeg State," a tribute to the fake wooden nutmegs once sold by peddlers, has given way to the more respectable "The Constitution State," now on many license plates. P. T. Barnum, born poor in Bethel, established in oriental splendor in Bridgeport, would have subscribed to both mottoes with pride. He was a magnificent showman and an exemplary citizen, trickster and honorable mayor, shopkeeper, journalist and author of a best-selling, if self-serving, autobiography. Barnum kept the freewheeling spirit of Jacksonian democracy afloat. In one stroke of civic ingenuity and real estate savvy, he established East Bridgeport as an inviting situation for industry—which leads me to contemplate our gritty cities in cyclical decline, in perpetual promise of recovery. Urban renewal is an industry in itself, never envisioned in P. T.'s age of The City Beautiful.

Yet another legend, "The Munitions State": our cities profited in war—guns, not butter. The Colt revolver was the earliest on the market in the Revolutionary War. The rivers that once drew settlers to the fertile valleys provided water power for the manufacture of clocks, corsets, ammunitions, machines, and machine-made parts. Prosperity invited the immigrants from Ireland and Germany, to be followed in World War I by the Italians, Hungarians, and Poles. During World War II it was said that there were more Hungarians in Bridgeport than in Budapest. That war brought the Puerto Ricans and African-Americans from the South, plenty of work in the factories. The *New York Times* recently ran an article on the Latinization of Hartford, which has perhaps the largest population of Puerto Ricans in the country; but the jobs so many came for went south or disappeared with cutbacks in government contracts. It's little comfort to the present wave of Russians, Serbs, and Asians to look back on a time when Czechs, Irish, and Italians had the comfort of their neighborhoods, their parishes, their temples; that the cities were alive with polkas, jazz, the beat of marimba bands. For many new immigrants, the balm of our classroom multiculturalism must seem a distant text, an instructive TV documentary.

Distressed industrial cities with desolate Main Streets can be found across the country, but Connecticut, which the census at the end of the last century counted as 79 percent urban, is distinctly marked by its urban and suburban divide. Greenwich is still listed as one of the richest towns in the country, while the poverty level grows in Bridgeport, Waterbury, Bristol. Connecticut is a small state set between the dominant cities of New York and Boston, but it's the proximity to Manhattan that lends western Connecticut the tone of enviable suburbia. Just a commuter ride away, you can have it all— the Colonial, the Tudor, the Pomo estate, the protection of the picket or deer fence, the American Dream of lawn, pool, three-car garage. And you know, it is splendid: in the spring, the display of azaleas at the dooryards of North Stamford, the dogwood on Green-field Hill, or the blaze of autumn along the majestic street of authentic colonial houses in Litchfield. Splendid and expensive. The postwar developments, ranches, and splits of the fifties are less grand. Settled into a fitting scene for the pursuit of happiness, they should not be patronised in Hollywood movies, denied their reality. So we have the forever struggling cities and the bucolic pleasures of sub-urbia: separate communities, striking inequality. We must wonder if the folks on the hill ever stop by the new housing replacing the crime-ridden slum of Father Panik Village in Bridgeport, or the depressed streets of Waterbury. I met a young woman in my native city, which is Bridgeport, a woman so confined to the one street of her project that she did not know there was a body of water, Long Island Sound, a half-mile away—forget the chic of Westport, the elegant restraint of Darien. It's possible that each morning the commuters coming into Manhattan pass the tenements and projects of East Harlem and have never seen the black or Hispanic communities in Fairfield County.

Once upon a time, at the end of the seventeenth century, there was a company of men called The Hartford Wits who wrote mock epics as well as paeans to a grand American future, believing poetry would do the trick. Impossible to conceive of their hopes or their hubris. The Wits must never be confused with "The Sweet Songbird of Hartford," Lydia Sigourney, once the most popular poet in America, whose sentimental dirges "A Dying Mother's Request," "The Time to Die," were much concerned with the consolation of the grave. For writers of Connecticut enlightenment, we must look to Nook Farm, that rarefied enclave in Hartford that harbored both Harriet Beecher Stowe and Mark Twain. Mrs. Stowe, of the Connecticut preaching Beechers, returned to native ground as the celebrated novelist of *Uncle Tom's Cabin.* Ever vigorous, she wrote *House and Home Papers* for *The Atlantic,* advising on home management and decoration, the brave abolitionist now the Martha Stewart of her day. She was a practical woman, and I have always wondered what she thought, really thought, of the Twains' place across the way— mahogany porches, nineteen rooms, seven baths, walls and ceilings stencilled by Louis Comfort Tiffany. Surely the excesses of his mansion, the intellectual vigor and dead-on gentility of Nook Farm led to his contemplations of Hannibal, Missouri; to Huck's horror of the Widow Douglas's attempts to "sivilize" him, "so when I couldn't stand it no longer, I lit out." I also credit the high-minded literati of Nook Farm with the creation of Twain's Connecticut Yankee: "So I am a Yankee of the Yankees—and practical; yes, and nearly barren of sentiment, I suppose—or poetry, in other words." Would he have listened to the correction of Wallace Stevens, poet and insurance executive of Hartford?

The poem refreshes life so that we share,
For a moment, the first idea . . .

But Twain's Yankee declares his strength to be invention: in the factory he "learned to make everything: guns, revolvers . . . all sorts of labor-saving machinery." Which brings me back to my grammar-school pride learning that the cotton gin was invented by Eli Whitney in New Haven; my posterboard project attempted to show how the seeds were separated from the fibers; samples of my father's cotton shirts were affixed as the end product. I never knew that Whitney lost money on the gin and turned to firearms for profit. My best friend informed Igor Sikorsky, a guest at her family's table, that Russians ate with their fingers out of a communal pot. So much for our childish understanding of Yankee ingenuity and gentle manners. Many years later I discovered that Buckminster Fuller invented his Dymaxion car in the old Locomobile factory down by Seaside Park, where the Golden Hill Paugussett are now seeking a permit for a casino.

The arts constitute a major entry in the history of Connecticut—shows tried out for Broadway in New Haven (that proximity to the metropolis again), the Long Wharf and the Westport Country Playhouse, Hartford Rep, the O'Neill Theater in New London. Art colonies blossomed on the railroad line—Cos Cob, a picturesque settlement for American Impressionists, Childe Hassam in residence; Willa Cather stopped by. Silver Mine, Saybrook. The studio of Alexander Calder nestled just off the road in Roxbury; Josef Albers, émigré from the Bauhaus who wrote the color-field bible, settled in Orange, which, to his delight, bore a green highway sign; the great photographer Walker Evans lived, while teaching at Yale, in Old Lyme. Connecticut, overpopulated with artists and writers, sports an embarrassment of educational riches: Wesleyan, Trinity, Fairfield, Yale, of course, and UConn, with women warriors who play the Ivies right off the basketball court, and Bridgeport University, now run by the Moonies. We're awash in culture, with the Wadsworth Athenaeum, perhaps the oldest museum in the country, Yale Art Gallery, the Peabody Museum, the Mashantucket Pequot Museum, which presents the history of the eastern woodlands, ice age forward, with cultural displays of the tribal nations. As I return to a favorite painting in the Center for British Art, a George Stubbs handsome steed with young master, or delight in the carving of a Connecticut highboy, I wonder at my privilege, knowing that the pleasure I take in our prized colonial furniture and I. M. Pei's translucent marble walls of the Beinecke Library is not easily available to everyone. I don't know if my distress at the cultural divide in this country is simply banal, the way we live now and have lived since the vulgarities of the first traveling circuses were not discussed in the parlor.

Politically, oh, I've been dodging this one: "The Land of Steady Habits," a phrase that conjures up the Puritan past, might still be applied to Connecticut for its fairly conservative politics—at the moment a Republican governor, John Rowland, and Democratic senators (Dodd and Lieberman), but what a parade of colorful gents from both parties. J. Henry Roraback, a businessman and lawyer, never ran for public office but dominated the Republican party until the Depression, when Wilbur Cross (D), dean of Yale Graduate School, became governor while still editing the *Yale Review*. Prescott Bush (R), the senator from Pan-Am, begat the dynasty; Governor John Davis Lodge (R), whose wife, Carlotta, danced for the Italian vote; Senator Clare Boothe Luce (R), something of a carpetbagger; Governor Grasso (D)—not a gent, our Ella, a woman of vision; and Abe Ribicoff (D), our distinguished Jewish governor. It's entertaining to think of Barnum as mayor of Bridgeport and liberal state legislator, but the star of all our politicos is surely Jasper McLevy, the Socialist mayor of Bridgeport, not much of a Socialist as it turned out, but an honest man, a plain man beloved by the workers. What a romp Twain might have made of his Scotch thrift, of his idealism worn to threads during the Depression! But my, was he honest! As I write this, Joseph Ganim, the mayor of Bridgeport, has been convicted of sixteen charges, a dazzling array including racketeering, bribery, kickbacks; the mayor of Waterbury is being tried for corruption and unspeakable sexual crimes against little girls. The last three mayors of that beleaguered city have all conducted city business from jail. And then again an aide of the governor's is under investigation and the governor himself is in a bit of a pickle. Corruption in Connecticut is hardly a new story, but at this moment we are in need of Walt Kelly, our inspired cartoonist of political scoundrels, or of a Third Awakening, or perhaps a revival of Barnum's Great Moral Show, in which he aspired "to make the world *better* for my having lived in it." Though we must not forget that P. T.'s first big kill was with the lotteries.

Politics aside, it's a grand small state, full of decent people who might be perfectly happy to reinvent themselves given a little less gentrification, a little more civic responsibility. Long gone is the burning pit of God's wrath, but we might look again at the idea of the state of the state, draw up new Fundamental Orders (or protect the constitution of these United States). To go back to the Pequots, they are currently in litigation over a fellow stealing their website, but they are well set up at Foxwoods in Ledyard. The Grand Pequot Towers rise above the fields of eastern Connecticut like Camelot, with spas, pools, gaming tables, average attendance forty-thousand a day, 4.9 million square feet, nightly entertainment competing with the wonders of the Mohegan Sun in Uncasville. Casino as reparation or retribution? Take your chances not far from the insurance capitol of Hartford. It's fun and no more chancy than your number coming up on an actuarial table.

Where are you from? The question we're all asked when traveling. I'm quick to explain I will never be a real New Yorker, not a big-city girl. I'm from Connecticut, from a gritty city that prospered on wars, from a small state that maps many a postindustrial problem, from a landscape of American plenty, wit, and ingenuity, replete with hometown loyalties, and, like much of the country, in need of repair.

DELAWARE

THE FIRST STATE

Eric Zencey

L aw, in the broadest sense of the term," Montesquieu wrote in the famous first sentence of *The Spirit of the Laws*, "is a necessary relation that derives from the nature of things." The nature of some things is different in different places, and Montesquieu, first thinker to dig sociologically into law, counted legislative perfection as one of them. He thought the best laws for any particular society would be shaped by its physical and social character—by its commerce, its religion, its wealth, morals, and manners, by its climate, and even by its soil. Soil type determines prevailing occupations and (this, a hundred years before Marx) therefore the prevailing mentality, the dominant character, of a people.

Delaware is made up of three counties, each underlain by a different type of soil. New Castle County, which pokes northward across the fall line into the Piedmont, is mostly clay. Kent County, farther south, is loamy. Sussex County, where Delaware meets the ocean along twenty-three miles of nearly unbroken beach (there's one inlet, to a large, shallow bay), is sand. Following Montesquieu, we'd expect the laws of the three counties to differ, and not just in such mundane matters as what kind of septic system you're required to have.

Most Delawareans haven't heard of Montesquieu, but they appreciate the substance of what he said. Delawareans generally believe that the Chesapeake & Delaware Canal—a deep-draft, flat-water route for shipping between Baltimore and Philadelphia that runs east to west across the skinny neck of the state—marks a boundary between places where the spirit of life, if not of the law in all its particulars, is different. Above and below the canal, they say, even the weather changes. (Maybe it does: Delaware below the canal is due east of the Chesapeake Bay. Delaware north of it isn't.) Not too far north of the canal, water power and that clay soil made manufacturing more attractive than farming, giving a boost to mercantile over agrarian types. Citizens of northern New Castle County are residents-in-full of the BoWash corridor, whose defining arteries—railroad, interstate, airline—bisect the northern corner of the state. Two-thirds of Delaware's population (480,000 out of 780,000) live in New Castle County, on one-fifth of the state's land (438 of 1,982 square miles). The resulting population density (more than 1,000 per square mile) exceeds both India's (775) and China's (328).

Below the canal, towns of any notable size still have grain silos and a farm-machinery dealership and a veterinarian who'll come around to tend your animals in situ. As a child growing up in the shadow of the high-rise bridge that carries the DuPont Highway across the canal, I was regularly shaken awake in the small hours of the morning by tractor-trailers pounding their way north to market, carrying produce to Philly and New York before dawn. (As the trucks climbed the old bridge, downshifting with their regurgitive roar, they'd hammer the expansion joints, banging their weight down through the concrete piers all the way to bedrock, whence it would shiver up through my parents' house to sway my bed. It was comforting, once you got used to the noise.)

With its agricultural south and mercantile north, Delaware encapsulates the main economic division of the Civil War—fittingly enough, as it straddles the Mason-Dixon line and was a slave state that stuck with the Union. My parents' house dates from the 1840s. Above its kitchen are two tiny unheated rooms, reachable by a dark and twisting stair. We called them "servants' rooms," though in antebellum Delaware most servants would have been slaves.

Delaware is the second-smallest state, after Rhode Island. Delaware is the second-flattest state, after Florida. Too much shouldn't be made of this twice-also-ran status, but I think it contributes to a sense among Delawareans that true distinction lies elsewhere. (Delaware, "The State That Started a Nation," was first in one thing: signing the Constitution. Its representatives knew that the colony was too small to have any chance of standing alone, and they'd have signed anything that threw their lot in with New York and Virginia.) The state occupies about one-third the peninsular landmass that divides the Chesapeake Bay, on the one side, from the Atlantic Ocean, the Delaware River, and the Delaware Bay on the other. The peninsula is known by a simple compression of the names of the states that share its administration, Delmarva, a name even a schoolchild could mark as unimaginative.

Perhaps because I encountered it so regularly as a schoolboy, the shape of the state on a map seems to me geometrically archetypal. It ought to have a name: that precisely curved top, that straight back, that flat bottom. The map shapes of Pennsylvania and Maryland clearly have something missing—a shelf-slot out of Maryland's eastern shore, a smooth semicircle gone from Pennsylvania's southeast corner—but the only holes in Delaware's outline are bays and marshes. On the map Delaware is strong-backed and roundheaded, a blend of regular, precise line and craggy natural feature.

Since 1979, when the number of Delawareans actually declined, population in the state has grown faster than the national average. It isn't that Delawareans are especially procreative. Much of the growth has been influx: Delaware suddenly became attractive in the early

1980s. A spurt of development began in New Castle County and pushed southward down the peninsula, across the canal, chewing up farmland at something like three-thousand acres per year. The face of the landscape changed. Roads that were pleasant lane-and-a-half country drives became four-lane, jug-handled throughways, with traffic lights and chain-link fences and Jersey barriers. Entire towns were paved over, bypassed, or had the life otherwise resected out of them by automotive culture. Others were surrounded by condos and town houses and malls and starter mansions, becoming oases of anachronism. The town house/condominium represents a late stage in the architectural succession of farmland into mall-and-sprawl urban "core." Seeing rows of them emerge from soybeans is depressing.

The spine of the Delmarva Peninsula rises only a few dozen feet above sea level. This lack of altitude means that Delaware's transition from land to water is often gradual and ambiguous: along the bay and river the shoreline is mostly tidal marsh. There are forty-thousand acres of it in Kent County and almost again as much in New Castle, an intricate, nearly unmappable coast. Some individual marshes exceed a thousand acres in extent. Others trace their way across the state, banking the courses of flat, slow-moving streams, threading into farmland, snaking their way inland until you can come upon them by surprise, far from the ocean. A tidal marsh has a quiet, vital beauty. Freshwater mixes with salt, the water rising and falling with the tide, forming channels broad enough to pole a boat upon, lapping at the mud-clenching roots of cattails and of tall, papery-tube-stemmed marsh grass. The mud smells of methane, an aroma that marks a common root to "fecal" and "fecund."

One such marsh outside Delaware City is called The Dragon for its shape on a map. When I was a boy its tidal gates were closed in winter, and for a few cold-snap weeks you could skate on it, playing boundaryless pond hockey on its open channels. You could skate at night, in the moon's semidarkness. Take for a puck an old soda can, which rattles across the ice when you hit it, revealing itself by sound. Use for a goal any convenient marker: this or that muskrat house, a pair of sticks laid parallel, a line etched with the heel of your skate. When the puck skitters off into the darkness let one among your number retrieve it uncontested. Trace his progress against a far horizon of chemical plants lit up like phantom cities, all stack and tube and pipe. Play until your ankles hurt, your feet hurt, your lungs hurt. Afterward, warm yourself by a fire. Quiz the older boys about cars, about what it is they try to do with girls.

You can say only so much about Delaware before getting around to the Du Ponts. "The Company State" is what Ralph Nader's study group called it, criticizing the ease with which public authority has been wielded privately and familially throughout its history. Eleuthère Irénée Du Pont came to Delaware from France and in 1802 built a mill at Hagley on the Brandywine, where he manufactured black powder, founding the company that would become a corporate giant, giving the world nylon, rayon, Orlon, Dacron, and all manner of chemical and textile progress. The original mill site is a museum today, kept in a state of perennially scenic desuetude. Schoolkids ride past in open buses, touring the ancient works, learning the origins of Du Pont wealth, learning the word "jitney."

In the last-gasp heyday of the industry, before the invention of dynamite in 1866, the operation at Brandywine was the largest powder works on five continents. It had a dozen separate water-powered mills, each with a pair of huge stone wheels operated from the common millrace. The buildings were laid far enough apart that an explosion at one wouldn't automatically send up the others. Each was made of treble-thick stone on three sides, wood frame on the last, a form that directed the regular accidental blasts out over the stream and forest. I remember seeing some sort of hagiographic film on a grade-school outing: an actor impersonated the original Du Pont in a beret and buckskins, scowling when his muzzle-loader misfired, costing him some geese on the wing. "Thees powdair ees no good!" For years afterward I thought that I, too, would find my life's calling and the kernel of a great fortune in some crucial act of frustration, and I kept myself open to it, waiting. A lot of Delaware schoolkids visit Hagley every year. A lot of them probably get the same idea. This might explain something of the Delaware character.

Pierre S. duPont IV ran for, and won, the position of governor of Delaware in 1976. Six-Pacque Pete, the newspaper columnists called him, catching typographically the irony of the scion's posing as just folks for the purposes of electoral politics. "I'm going to vote for him," my friend Jimmy said, a sentiment shared widely among the bricklayers and apprentices I worked alongside summers out of college. Some of my construction buddies were impressed that Pete had once climbed up a three-story scaffold to shake our hands. Not Jimmy. He had a sense of reverse noblesse oblige: "They own the damn state. They should have to run it."

I left Delaware in the 1970s and returned occasionally over the next decade. I recall thinking on one visit that the New Castle County Planning Commission should be rounded up for questioning and maybe indictment, because there was no rhyme or reason to what had happened on their watch. Strip malls here, housing developments there, corporate "campuses" someplace else, with acres of fresh concrete and tarmac to connect it all. If you were told, "Design a landscape to hold 1,000 people per square mile," and you were beginning from scratch, or even from where Delaware was twenty years ago, you wouldn't produce what's there today. Incremental choice driven by private greed has produced a result that suits no one well. Overall road construction in Delaware in the 1980s and 1990s could have been measured in Global Warming Units. And the growth continues: in July 2002 Nicholas DiPasquale, the outgoing head of Delaware's Department of Natural Resources and Environmental

Control, said that the biggest threat to the state's environment wasn't toxic stuff from the chemical industry but suburban sprawl. "Vinyl [is] popping up all over the place."

In 1839 the Congress of the United States saw fit to abolish punishment by whipping and pillory, but then, as now, their enlightenment reached only to crimes within federal jurisdiction. Delaware law abolished the pillory much later, in 1905. The whipping post was retained, though in 1889 a law had been passed holding that "hereafter no female convicted of any crime in this state shall be whipped or made to stand in the pillory." A law passed six years before that (really, it's hard not to think of the 1880s as the Golden Age of Delawarean Jurisprudence) prescribed that "in case of conviction of larceny, when the prisoner is of tender years, or is charged for the first time, the court may in its discretion omit from the sentence the infliction of lashes." When lashes were not discreetly omitted, statute required that "the punishment. . . shall be inflicted publicly by strokes on the bare back, well laid on." The second (1958) edition of *The Delaware Citizen* (a standard good-citizenship text used in a course required of all students at the University of Delaware until 1968) lists twenty-four crimes still punishable by public whipping.

The list, with lash count, is instructive:

Poisoning with intent to murder, 60.

Maiming by lying in wait, 30.

Assault with intent to ravish, 30.

Wife beating, 5 to 30.

Robbery, up to 40.

Assault with intent to rob, up to 20.

Burning a courthouse or office where public records are kept, 60.

Burning a vessel, mill, granary, church, school, etc., 60.

Breaking and entering a dwelling in daytime, with intent to commit a crime, 20.

Larceny of horse, ass, or mule, or larceny by breaking a lock, 20.

Knowingly buying, selling, or receiving a stolen horse, ass, or
    mule, 20.

Embezzlement by carrier or porter, or by cashier, servant, or
    clerk, up to 20.

Willfully and feloniously showing false lights to cause a vessel to
    be wrecked, 39.

Perjury or subornation of perjury, 40.

Interestingly, a legislature capable of the fine distinctions necessary to calibrate one malefaction at thirty-nine lashes and another at forty had nevertheless not got its own capacity for myopia fully under control, for the last whippable crime in the list is "tampering with, altering, or destroying legislative bills or acts, 10 to 30 lashes." Is shortsightedness the reason lashes are earned for "poisoning with intent to murder," but not for manslaughter, for "maiming by lying in wait," but not for maiming by direct and passionate assault? I don't think so. Here the law reveals agrarian, loamy roots: the farmer has measured all too well the distance between plan and effect, seed and harvest, and learned that intent, not result, is where character is revealed. It would have been a merchant, not a farmer, who said "the road to hell is paved with good intentions."

Also notable is the interchangeability at law of horse, ass, and mule. The rich rode horses, the poor rode mules; the spirit of the law in preautomotive Delaware was commendably egalitarian. And none of your hairsplitting sophistry for these people, no sir: receiving stolen property is as bad as the theft itself, getting people to lie the same as lying.

The third (1967) edition of *The Delaware Citizen* omits this suggestive list and notes merely that while the number of whippable offenses stood then at seventeen, "a prisoner has not been whipped for years." I recall that during my adolescence some unfortunate trespasser against the public peace and dignity chose a whipping over jail, and that his choice prompted an outcry that eventually got the law changed. This would have been sometime in the 1970s. And who knows? If case law in Delaware's Court of Chancery had evolved to define corporate officers as executors, administrators, and guardians of a collective trust, and if Delaware statute still held that "fraudulent misapplication or conversion of funds by executors, administrators, [and] guardians" was punishable by "up to ten lashes, well laid on," how many corporations chartered in the state would have gotten involved in the pump-and-dump stock scandals of the 1990s?

In volume one of his *History of the United States During the Administrations of Jefferson and Madison*, Henry Adams expatiates on the character of the New England States, the middle states, the Southern states. He doesn't specifically mention Delaware but part of the description of Pennsylvania does the job: "If its soil bred little genius, it bred still less treason." "Pennsylvania was never smart, yet rarely failed to gain her objects, and never committed serious follies." "[T]he state made an insignificant figure in [national] politics. As the nation grew, less and less was said. . . of interests distinct from those of the Union."

Delawareans, too, easily take national interests as their own, and mostly the nation has been interested in the business of making money. This Delawareans have done with some vigor since the passage of the Financial Center Development Act of 1981, which was designed to make Delaware "the Luxembourg of the United States for banking and finance," as a spokesman at the state's Division of Economic Development proudly announced. Among other things, the law removed the usury caps that had been in place on interest charges. The prime rate was floating around 20 percent back then. Suddenly every bank and credit-card company in the country needed to have offices in Delaware. Long accustomed to flag-of-convenience incorporation because of the breaks it gives to corporations (that DuPont influence), Delaware saw some major players

(MBNA, Chase Manhattan) establish a more-than-symbolic presence in the state. That influx drove other changes, developments that rippled through the economy, sending town houses crawling into soybeans as far south as Middletown, an hour's drive from the corporate Valhalla of Wilmington.

The Financial Center Development Act did what it was supposed to do. A writer can feel envy that mere words on a page should have such effect in the world.

The character of a citizenry shapes the law, and law returns the favor. What sort of society did the Financial Center Development Act presume, and therefore help to make? Not one in which every nonhuman species is thought to be at least as precious as a legislative bill or act. Not one in which a healthy landscape is understood to be a public boon, parts of which an individual might hold in trust for all. Not one in which a landscape can be poisoned or maimed. Not one in which the soil is understood to be our culture's conjugal partner, needing protection from ravishment and abuse. Not one in which the landscape is at once the public's granary, church, school, and its chief repository of social and genetic wisdom, of records that ought to be preserved for no better reason than that someday, for some reason, someone might need to consult them. No, in Delaware as elsewhere, the landscape made by law is fit for the typical modern consumer-worker, who is not so much a citizen or a townsman—but an atomized particle in a mass, a human who asks nothing more from an ecosystem than the opportunity to ignore it—to be sped on good roads from job to home to shopping, and, in summer, on an occasional trip to the beach. To the commercial mind, the landscape is an amalgam of properties, nothing more—just as the public interest is (apparently can only be) the quadrennial summation of individual greeds and conceits.

First Staters are first and foremost American. Whatever Americans are privately, our chief public face shows that we are a race concerned with getting and spending, a race for whom any activity is improved if somehow the use of more and more fossil fuel can be made essential to it, global warming be damned. By what false light were we distracted, brought to hazard on this shore? If things go well for the planet, our children's children will view our ownership and use of internal-combustion engines with the same mixture of distaste and unsympathetic judgment we level toward those among our ancestors who once owned human slaves: "Granddad had two cars and a riding mower and a *speedboat?*"

"Love the sinner, hate the sin" is the motto of some churches. By this light I try to love the land and hate the forces that deface it. In many, many places in Delaware this is not hard to do. There is beauty there still, in places yet untouched by the press of hurry and scurry and assaultive population growth. There are some few towns holding communities that have kept themselves alive in unbroken succession for hundreds of years. There are wide bright beaches and broad shallow bays. There are forests and glens and quiet streams. There are wildlife refuges where migrating geese assemble in honking, noisy multitudes (Delaware underlies a major flyway). And there are those marshes, those magnificent marshes, protected (more or less) by state as well as federal law, where the great world ocean laps at one of its local limits, and where a soda-can puck sent sailing into the night can seem to rattle on its way forever.

FLORIDA

FINDING FLORIDA

T. D. Allman

Infusing everything is the enigmatic quality of Florida. Is it water or is it land? And where does one stop, and the other begin? Imagine a geographical feature four-hundred miles long, more or less the shape of Italy. Only at the top, instead of the Alps, it's the Okefenokee Swamp. At the bottom, the Everglades commingle water and land so equivocally a man could go mad trying to figure out which is which—if he isn't eaten by an alligator, or mauled by a panther, first.

Florida's loftiest point is an accident of political cartography, a hillock on the Alabama border 345 feet high. Ninety percent of peninsular Florida is less than 150 feet above sea level. Most of Florida's eighteen million people—nearly the population of Australia, and growing fast—live only a few feet, often only a few inches, above sea level. Florida's lowness is matched by the shallowness of the adjacent seas. The loss or gain of a thirty-story condo would scarcely be noticed along Florida's Atlantic or Gulf coasts. Yet if the seas rose that much the entire state would disappear. If, on the contrary, water levels fell that much, Florida would nearly double in size. It would extend itself halfway across the Gulf of Mexico.

Florida could be everything. Florida could be nothing, and this macrogeological equivocalness plays itself out in every Florida backyard. Build a swimming pool, and one morning you'll find an alligator there, brunching on your fox terrier. Fell that pine barren, and open a theme park; transform that scrubland into suburbia. Then watch while the sinkholes swallow up your Florida fantasy, while the palmetto bugs—Floridaese for giant flying cockroaches—find countless unsuspected ways to infest your life. Trying to shape Florida is like playing with play-dough: take the goo; mold it to your dream. Then watch the dream morph back into goo. People are constantly ruining Florida, and Florida is constantly ruining them back: that's Florida's oldest, and defining, historical theme.

Ponce de León was not—repeat, not—looking for the Fountain of Youth when he spotted Florida in 1513, but he was hoping to do something just as loony. In Florida's mush, he dreamed of re-creating feudal Castile, complete with serfs. Florida's various "Indians"—Calusas, Timucuans, and the rest—did not take kindly to enslavement, making the importation of African slaves ultimately necessary. The alien microbes the Europeans carried in their lungs, blood, and semen in any event doomed them, but while they could these original Floridians gave as good as they got. In 1521, an Indian arrow turned Ponce de León into the very first of Florida's failed property speculators, but it was Florida's microbes, festering in the wound, that actually killed him, making this arguably Florida's first celebrity homicide.

Hernando de Soto, Florida's next famous conquistador, marched up the peninsula looking for gold, then lost his way, his reason, and finally his life wandering aimlessly in the wilderness. De Soto and his many imitators never found gold because Florida, which is composed principally of porous limestone, has no metals. No iron, no copper, no bauxite, no lead—no gold. Florida also has no water power, in spite of all that water. That's because water, to be useful, must flow downhill. Think of ancient Egypt; think of Niagara Falls: civilization as conventionally defined cannot develop without metals and rushing water.

Florida consumed expedition after expedition. The Spanish didn't finally establish a permanent settlement there until 1565—and then (adumbrations of the Cuban missile crisis four-hundred years later) only because they didn't want the rival superpower, in this case France, to get ahold of it. Florida's real founder was a mass murderer named Pedro Menendez de Aviles. He tricked hundreds of shipwrecked Frenchmen into surrendering, then lured the defenseless castaways behind sand dunes where he cut their throats.

Florida was Spanish for nearly 250 years; never once did the Spanish manage to make it pay. This was in part because Florida's climate is nearly as bizarre as its geology. Except for a fringe at the top, centering on Tallahassee (which is why Florida's antebellum slaveholders ultimately put the state capital there), it's too far south and soggy for cotton, let alone the other cash crops that would make the rest of the United States the most abundant agricultural as well as industrial producer in history. Yet Florida is also too far north for easy exploitation of the great tropical plantation crops: no bananas, no spices, no indigo, no coffee, no rubber plantations flourish in Florida because, climatically, the place is neither temperate nor tropical. Instead you get the worst of both worlds: ten months of sweat followed by those spells each winter when the killer frosts kill the citrus, the tourists shiver in their flimsy resort wear and, in Sarasota and Bal Harbour, Florida society women take their mink coats out of storage, and dress up like Katherine Harris. It has actually snowed in Miami, but Florida's defining meteorological event is the hurricane, sweeping away all before it, including reason and dreams.

Florida history becomes U.S. history with the arrival of another conquistador, this one named Andy Jackson. The independence of the United States in 1783 opened up a glorious destiny for free white men like Jackson and his followers. It was a darker event for Indian tribesmen, black slaves, and people of mixed race. Faced with the insatiable land hunger (and guiltless racism) of the rising American yeomanry, runaway slaves and Indians facing extermination found refuge in Spanish Florida, though not for long. In 1814 Jackson—unable to tolerate the spectacle of multiracial, multiethnic liberty on foreign soil so close to the United States—marauded into Florida, massacring black and Indian civilians, kidnapping and killing British subjects, and making himself an American hero celebrated from New Hampshire to the Carolinas in the process. Following a series of illegal, unprovoked U.S. attacks—including the massacre of more than two-hundred black men, women, and children who tried to defend themselves at a now forgotten place in Panhandle Florida called "Negro Fort"—the Spanish meekly ceded Florida to the United States. Contrary to what you were taught in grade school, the United States never bought Florida. It mugged Spain, then inserted a clause into the treaty of cession by which the U.S. government agreed to pay its own citizens, who had trumped up charges against Spain, the monies they claimed to be owed.

Florida, not the Wild West, was where America's longest, bitterest Indian wars were fought. The U.S. Army's most formidable adversary—and Florida's first great defender of civil and human rights—was the Seminole resistance leader, Osceola. By then Florida's original inhabitants were long since exterminated. The Seminoles—far from being the tribal Indians we vaguely remember them as being—were a civilized, multiracial people. Osceola was, like his antithesis Jackson, a child of the American frontier—the son of a white Georgia father and a Cherokee mother. Like Jackson, he was also a military and political genius, but unlike "real" Americans, Osceola turned out to be a loser, in part because he respected the rules of civilized warfare. Lured to a parley, he was tricked into capture when U.S. forces betrayed their flag of truce. When Osceola died in

U.S. military custody, his American doctor cut off his head and kept it as one of the first Florida souvenirs. Resistance to U.S. land seizures continued until 1858, when the last of the Seminoles, except for a few who fled deep into the Everglades, were hounded out of Florida along the Trail of Tears.

Under U.S. rule Florida become one of the most unequal societies ever seen. According to the U.S. census, by 1860 there were about 160,000 people in Florida. Of these, officially, 77,000 were "Negro slaves." Florida had been seized from a foreign country; its inhabitants had been scattered to the wind, in order that fewer than 25,000 American white men and their families might use a subject labor force imported from Africa to exploit Florida for their exclusive benefit. Yet Florida never would be safe for its slave-owning freeholders. In all, less than sixteen years elapsed between Florida's admission into the Union as a slave state, in 1845, and the outbreak of the Civil War. Florida earlier had rebuked the golden illusions of the conquistadores. Now the Jacksonian dream of a white democratic slaveocracy turned to muck, too, as the Union Navy assaulted Florida's indefensible shoreline, and Florida's Confederate governor committed suicide.

Those who imagine that Florida's peculiar role in national politics is something new should revisit the fateful presidential election of 1876. Democrats won the popular vote, both nationwide and locally, but the Republicans stole the presidency by manipulating Florida's electoral votes: the vote-grabbing was particularly egregious in Dade County. In return for letting their losing candidate, Rutherford B. Hayes, take office, the Republicans abandoned their commitment to Negro enfranchisement, racial integration, and civil liberty in Florida and the rest of the South. The consequences of this corrupt deal, which put an unelected president into the White House in return for ending Reconstruction, would be dire and long-lasting. In Florida, as elsewhere, a racist counterrevolution would ensure that white supremacy would be maintained for generations at the cost of systemic political and human injustice. The price paid in cultural stagnation and economic backwardness would be enormous, too.

Until the very end of the nineteenth century, Florida's uselessness remained its decisive factor. For more than three-hundred years, no one had been able to figure out a way to make the place profitable. But then, thanks to the Industrial Revolution, America—or at least America's robber barons—got so rich it didn't matter anymore. At the height of the Gilded Age, Florida became a wonderland, where people dispensed fortunes they'd made up north. What cars were for Detroit, and oil was for Texas, throwing your money away turned out to be for Florida—the economic activity that determined its identity and defined its soul. To this day it's what links the Palm Beach millionaire on his yacht and the Ocala retiree on his shuffleboard court. One is squandering, the other is eking out, money that both made somewhere else.

Florida's newest conquistador was Henry Flagler, one of the greatest of the great tycoons. Flagler wanted Florida to be a combination of Monte Carlo and Tahiti. Such a Florida did not exist, so Flagler created it. Mangrove swamps, where the loudest sound had been the buzz of mosquitoes, were reshaped into South Seas paradises where dancers swayed to the rhythms of ukuleles and castanets. Where egrets once nested, golf balls now flew over the formal gardens of Renaissance villas. Flagler reshaped more than the land. He reshaped the very idea of Florida. In the mind of America he transformed one of the rainiest places in the country into "The Sunshine State." He originated the notion that all the ills of America are somehow linked to temperature: if we only moved someplace warmer, we could escape the incoveniences, injustices, and divisions of our society, and live in a Florida-America where there was never any snow to be shovelled, and everyone was just like us.

The backbone of Flagler's empire was his Florida East Coast Railroad. Ultimately it would stretch to the very extremity of the peninsula and then, following the Florida Keys, leap from island to island all the way to Key West, only ninety miles from Cuba. Why was this great construction project pushed so far south at such great expense? As Flagler discovered, not even his Palm Beach palazzo was far enough south to escape Florida's winter chill. A generation earlier, gold had propelled the transcontinental railroad west to California; the Florida railroad was impelled south by the search for a place within the continental limits of the United States where the mercury never, ever, dipped below 32 degrees Fahrenheit.

Flagler set off a speculative boom in Florida real estate that made more people richer, quicker, than the California gold rush ever had. Then, beginning in the 1920s, retribution swept down on Florida from both north and south. The New York stock-market crash was devastating for Florida's speculators, but that was only half the catastrophe. What the Roaring Twenties had built, the roar of hurricanes now blew away. One after another, the killer storms struck— swamping Miami, breaking Flagler's railway as though it were a prop in a cheap disaster movie. Florida had been a backwater of the Spanish Empire, a strategic liability to the Confederacy. Now Florida was a backwater again.

It would take something more than the rotation of the economic cycle from bust back to boom to restore Florida's fortunes, and then transform it into the pivotal state it is today. A complete reorientation of America's national life—south toward the sun, financed by massive government transfer payments—would be required to transform Florida into a place where millions of newcomers would choose to act out their life dramas on a year-round basis. Beginning with the New Deal and World War II, that's exactly what happened. The government in Washington unleashed a year-round tidal wave of money flowing into Florida. Thanks to Uncle Sam, poor whites and poor blacks would get food stamps. Migrants from the north would be given the Interstate Highway System to speed them and their Winnebagos, like latter-day pioneers in motorized covered wagons, to the Promised Land of trailer parks and sunshine. Generous government financial benefits for anti-Castro refugees from Cuba would subsidize the Cuban success story. The rich, never to be left out, got the Intracoastal Waterway, built at taxpayers' expense by the U.S. Army Corps of Engineers, to ease the passage of their yachts south each winter. Social security payments provided the recession-proof, nonseasonal financial underpinning for what became America's fastest-growing big state.

The conquistador of this new Florida was Walt Disney. He was to this new post- (actually never-) industrial, Sun Belt Florida what Flagler and Jackson earlier had been to the state. His gigantic Florida theme park, Disney proclaimed, would be founded on "the ideals, the dreams, and the hard facts that created America." Critics would claim that, inside Disney's brave new world, America's ideals were transformed into mindless conformism, the American Dream into a Smiley Face travesty. No one, however, could deny that Disney World exemplified "the hard facts that created America." Disney World was a land grab that would have done Jackson or Flagler proud. Like them, Disney imprinted his idea of America on Florida. Here was a Florida, an America, where nothing was left to chance in Adventureland—a country where even the presidents were robotic. Meanwhile, an hour's drive away, America's astronauts were getting ready to soar from Florida to the moon.

Even as the moon was Americanized, and the American Dream was Disneyfied, Florida's permanent themes resurfaced. In early January 1959, Fidel Castro entered Havana, and the tropical, Latin, Caribbean side of Florida's destiny reasserted itself. Thanks to Castro, but thanks also to decades of unremitting U.S. hostility to him, Miami would be transformed from Florida's biggest tourist town into a world-class metropolis. Meanwhile millions of "real" Americans, surging into Florida from the north, were reproducing all of America's homegrown complexities. Florida was also on the cutting edge of globalization, thanks to tourism and drugs, which were to this latest new Florida what bootleg whiskey and the slave trade had been earlier. It remained only for the Bay of Pigs invasion (planned and partly run out of Opa-Locka, near Miami) and the ensuing missile crisis to bring America's "Escape State" into the fulcrum of the closest we, and the rest of the world, have ever come to nuclear holocaust. The Russian missiles, had they been fired, would have hit Orlando.

By the unforgettable year 2000, Florida had become the crucible of every human change reshaping the United States, from the aging of America to our transformation into a multicultural society. It was where revelatory dramas were acted out. With hanging chads, Florida made the second Bush presidency, and hence the second Iraq war, possible. With anthrax in envelopes, Florida played its role in making terrorism a hometown phenomenon. The Islamic fundamentalists who flew into the World Trade Center had attended flight school in Florida. After 9/11, the Afghan air war would be run out of McDill Air Force Base, near Tampa. As the new millennium became darker, quicker than any pundit had foreseen, the now retiring baby boomers kept surging into Florida, lured by the dream of a Florida respite. Meanwhile in Hollywood—Florida, not California—the sexy francophone spokeswoman for a weird cult announced it was cloning babies and, up in Fort Walton Beach, millions of tiny frogs emerged from the earth to take over the Panhandle Animal Welfare Sanctuary (PAWS).

Florida always has been a mirror of America, but what does it show when we look into it? It shows things that, like it or not, have always been true about us and our country. Whether it's Al Gore or Osceola, Florida shows us that America always has been a nation of losers as well as winners—and that when it comes to politics, and many other things, Americans often play rough, and do not always play fair. It continues to show us what was true in 1876 and 1821: in this remarkably adaptive country, racism still colors almost everything, and inequality forever dogs us no matter how rich our country gets.

Florida shows us that it's hope, not justice, that keeps America from flying apart. Next time you're driving around Florida, and get stuck in traffic because a bridge has opened to let someone in a $100,000 boat go deep-sea fishing while all the poor lugs stuck in traffic have to go to work, look into the faces of the people stuck in the cars. You see no anger; you see no jealousy. No one complains that rich people in boats have right-of-way over average people in cars, because everyone in those cars believes someday they'll be rich. They'll be driving a big boat, and the bridge will open for them.

That's the promise of America. And isn't it true that, perpetually in America, enough things go well enough for enough of us that, by and large, the dark swaths around us are best left as they are?

GEORGIA

A TWISTED ROAD

Jim Grimsley

There is a Georgia landscape that I love, but it is a landscape of the interior, of the vault beneath shade trees or under the canopy of a forest. The Georgia that one can admire is a green land through which runs a twisty road, a journey over hilly country where the parade of houses is occasional, where other roads branch off from mine, heading into a green that is full of hiding places, that is a multitude of enclosures in which live modern Georgians, modern southerners.

The state is a forest, green and deep. There are 140-odd counties of Georgia, each one a different reflection of Georgia unique unto itself, so intricate that a person could tell the story truly only by living in each place.

Where I live, the city and the country collide. My home city is Decatur, the small old town that a century and a half ago disdained to become Atlanta and instead became Atlanta's next-door neighbor. This is a layer of the truth that could be peeled further for more onion; in fact, Decatur refused to become Terminus, a joining of railroads, and it was Terminus that became Marthas-ville and later Atlanta, a name that is as certain as the fact that no one really remembers who made it up or where it came from.

Our history here is like that—curious, somehow as ornate as the word "Atlanta," and equally as inexplicable in its origins.

We Georgians are the heirs to ideas that are so contradictory as to be schizophrenic, living in the shadow of events that will continue to color our history for the century to come, and likely beyond. We live in the United States of America, which we are proud to claim as the home of the free and the land of the brave, but which is no longer so free as it was, though it is likely as brave as ever. As southerners we live in a land where a white person will tell you he is born to be free and raise hell and yet will likely raise his beer can to the battle flag of the old Confederacy, as if that is the idea of freedom that he meant all along. We live in a land where a black person must live in the memory of slavery that still roots and flowers in the landscape.

The ideas of freedom and equality have always offered peculiar flames to the moth of the human spirit, bumbling through the air. The idea of freedom burns us even as we seek to attain it or claim it for our own. Our country likes to remind itself of the intricacy and beauty of the documents that laid down our democracy, but we too often forget that inequality and lack of freedom are also codified in these documents. Slavery was part of the design from the beginning; slavery was part of the landscape even while different groups of people struggled over the idea of freedom and what it meant. Slave-owners shaped and signed our Declaration of Independence; slave states were among those insisting that a Bill of Rights be added to the Constitution before it be ratified.

This history being common knowledge, one should focus on the schizophrenia of the two ideas—that a country that once allowed chattel slavery as a legal practice should ever call itself free—for it is a certainty that this country, with such a blindness in its perceptions, is never likely to be free of its past. In Georgia, we see this to be the case. Black people look to the past and see the pain of their own bondage; white people look to the war that ended the bondage as if the war was penance for it, or should have been. Each group takes what ideas best suit its needs and makes of them what it wishes. Georgians, like nearly everybody else, are remarkably adept at learning to remember what they want to remember and to believe what they want to believe.

The focus is always on the freedom of the individual and much more rarely on equality. In fact, we celebrate the somewhat contradictory notion that, in order to allow people to be free, we must accept the fact that they will never really be equal. In order to allow an individual to express his business sense, for instance, he must compete in a free market and, through competition, prove himself better or worse than others.

The look of equality in Georgia is much like it always has been. We do not look for equality, in fact; we look for a carefully managed inequality, which will supply us with the kinds of difference to which we have become accustomed. From this system we require the necessary labor for our chicken-processing plants, hands for the peach and peanut harvests, cleaning people to clean up all the big buildings in all the towns and cities. We create the inequality that we require, and we explain to ourselves that, in a free country, a person is free to do better, or to do worse. How can some do better if some don't do worse?

In this we are like our neighbors in the Carolinas, in Alabama; we are like New Yorkers in this; in fact, we are like everyone. Certain kinds of optimism, like socialist ideas, have fallen so thoroughly out of fashion that we are left only with our freedom, the freedom of the predator to take prey, the freedom of the strong to control and divide the weak. Certain ideas, like the notion that civilization should not reward differences in status to such a great degree, are being lost.

Georgia is a market, selling itself and all that it contains. Being a free market, Georgia applies as few constraints to competition as possible, in order to maintain a healthy economy, a notion that is very rarely examined in any detail. A healthy economy is one that is always growing, like a cancer. The contradiction somehow goes away in daily expectations. The idea is that competition is good for business and good for the market—but only competition of certain kinds. Businesses compete; labor labors for business. In Georgia, as in many states, labor laws favor the employer to the degree that, while business is free to organize in various ways, labor is not.

These days, the individual Georgian could be anyone. Possible selves are offered continuously through entertainment of all kinds available to any Georgian, even in a trailer parked at the end of a red-clay dirt road in the deepest piney woods south of Macon. Only the most determined isolate can escape the reach of the satellite and the Federal Express van these days, and therefore any trailer in the woods might be anything, a corporate headquarters, a laboratory for illegal drugs, a massage parlor, home to a child pornographer. The individual Georgian could be an Atlantan from Minnesota, educated in Colorado, here in Atlanta in middle management for a corporation that recently relocated him or her from a job in New Jersey, who plans to live here for four or five years before taking a job somewhere else, maybe California or Texas. Could be a Korean businessman, maybe at the corner grocery or the local convenience store. The individual Georgian could be a gut-busted beer swizzler living in Mom's swayback house on the back streets of Douglasville, or a newly arrived cross-dresser in Savannah, looking for midnight in the garden. The individual Georgian is the deepest forest, the most elaborated of all the interior spaces of Georgia itself.

The Georgian could be homeless, nearly invisible on the street, as if the grime on clothes and skin were a kind of camouflage; the Georgian could be a citizen of the sidewalk, existing on nothing, as free and equal as the rest of us, and hungry out of some personal failure of some kind, tragic but inevitable. Let freedom ring.

Does one measure a territory like a Georgia by its successes or by its failures? Even in framing the question this way, the defeat of equality becomes inevitable. We focus on the wealthy, the happy, the suburban, the elite urban, the possible mobility from one class to another, the fact that an individual is free to make a better life. Or we focus on the suffering, the poor. We focus on the fact that some will always do better and some will always do worse. The idea of a true pursuit of equality, of sharing a community and resources more equally, is rarely considered.

Writing a century ago on this subject of Georgia, W. E. B. DuBois wrote the following:

> To the employer a working man is nothing but a profit-producing animal and he doesn't care a snap of his finger what the animal's color is—white, black, red, brown, or yellow; native or foreign born; religious or unreligious—so long as he (the worker) has strength enough to keep the logs coming and the lumber going—that is all the bosses want or ask. It is only when they see the slaves uniting, when all other efforts to divide the workers on the job have failed, that we hear a howl go up as to the horrors of "social equality."

Today's Georgia laborer may more likely be a fast-food worker, or a systems analyst, or a sales representative, or a clerk/receptionist at an HMO; may be African-American, European-American, Asian-American, Latin American, Native American; the elegance of the principle is that it need not change. Whatever differences exist can be used to divide laborers from common cause with one another.

What is certain about DuBois's statement, and certain, at last, about his small hope that this difference of racial hatred might be overcome, is that the statement holds true today to an even greater degree, and that the differences of hatred and division have never ceased to thrive in all the century since he wrote.

At the end of a prosperous century, facing an uncertain

millennium, glutted on the goods of the world, we are in fact worthy of all our differences, especially in that we cannot let go of them.

What is the use of freedom if we are not willing to be equal as well? Since it is clear that equality is not interesting to any of us, how are we to survive as more and more of us crowd this state?

Once I spent a terrifying month in another landscape, in Wyoming, in treeless plains where I could see for miles on all sides, every storm crossing a field, every car or truck making the curve past the distant ridge and sweeping along the long bow of it around a field as vast as my old hometown, over a bridge and a creek that snaked thin and circumspect beneath the wide sky. In such an open landscape, with that appalling breadth of heaven overhead, maybe all people are humbled by their puny scale compared to the big things like wind and grass and earth. But in Georgia, in the mazes and labyrinths of green, the wind moves only as distant leaves, one tree blends into another, and our eyes are trained to see the small differences in our small interior spaces, among the leaves; maybe that's the reason we persist in seeing only the differences between ourselves and others.

HAWAII

THE ALOHA STATE

Lee Siegel

L ove is big business is Hawaii. It's our most natural resource and reliably marketable export commodity. Once we had sandalwood, then whale blubber, and then sugarcane and pineapple. But now it's romance, more fragrant than sandalwood, sweeter than sugar or pineapple, and whale blubber can't even compare. Based on an AOL poll, a recent issue of *Travel and Leisure* magazine, announcing that Hawaii is considered "the most romantic place in America," deemed Honolulu the best city in the United States in which to "pop the question, take a romantic walk, or enjoy a honeymoon."

Romance is indigenous and well-suited to these islands of equable breezes and perennial sunshine—it readily germinates, blossoms, and bears fruit both in the wild and with controlled cultivation. To sustain our economy under the decline of agricultural and military revenues, the Hawaiian tourist industry harvests, processes, and packages the varieties of romantic love that flourish here for consumption by the millions of tourists who visit each year. Many of them come for the very same reason as the humpback whales—to mate.

"Hawaii" a promotional brochure for a locally-based international wedding service typically proclaims, is "the Most Romantic Place on Earth." The company arranges nuptial ceremonies in English and Japanese "on a secluded beach of golden sand or beneath a tropical waterfall at affordable prices starting from $69.00." If you're already married, this firm, like its many competitors, can provide you with a second, third, or whatever honeymoon, or an anniversary package tour. And if you're cheating on your spouse, or not married and not necessarily planning to be, they've got "a fabulous getaway for romantic lovers who, regardless of their budget, recognize the value of celebrating their love affair in a setting that only beautiful Hawaii can offer. Hawaii is for lovers!" Hawaiian automobile license plates identify this archipelago as the Aloha State. "Aloha," as everyone who visits here must inevitably hear, means not merely "hello," and "good-bye," but also "love" and "I love you." Between the Aloha Academy of Golf and Aloha Yard Service, the yellow pages edition of the Oahu telephone directory lists almost three-hundred businesses or institutions names Aloha something-or-other, including Aloha Bridal, Aloha Beautiful Weddings, Aloha Chapel, Aloha Pregnancy Counseling Center, Aloha Escorts, and Aloha Strip-O-Grams of Hawaii (not to mention Aloha Bail Bonds and the Aloha Rehabilitation Center). The directory itself is called "The Paradise Pages."

Hawaii has evoked idyllic reveries and hopeful dreams of love, erotic fantasies in which amorous fulfillment comes easily and naturally, since the very beginning. When Captain James Cook happened upon this chain of islands in the middle of the Pacific on the morning of January 18th, 1778, jubilant natives, enthusiastically shouting "aloha," surrounding his ships in canoes full of gifts—pigs, breadfruit, sugarcane, sweet potatoes, and naked women with "countenances open and agreeable," who, according to ship surgeon William Ellis were "remarkably anxious to engage themselves to our people." While "aloha" out of the mouths of the men may have meant "hello," the women's alohas apparently declared "I love you." Fearing that "connection" with them would bring the "Venereal Complaint" to the uncharted islands, a sober Captain Cook tried to prevent the females from boarding his ship. But Polynesian passion proved too potent a power to control. Voluptuous wahines, curious and playful, giggling and seductive, clambered aboard the *Discovery* and the *Resolution* to gleefully make love to the visitors. And then there was nothing Cook could do to restrain his love-starved seamen from going ashore for more of the lush pleasures of sweet romance in the isles of Aloha.

A year later, having returned to Hawaii from the cold north, Captain Cook was beaten and stabbed to death by peeved natives on Valentine's Day. Reports divulging that the Hawaiians had eaten his flesh put a damper on visits for a while. But, some fourteen years later, when Captain George Vancouver, sailing into the Kealakekua Bay, the very place where Cook had been killed, discovered that the women of Hawaii were as eager as ever to make love with foreign men. Young Thomas Manby, master's mate on the ship, described the reception: "By sunrise the vessel was surrounded by canoes, every one freighted with the choicest part of creation, the female sex. . . In a moment our decks were crowded with young, good-natured girls, whilst the surface of the water around us was covered with some hundreds soliciting admittance. Our bark instantly became a scene of jollity and all was pleasure and delight."

Still today when you embark from an airplane in Hawaii there are dark-haired, barefoot local girls, clad in pareus, with flower wreaths around their heads and floral garlands around their necks, to greet you. They hold placards identifying their employers—"Aloha Vacations," "Paradise Tours," "Romance Hawaii," and the equivalents in Japanese. Once you identify yourself as a pre-paid client of their particular tour company, a lei is draped around your neck and, for the first of many times on your visit, you hear the magic word: "Aloha."

Received on shore by a "pretty, good-natured girl" named

Macooah, one of the many spry queens of the old chief Enemoo, Manby was fed fruit and coconuts. Other nubile, "uncivilized brunette[s] in a state of nature" joined in the fun as, after adoringly adorning him with flowers, Macooah proffered hospitalities that the employees of Aloha Vacations and Romance Hawaii have let fall into neglect: "She then nearly undressed me to observe my skin," Manby reminisced: "Two hours I reveled in ecstatic enjoyment."

Three weeks later, upon his departure from Hawaii, Manby gave his charming chiefess "a few beads, ribbons, and other trinkets" to assuage the sorrow she displayed over his farewell. The last "aloha" left Manby with a certain romantic nostalgia that has endured as a sentiment associated with having made a visit to Hawaii. Almost two-hundred years later, Ricky Nelson echoed the young sailor's wistfulness:

Pretty Polynesian baby over the sea,
I remember the night
When we walked in the sand of Waikiki,
And I held you oh so tight.

A yearning for paradise and the dreams of it which have infused Western consciousness ever since the Enlightenment constrained us to abandon the notion that the Biblical Garden of Eden exists somewhere as a geographical reality, informs all conceptions of this seagirt paradise, the most remote place on earth. There is a prevalent fantasy, that pre-contact Hawaii was like that primordial garden wherein man and woman, unashamed of the nakedness of their bodies and of the desire natural to their flesh, enjoyed an unmitigated pristine pleasure. *N ān ā I Ke Kuma*, a book dedicated to elucidating pre-Western cultural norms for contemporary people of Hawaiian ancestry wishing to revive those preciously traditional values (or maintain what remains of them), insists that "the sexual act [in ancient Hawaii] was accepted without shame as both creative and as a source of supreme pleasure. It was sacred, but it was fun too." The text explains that children began to indulge in sexual intercourse as soon as they were physically capable of doing so. As boys were counseled by their grandfathers as to how to please a woman, so grandmothers taught little girls "how to touch and caress a man and make him happy." And, to that end, how to make their vaginas perform 'amo'amo ("wink-wink"). Grandmothers deflowered their granddaughters in childhood so that first experiences of lovemaking would not be painful. Le'a, the Hawaiian word for orgasm, denotes not only sexual gratification, but pleasure more generally, and happiness more far-reachingly still. "Hawaiians knew intercourse as an ecstacy in which na ūhā 'olina ('the thighs rejoiced'). They knew it as warmth and companionship and merriment." Most ancient Hawaiians, furthermore, had their own mele ma'i ("genital chant")-Queen Liliuokalani's mele ma'i prasied and immortalized her vagina as 'anapau ("frisky").

Conceiving of sexuality as an energy inherent in all things, animate and inanimate alike, native Hawaiians, it is nostalgically supposed, had a thoroughly erotic perception of their topography and its geology. "The ancient name for this place," a friend knowledgeable in traditional lore told me as we drove past Koko Head Crater, "was Kohelepelepe. That's Hawaiian for 'fringed vulva.' The crater is the imprint of the vulva of Kapo, the sister of Pele, the volcano goddess. It was a flying vulva, and Kapo used it to lure the pig god here. It flew from here to Kalihi. It hasn't been seen again since the haoles arrived."

To these Happy Isles where bare-breasted "brunettes in a natural state" with frisky winking vaginas and virile chiefs with rejoicing thighs once sang genital chants, danced the heated hula, and merrily made sacred love, came the haole—the panting, bloodless white foreigner to whom sacred and fun were antonymous. First the explorers, and then the sandalwood traders and whale hunters, imported venereal disease and the capitalist system that perverted love into prostitution and subverted the holy into the profane. And then the Christian missionaries introduced the superego into this sexy Eden where there had previously been a complicity between id and ego, where the pleasure principle had gone unchallenged by reality as we have constructed it. But while Hawaiian soil has been hospitable to trees bearing juicy mango and sweet papaya, the tree of the dry and bitter fruit of the knowledge of good and evil seems to have been better suited to colder, darker places.

Captain John "Mad Jack" Percival, commander of the first U.S. warship to dock in Hawaii, showed up in 1826 only to discover that the Hawaiian chiefs, having converted to Christianity, had outlawed prostitution. His men got drunk, rioted, and rampaged through the streets of Honolulu. When Mad Jack threatened to permit such behavior to continue unless the chiefs rescinded their prohibition against fornication, the Hawaiian leaders, realizing that their economic relationship with the United States was in jeopardy, acceded. For the sake of big business, Hawaii once again became a place to come for sex and love, for shameless fun and high romance.

The Hawaii Visitors Bureau would certainly support the view that despite the efforts of puritanical churchmen to eradicate the inherent Hawaiian lack of shame and proclivity for carnal delight, Hawaii remains a lovers' paradise. A locally published guidebook, *Hawaii in Love*, providing information on each island's most "romantic spots," invites visitors to indulge in the fantasy of the eternal Hawaii of romance: "Imagine a land, sensuous and warm, where desires dance untamed, no strings—and no sins—attached. A place where lovers rendezvous on rainbows; where gods occasionally mate with mortals, plants have passion, and rocks can copulate." Having observed a lot of rocks in Hawaii, I can attest that if they do in fact copulate, they do it very, very slowly.

My own fantasies of romantic Hawaii were fostered over fifty years ago when, going to dinner with my parents at Don the Beachcomber's Polynesian Restaurant in Hollywood, California, I'd gaze at the portrait of the stunning bare-breasted South Seas siren as painted on black velvet there. Behind her, the full moon's reflection shimmered in an enchanted sea cove. Every fifteen minutes, it rained outside the restaurant windows: bamboo, fern, and birds of paradise, the crimson phallic protuberances of anthuriums and yawning vulvic orchids, all glistened with delicate droplets from these automated tropical showers. Erotically exotic perfumes of pikake and plumeria laced the air; and there was the dulcet sound of ukulele and a honied voice in lilting song:

I want to go back to my little grass shack
In Kealakekua, Hawaii
I want to be with all the kanes and wahines
That I used to know long ago

When, in 1955, at the age of ten, I came to Hawaii for the first time with my brother, mother and grandmother, the moon wasn't quite as luminescent as it had been in the painting on black velvet at Don the Beachcombers. And the only naked breasts I got a glimpse of here were the sagging pale ones I saw when I opened the door to the bathroom in our room at the Moana Hotel to inadvertently discover that my grandmother was changing into her bathing suit.

Hawaii was, however, despite the relatively minor disappointments, perfectly romantic, even (if not especially) for a boy of ten. Love was in the air at the luau at Don the Beachcomber's Waikiki copy of his original Hollywood establishment. Listening to the emcee's song, I couldn't help but get a big crush on one of the little girls in the line of young hula dancers whose grass skirts were made of cellophane and whose ornamental bras were formed of diminutive scallop shells:

I love a pretty little Honolulu hula-hula girl!
She will surely make you giggle
With her naughty little wiggle . . .
Her oni-oni motions
Stir up my emotions . . .
My Hawaiian hula-hula girl . . .

Even though, subsequent to the dancers' final "aloha," I never saw the nine- or ten-year-old brunette again, after leaving Hawaii I probably thought as much about her as Thomas Manby thought about Macooah or Ricky Nelson about his pretty Polynesian baby. In ancient Hawaii her grandmother would have already have taught her everything there was to know about love. I succumbed to the romantic nostalgia. Hawaii had lived up to the promises made on the Pan Am poster that, after my return home to California, I put up on the wall of my bedroom: "Your Hawaiian adventure is sure to give you a taste of the romance of ancient life on dreamy island shores."

When I stayed at the Moana Hotel in 1955, four years before Hawaii became a state and one year after Burt Lancaster had made love to Deborah Kerr on a Hawaiian beach in *From Here to Eternity*, we were required to change from our bathing suits and flowered shirts into coats and ties in order to go into the beach-side Banyan Court of the hotel where a Hawaiian orchestra played, and a large Hawaiian woman, bedecked with flowers, sang sweet love songs. It was from there that the radio show Hawaii Calls was broadcast for so many years to enchant Americans all across the nation with the amorous sounds of the South Seas. The Hawaii of the Moana, the place where the romantic likes of Mary Pickford and Douglas Fairbanks, and Carol Lombard and Clark Gable, had once vacationed, was still rather elegantly romantic. My mother danced with Charles Boyer there.

I went to the Banyan Court for a drink the other night and, while many of the same songs are still sung there, there are no coats or ties.

In 1955 my mother dressed my brother and me up like adults; now all the adults are dressed like children. They wear shorts, sneakers, baseball caps, and tee shirts that say things on them like "Official Bikini Inspector," "I Got Lei'd in Hawaii," and other phrases that insinuate a Hawaii where, while sex may still be prevalent fun, romance may be going the way of sandalwood and whale blubber. Although lovers strolling along Kalakaua Avenue in front of the grand old hotel often hold hands, they are usually carrying an ice-cream cone or a diet soft drink in the free hand.

Or maybe it's just me. I've lived here for almost thirty years and it's as easy, I suppose, after such a long time, to become inured to the romance of Hawaii as it is to the perfect weather. Since moving to the state that *Travel and Leisure* magazine has designated as the most favored place in the United States in which to "pop the question, take a romantic walk, or enjoy a honeymoon," I've been divorced twice. Inasmuch as the same poll cited New Orleans as the best place in America for "steamy encounters," I must assume that "pop the question" in Hawaii does not mean to ask "Would you like to have sex with me?" but rather "Will you marry me?"

Seated near me at the Moana bar there was a couple drinking Blue Hawaii cocktails, each garnished with a pineapple slice, vanda flower, and a back scratcher. "Where are you from?" inquired the sun-burned man in a flowered polyester shirt that Douglas Fairbanks would never have been caught dead in. That question, no doubt heard for the first time by Captain Cook two-hundred twenty-five years ago, is routinely posed to every haole here. When I informed the visitor that I live here, his wife beamed: "It must really be some-thing to live in paradise." She divulged that they lived in Iowa and had, ever since getting married twenty-two years ago in Cedar Rapids, dreamed of coming to Hawaii to reaffirm their vows: "And it's been even better than our wildest dreams. We had the ceremony at sunset on the beach near Koko Head Crater, an authentic

Hawaiian wedding with lots of flower leis, pineapple champagne from Maui, and real live parrots. Our minister, Reverend Jimmy, blew a conch shell just like they did in ancient times. And his wife, Laia, danced the hula for us."

When the singer, looking in her muumuu and leis not unlike her 1955 predecessor, asked how many people in the audience were newly weds, it was not only the Iowan newly re-weds who raised their hands. "Anyone celebrating an anniversary?" brought more hands up. "This song," the Hawaiian entertainer announced, "is dedicated not only to you, but to everyone who's in love."

> Love sweet aloha . . .
> Now that we are one
> Clouds won't hide the sun,
> Blue skies of Hawaii will smile
> On this our wedding day.

The song brought joyful tears to the eyes of the woman from Cedar Rapids. Tenderly placing his hand on her arm, the happy husband reiterated for me the epitome of all that's imagined, believed, and marketed—all that's said and written—about the Aloha State: "Hawaii is the most romantic place on earth."

IDAHO

STILL KICKIN'

Judith Freeman

I'm sitting in a senior center in a small town in Idaho, population 380, in the middle of farm country. All the men are playing pool, big suspendered fellows and little wiry old farmers leaning on their cues. The women are already seated at the long tables, waiting for the lunch that's about to be served. Every once in a while one of the men thunks one of the women in the head with his pool cue as he maneuvers for a shot in the tight space, and somebody yells, "Hey watch out, yer bangin' her," or "Canchoo use a shorter cue?"

Outside it's warm, very warm for December, not a good sign for this country in the grip of a drought that's stretched on for years. A block away, in one of the only businesses still open on Main Street, the proprietors of the sandwich shop are waiting for the few lunchtime customers to dribble in.

Lunch at the senior center is $2.50, unless you're underage, which I (gratefully) still am, and then it's $3.50. Today I'm the guest of my friend Pearl, who's eighty-five, and her sister-in-law Doris, who just turned ninety. Besides lunch—fried chicken, mashed potatoes, gravy, and peas—there's to be entertainment today, a man who sings karaoke-style to country-and-western tapes and talks about the wild elk he befriended and named Elvis. He's brought a stack of his cassettes and videos to sell. They sit on the table behind me. I can make out only one title on a video: it looks like *Still Lickin'*.

We've been living in this town for a number of years, my husband and I, but recently we sold our place in town and bought an old homestead in the country. The land is so dry nothing grows on it except a kind of drought-resistant native grass, cultivated for the seed that the government buys to replant areas burned by recent wildfires. We inherited a windbreak of dying trees, fields infested with noxious weeds, broken fences, and a pond that hasn't had any water in it for seven years. On windy nights, the rattle of old equipment abandoned in the fields and the thrum of an antiquated antennae run beneath my dreams.

Since we bought the place, I feel I have more in common with these elderly people. We're all committed here, so to speak, located firmly on this spent soil.

"There are only two kinds of music as far as I'm concerned," the entertainer is saying. We have all marched dutifully through the feed line and are now devouring our food as the program begins. "There's country, and then there's western." He has come to the right audience, I can tell from the appreciative laughter. I'm facing the wrong way, however, and can't see him. I have to settle for his songs, which are many, if not varied, each one delivered to the same electronic beat of the boom box that backs him, each a twangy ode to the West. Elvis is his hero, and he takes a no-holds-barred approach to belting out his imitations.

It takes a long time to drive across Idaho: it's a big state, and there are few roads to take you east-west around the vast national forests and wilderness areas that make up the center of the state. It's easy to think of it as a divided region due to its geography.

People will tell you there are really three states in Idaho, not one: there's the piney, lake-studded north—the so-called panhandle, where Randy Weaver and his family lived until agents from the Federal Bureau of Alcohol, Tobacco, and Firearms killed his dog, his teenage son, and his wife as she stood in the doorway of their house holding their infant daughter—a tragic episode that for many has come to represent the violent abuses of the government.

Then there's the southern farming country, a region dominated by conservative Mormons who in many ways are more aligned with Utah than Idaho. And then there are the rest of us—the dirt farmers and dreamers, the real and would-be cowboys as well as the urbanites who live in the growing cities of Coeur d'Alene, Boise, Pocatello, and Moscow.

Some would argue that there's a fourth state within the state—the wealthy, liberal enclave of Sun Valley, where Bruce Willis and Demi Moore, Arnold Schwarzenegger and Tom Hanks park their jets and Hummers. And, lest we forget (which we usually do), Idaho is also home to sovereign tribes—the Nez Perce, Shoshone-Bannock, Northern Paiute, Kootenai, and Coeur d'Alenes, each with their own reservation.

We are an odd lot, and we know it. What can you expect from people who put FAMOUS POTATOES on their license plates? "If there was ever a state that needed some PR," someone said to me recently, "it's Idaho." Sad to say, but true. As the twentieth century came to a close, we became better known for white supremacists than spuds. The question is, do we deserve such a reputation?

"This here's a song my son said I ort to have called 'Taco Belle,'" the country-and-western singer says with a chuckle, launching into a ballad about a Spanish senorita glimpsed one never-forgotten night, her dark eyes a haunting memory. The oldsters by now have finished their meals and moved on to dessert, store-bought angel food cake with two stewed apricots sitting like orange yolks upon a little pillow of Dream Whip. Their attention seems to be drifting.

It's hardly worth noting that everyone in this room today is white. Like much of Idaho, this town has no racial diversity—it's a hard place, bitterly cold in the long winters, and now mostly populated by the elderly who haven't managed to leave like the many who did when the sawmill shut down in the late seventies. Sixty miles away in Sun Valley, things are different. There, a vibrant population of Mexican immigrants keeps the economy running, as they also do in the farming areas throughout much of the state. We're one of Sun Valley's bedroom communities. There are no jobs here, not for Mexicans or whites. Our town has been dying for years.

It's a beautiful state, Idaho. As lovely as they come. Acres of wilderness, wild rivers, mountains, thick forests, and a small human population—in short, a place where a guy or a gal can still get away from it all and live out some sort of Western Mythic Dream. The problem is, everybody has a different idea of what that dream entails. Almost 70 percent of the land in Idaho is government-owned—most of it federal—and lately there's been a lot of disagreement over how that "public" land should be used: wolves, or no wolves? Mining and logging, or recreation and conservation? All-terrain vehicles and road cutting, or closure of wilderness to vehicles? Cows on public lands, or an end to "welfare ranching"? Should we take out the dams and hope the salmon return, or keep pumping that power? The debates grow ever more heated, with no resolutions in sight.

"I'm a'gonna to cue up my Elvis video now," the singer says. He means the elk he's named after his singing hero. As we look at images of a huge bull elk standing in a pristine forest, he explains how he's killed seven or eight of these magnificent animals in his lifetime. In fact he was writing a book on elk hunting when this particular elk wandered down out of the mountains one winter and befriended him in exchange for some hay. He got the idea to make a video—"clean family entertainment"—on which he would tape

Elvis eating hay out of his hand while he sang him some songs. The video was so successful it landed him a front-page article in the *Wall Street Journal*. "You all have heard of that paper, haven't you?" he asks the seniors. There's a murmured response, not really a yes or a no.

"Well," he adds, "it's real important back there in the East."

Back there in the East, Idaho is a kind of easy joke: say "Boise" on late-night TV and get a laugh. It's easy to think of Idaho as a blank state, a place devoid of culture and identity. Most people don't know that Ezra Pound was born in Idaho, in a small mining town called Hailey, not far from where Ernest Hemingway lived in Ketchum and where he later committed suicide. You could say that twentieth-century American literature was born in Hailey and died in Ketchum. Both Hemingway and Pound were fond of Idaho. Later in his life Pound used to sign his letters "The Idaho Kid." He must have liked the idea of claiming Western roots, even if he did leave the state before he was two.

They're our most famous citizens—Hemingway and Pound. Idaho isn't a state known for its writers, unlike, say, neighboring Montana. In other ways it doesn't have the same cachet, suffering as it does from the twin curse of spuds and white supremacists.

Yet Idaho is one of the fastest-growing states in the nation. Most of the newer residents are "whites in flight"—Californians looking to get out of crime-ridden cities, people who want to start over again in a new place—like Mark Fuhrman, the LA cop charged with racism during the O. J. Simpson trial, who moved to a small farm in northern Idaho and now hosts a popular radio call-in program focused on crime. He didn't help our image any. Nor has James "Bo" Gritz, the former Green Beret who brokered the surrender of Randy Weaver and went on to buy a large tract of land in northern Idaho (named "Almost Heaven") in order to sell lots to disgruntled anti-government types like himself.

It's easy to believe all the bad stories about Idaho and racism—but only if you think that what you hear in the world of sound-bite news is the whole story. It's true that Richard Butler and his Aryan Nation cohorts started a compound in the early 1980s near Hayden Lake devoted to preaching racial hatred and that within the remote forests of the Northwest a whole assortment of outlaws and oddballs have taken root.

What is less well known is the fact that Butler and the people he attracted weren't actually from Idaho. They were outsiders, come to spread their stain on a state they perceived as fertile white country. But the people of Kootenai County fought hard against them. Over many years, ordinary citizens united to resist Butler's message of hatred. Finally, in 2000, with the help of a lawsuit filed by a woman and her son who were attacked by Aryan Nation guards, the compound was closed down and taken over by a local college. All the buildings have been razed, as if to detoxify the site, and a new campus is taking shape devoted entirely to promoting a message of peace and racial unity.

But then that's the story of Idaho that doesn't often get told.

"I thought Elvis had died," the singer is saying, " 'cause I didn't see him for a few years and elk don't live very long in the wild with hunting and all. But then this spring I thought he came back. At first I wasn't sure it was him. So I went out in the woods to try and figure it out and took my camera along. That's me there, singing him a little song. It's called 'Still Kickin'.' That's the title of my new video. I hope y'all will buy it."

I look at the stack of videos. So it's not *Still Lickin'*, as I'd first thought, but *Still Kickin'*. It occurs to me this is a good motto for Idaho, given all its difficulties over recent years with different factions trying to figure out how to live with each other. However, I've been told that state officials have recently thought of a different motto for its new ad campaign for the state: IDAHO: THE WAY AMERICA USED TO BE.

I have to think about this. Because if Idaho is the way America used to be, how does it fit with the way America is now?

Rural Idaho has been losing population for some time now while the cities are growing. Our community had 1,800 people living here in the 1920s, as opposed to 380 now. It's true in many parts of the state. Towns are dying out. Farms are failing. Jobs are scarce. People are struggling, and they're looking for somebody to blame. Many have taken to the woods to live more self-sufficient lives.

Idaho has *lots* of woods and out-of-the-way places. Out in the less populated regions is where you find the constitutionalists and states'-rights advocates, the antitax people and militiamen and survivalists, those trying to live off the grid and fly just below the government's radar. With so much unemployment—so many disgruntled former miners and loggers—people are ready to hear about how you shouldn't have to pay taxes—how the Democrats want to take your guns just like they took your jobs. Government isn't much liked hereabouts. As one local militia leader over in Blackfoot put it, "Know what your legislator looks like: you may have to shoot him." The state has pretty much become a Republican stronghold, where even a Republican ex-governor has gone on record saying he's worried the two-party system is in danger.

People here in Idaho will tell you there's no future in farming except for big corporate farms and maybe they're right. Maybe the cities are our future, and the huge agribusiness pig farms and dairies—the so-called "cafos" (confined animal feeding operations) that have moved in from California, thanks to the low level of regulation in Idaho, and now plague communities with their foul smells and pollution. But farming is so much more than farming—it means families, solid citizens, a commitment across generations. It could be that the West is breaking down, with people and agribusinesses moving in from cities because land is cheap. It's just economics. What the West used to represent was freedom—and cheap land. Now, if you have enough money, you can buy a piece of that freedom. It comes with privacy, safety, and good air.

For some people anyway. Because there doesn't seem to be much of a place at the table for the working poor of Idaho. The move-ins, with their city ways and disposable income, tell the native loggers and miners and ranchers that the way they did things in the past is wrong and they are going to show them the new, better way. But some of the old-timers don't want the new ways. They just want to go on feeding their families and working the jobs they've always liked. They suspect that the newcomers are insatiable consumers, and the thing they now want to consume is "beauty"—the unspoiled, carefully managed beauty of the land others live by.

For many of the people moving into the state, there is a serious disconnect—"nature" is their new playground. They don't like hunters because they don't want wild things killed. Yes, the wolves have been successfully reintroduced and that makes environmentalists happy. But within the wilds of the massive Frank Church Wilderness Area and adjacent regions, the wolves have reproduced more successfully than anyone thought and will soon be "delisted" and this worries people who prefer to think of wildlife as children, in need of supervision—not unlike Elvis the elk, who has been turned into a sentimental character by an elk-hunter turned big-daddy video crooner.

In so many ways Idaho isn't ready for its new motto—THE WAY AMERICA USED TO BE—because Idaho is very much like America is now, full of rifts and divisions and fears. What has sustained us is an innate decency, the wish to do right by each other, and a creed of self-reliance that seems bred in the bone.

I see this in the faces of the seniors surrounding me. Here in Idaho, there is an ethic common to the West—still very much alive— whereby a man is judged not by his skin color or wealth but by his character. There exists old-fashioned hospitality and generosity—a large-heartedness to match this big country.

"Thank the lord for you seniors," the singer says, wrapping up his program. "I been travelin' around this state, visiting senior centers, and you've been my best customers. I got plenty of my new videos for sale today. I hope you'll take one home and keep a little bit of Elvis with you."

It could be my innate skepticism, but I walk out wondering, did old Elvis really return, like the original Elvis come back from the dead, or is it a case of opportunistic revival for the sake of a new video? In the end, it doesn't matter. The videos don't sell. Nobody here has that kind of disposable income.

What they do have are memories of a place where a family could make a living off a small farm. Now it takes ten of those farms to do the job (unless you're low-tech, thrifty, and resourceful). They remember also when the streams still ran, before they were straightened and degraded by decades of abuse. They remember the fish that swam in those streams, now long gone, and how the sage hens and pheasants once were abundant. They can recall the days when there were real fiddlers among them, not canned music, times when their town was alive with dance and song and thriving businesses. It's a world most of us won't ever know. Unless we make it happen again.

Maybe that's why most of us have come here, or stayed—because we believe in the possibilities. In an increasingly managed world, Idaho is still one place where you can find freedom and space. As the novelist Denis Johnson, who lives in Idaho's panhandle, put it, "You come here with a vague notion of getting away from it all. Then when you get out into the woods, you see how wonderful it is to be self-sufficient to any degree, how essential it is to being human."

The truth is no one really knows who's out there in the woods of the Northwest—harmless nature lovers? Or more dangerous types—people Gritz has called "Spikes"—Specially Prepared

Individuals for Key Events. Perhaps those woods are the domestic equivalent of the "Arab Street"—the place where homegrown resentments are festering. What is certain is that this isn't a regional problem, it's a national one. We must count on our civility to bring us through whatever lies ahead. As a nation perhaps we can aspire to live up to the sentiment expressed in the signs posted in the north during the turbulent eighties and nineties: IDAHO: IN IT TOGETHER, TOO GREAT TO HATE. That would be something worth striving for.

ILLINOIS

NOT JUST ABOUT GANGSTERS
AND GRASSLANDS

Ana Castillo

The state surrounding my city, my hometown, place of my birth and where I have lived most of my life (although I have left time and again; as you will see, my ambivalences shall be immediately evident) was always alien to me—and alienating; a place that (unlike myself) didn't have much use for ambivalences. Black and white both city and state. Overwhelmingly white—was and is. They did away with the Indians a long time ago, almost at the start. As for the black descendants of slavery and the "others" who came to reside there—coming up to work in the fields, railroad, stockyards, steel mills, any dirty job that was to be had— they were never given any real attention, much less credit for it.

Therefore, from within the walls of Rome (as it were) where I came along, about around the middle of the twentieth century, having no relationship to "down state" or the rest of middle America, I write this today the same way I most assuredly would have sat down in the sixth grade to write a social science report for Miss Inglesby at Jackson Public Elementary. I put on my hose and nice Sunday clothes and brushed my hair, as if I were on my way to the capital of Springfield to look up the records of the founding fathers and I took a trip down to State Street to the Harold Washington Library. It is a monster of a monument to the city's only black mayor (and what a mayor he was), with gargoyles passing themselves off as owls looming down at passersby—interesting touch on a notable contribution to a city with a formidable near-revolutionary attitude regarding its architecture. "Revolutionary" in terms of style and form and "near" because of lack of sentimentality or nostalgia about . its constructions. (It must have been the trauma of the Chicago Fire. But then they still preserve the Water Tower, one of the few structures that survived it, so who knows.) Unlike other cities in the world, New York, Istanbul, Mexico City, that hold on to buildings a very long time, long past their functionalism and even safety, here the contracts get set up, the politicians give the green light like pharaohs determined to remake the kingdom in their own image, and the hailed architectural statements of the last era are likely to be knocked down tomorrow and replaced with something entirely new—and often suspect.

In the last decades Chicago has been undergoing one of its biggest building booms. Down goes the abandoned Goldblatt's store. The rear end of an old theater is demolished while the Sullivan-on-opium-like facade is saved for a new building behind it. Your mother's house is demolished and up comes a condo complex or soft loft building or a row of town houses bought up before they are even completed by the influx of mostly white, white-collar, young upwardly mobiles, children of the White Fright of the fifties, sixties, and seventies, I imagine. Just as fast, the ethnically and economically divided neighborhoods for which this city is noted, that gave it a provincial and working-class reputation, are disappearing.

It actually started a while ago, Chicago's centennial face-lift. An example was the battle Mayor Daley (the first) had with the residents of the neighborhood known as Little Italy when he started the building of a University of Illinois campus smack down in the middle of town. The residents seemed to have won their fight in part by rescuing at least some of the old neighborhood. But today, Little Italy and Greek Town (which also borders the sprawling campus that continues to swallow up surrounding areas), with the exception of a few restaurants, exist in name only. In name only is another historical building, not for its structure but for what it stood—Jane Addams's Hull House. The remaining portion, a mere fraction of the original mansion (and I ought to know since I was among the countless minority children that benefited from its services "back in the day" as might be said in youth vernacular), stands on the UIC campus as a museum.

This is the area where I grew up, located near everything, the center of the world, the navel of the city, control tower for the Midwest. A scant bus ride to downtown, the Loop, State Street, the grandeur of Michigan Avenue and its Magnificent Mile. Around the corner from the famous Maxwell Street Market, begun at the end of the nineteenth century by an early wave of Jewish and Irish and later Italian merchants. Those who came to purchase *bacalao* and tailor-made suits were serenaded on electric guitars crying the blues, music brought up from the South that became synonymous the world over with Chicago as much as its pizza and gangster era (and today for its nasty reputation for violent crime, pristine skyline, as well as a basketball team led by a certain *superathlete* that won six national championships). Today Maxwell Street has been relocated just west of its original location and divided into two main merchant camps: the Mexicans and the blacks, with a few other immigrant vendors signaling that they too are digging stakes for good in Sweet Home Chicago.

The city in which I was born, as it grew in industry and population, was noted for its high-rises and skyscrapers—one that held its own for a while as the tallest on the planet. If such a thing as a natural mound, hill, or mountain existed it was only a rumor to the native Chicagoan—a Hollywood illusion that may have been seen on the black-and-white screens of early TV or the great big ones of such ornate and impressive theaters as the Oriental downtown. No, I lived within the invisible boundaries of an organized and determined metropolis. For more than the first half of the twentieth century, if you were born there you stayed. Those who arrived rarely left. (Whites were leaving of course, creating what they hoped would be the antiseptic city antidote known as Suburblandia.)

If I thought of Illinois at all, it was in school during a history lesson and it was white in complexion as much as it was panoramically flat, not an alluring combination for the likes of me. When I was small I was unfamiliar with the railway system that transported imports and exports and movie stars and dignitaries before O'Hare Airport existed (and which is now considered the world's busiest). We also did not have an automobile to take Sunday road trips outside of the city, so without eyewitness experience any school report on the state would have turned out the travails of the frontier, the story of the early French settlers and fur trappers, Lincoln who freed the slaves, farm life, the settlements of the Mormons and Lutherans, and as I said, scarcely a mention that anything real exciting had transpired since the late 1800s after John Deere had invented his plough.

No surprise then perhaps that researching "Illinois"—checking out the new main library with the Gotham City gargoyle sentries but also a much more modest but equally gratifying new one in that "We-Are-the-World-Via-Our-Neighborhoods" kind of way—a second and even third perusal of the bookshelves scarcely revealed any more than what I'd learned in the sixth grade. "I'm afraid what we have mostly are books on the frontier," one librarian said to me. "Have you tried the Internet?"

Well, with that attitude it is little wonder that writers fear the extinction of their books.

So, forced to return to the seclusion of my room to accomplish the task set before me long after Miss Inglesby (who always said I had promise of something or other), with only a handful of books, some dusty, a couple reeking of homework assignments and Nelson Algren's and Studs Terkel's takes on the city for good measure, I dug through my memories and plugged in a borrowed laptop and took the request to speak on the state as well as my hometown not only as a challenge but as an opportunity to find out once and for all what makes Illinois tick at the start of the twenty-first century besides wheat.

Chicago, the world-class city it has made itself into, chugged along—not like "the little engine that could" but like the sturdy and unpretentious "city that works" (long before it was so ordered by one of the country's larger-than-life politicians, Mayor Daley or "Mare Daley" as local political satirist Aaron Freeman might say, thinking as a kid himself that it was a term synonymous with "leader of the city"). As much as the city thinks of *himself* (apparently the city of "Big Shoulders" has traditionally been considered masculine, while on the other hand "The Prairie State" of plains and passive bodies of water is seen as feminine) as set apart from its surrounding area, it is an offshoot of the Midwest.

Geographically, Chicago, if you could see far enough in any direction past the high-rises, you'd find is also flat. Then there is the immensity of the body of water that flanks it all along one side, which obviously obliterated any possibility for growth to the east. Lake Michigan—a Mediterranean Lite on some blue-sky days in June—is Chicago's splendid little secret. You have to see it to believe it. While it looks like the sea it is not the sea. It does not give the yachts and sailboats that jam its docks in summer passage to China or even to Mexico. Rub your eyes and look again, it's a lake. But unless you've seen it on blue-sky days when the waves call to swimmers and yacht owners and Jet-Ski lovers and lunch-cruise boats for tourists at the newly redone recreational center of Navy Pier, or on a gray January day when the sight of such a huge body of water that has been frozen in mid-wave is equally stunning—although of course, not inviting—you would not think of Chicago as a beach town. But it is.

Chicagoland, as it is called outside the official peripheries of the city, has grown, westward, northward, and southward, spilled out into suburban enclaves, small cities, and smaller towns which, in my opinion, came from White Flight, the desire to escape the intensity of urban life as well as the jobs made possible by the Age of Industry (rather than urban entities unto themselves aspiring for personal recognition). The next largest city after Chicago, Rockford, has a population of around 150,000 compared with Chicago's close to 3 million. No, anywhere in the world, a person born way down state, close enough to Missouri let's say, soldier or tourist or business traveler, when asked from where he or she hails, is not beholden to reply with Decatur or Peoria or even Evanston. Without questioning whether there might be the slightest exaggeration in the response, they hold on to the helm and ground him or herself with a simple "Chicago."

But while Chicago is a city that holds its own in the world, it and Illinois bottom-line, end of the day, no use denying it, linked in all the good and bad ways that cities live out their fates on the land on which their founders commenced their ambitious planning. Whereas eighty years ago or so the diligent Illinoisans may have had not much else to discuss but the commerce of soybeans and lumber and livestock, the state presently maintains its economy with, among other major industries: food, petroleum, textiles, chemicals, electronics and appliance plants, coal and metal mining. And of course, while those plants keep Illinoisans employed, they also contribute mightily to an unhealthy environment.

Not less threatening, but as important to note, is the connection of the Manhattan Project at the University of Chicago, when Enrico

Fermi and fellow brilliant minds, spurred on by the horrors committed by the Nazis, split the atom. Today Illinois is home to thirteen nuclear power plants, twelve of which are in operation.

In all the good and bad ways as I say. Bad were the riots in Springfield, the capital of the state. Good was the result of the birth of the NAACP the following year in 1909. But it was not the last riot nor was race the only cause for major unrest in the city (see: the 1968 Democratic Convention in Chicago).

(Of course, that year must've been particularly charged by a Saturn or Uranus influence, the Age of Aquarius or something cosmic, since no place on the planet was safe from chaos in 1968.)

I was a kid then and from our back porch we got a clear view of the National Guard swarming out to quash the protestors. We also were able to witness entire neighborhoods being torn down to make room for the University of Illinois, an urban campus that now has a student enrollment of nearly twenty-five thousand. There are sixty-eight colleges and universities in the state. In addition to the twenty-five thousand urban academics above, DePaul University (the largest Catholic university in the country) hosts another twenty thousand students. There are also such noted institutions of higher learning as Northwestern, the University of Chicago, the School of the Art Institute and Loyola, and, down state: University of Illinois at Champaign-Urbana. It was at this latter institution that a faculty member reconstructed the materials DNA and RNA.

No discussion of Chicago can go without a mention of Al Capone who hailed from Cicero, Illinois, but let's hear it now for the township of Cicero's own former president, Betty Loren Maltese, for upholding local tradition: she was recently prosecuted for racketeering and has just started doing jail time. And while we are remembering convicted politicians there is former Republican Governor George Ryan's recent parting act—unprecedented, controversial, and his right to do it—a blanket commutation of 156 death-row prisoners.

The state may have had a reputation as leaning toward Republican while the city maintained its loyalty to the people and stayed Democrat. But after the daily televised "council wars" during Harold Washington's first office term exposed some of the more blatant divisions of power on the basis of race and gender, I got to know firsthand how a German or Irish Chicagoan must have felt seeing one from their own community who had managed against all odds to be voted into political office be accused and carried off to prison for misusing his post, when I recognized an old college mate turned alderman on TV during the Silver Shovel exposé. It wasn't that he was accused and soon imprisoned for accepting bribes that seemed so unconscionable given the name of the game in politics. But to find out that Ambrosio Medrano took money in exchange for permitting toxic waste to be dumped in his community left me horrified.

Yet, upon his release, he came out and tried to run again.

Chicago is the "city that works" but so does the rest of the state and not solely by its agriculture, which distinguishes it. Illinois hospitals employ over a quarter of a million individuals while in Chicago alone the Medical District extends over 560 acres, consisting of hospitals, biotech labs, schools, and other medical-related facilities.

Factories, not field work, brought my own Mexican relatives to Chicago in the twentieth century. Over a hundred years ago Chicago was a center for labor organizing that guaranteed the worker in the country an eight-hour day. But the laws that were established to protect the safety and health of workers in the eighties, along with a desire for huge profits, pushed companies to locations around the world where labor was cheaper and there were no unions.

Immigration continued and continues, if not for the promise of employment, also for political reasons. Most recently Eastern Europeans, Central Americans, South Africans as well as the Asian populations have also grown, and there are new residents from the Middle East. In other words, from all over the world.

But whites still make up nearly three-quarters of the state population.

The state once reflected the religious convictions of the Mormons and the Lutherans (while it dismissed the religions of the black slaves and Indians). In the city, Catholics more or less made a visible claim to it by constructing churches everywhere. Here and there the Greek Orthodox and Russian communities were no light-weights in impressive steeple building. Jews, too, were visibly present early on. Chicago also became the home of destination for black Muslims. Winnetka is where you'll find one of the most breathtaking structures anywhere, in the form of the Baha'i Temple. Everywhere, many other religious and spiritual groups and institutions enjoy currency.

On the subject of diversity, despite the nearly alarmist statistical reports that Hispanics/Latinos are taking over the whole country, the last census bore out the fact that they made up about 12 percent of the population, blacks somewhat more and Asians somewhat less. The figures within the city are somewhat higher. But that's the way immigration is during the Age of Globalization—with people from all over the planet relocating to the United States for all the reasons the pilgrims moved to these lands seeking safe haven, new opportunities, and a new way of life.

If you have a little surplus cash or if your father did before you, you may have yourself a nice summer home. But in Chicago, you are just as likely to have it in one of the states that surround Illinois, like Nelson Algren did in Michigan or the Indiana Dunes and where he once took the Parisian intellectual Simone de Beauvoir to rendezvous. But if you care to stay within the parameters of the state you might find a great deal of it has been put aside for leisure and recreation in the form of state parks, tree nurseries, fishing and hunting, nature preserves, and (why not, if it brings in revenues) the riverboat casinos.

Chicago and the state—not the oldest, not the largest, not the most impressive and intriguing or not the most sublime by any measure—at the start of the twenty-first century stand on their own androgynous, talented, and unassuming legs quite well.

Let's take an ever-so-brief and most definitely incomplete survey and try to count the ways of more of the good and the bad and the ugly, the push-pull of this place that, for me, encapsulates a whole state: *Sister Carrie* and Mother Cabrini; public art, Picasso, Calder, Chagall, murals, and the Buckingham Fountain; museums from A-Z; Sue the T-Rex; Jesse Jackson Moments here and abroad; what's snow to cold; steady temperatures for a week in 1989 of 80 below with the windchill factor; the Heat Wave of '95 that took five hundred lives; the Chinese New Year Parade if you can get parking; Ravinia; more bridges than Paris; subways that become elevated trains; José Clemente High School; Malcolm X; Cabrini Green and Marina Towers; Lyric Opera House the night Maria Callas broke everyone's hearts there with her voice; the Green Mill; poetry slams; Second City; Chaka Khan when I heard her in a bar on Rush Street just before she became CHAKA KHAN; Mies van der Rohe buried two blocks from me in Graceland Cemetery; Siskel and Ebert; the Busy Bee Restaurant and the Pump Room; Harry Carey; Lorraine Hansberry and David Mamet; Steppenwolf Theatre; *Grease*; pizza (does bear mentioning again) and not hot dogs but Italian beefs; 1986 Super Bowl; Sears catalog, Second World's Fair 1933, and the debut of the Ferris wheel; the Cubs in 1906 and not so much since; loyal sports fans; Steelworkers of America-CIO; murderer of eight Filipino nurses turned transsexual in prison; *Notes of an Anatomist* and Children's Memorial Hospital; Galena, Illinois; Koko Taylor; *Playboy*; White Sox, 1959; Bozo's Circus; Riverview Park; John Gacy's execution in Joliet, Illinois, in 1994; in memory of the Shawnee, Black Hawks, and Pottawattomies; Chicago Black Hawks; Lincoln's home state and Reagan's birthplace; Dillinger and the Biograph movie theater that remains in operation; Senator Dick Durbin who voted against the Iraq War Resolution; the State of Illinois Center in downtown Chicago; the transplanting of the Healy Road prairie; the Mexican Fine Arts Center Museum radio station; Marshall Field's Department Store; Black Panthers; *Da* Bears; Oak Park: Hemingway's birthplace and Frank Lloyd Wright legacies; the Chicago Coalition for the Homeless; before: L. Frank Baum, Richard Wright, Gwen Brooks, now: Turow, Bellow, Peretsky; Bookman's Corner Used Books on Clark Street; twenty-four-hour *taquerías*; Masonic Temple; *Chicago Tribune* and the *Chicago Defender*. To give Martin Luther King the last word: "If we can break the backbone of discrimination in Chicago, we can do it in all the cities of this country."

INDIANA

THE HOME STATE

Richard Lingeman

Ain't God good to Indiana!
—Abe Martin (Kin Hubbard)

W here're you from? Americans say. Everybody has to be from someplace. I'm from Indiana and I've spent a lot of my life trying to figure out what that means, if anything, about who I am.

As an exiled Hoosier who's lived in Manhattan for forty years, I can tell you that being from Indiana never got me much mileage at social gatherings. To native New Yorkers (yes, there are some; I know several personally) Indiana is part of the great amorphous geopolitical blob called the Midwest. The most recognition you'll get is, "Oh, Indiana. I went through there once." I get another reaction when someone pries out of me the name of my hometown, Crawfordsville, population 15,000: "What's that near?" (Answer: Indianapolis.)

In his novel *Cat's Cradle*, famous Indiana author Kurt Vonnegut, Jr. sets down this exchange:

> "My God," she said, "are you a *Hoosier*?"
> I admitted I was.
> "I'm a Hoosier, too," she crowed. "Nobody has to be ashamed of being a Hoosier."
> "I'm not," I said. "I never knew anybody who was."

Kind of faint praise when you think about it, but I've never been ashamed of being a Hoosier. I'd go as far as to say I'm proud of it. I persist in my belief that there is embedded in me a strand of DNA labeled "Indiana." To isolate its traits I must first isolate Indiana's identity, which is not easy.

In popular music Indiana is identified with *home*. I refer you to "Back Home in Indiana," which is sung every year at the opening ceremony of the Indianapolis 500 Mile Race before 500,000 fans and a vast TV audience. There was a movie with that title in the 1940s—about harness racing, a sport that used to carry an Indiana stamp as thoroughbred racing does a Kentucky brand (thus, "My Old Kentucky Home" on Derby day).

Actually, "Back Home in Indiana" is a derivative song. You remember the chorus:

> Back home again in Indiana
> And it seems that I can see
> The gleaming candlelight
> Still shining bright
> Through the sycamores for me, etc.

That business about the candlelight, sycamores, etc. was lifted from the state song, "On the Banks of the Wabash," by Paul Dresser, who was a leading popular songwriter in the 1890s. He has a bridge named after him in his birthplace, Terre Haute, located on the banks of the Wabash sixty miles southwest of Crawfordsville. Indiana has turned out some great pop songwriters—Dresser, Cole Porter, Hoagy Carmichael, John Mellencamp, Ned Rorem. (My apologies to Rorem for listing him with the pop group, but I don't know any other Indiana-born art-song writers.)

Paul Dresser was the oldest brother of Theodore Dreiser, Indiana's greatest novelist (though, in fairness, I should say that some people in Indiana think Paul was a better songwriter than Theodore was a novelist). Paul changed his name to make it sound less German. Unlike Dreiser the grim naturalist, author of *Sister Carrie* and *An American Tragedy*, Paul was a soppy sentimentalist. Tears would run down his plump cheeks (he weighed three hundred pounds in his prime) as he composed sad ballads about letters that never came and mothers who were keeping a light burning in the window for wandering boys. In his heyday he was considered Tin Pan Alley's leading exponent of the "home song," and "Wabash" is one of the enduring examples of the genre, up there with Stephen Foster's "My Old Kentucky Home" and "Old Folks at Home."

According to Theodore, the Wabash song come about because he urged his big brother to write about a river as Foster had done so successfully. Paul challenged him to come up with a verse so he dashed off what became the opening lines of Paul's song: " 'Round my Indiana homesteads wave the cornfields / In the distance loom the woodlands clear and cool." (Paul wrote the chorus, including "Through the sycamores the candlelight is gleaming.")

I suspect this "home" concept in American popular culture goes back to pioneer times. Pioneers were "*homesteaders*," after all, *settlers* yearning to be *settled* on a plot of fertile Indiana bottomland.

During pioneer days—a very influential formative force on the Hoosier character—another link of Indiana DNA emerged: that nickname *Hoosier*. There are a lot of theories about the origins of the name. Some say it comes from a greeting people called out when a stranger approached their cabin: "Who's here?" which came out "Who's hyer?" in the southern dialect common among Indiana's early settlers. Others hold, however, that it was the cry of boatmen along the Ohio River. And still others say it referred to toughs known as "Hushers" because they would shut up anybody who mouthed off to them. Finally, there is a school that says the word comes from a dialect of Lancashire, England, and means a bumpkin, a rube, which come to think of it describes my self-image when, at social gatherings in New York, I identified myself as a being from Indiana.

Actually, I think Indianans felt they needed a nickname like "Buckeye" (Ohio) or "Sucker" (Illinois, I think) but were unable to come up with one until a popular poem called "The Hoosier's Nest" appeared in the Indiana papers in the early 1830s. A desperate state embraced the word and then put out all those suspiciously contradictory cover stories about what it meant.

The world was given a large dose of Indiana propaganda in the 1986 movie *Hoosiers*, in which Gene Hackman coaches a tiny town's high school basketball team, which miraculously beats the powerful big-city school to win the state championship.

The movie was based on a true story that had become a legend in the annals of Indiana basketball. In 1954 the obscure crossroads of Milan (population 1816, near Cincinnati, Ohio) won "the state," as Hoosiers called the one and only championship.

Alas, such miracles are no longer possible. After the movie came out, the state athletic association reorganized the tournament into Division A, B, C, etc., according to school size. There was a lot of opposition to the association's move at the time. They were killing a dream very important to Hoosiers, who believe small is better than big. Every town imagined that somehow it would produce a state championship team. Winning a Division C championship just isn't the same.

In my day, every little village had a team and a school gymnasium, and every garage or barn had a basketball hoop affixed to it. Now the village high schools have vanished, and the kids are bused to consolidated schools. But you still see the hoops.

Basketball probably became so popular because of Indiana's long, cold winters. It gave kids an indoor sport to play or to watch on Friday nights, followed by a dance. But these games were entertainment for grown-ups as well. The townspeople packed the gym and rooted with a hoarse passion for the locals. And on Saturday the game was chewed over in every barbershop and café in town. As John R. Tunis writes in the definitive young-adult book about Indiana basketball, *Yea! Wildcats!*: "They say a man talks basketball in this State for an hour after he's dead."

As for *Hoosiers*, I first saw it while visiting my mother in my hometown, Crawfordsville. (Hoosier factoid: Crawfordsville won the very first state tournament in 1911, the same year that the first five hundred-mile car race was held at the Indianapolis Speedway.) *Hoosiers* played at the Strand Theater for an all-time-record three months. Parts of it were filmed in the county, and people went again and again to see their little patch of Indiana exposed to the entire world.

Also, I believe people felt they were looking at themselves in the mirror. *Hoosiers* celebrated Indiana values—hard work, true grit, small against big, loyalty to home and family.

These conservative values of course are not unique to Indiana, but they are as much a part of the state's character as basketball is. Take the work ethic. When I worked one summer vacation at the Alcoa plant in Lafayette, I remember the farm boys actually boasting about how hard they worked. "Shee-it," they would say. "I can outwork you any day!"

According to Dwight Hoover's *A Pictorial History of Indiana*, the state's "fundamental value system" includes a belief in "individual effort, self-determination, work, religious institutions, and patriotism."

Those were the core values Robert S. and Helen Merell Lynd identified in their sociological studies of Muncie, *Middletown* (1929) and *Middletown in Transition* (1937). In the mid-1970s, another team of sociologists headed by Theodore Caplow replicated the Lynds' questionnaires and concluded that Muncie's young people were "as strongly imbued with religion, patriotism, and the Protestant ethic as their grandparents were at the same age. . . ." This study, *Middletown Families*, is subtitled "Fifty Years of Change and Continuity." Here's what Caplow et al. have to say on that subject:

> Change, for Middletown, is something flowing irresistibly from the outside world. Continuity is furnished locally. The outside world continuously proposes new ways of living and thinking. The local community steadfastly resists most of these suggestions and modifies those it adopts into conformity with its own customs. . . .

Although Indiana regularly sends liberal Democrats to Congress, it's still a pretty conservative state. There's a strong labor movement (the socialist leader Eugene Debs hailed from Terre Haute) and the economy used to be dominated by steelmaking and manufacturing. Nevertheless, the rural counties dominated the state legislature for many years until redistricting let in more city legislators.

Recently the outside world has been telling Indiana it's time to change its way of doing business. The *Indianapolis Star* ran a lengthy series of articles on the state's economic decline. The paper, owned by the ultraconservative Pulliam family until 2000, published a list of twenty-five downside economic indicators: between 2000 and 2002, Indiana lost more manufacturing jobs than any other state; personal income dropped from seventeenth to thirty-third from 1965 to 2000; personal bankruptcies increased at double the national average; the state led the nation in the rate of home foreclosures in 2002; per capita personal income has fallen to 91.1 percent of the national average.

Another article in the series analyzed the historical roots of Indiana's economic failures. The chief culprits were: "Hoosier caution and resistance to change" and stick-in-the-mud political leaders, said the author, Norm Heikens. Hoosiers have been resisting change ever since the first settlers arrived. A majority were from the southern upland states and they were "agin' " high taxes and any-thing else that would interfere with their way of life. For example, when the general assembly tried to promote dam and sawmill con-struction to boost the pioneer economy, they opposed the plan, saying the dams would interfere with canoe traffic.

Rather than building new businesses, Indiana settled for hosting branch plants. The state once had a thriving auto industry, and Indi-anapolis could have been another Detroit. Between 1900 and 1920, there were 200 carmakers in the state, out of 2,200 nationwide. Con-solidation by the present Big Three, of course, knocked out a lot of those companies, but the state didn't help, Heikens reports; "long established, ultra-conservative" industrialists, fearful that the high-paying jobs in the industry would attract swarms of foreign workers, resisted. And so all those glorious Indiana-based marques—Auburn, Dusenberg, Cord, Stutz, Willys-Overland, Studebaker, went out of business one by one between 1930 and 1963. Meanwhile, conservative politicians rejected federal dollars for local improvements, and rural legislators blocked urban development, allowed out-of-state banks to gobble up local ones, fought "one-person one-vote."

In addition to the elimination of manufacturing jobs, the Indy *Star*'s diagnosticians discovered a serious brain drain. The state has two world-class universities, Purdue and Indiana, but the best and the brightest of their graduates tend to abscond with their diplomas.

The present Democratic governor, Frank O'Bannon, unveiled a $1.25 billion "Energize Indiana" plan to encourage development of high-tech and life-science industries in order to keep the brains and create jobs to replace those lost by the flight of manufacturing.

Lots of other ideas for saving Indiana are in the air, according to Heikens. One is to create a culture that's friendly to creative people and encourages bold entrepreneurs. "Silicon Valley on the Wabash" is the idea. Richard Florida, author of a well-received study on the importance of unconventional, creative people to a city's business climate, *The Rise of the Creative Class*, suggested that the state create a new culture "that's open to eccentric, different-thinking, some-times-weird people." Soho in Indianapolis?

Well, the lack of such a creative culture was one of several reasons I left Indiana and ended up in New York to become a writer and editor at a left-wing weekly. Those activities could not be pursued in Indiana.

Let it be said that Indiana produced a lot of creative people in its day, particularly authors, a sample of whom includes Edward Eggle-ston, Booth Tarkington, Gene Stratton-Porter, Charles Major, James Whitcomb Riley, Theodore Dreiser, Janet Flanner, Ernie Pyle, Jessamyn West, Ross Lockridge, Jr., Marguerite Young, A. B. Guthrie, Jr., Kurt Vonnegut, Jr., and Dan Wakefield.

It has also spawned a plethora of humorists and comedians, e.g., Abe Martin (Kin Hubbard), George Ade, Red Skelton, Herb Shriner, Jean Shepherd, David Letterman. "Why are there so many funny Hoosiers?" a man once asked me after a lecture I gave. I was stumped for an answer. The high limestone content in the water? Something in the pioneer tradition with its shivarees and tall tales and cutting "proud" people down to size? It probably traces back to the "Hoosier" hoax, which people are still chuckling about.

My hometown produced seven published scriveners in the late nine-teenth century, including General Lew Wallace, author of the best-selling warhorse *Ben-Hur*. (Those seeking further information should consult Dorothy Ritter Russo and Thelma Lois Sullivan, *Biographical Studies of Seven Authors of Crawfordsville, Indiana*, Indianapolis, 1952.)

According to Richard E. Banta's anthology *Hoosier Caravan: A Treasury of Indiana Life and Lore*, in the period between 1947 and 1970, 3,000 Indiana authors published some 15,000 titles. No mention of which of them were any good.

The reason I say that is that Banta, who lived in Crawfordsville, mentioned a best-forgotten book that I wrote. I suspect he included it because he was a kindly man and wanted to boost still another Hoosier author.

Well, I've written other—I hope better—books since then and no longer have family ties to Indiana, and my visits grow increasingly rare. The state now exists for me primarily in memories. I have recurring ones of the land: the rugged gorges and placid creeks in the Shades of Death park; the serenity of New Harmony, a Utopian community built by the Rappites; the architectural surprises of Columbus, where the Cummins Engine company commissioned great architects such as Cesar Pelli, Eliel and Eero Saarinen, and Edward Larrabee Barnes to build churches, schools, and public buildings; the *centrality* of the Circle in Indianapolis with its towering Civil War monument, symbolizing the state's middleness.

I remember as a boy walking through still Indiana woods in spring searching for morels, the redbuds and tulip trees in flower, May apples underfoot.

Theodore Dreiser titled the Indiana essay he wrote for the 1920s *These United States* "Indiana: Her Soil and Light." Nature was a strong part of his memories. His family was dirt-poor and bounced among four towns, treated like pariahs by local snobs and gossips. Yet in his autobiography, *Dawn,* he tells of his discovery of nature as a boy rambling through fields on fresh summer mornings.

Soil and light. My final Indiana memory is of driving through countryside on a summer evening—faded red barns and white farmhouses, green rolling fields thick with corn, lit by the slanting golden light of the setting sun. There is such an aura of peace and fat contentment in that picture. That's my Indiana home, I guess. Or was.

Indiana: a great state to be from.

IOWA

COMMONSENSE IN THE HEARTLAND

Frank Conroy

I drove across Iowa last October—from the southeast, where I live, to the northwest and a lovely town called Storm Lake. It took five hours. To cross the entire state east to west, from the Mississippi to the Missouri, takes perhaps seven hours. North to south, along the banks of either river, let's guess at six hours. (I've never done it.) A big state. Fifty-six thousand, two hundred and ninety square miles, to be exact, with a population of something like three million people. I took the blue highways for the most part—the local roads—and drove through dozens of quiet little towns and villages where the displays of patriotism were discreet. No extra flags flying that I could see, only the messages on the church boards, or in the signs in front of a used-car lot, or on the marquee of old, converted movie theaters. GOD BLESS AMERICA. UNITED WE STAND. AMERICA THE BEAUTIFUL. Very few people were out and about. Traffic was almost nonexistent. I had the sense that the state of Iowa was marking time, thinking, reflecting, attempting to absorb the events in New York City and Washington, D.C., not sure yet what to make of it all—except, of course, that it was tragic.

Iowans are not, in general, jumpy people. They work in the long cycles of agriculture, and are in general patient, careful, and moderate in their thinking. They are rich, not in cash, but in equity. The plant protein produced annually in Iowa is enough (if not converted into animal protein) to meet the annual nutritional needs of the entire population of the United States. Iowans have time to take the long view. They do not need to, nor are they disposed to, jump the gun. Their topsoil is the richest and deepest in the world, water is plentiful, and the sun can be counted on to shine. They know they are blessed and they know that much of the world is not, and lives in misery. They are religious, generous, responsible, hardworking people, for the most part, slow to anger, slow to suspiciousness and slow to show their feelings.

Beyond agriculture we have a significant light industry—manufacturing, scientific and medical research, electronics, food processing, and other economic engines. It is a big state, as I've said, with more going on than is generally appreciated. These generalizations are dangerous. But I'm going to risk a few anyway. As I write, in January 2002, it seems that people in Iowa are getting angry about a number if things. A slow burn, you might say, building rather than fading.

The state of the economy has created unease, but not anger. Certainly the severe cutbacks in education (traditionally a closely watched and highly valued concern) have unsettled many people, and the prospect of higher state taxes pleases nobody, but Iowans have been through tough times before. The interest rates of the 1970s were particularly hard on farmers overextended in terms of debt—those who were in the midst of expansion when the hammer fell—but after a while things settled down, and fewer people went under than had been feared. In the Midwest it's a bit easier to hunker down and wait out the rough patches than it might be in the faster economies of California or the New South, for instance. Iowans remain disappointed about the economy, but that's the extent of it.

What's bugging them, then? Two things in particular—television news and various unanswered questions. They are beginning to feel used in ways that they have never felt before, and indeed probably never thought possible.

Rural people read their local newspapers closely, and most papers in Iowa dropped the World Trade Center story, and the Afghan stories, into the back pages as soon as new information grew thin and press releases repetitive—which is to say pretty quickly. Front pages once again dealt with local matters, which was doubtless reassuring for a lot of folks.

Yet how many times have the Twin Towers fallen on television, week after week, month after month, like some endless loop from an avant-garde film? How many thousands of images of Ground Zero have been shown, as if the network producers had fallen into a pathological repetition compulsion? How many simple-minded diversity-conscious spots of people saying "I am an American" (and nothing else) have been foisted upon us by the Ad Council? How many funeral services, memorial ceremonies, viewing platforms, and icons of death are sufficient? Will they keep on forever? Why are they doing it?

Ah, yes. *Why?* There lies the rub.

You won't find anyone in Iowa who thinks America should not have taken action after September 11. President Bush's rating in our polls is very high, presumably as an expression of patriotic solidarity in challenging times. And yet many midwesterners are starting to chafe under the commercialization of the event. We have known for some time that the East Coast is self-absorbed, that it assumes that nothing elsewhere means very much, and some allowances are made for that, but the relentless choreography of fear and catastrophe broadcast daily by CNN are now understood to be simply ads for CNN itself. They will try to keep us jumpy and nervous in order to make money. That is the *why*. In rural areas it is not easy to follow

Laura Bush's advice to turn off the television set. Why should not CNN and the others stop fear-mongering instead? Even as AOL–Time Warner et al. celebrate patriotism, they exploit it.

Cynicism is rising in the Midwest. People know that certain controls in the flow of information during military operations are appropriate, and while they do want to know what's going on, they want the information that can safely be released. Instead they get smoke and mirrors, secrecy as reflex, and flat-out disinformation from their government. The self-satisfied dandyism of Secretary of Defense Donald Rumsfeld, who acts as if nothing more is going on than his clever dueling with the press corps, is becoming irritating.

How can we resist cynicism when, after the videotapes of Osama bin Laden have been made public, we are told that suggestions that the tapes might have been tampered with by the United States are ridiculous, desperate, and entirely groundless, yet not long afterward American warplanes drop leaflets over Afghanistan containing a doctored photograph of a beardless Osama dressed in a Western suit and tie? An action defended by both the Pentagon and the State Department. The contents of the leaflet were created by Charlotte Beers, sometime high-flier at the advertising agencies of J. Walter Thompson and Ogilvy & Mather, present undersecretary of state of public diplomacy. Discussing her government job with a reporter at *Business Week* Ms. Beers explained, "The whole idea of building a brand is to create a relationship between the product and the user.... We're going to have to communicate the intangible assets of the United States—things like our belief system and our values." Things like lying to people, some Iowans might ask? Belief in the propagation of outright falsehoods? Do the lies extend past Afghanistan? Does the "communication of intangible assets" involve other kinds of lies told to Iowans, to Americans, and to the world?

In this kind of atmosphere, forbidden thoughts arise. Is the worldwide network of terrorists as organized, efficient, and united as we have been told it is? Is it perhaps *not* a cohesive force, but a string of poorly organized, inefficient groups with different concerns and different goals? Was the apparent precision of September 11 to some extent serendipitous, as bin Laden himself suggested in tape No. 2? Was the deranged shoe bomber who attempted to light his fuse at his seat rather than in the toilet part of an organized and efficient terrorist cell? Was the anthrax sent by a homegrown nutcase? What is the degree of danger to the United States? What is the proximity of the danger? Why cannot the government tell us anything?

More questions. Why announce a continuous alert without announcing the nature of the danger? The policy seems irrational, unless its purpose is to sustain nervousness in the people so that the executive branch can continue its incremental consolidation of power. Why use military tribunals except to increase the power of George W. Bush, commander in chief? Why move forward in the attempt to strengthen confidentiality and reduce further access to presidential papers at this particular moment in time? Should war powers redound to the president, or does the situation more closely resemble a new kind of international criminal conspiracy?

Whenever I drive around Iowa I make it a point to go into the small towns and look for the places people go to for coffee and small talk. An off-the-interstate "downtown" McDonald's (very often bright, clean, cheerful, and above all climate-controlled places), a luncheonette, a supermarket cafeteria/deli (big in the Midwest), or a pizza joint. Typically I'll sit near a table of old-timers, or farmers, or people on their lunch hour, and keep my ears open. People glance up, nod, usually smile, and leave you to your privacy. Over the past few months I have heard every one of the questions above quoted, floated, alluded to, repeated, or simply asked at one or another of these gatherings. One by one, mind you, dropped into the general conversation as you might dunk the last bit of your donut into your coffee. I can well imagine the reaction of a typical group if the questions were all lined up in a row and asked one after the other as I have done here. "Now, just hold on a minute, sir. Try to calm down. You make it sound like some kind of revolution or something. Things ain't *that* bad." And of course the observation is correct and very Iowan. This is *America*, the subtext goes. There will always be dangers and alarms and excursions of one kind or another, but this is a country with deep reserves of faith and inner strength, a beautiful society that will abide, come what may, a true wonder in the world.

Iowans may be saddened—indeed, how could anyone not be saddened by the sudden eruption of barbarity in the midst of the civilized world—but they are not afraid. Not even remotely. A little cautious, perhaps, but strong as ever. They are pissed, but they are calm.

Kansas

The Other Side of Oz

Antonya Nelson

The most famous tornado in history was unleashed in 1939. It happened in Kansas. *The Wizard of Oz* begins in sepia-toned, quasi-realistic, dusty, rural Kansas; Dorothy Gale, it must be assumed, doesn't understand the full extent to which she is chafing against the large and limited landscape. The combined forces of misunderstanding and fear drive her down the road, running away with her maligned little dog. A kindly carnival swindler encourages her to scoot home as the storm is about to hit, but, alas, his advice comes too late. In Dorothy's delusional state, she casts away her black-and-white manacles, inhabiting, post-tornado, the psychedelic terrain of her own imagination, that place over the rainbow she'd been previously dreaming about. It's a vast expanse, her imagination, peopled by farm figures and fantastical creatures, played by highly costumed members of her family and neighborhood, and none of them any less devilish or flawed than they were back there. Her unconscious desire, made manifest by the tornado that knocks her flat and sends her into herself, is to escape her world; by the end of the film, she's ready (eager) to return to it. Even her name contains the Jekyll and Hyde-like aspects of her impulses, a pairing of the prosaic Dorothy and the

stormy Gale. The unconscious sends her away from, and consciousness restores her to, Kansas.

Why Kansas? Situated in the nation's geographical center (no state,
surely, is as distant from either ocean coast or foreign borders, the
navel of the contiguous country), it is by reputation an undramatic,
"flyover" piece of the country, flat (flatter) than a pancake, its largest
city no more than 300,000 people large. But alongside this drab
pigeonholing, Kansas is also the locus of the nation's most devastating cyclone activity, generating more F5-scale twisters than any
other state. That this particular position, this meeting ground for
strong differential air masses, so-called supercells, also renders Kansas
the state most thoroughly insulated seems compellingly contradictory. You could feel safe there. Or trapped. Dorothy Gale seems to
have felt both. A force of nature arrived to lift her out of that place,
while simultaneously teaching her its value. The two most infamous
lines of dialogue in the film reiterate the paradoxical lesson Dorothy
Gale learns: "I don't think we're in Kansas anymore!" she exclaims
naïvely, fearfully, excitedly to little Toto. How often the film's viewers
have taken up this sentiment, using it as shorthand to designate a
new world or experience—one of thrilling Technicolor mystery,
patently *un*Kansan. Balancing this utterance, of course, is the film's
coda: "There's no place like home."

In a landscape as insular and unvarying, one lacking much besides
grain elevators in its vistas, one whose horizons are shimmering
mirages at the distant edge of vision, it's interesting to consider the
variety of swirling upheavals that have struck the place over time, the
twinned binary forces operating, it seems, in some odd symbiotic
measure. The special effect of the approaching tornado in Dorothy
Gale's ochre-tinted home is a near facsimile of Kansas artist John
Steuart Curry's painting *Tornado*. The decidedly vertical terror is fast
approaching across the unrelentingly horizontal life, its effects unques-
tionably cataclysmic, the foregrounded family scurrying for cover.

"Bleeding Kansas" entered the union as the thirty-fourth state on January 29, 1861. Its current reputation is conservative, both politically and socially. But its history is as explosively charged as its weather. On either side of statehood, the territory was home to extraordinarily savage battles between abolitionist Jayhawkers and the proslavery Border Ruffians of Missouri, passionate skirmishes between people divided on the subject of slavery, a kind of miniature version of, or prologue to, the Civil War itself. Two famous raids stand out, one from either side of the two forces at work in the region: John Brown's 1856 massacre of proslavery settlers at Pottawotamie Creek (five deaths) and rogue Confederate Captain William C. Quantrill's 1863 bloody raid on abolitionist mecca Lawrence, where his men (among them adolescent Jesse and Frank James), killed 180 people, sacked the town, and burned most of its buildings. During the Civil War proper, Kansas contributed a greater percentage of its male population to the Union Army than any other state—nearly 5,000 (25 percent) more men than requested—and sustained the highest mortality rate—more than 61 percent.

That the statistic surprises is significant. Kansas is a state by both geography and popular conjecture neither north nor south, not western or eastern, oftentimes denied placement even in the category of Midwest (more than one Ohioan or Iowan or Michigander has told me in no uncertain terms that Kansas is not a member of the Midwest club). Situated dead-center, as landlocked as could be, a vast plane of plains and mostly empty, it is its own innocuous, undesignated place. To name it beautiful is to embrace a contradiction, to appreciate the aesthetic of absence: of people, of glamorous animals or geologic protuberance, of large bodies of water or thick forests or startling architecture, of cliffs or coasts or any other wonder, natural or man-made. World's Largest Hand-Dug Well. Biggest Ball of String. Birthplace of Bob Dole. Place where occasional tempestuous opposing forces acquire a kind of critical mass.

A hundred years after the nation's first civil war, when Kansas had been the site of a prescient wave of U.S. race battles, the second wave rolled in, this one also heralded by a Brown, the first having been John, the next Linda. In 1954, an African-American third-grader in Topeka became the subject of the Supreme Court case *Brown v. Board of Education,* which overturned the "separate but equal" education policy that the nation had until then operated under; thus, the systematic desegregation of public schools was begun.

Flash forward to the year 2000, when the Kansas Board of Education made headlines once again, this time as it declared evolutionary theory—and the big bang theory, as well—optional in the state's science education standards. Under this order, local school districts would decide for themselves what was—and wasn't—taught about the origin of the universe and man. *This* is the Kansas that the coasts know best, the state littered with handmade antiabortion billboards, these and the waving American flag, land of prim countenance and humorless sensibility, morally frightened and politically conservative, holding tight as a fist to old-fashionedness as if to preserve it for the remainder of an ever-loosening, dissipating nation.

If not for this reputation of stubborn innocence, stern naïveté, circumscribed Christianity, Truman Capote would never have located his true-life source story for *In Cold Blood.* The story's drama depends on the arrival in the heartland of the big bad forces of beyond, the cyclone spinning toward the hapless farm. It achieves its epic proportions because the forces are in such stereotypically polar opposition. Two murderous prison escapees descend into the wholesome homestead of the Clutter family in Holcomb, Kansas, and wreak absolute havoc. It's particular, true to a place and time, but it's also emblematic of the ongoing struggle both personal and societal, the towering incendiary power of darkness and depravity and death as it strikes the virtuous, innocent garden; moreover, it is an assault on image and icon, as if a bucket of blood had been thrown upon a

Norman Rockwell original. The extreme terms of the encounter, sinners and saints, taints all subsequent byproducts of it. Truman Capote understood that his own flamboyant presence in Holcomb in the wake of the murders was another kind of shock to the Kansas system; he brought along Harper Lee, emissary of moral decency, to soften the blow. But a great deal of the book's—and the later film's—power relies upon Capote's ability to identify with one of killers, to make intimate contact with the dark force that wishes to over-shadow a certain band of light.

The encounter—the irresistible force, the immoveable object—is what creates action, reaction. Kansas seems peculiarly the site where torrential force touches down momentarily, famously, then disap-pears back into the sky. Carry Nation swung her intemperate axe here; extraordinary superhero Superman was dropped from above into the Kents' Kansas farm to be raised under their all-American guidance. Allen Ginsberg's "Wichita Vortex Sutra" takes as its subject the swirl of contradicting images, the dizzying vision of the country at war (composed in 1966, at the height of U.S. involvement in Vietnam) in contrast to the "brown vastness" of Kansas going about its blasé business. The poem is cluttered with the material of war (airplanes, in particular, since the manufacturing hubs of Boeing, Cessna, McDonnell Douglas, and Beech were located in Wichita) but punctuated with the notion of "emptiness," with the "long presence into this Vortex named Kansas." Void and vortex, at once. In the piece Ginsburg frequently references the innocent Kansas girl. The inno-cence, one understands, is both prized and scorned by the poet. Nascent Dorothy Gale, your standard insulated youth.

The state manufactures wheat and beef, the essential components of that famous American sacrament, the hamburger. The wind blows through the amber fields of grain, which wave the stench of the feedlot across the truck-laden highways. Those trucks are headed elsewhere, bearing the products of the so-called heartland.

I don't live in Kansas anymore. I went to the mountains, I went to the ocean, I went to the big city. I went to all the places that weren't Kansas. But when I was young, before I saw *The Wizard of Oz* on television, I had my own tornado. My family was in a tornado, six of us, if you count my sister in utero. The story of it has dominated my youth, my sensibility, my family's sense of itself, for the thirty-eight years since its dramatic inception. This tornado lifted my family from our suburban street, encased in our Ford station wagon, and turned us onto our collective back like a bug. Then, strangely enough, the tornado reached down and lifted our car once more to right us. Flatter, yes, but restored to our wheels, bodies more or less intact. Inside were: my father, my mother—eight months pregnant—two of my brothers, a family friend, and me. My brother David and I were in what we called the "way back," two facing seats in the rear that folded down to create cargo space, up to accommodate children. This was where the youngest always sat.

It was 1965; we lived in Wichita. We'd been out to dinner, a rare occasion in my financially strapped family, when the storm began. Candles were lit, the mood was festive. There was neither a tornado watch nor warning in effect. As we drove home, lightning struck in a field beside the road, one thick vertical bolt still imprinted in my memory, sizzling. My father remembers electric lines suddenly snapping at the pavement, whipped by the wind from their poles. My older brother saw a roof unpeel itself from its house and fly off. All around us the lush late-summer trees thrashed, the road coated with their leaves. It was dark dusk, the peculiar green of tornado weather, which is not unlike that sickly black-and-white pallor Dorothy Gale lives under before she lands among the Munchkins. My father steered us into a parking lot, where we parked among the empty cars. Their owners stood inside the Baskin-Robbins ice-cream parlor, a horrified audience whom we could see through the plate-glass window whenever lightning lit the air. Amidst the many rows of unoccupied cars, ours alone, full of us, was singled out by the storm.

Through the way-back window my two-year-old brother flew, sucked free of the vehicle by the wind. He cried for our mother, who, by some maternal miracle, had made her hugely pregnant way over two sets of seats to spread her arms, winglike, above us. The glass she took left a series of suture scars like small slugs crawling from wrists to shoulders. What must she have thought when my brother disappeared? What must he have thought, out there on the asphalt with a drinking straw driven into his cheek?

When the tornado had dropped us the second time and spun away, we fled our wrecked car for someone else's. In that untouched car we waited, my mother bleeding on the backseat as she held tight to my sobbing younger brother, my older brother furiously sounding the horn, me beside him on the front seat needing so badly to pee I thought I'd wet myself. I was four, and my immediate concern was that imminent disgrace. That's what I remember of the arrival of the ambulance, at last, of the photographer who took my picture as I was loaded into its chamber, of the ride to the hospital, of the gurney trip to our room, of the entrance of my terrified grandparents: fierce and growing pressure on my bladder, embarrassment of bursting.

We survived. My father's shoulder was injured, my mother had her stitches. My older brother wore a turban of gauze for a week or so; my younger brother has a tiny dot on his face where the straw punctured it. The baby was fine, born six weeks later at the same hospital. Now there's a Dillons Food Store where we were lifted and smashed down and lifted once more; my father prefers its selection to Safeway's. Whenever I'm back in Wichita, I enter that parking lot without a lot of internal fanfare.

Which is not to say that our tornado hasn't left a memory. It is, I think, if not responsible for, then metaphorically accurate about who we were and are, as a family. The photograph of my father hefting me—YOUNG TONI NELSON WITH UNIDENTIFIED MAN! read the caption accompanying the AP wire photo—shows us bleeding and scared, him without his glasses, me with my flowered dress hiked up. This survived nightmare taught us, early, to treasure our continuing lives together. To treasure and to fear, a tricky line to tread. "Lucky!" people would exclaim to my father, after the disaster. His response? "What's so lucky about being the only car hit in a parking lot full of cars?" In his mind, it wasn't luck. And in his mind, I know, it was also luck. We are not a religious clan unless you want to call family a religious affiliation or institution, in which case, we are devout. We are blessed by its existence; we suffer under its weight. It brings us pride and guilt, in nearly equal portion.

We gather at least twice a year in full complement, and more often than that in smaller sects. Our lives have been guided by the notion of gathering. We do this in Kansas. Still the large crumbling family house (8,400 shabby square feet), with all of its rooms and nooks, those places to get lost and to get found, as well. We gather there in the winter, over Thanksgiving or Christmas, occasionally for a birth or funeral, and in the spring, for our breaks and breakdowns. There's an attic apartment, for when a midlife or adolescent crisis occurs, for divorce or bankruptcy or flunking out, a quiet garret, perfect (if slightly chilly) sanctuary. Among my siblings, following the tradition we witnessed growing up, we welcome into our far-flung homes the angst-ridden, the undecided, the suicidal, the merely at-loose-ends. We gather into our family tribe new members—the inlaws whose own families do not demand as much attention as ours. We also adopt the random unrelated who need a group, best friends and graduate students and co-workers and neighbors, people who find themselves pulled as if by centripetal force into our midst.

We gather around the capacious dining-room table and laugh, drinking; we split into pairs and take walks, gossiping. We are lucky.

We are unlucky. We are average, universal. We are dysfunctional, intact. Three of the five in my sibling pool are deeply ensconced in the business of studying human trouble—I write fiction, and one brother and my sister are psychologists. We are constantly interrogating our own history while learning the histories of our characters or patients, most especially in relationship to their families. Our inclination to gather, I think, has directly to do with our early experience in being nearly torn asunder. That tornado might have sent us flying from its center; instead, it seems to have made us turn inward toward the eye of its power, seeking each other continually.

And what are we seeking, exactly? Perhaps a sense of consequence in a landscape that doesn't often assert it. In the center of the country, the Kansan is aware of the vast span of time and space just outside the window, the world out there that insists an individual is just too tiny, too lost in the billions and billions of like types to matter in the least. It can make you dizzy with meaninglessness. If having survived a tornado might have convinced some people of the presence of a benevolent universe, it confirmed my parents' belief in an utterly indifferent one. In the face of such indifference, how then to find purchase, to care enough to keep living, to rise out of the existential bed and go on?

"You don't make war on your family," my wise uncle once told me, his apparently only rule; all of the others he was happy to break. We must have an encoded list of commandments, never stated, merely known, passed, it seems, genetically. Over this most recent summer visit, my sister and my daughter and my grown and not-grown nieces and my uncle's wife and my sister-in-law and my mother all stood around back-to-back in the Wichita kitchen with our shoes off, deciding how tall we were. Outside, a storm brewed; we listened for the city siren that would warn of a tornado here in tornado alley. Meanwhile, we were one inch shorter than, or two inches taller than, or up to the waist of, or nearly a head distant from, or much smaller than, one another; there wasn't any other measure, no other mirror aside from ourselves. We have hosted each other's lowest and highest moments; our children one and all love babies, all want to hold the baby, whoever that baby might be. It is a fierce and confounding and paradoxical allegiance, like a religious belief, like a force of nature.

KENTUCKY

A BOX OF BLUEGRASS

Dwight Allen

This spring, in a certain town in southwestern Connecticut, a fourth-grade boy brought a box of bluegrass to
school for his research project on Kentucky. That was all
he brought. He didn't bring a pack of cigarettes or a bottle of
bourbon or a bottle of caffeine-laced Ale-8-One ("Kentucky's Soft
Drink," since 1926) or a jug of moonshine or a losing pari-mutuel
ticket from Churchill Downs. He didn't bring a nickel bag of marijuana (one of Kentucky's major cash crops) or any of the painkillers
that some doctors in the mountains of eastern Kentucky so promis-
cuously prescribe. He didn't bring a basketball or a piece of fried
chicken or a chunk of coal or a round wheel of aromatic cheese
made by Gethsemani monks. He didn't bring a poem by Robert
Penn Warren or a story by Bobbie Ann Mason or a song by Loretta
Lynn or an inspirational audiotape made by one of Kentucky's fundamentalist preachers. All he brought was a box of *Poa pratensis*, a
short, nutritious, dark green grass that thrives where the average
daily temperature in July doesn't exceed 75 degrees Fahrenheit.
Bluegrass, which is produced in seed form primarily in Oregon,
flourishes in Kentucky horse pastures during the spring, but it

quickly burns out in the summertime. A Louisville lawn-care expert I know says that only "old-timers" seed their yards with the stuff and that only a summer of constant rain will keep it green.

Near Hyden, in the mountains of southeastern Kentucky, Silas House pulls the car into the parking lot of a yellow-brick Pentecostal church. He needs to stretch his legs and smoke a cigarette—mostly the latter. Silas is thirty-one and the author of two novels, *Clay's Quilt* and *A Parchment of Leaves*, both of which are set in southern Appalachia, where he was born and raised and has never strayed far from. He has high, sharp, Indian cheekbones (he is one-eighth Cherokee; the rest is mostly Irish) and penetrating blue-gray eyes and short, light brown hair that runs away from his broad forehead. He has told me that he has a spiritual side and an intellectual side and a honky-tonk side. His intellectual side he does not flaunt. "If you're a writer around here and you're a little successful"—his first book sold well enough that he was able to quit his job as a mail carrier— "you're always in danger of being seen as getting above your raisings." He is less conflicted about his honky-tonk side. He loves to dance, and will do it stone-sober (or otherwise) pretty much anywhere. His books are full of music, including the jump-and-shout Pentecostal church music that he heard on Sundays as a boy. (He no longer belongs to the church of his parents or to any other denomination, though he says without hesitation that he believes in God. Judging from his novels, one place his God is to be experienced is in the Kentucky mountains, in spots unspoiled by coal mining.) Last summer, Silas won a clogging contest in London at the World Chicken Festival. (London is a southeastern Kentucky hub on Interstate 75, just north of a speck on the map called Lily, where Silas lives with his wife and two daughters.) He said a woman once asked him to teach her how to clog and he said he couldn't. "It's just something you naturally know how to move your feet to."

When Silas was growing up, he spent the summers in Hyden, among his mother's people. Earlier, he took me into town and showed me the courthouse where the man who shot and killed his favorite uncle, a coal miner, had been tried and acquitted. ("It was over a card game.") Then, after we drove by the Richard M. Nixon Recreation Center—Nixon, disgraced but unrepentant, came to staunchly Republican Hyden for the dedication in 1978; the only Kentucky politician of note to show up for this event was Albert (Happy) Chandler, the garrulous former governor, who was by then a sort of state mascot—Silas took me to the hollow where his cousins had lived, where he'd played in the creek and ridden around on a fat-wheeled ATV and wandered the mountainsides among the redbuds and dogwoods and serviceberry trees. A few years ago, a coal operator bought all the property in the hollow belonging to Silas's family and built the sort of mansion that wouldn't be out of place in suburban Louisville. The property is fenced and gated. Silas says he doesn't mind the house, but he hates the estate-style fence. The fence is a defilement, a stick in the eye.

Silas drags on his cigarette, looks toward the creek on the other side of the road. He says that whenever he is in Hyden he feels "a powerful, almost physical connection" to his ancestors. The feeling is like an electric current running through him. He says he can feel all the poverty and trouble his people have lived through. He also says that it's important that I—a native Louisvillian who grew up in money, who has lived out of state for years—know that while his people were impoverished they weren't miserable. He says that some readers are disappointed that the characters in his novels aren't more downtrodden. "I make it a point to create characters who aren't defined by their economic circumstances. You can be poor and happy, you know."

Driving through the hills toward Big Creek on Route 118, a narrow, sinuous road that follows an Indian trace, seeing an old man in overalls and broad-brimmed hat sitting by himself at the edge of a garden patch, I think of a passage from James Still's 1940 novel *River of Earth*. It is part of a sermon delivered by Brother Sim Mobberly. The preacher says, "I used to think a mountain was the standingest object in the sight o' God. . . . These hills are just dirt waves, washing through eternity. My brethren, they hain't a valley so low but what hit'll rise again. They hain't a hill standing so proud but hit'll sink to the low ground o' sorrow. Oh, my children, where air we going on this mighty river of earth, a-borning, begetting, and a-dying?"

Still, who was known as the dean of Appalachian writers, was an Alabaman who spent the last seventy years of his life at the Hindman Settlement School, in Knott County, forty miles east of Hyden. Silas and I visited the school and Still's grave. Silas had met Still when he was a student at the school's Appalachian Writers Workshop. He said Still, who died in 2001 at the age of ninety-four, had given him a couple pieces of advice, one of which was "Be still." (The older man wasn't proposing that Silas model himself after him, though Silas did take the title of his second book from a Still poem.) Looking at the inscription from Job on Still's gravestone—"The range of the mountains is his pasture, and he searcheth after every green thing"—I thought of something I'd heard a preacher say on the radio the previous day: "Even if you're standing still with God, you're taking a step with him." I pondered this holy-roller koan, and wondered if I could be happy in the stillness of Hindman. I guessed I'd be driving a lot into the next county to buy my Fat Bastard chardonnay. You can't get Fat Bastard chardonnay or any other kind of alcohol in Hindman.

On a humid Thursday night in June, I'm watching standardbreds trot around a Lexington harness track called The Red Mile. I'm there with two local writers, Michael Kelsay and Ed McClanahan, and Ed's wife, Hilda, a Belgian, who teaches piano. Mike and the

McClanahans live around the corner from each other in a leafy old neighborhood just east of downtown. Neither Mike nor Ed has a congenital interest in horse racing, though Ed's father, who operated a shipping business in Maysville, on the Ohio River, briefly owned a thoroughbred named Hylo's Hoop, and Mike, in his student days, briefly entertained the thought of making a living by studying the Racing Form and betting on obvious winners. For her part, Hilda loves animals and has informed Ed that she won't place a bet on a horse whose driver whips it. Ed tells his wife that since every driver whips his horse, Hilda won't be able to bet. Hilda, who is tall and beautiful, says, "Hmm."

Mike, who is forty-five and married to a lawyer from Louisiana, spent his first sixteen years in West Virginia but considers himself a true-blue Kentuckian. He is the author of a novel entitled *Too Close to Call*, about an unemployed, substance-abusing, small-town Kentuckian who decides to run for mayor. It is elegantly written and sharply satirical, and, as Mike happily acknowledges, it owes something to the work of Ed McClanahan. Ed, who is seventy, whose checkered academic career included a long frolic on the West Coast, is the author of, among other books, *The Natural Man*, a whimsical, earthy, hilarious, profound novel about growing up in a small northern Kentucky town, and *Famous People I Have Known*, a very funny memoir in the form of essays about hippie culture and his late friend Ken Kesey and Kentucky musicians you've probably never heard of. Ed and Mike are somewhat anomalous figures in Kentucky literature, whose mainstream tends to celebrate, sometimes piously, rural values. Though their feet are planted in the clover of central Kentucky, Ed and Mike's comic sensibilities lead them off the beaten path. They are attracted to losing causes—Mike's passion for the professional basketball team at the University of Kentucky aside—and they are not above poking fun at themselves.

While it goes without saying that Ed and Mike are not joined at the hip, it should be noted that they share a dentist, a man who grows fruit trees in Colorado when he isn't filling cavities in Kentucky, and that the dental chair they sit in is also sometimes occupied by the governor of the state, Paul Patton, a Democrat, whose career recently ran into trouble when a nursing-home operator in Hickman County accused him of providing official favors to her while they were having an affair and of retaliating against her when the affair stopped. Kentucky is a small state, a mere four million souls, and it seems uncoincidental that a couple of its novelists have a connection to the man known as the Love Gov, who is soon to be succeeded either by his attorney general, Ben Chandler (the grandson of Happy), or a Republican congressman named Ernie Fletcher. Ed, it turns out, has a slightly more than passing acquaintance with the Chandlers. His father sometimes did business with Happy when Happy was governor. When Ed's first son, Jess, was born, Ed was living in California and he wanted to give Jess a middle name that would be redolent of Kentucky. He chose Chandler.

Ed is talking about how a wayward pinto pony named Betty that his parents bought for him when he was seven ran him under a low branch on a walnut tree and nearly beheaded him, and then he is talking about how Betty's replacement (a biter also known as Betty, who "frequently mistook me for an apple") tried to dump him at the Bracken County fair, and then he notices that Hilda is missing. We scout the concrete apron in front of the grandstand for her. It is the seventh race and Ed has his money on a Kentucky-bred pacer named Stoney Lonesome. Mike places a last-minute bet with a mobile wager vendor and we watch our horses pull their sulkies around the red clay track. In the distance, shining under an ample Kentucky moon, is downtown Lexington, with its cluster of high-rise office buildings and its ancient churches and the house of roundball worship known as Rupp Arena. All our picks finish out of the money. A few minutes later, Hilda appears, beaming with the news that she has just spent some time with a horse. In fact, a man, a trainer perhaps, noticing her interest, has tried to hire her as a hotwalker and groom. Ed is happy to hear she turned him down.

On the way to Louisville, I listen to a Kentucky-born country musician named Gary Stewart, a favorite of Mike Kelsay's. Stewart's songs, mostly about drinkin' and honky-tonkin' and divorcin', are exuberant and heartbreaking and darkly funny. "I've got this drinkin' thing," he moans, "to keep from thinkin' things." Stewart delivers his honky-tonk numbers like a Pentecostalist on fire, but songs about religion and redemption don't seem to be in his repertoire, a fact I can't help noting as I'm driving by Southeast Christian Church, on the outskirts of Louisville. From a distance—and up close as well—Southeast Christian looks like a convention center with a cross on top. It has twenty-two-thousand members and a triple-deck sanctuary that seats nine thousand. (Those in the upper reaches can watch the proceedings on the jumbo TV screens above the altar. They may or may not notice the security professionals who shadow the ministers.) A preacher I know refers to the church, which has an Activities Center that rivals Rupp Arena, as Six Flags Over Jesus. Being inside—at least this was the case when I visited on a desultory Saturday afternoon—is enough to make you want to get back in your car and crank up Gary Stewart.

Southeast Christian is descended from the Cane Ridge Meeting House, a log church built in 1791 outside Paris, in Bourbon County. It was here in 1801 that Barton Stone, a Presbyterian minister who later broke away from his sect to form the Christian Church (Disciples of Christ), organized a revival meeting that attracted twenty thousand people, not excluding a fair number of hecklers and layabouts and romantic opportunists. At the time, Kentucky, which constituted the western edge of the nation, was inhabited almost entirely by nonbelievers.

I visited Cane Ridge after I read an essay about it by Philip Ardery in his memoir *Heroes and Horses: Tales of the Bluegrass*, published in 1996 by the University Press of Kentucky. Mr. Ardery, who is now eighty-nine, was baptized in the Paris First Christian Church when he was seven. He was wearing a white linen suit and was fully immersed in the church's marble tub. He later joined the Episcopal Church. All four of his children escaped immersion.

A lawyer and longtime Democratic party activist, Mr. Ardery lives with his wife in Rolling Fields, the Louisville neighborhood where I spent much of my youth. It is a wealthy neighborhood, though the brick and frame houses, built in the forties and fifties, are modest compared to the castles that have lately risen from farmland beyond the eastern edges of the city. It is a neighborhood in which Episcopalians and Presbyterians and Catholics and Jews live, but it is not a neighborhood that harbors many Democratic party activists. When Mr. Ardery ran for Congress in 1952, he lost his home precinct by five to one.

When I went to see Mr. Ardery this summer, we sat in his sunroom and he closed his eyes the way a preacher waiting for inspiration might and told me stories about the Bourbon County farm where he grew up and about his father (a circuit court judge who stirred up the local branch of the KKK in 1928 when he campaigned for Al Smith, the nation's first Catholic presidential candidate) and about Happy Chandler (who in 1955 took the governor's oath of office in Judge Ardery's farmhouse) and about his old school chum Ed Prichard (a brilliant, arrogant, Harvard-trained lawyer who served in the Roosevelt administration and in 1949 was convicted of ballot-box stuffing in Bourbon County, partly on the testimony of Judge Ardery). Mr. Ardery told me about how, when he told a Franklin County tenant farmer whom he had defended in a murder trial that he could get the verdict thrown out on appeal, the man had said, "Oh, Mr. Ardery, I think my sentence is about right." Listening to Mr. Ardery's stories, narrated at a mellow central-Kentucky tempo that allows for digressions (the definition of a pervert in Kentucky, he says, is "a person who prefers sex to basketball"), I recalled Silas House saying how happy he was as a boy sitting at his Hyden uncle's knee, listening to his stories. When I'm in Kentucky, listening to my friends talk about their farmer-dentists or about the creative campaign tactics of this or that gubernatorial candidate or about the smell of a tobacco barn in drying season or about how a Louisville cab driver wouldn't let a certain pipe-smoking local celebrity into his cab because "him and his big head wouldn't fit," I realize how much I miss my home state. When I'm back north, I especially miss the sound of those voices.

LOUISIANA

HAMMERING DOWN I-25

James Lee Burke

M ost of my literary effort has been spent writing about the South and the American West. Geographically, I have always felt at home in either region. But the historical era with which people my age identify is less easily defined.

Americans of my generation, those born in the Great Depression, are transitional people, and as a consequence we tend to look at the historical calendar in the same way the two-faced Roman god Janus looked back at the preceding year and forward at the one to come. Because of the privation of the times we were born into, we throw away nothing, consider the wasting of food a theological offense, and consider most financial institutions suspect. In some ways we feel we are sojourners in the present, with invalid passports, a bit suspect ourselves for the attitudes we hold.

George Orwell once described England as a protean creature, stretching ceaselessly into the past, forever changing, forever the same. I think the same could be said of the United States. The changes I've witnessed in my lifetime are enormous. But the strength, resilience, courage, and compassion that are inherent in every aspect of the American value system remain unchanged. Unfortunately, our greatest weakness and vulnerability is still with us too—namely, our willingness to place our faith in charlatans, flag-waving demagogues, and upscale hucksters who would turn the Grand Canyon into a gravel pit.

When I was a child, southern Louisiana was a misplaced piece of Caribbean culture where more people spoke French than English, almost all the dirt roads and state highways were canopied with live oaks, and each morning came to you like a gift, filled with birdsong, smelling of chicory coffee, ponded water, spearmint growing in a brick courtyard, night-blooming flowers, lichen crusted on stone, moldy pecan husks, and fish spawning in the bayou. Time was static, and the salmon-colored vault of heaven over our heads was simply an extension of the idyllic natural world into which we had been born.

In his autobiographical book *The Air-Conditioned Nightmare*, Henry Miller wrote of his visit to New Iberia during the Second World War and of the innocent way of life that characterized New Iberia's Acadian people, whose cypress cabins and houseboats and pirogues along Bayou Teche were shrouded in mist in the predawn hours, and the only sounds were fish flopping in the lily ponds.

Of course, the old injustices were here, too: massive illiteracy, rule by the plantation oligarchy, the denial of equality to people of color, wage exploitation of the poor, the great discrepancy between the haves and the have-nots.

The irony is that in many ways the deleterious aspects of early Louisiana society have found greater permanence in the present than the Edenic world described by Miller. For the most part, the plantation oligarchy is gone, but it has been replaced in economic and political influence by the petrochemical industry.

This essay isn't meant to be an attack upon the oil business. My father worked for a pipeline company most of his adult life. I was a landman for Sinclair Oil Company and a surveyor on the pipeline and briefly a laborer in what is called the oil patch. Oil people are like

Roman legionnaires. They're the cutting edge of an empire. The grunts who actually produce the oil and natural gas out of the ground are the hardest-working, most stoic and fearless people I've ever known.

But petroleum corporations are totally pragmatic, if not amoral, and they do business with baseball bats. In the Hollywood film *The Formula*, Marlon Brando plays the role of a morally insane Texas oilman. One of his colleagues says something to the effect of, "These damn A-rabs is sure causing us a mess of grief, ain't they?"

As I recall, Brando replies, "Son, haven't you figured it out yet? We are the A-rabs."

The petrochemical industry in Louisiana is Louisiana. What that translates into is the second-worst environmental record in the United States. The governor of the state threatens, on television, to investigate volunteer attorneys who take on the cases of poor blacks whose communities have been used as open-pit dumping grounds for waste haulers throughout the South. For years our waterways have been considered among the most polluted in America.

This is the new world of Wal-Mart and the ubiquitous strip mall. The state roads and the parking lots of discount stores are literally layered with trash, thrown there by the cavalier, whose self-congratulatory hedonism is a form of anti-confiteor. Drive-by daiquiri windows are not only legal but under Louisiana law the owner cannot be punished for selling to minors as long as the infraction is committed by his employee.

I think the old plantation oligarchy would doff their hats in tribute to the public servants who have helped create a disparity in the quality of life here that has no peer outside the Third World.

My first trip into the real West was at age fifteen, when my father bought me a dollar watch and put me on a Southern Pacific sleeping car bound for a summer of trout fishing in Colorado's Sangre de Cristo Mountains. I woke in the Pullman berth around 4:30 the next morning near Raton Pass. That particular dawn was marked by the most beautiful sunrise I have ever witnessed. The mesas were enormous and pink against a night-black sky, the hillsides a velvet green that seemed soaked in blood. When the train stopped before the long pull up Raton Pass, I stepped down from the vestibule into the coolness of the dawn and the good smell of the creosote in the railway ties and woodsmoke rising from the stucco houses in the valley. In the hiss of steam from the locomotive, the rattle of the ice and mail wagons across the train platform, I felt I had stepped through a hole in the dimension, back into the world of Doc Holliday and Wyatt Earp when they pursued the Clanton-McLaury gang into Colorado after the shootout at the OK Corral.

Up the grade lay the old mining town of Trinidad, the gateway to the Rocky Mountains, its cobbled streets specked with frost, its nineteenth-century buildings softly lit in the morning light. The past was right at the end of my fingertips.

My wife and I have made that trip, over and over, for exactly forty years now, except today we continue on up Interstate 25, through Colorado and Wyoming, and then into western Montana, where we live half the year. But the two-lane road that followed the South Platte River north from Denver through meadowland and cottonwoods is now a highway swarming with cars that drive close to eighty miles an hour, many of them SUVs burning gasoline as though there were no tomorrow.

My wife was in a hospital in Missoula, Montana, undergoing tests the morning of September 11, 2001, and I was in the waiting room, watching the news on CNN, when suddenly the cameras cut to the attacks on the Twin Towers. I will never forget the images that came through the television screen that morning, and like all Americans who were alive the day President Kennedy was murdered or the Sunday the Japanese bombed Pearl Harbor, I will always remember what I was doing at that particular moment. I felt my chest contract and my eyes water, and even though I was sixty-four years old, I felt the same sense of shock and fear and, ultimately, horror, that I had felt as a five-year-old child when, at 1:05 Central Standard Time, in a small café run by an elderly man from St. Martinville named Mr. Goula, a small, brown, wood-cased radio with a tiny yellow station indicator announced that the Second World War had just begun.

During the six weeks following the September 11 attacks I think I slept two nights. I could not rid myself of the images of the people who held hands and leapt to their deaths to avoid burning in the flames. Or of the firemen and police officers who went up the stairwells of both buildings, knowing in all probability they would be crushed to death or buried alive. How loving and how brave do human beings get? The answer, I think, is in the images of those desperate souls who held hands in their last moments and those courageous men who plunged upward into darkness and flame in order to save lives at the cost of their own.

Before his death, Adlai Stevenson made a statement about the level of humanity that characterized the foreign policy of the United States immediately after World War II. We were the only nation on earth that possessed atomic bombs. We could have turned the planet into a slave camp of watchtowers and concertina wire if we had chosen. Instead, through the Marshall Plan, we rebuilt the countries of our enemies. As Stevenson pointed out, no nation on earth ever acted with as much humanity.

But today, as I fly-fish the almost mythic Blackfoot River of western Montana, I realize I am seeing perhaps the last of the wilderness areas that for most of us geographically define the historical United States. Extractive industries wait like a starving man at a banquet table, knife and fork at the ready, to rip into virgin lands. Every justification is offered: jobs, tax revenues, and, most perversely, national defense and what has come to be known as "the war on terrorism," which seems to have replaced the old slogan "the war on communism."

I believe every individual has a special place in his or her heart that he or she creates out of the aggregate of that individual's experience. I liken it to a stained-glass cathedral visited by the people who are emblematic of our lives, the virtues and qualities we hold dear, even the weaknesses and the frailty of moral vision that give us our humanity. The special place where I live is full of Americans who to me are heroic: Dorothy Day, the Maryknolls who were martyred in El Salvador, Molly Brown, Joe Hill, Thomas Jefferson, Woody Guthrie, the women and children who died in the Ludlow Massacre of 1914, Audie Murphy, and Flannery O'Connor. And once again, the great irony is that the bravest people I've ever known are people who are so humble and nondescript you cannot remember what they look like ten minutes after they leave a room. But in the final say each of them is a descendant of Natty Bumppo.

Let the revisionists and denigrators say what they will. This is a great country and it's an enormous privilege to live inside its borders. The egalitarian meritocracy that Jefferson envisioned will probably become a reality in this century. In the meantime we'll continue to hear the shrill voices of those who despise the idea of a pluralistic society. Their message is vitriolic and filled with fear and hatred because they know they're on the wrong side of history. But they make handy point men for those who would grind up our forests, leach gold out of the rocks with cyanide in the Blackfoot drainage and drill for natural gas on the edge of Glacier National Park.

I hope the day comes when the degenerates and cowards who planned and paid for the attacks on the Twin Towers and the Pentagon are rounded up and given what they deserve, perhaps life terms chain-ganging on the hard road under the oversight of a few tobacco-chewing Mississippi gun bulls. I also hope the day will come when our national leaders will not lionize a collection of bedbugs and use the suffering of others to reinstitute a return to both cold war rhetoric and military spending.

But whatever happens, I will always feel a great pride in having been a participant in my country's national experience. The American story is an epic one, and all you need to do in order to see all its historical manifestations is to let imagination have its way for a moment or two and walk or drive through the older parts of our cities or across the countryside in the early-morning hours when the fog hides the present and reveals the past.

In the late fall my wife and I drive south on I-25, through the Big Horn Valley, on through Denver and Pueblo, and past the site of the Ludlow Massacre, where striking miners and their families were attacked by state militia and union-busters who worked for John D. Rockefeller's mineral interests. A tent city sheltering strikers and their families was set afire and machine-gunned. Thirteen women and children took refuge in a cellar under the flames. They died there, and today, between Trinidad and Pueblo, you can turn off I-25 onto a side road that leads you out on the hardpan toward the mountains, which are dotted with pinyon trees and turn a dark purple in the fall.

The storm cellar's still there.

When you lift the door and descend the stairs, I would swear you can hear the voices of the dead in the plaster walls.

Farther on, when you drive down Raton Pass south of Trinidad, you will see the ruins of a stucco mission tucked back in the hills to the west. It was built by Rockefeller, supposedly to rehabilitate his image after the killings at Ludlow.

What does it all mean? For me, the answer is simple. The potential in human beings for either good or evil seems limitless. When I return to our home in Louisiana, on Bayou Teche, a tidal stream on which members of my family have lived since 1836, I look at the red sun beyond the live oaks on the bayou, the smoke from stubble fires drifting off the fields, the hammered gold-and-purple light on the sugarcane, and in the gloaming of the day I want to see the moment caught forever inside a photographer's lens, before the land developers and the builders of strip malls and discount stores have their way with what I think are the gifts of both heaven and earth.

A character in Ernest Hemingway's *For Whom the Bell Tolls* says, "The world is a fine place and worth the fighting for." Saint Paul talked about fighting the good fight. I think both men understood the ongoing nature of the struggle and the fact that the contest is never over, the field never quite ours. To be a participant, though, in whatever small capacity, is nonetheless a grand and ennobling experience. Sometimes on I-25 I think I hear Woody Guthrie's voice on the wind. It's a wonderful feeling to belong to both the past and the future and to be linked in spirit and vision to those who perhaps represent everything that is good and brave and decent in the human family.

At least it has been for me.

MAINE

Heyhodedoodle-oh

Janwillem van de Wetering

Maine is big, and has a long coastline. I mostly know about the coastline where I live. There were, in the almost thirty years I have enjoyed life here, a few expeditions inland, cross-state to Montreal and Quebec City and New Brunswick. Bad roads, strange people, some holding shotguns, not loaded but broken open, and as I drove by the strange people kept one hand in one pocket, no doubt holding some perfectly good shells. I drove into a gas station and nobody came out to pump— yes, a regular pump, with a glass cylinder filled with orange-colored gas and a handle. I went in and there were strange people, one in a wheelchair. I said I needed gas and the person in the wheelchair asked why. Someone locked the door behind me and we sat around for awhile, looking at each other. "I am from away," I said, and a hairy person said, "No kidding." Were they going to rob me? After killing me of course? Any torture? Did I care?

I remembered my coastal neighbor, a gnarled man named Jezz, leaning down from the antique that he says is a tractor, after I shouted up that there was a dead raccoon in my pond. "In Maine, if you don't care," Jezz shouted, "it don't matter."

"Do I care?" I asked the wheelchair person.

"Kingdom come," he answered. Or maybe she answered. The person's voice was high but came from a hole within a stubble. The person and the other strange people bowed their heads and spoke in tongues. So did I.

"You praying too?" a hairy man asked from behind a counter stacked with sardine cans from long ago. "Sure as hell I'm praying," I said. The atmosphere lightened. "OK," the wheelchair person said. The store's door got unlocked. Ten dollars' worth of gas got pumped. I handed over two fives. "Covers it just barely," the hairy man said. Nobody shot me as I drove off.

So far for inland Maine. Stephen King has a camp in inland Maine. There's also the bright side.

LIFE THE WAY IT IS SUPPOSED TO BE the sign says just after you cross into the state, from *down-south*, or *allthemotherstates* as Mainers define the rest of the country, where life is not the way it is supposed to be. Don't you like that? I do, not so much because of its blatant arrogance, although there's that too, but because of the pleasant emptiness that starts behind the sign. Traffic begins to thin down just about at that waypoint. That's where home starts. "I'm home," I say to whoever is in the car with me. There's another good sign a hundred miles up the road. BE ALERT, THINK OF BERT. Bert who? Who cares Bert who? Bert wasn't alert. He didn't live to enjoy the Maine Coast, much longer than the two-hundred miles the schoolbook has it. More like three-thousand miles long, because of all the necks, coves, peninsulas, islands with bars that come up at low tide.

You know there are two types of Mainers? There are Mainers and there are From Aways. I'm a From Away. I have only lived here thirty years. Would I have born-here kids they would be From Aways too. From Aways are stupid.

Like Alex, who wandered in, late sixties, as a hippie-cum-flower-child-cum-homemade-Buddhist. For a day job he walked a chihuahua. The dog belonged to an old lady. This story is set in Bar Harbor. The "bar" in Bar Harbor is a stroke of glistening solid-looking gravel visible at low tide. It connects to an island. Alex walked Chi along the bar to the island that's mostly part of Acadia National Park. Alex, strolling along behind the hairy house mouse, got tired. He sat down and fell asleep. When sudden rain woke him the bar was gone and didn't return until many hours later. Chi dragged Alex home then, to a lack of welcome.

A beautiful coastline we have here, along a clean cold sea, dotted with the heads of seals, loons (an endangered species of large diving birds), eider ducks, and gulls. One is tempted to go boating. "Mind you always know exactly where you are," Jezz, my neighbor, after selling me his wooden sailboat, mumbled. Others confirmed the hint. Keep your finger on the chart. Check your instruments. Name the passing islands. Watch your depth. Know your weather. Even Mainers get lost here. The ocean isn't known to forgive too much foolishness. Lobstermen, out of fuel and without their cell phones, drift out forever. Scallop draggers with their iron bottom scrapers hoisted up too high turn over and sink in three-hundred-feet-deep seas. A cargo boat, loaded with sardines, rips her bottom on a razor-sharp ledge, loses her crew, and feeds happy mammals and birds.

Always stay in contact.

"How are you doing?" my wife's voice says in the phone and I say "I'm at Little Duck, the sea is like glass, watching gray seals diving near orange granite rocks, the seals aren't gray, they're sparkling green." "It is blowing hard here," she says. "Better find a harbor, see you alive tomorrow." Another Maine aspect. Different locations, different weather, no matter if the locations are less than ten miles apart. Various climatic zones cut into each other here so you never know what's what and what will be what and on behalf of what. There's the cat's-paw, a sudden blast of wind directed straight at your puny vessel as she putters along on a hardly moving sea, calm enough right now, but the paw, coming from the next cloud, has claws, and likes to topple the unwary.

Maybe that's why the open sea can be empty on a good day in the midst of the holiday season. Harbors like Camden, Rockport, North East and South West Harbors, Bar Harbor itself of course, Eastport on the Canadian border, and all the southern ports I can't remember the names of don't send out their million-dollar yachts too far. Directors, executives, brokers, takeover artists prefer picnicking in safe coves, their splendid Maine-made vessels tied to sturdy moorings, with the kids buttoned up in their life jackets and the chef cooking in the cabin, the wife watching TV down below, and the mistress up on the bow, one magnificent leg up at a 90-degree angle, one magnificent leg stretched out.

The dot that shows up in my binoculars, far out in the east, slowly approaching, most likely turns out to be a foreign sailboat. I was out in the bay at midnight once, rowing my cedar dinghy under a full moon when I was hailed by the skipper of a weather-beaten fifty-foot vessel that said AUCKLAND, NEW ZEALAND on the transom. Yachtsman wanted to know where he could have the girls dig clams for breakfast. Invited on board, I got introduced. The man had been a banker. Looking ahead one day and seeing nothing but repeats he sold out to his partners, bought the old two-master and wanted to sail to nowhere, possibly forever. But he knew he could never handle the boat alone, and that's when tourist Swiss sisters smiled down from the quay. That was years ago. The girls were older now.

A flat-bottomed boat, kept steady by huge oval sideboards, that showed up at my dock last summer, asking for drinking water, came from Hamburg. The crew, after covering their technology shorts at huge profits, were aiming, after exploring the Maine Coast, to go around Cape Horn, then settle on the Marquesas. "Where Gauguin lived, you mean?" "*Jawohl*," they said. They were going to paint too, and their wives believed in weaving. They talked about palm fronds.

Maine adventures. There's bear hunting, ridge running, coyote trapping (but coyotes have two litters a year and they're smart), otter watching (one visits my pond and barks happily when it sees me); there are turkeys between the sweet fern now. I got used to seeing four eagles at a time, and up to a dozen ospreys, but the turkeys are new. My Internet sources say American turkeys were extinct but were reintroduced from Spain, via offspring of genuine USA wild turkeys that some conquering don took home. Whatdoyouknow! Wild local turkeys defy my dog, calmly hop-march around the outhouse as my guardian barks, snarls, and drools.

Is this exciting country or what?

"Can't make money in Maine," Jezz tells new From Aways sniffing around for a shed on an acre.

I tell them that too. We have hardly any industry left. The last factory in Bangor, making high-end handbags for New York ladies, surrendered to China recently. The L.L. Bean sportsman catalogue, even when preferring to buy locally, adds more and more import products. The boat builders, sure, but commercial fishing licenses are hard to come by and the government buys fishing boats to take them out of production. The Maine-built multimillion-dollar yachts have a limited, possibly shrinking, market. So what do you do down here? Let's keep down the population.

"Still some room here," the new From Aways say.

"Tough climate," I say.

"If you must face the climate," Jezz says, "please bring your own money."

So that would be the retired crowd, which, by its very nature, tends to die out on its service. It gets quiet here in winter. "All by your lonesome," Jezz says. "And for the summer we have the black flies, oh, aren't them little pests wicked. Them don't sting, you know, they tear a piece off. Can hear them chomping as they fly home to tell the others. Bug spray? Hah." He whispers. "*Cancerous poison.*"

I nod. "And there are little bugs too, Indians call them no-see-ums. Big biters. And deerflies, ferocious, zoom around your head when you try swimming in our cold cold waters."

"There are them skeeters too," Jezz says.

"Dengue," I say. "High fever, unbearable muscle ache."

"Ticks," Jezz says. "Lyme disease we have now. That's a killer. Better cover up when you wander into them woods. This ain't no hotpants country."

I mention the hippie horse farm that closed down because the horses froze. It was 40 below.

"So why do you live here?" the newcomers ask.

True. I work and communicate with a PC. I could do that anywhere, as my brother pointed out while visiting briefly, experiencing rain, drizzle, and fog. If he had stayed I could have rowed him out of the cove to watch the sun set behind Blue Hill, driven him up Mount Cadillac on Mount Desert Island to be breathless while taking in panoramic views, showed him finback whales, the largest creatures ever to live on this planet, not thirty feet from the boat, taken him past miles of glowing blueberry fields, bought him a lobster roll for lunch. We could have walked with white-tailed deer on Swann Island, eaten home-baked ice cream pie on neighboring Frenchboro with its hidden safe harbor. There are the mysterious swamplands in spring (or any season) off Route 69; there is the empty Interstate 95, perfect pavement, park-like ever-wide shoulders, all the way to Canada and back. We could have flown to the inland lakes in a seaplane.

"The weather!" he said.

Sure we have weather. So we wait till it changes. Nobody has to camp out in the rain. We have houses here. Hot showers. Clean water that comes out of the well for free. Organic food grown on idealistic farms. Hormone-free meat. "Agua-culture" salads grow in a factory across the road. Salmon grows in pens in the bay, soon there will be haddock too. Lobster eggs, no longer eaten by the almost-extinct cod, produce good harvests. The state adapts.

"Taxes are high."

Very, I agree. So don't live here. So as not to pay high taxes.

"Hawaii," my brother said. "Go live in Hawaii."

Yes, I have been there. Hawaii, especially the big island, is heaven.

"You don't want to live in heaven?"

Nah. Maine is close to Europe, my old stomping grounds, six hours out of Boston, five hours out of Bangor if you can fly with the lobsters on the Xmas jumbo-cargo. New York is very close, and there is a train out of Portland now. Nice train. Montreal, I've been there for lunch, in a neighbor's plane.

Isn't that frightening? Soon the From Aways will invade us. The climate is changing. Snowmobiles were useless the last few mostly mild winters. Florida birds are coming in for the summer; I saw a giant egret in the cove yesterday. Vultures are common now, even in winter. A cardinal is singing as I write.

Up north, however, winters are still tough. I've been looking at maps. There are snowmobile trails there, into infinity and beyond (beyond being Canada). Looking down during the plane ride to lunch in Montreal there was the vast forest. True, there were nasty beetlelike machines scratching part of it away, but I read about paper-factory promises to replant the clearcuts. All-terrain vehicles can manage the snowmobile trails in summer. What grown-up boy wouldn't like to try that, dressed up as a space character in leather, helmet, gloves. "You're against ski-jets too," my wife says. Yes, when other folks ride them. Jezz says he'll come along as soon as I get one. As long as it's mine, Jezz says, for he is against From Away foolishness, although, as long as you don't care, it don't matter.

And yes, he helped getting rid of the dead raccoon fouling the pond. As for the strange inland folks, they did let me go. Good people (whether you get to know them or not), pristine exotic endlessly explorable coast, great state all-over. But please, let's keep that quiet. "There's taxes," Jezz says. "There's bugs," I say. "There's weather," all of us say. Can't make money in Maine. But then, can't spend it too easily either.

MARYLAND

THE WISHED-FOR STATE

Wayne Karlin

I t likes to think of itself as a microcosm of the nation: the
nation's capital embedded in its flank, its topography stretched
from eastern coastal marshes and beaches to western mountains; its economy marching inexorably from fishing, agriculture,
and factory to high-tech, service, and government; its history a
jigsaw fit of antebellum South to Unionist North; its demography
rural black and white to urban ethnic seethe.

But to see it, we need to start from one point, from, in fact, the aptly
named Point Lookout. It was the first sight the two shiploads of bedraggled, seasick British boat people who sailed up the bay in 1634 had of
their future colony, a blade-tip of land thrust into the confluence of the
Chesapeake and the Potomac. A nineteenth-century lighthouse still
stands there, just beyond a chain-link fence, though the place now
serves as a Navy tracking facility, part of the country's coastal
defense system: a notion that occurred too late to the Piscataways who
had stood along the banks watching those ships. "Just at the mouth of
the river," father Andrew White, the senior Catholic chaplain on the
first Maryland expedition, noted in his diary, "we observed the natives
in arms. That night, fires blazed through the whole country."

If now, instead of looking outward for threats, we turn our back on the waters, if we spin around and look inland, we see the land swell out from that point into the boulder-bordered flat of sand and cordgrass where, 228 years after White first beheld it, more than three-thousand interned Confederate prisoners would die of disease, starvation, and abuse. We see it widen into a delta latticed with estuarine lakes and creeks, grow thickly picketed with loblolly pines, clear into neatly furrowed corn and soybean fields edged by clapboard houses where descendants of slaves and plantation owners—the progeny of those two ships and that POW camp—live in complicated symbiosis, and then, seven miles from the point, we see my house, the point where I look out, near the buried ruins of the first settlement, itself sitting on the vanished town of Yaocomaco, given as a gift to the British by the deluded Kittamaquund, head chief of the Piscataway federation, who hoped that small morsel, tossed to the whites, would be enough to keep his people from being swallowed. From here, it is still easy to see how this place looked at the time when that village was still extant.

But if we keep looking, to the north, staring now through the uneasy eyes of Kittamaquund, straining to peer through mist into a future, we would begin to see the forests and marshes thin or vanish as the land widens and becomes encrusted with malls and stadiums and parking lots and red- and white-brick housing developments wistfully named Laurel Glen or Glen Laurel, and apartment and town-hice complexes called Avalon or Fox Run or Fox Die, and sculpted acres of turreted, crenellated McMansions, temples erected to themselves by a hundred thousand Gatsbys, all of it still following the Potomac and along the great network of the Catawba, the trail, now lying under the artery roads, a skein the snipers Malvo and Mohammed moved along, marauders unforeseen by the eyes looking out at Point Lookout for terror from beyond the sea, the two turning away from the frontier and barreling back east, heading in their murder-mobile to the ultimate drive-by, to the walled Beltway around the capital city, to what they also must have seen as an exemplar of the nation, even more so than the Twin Towers or the Pentagon. Sniping from the sparse woods and side roads flanking the high-tech mock-Mayan pyramids of the Interstate 270 corridor, the pikes and boulevards branching off the interstates and into the state, the strip-mall souks teeming with a new and hoped-for polygenesis, a Crewed, Bauered, Beaned, Anthropologized, baseball-capped, turbaned, burnoosed, longyi'd, ao dai'd, abayahed, kepahed, keffiyehed, latte-sipping, Fresh Fields–shopping, sushi-, Tam Yong Gong-, pho-, dim sum-, pasta-, burger-, freedom-fry-eating overweight booboisie that Mencken never dreamt of. The murderous pair shooting Jamaicans and Nicaraguans and Indians and Vietnam vets off benches and in front of Home Depots and Friendlys and Michaels and Texacos with the random, senseless fury of the uninvited; their route looping off north and east to the killing streets of Baltimore, city of Poe and Zora Neale Hurston, and H. L. Mencken and Lady Day, of Barry Levinson and John Waters, David Simon and Lucille Clifton, all visionaries and poets who saw and sang the pattern under the country's crazed buzz that was reverberating and dissembling now, sputtering and pulsing like bug-circled neon in the killers' skulls; the outlaw pair finally, traditionally, fleeing west to the first mountain blockade, the Blue Ridge, the Catoctins, where presidents squat on wooded peaks with prime ministers and squint out, uneasy and clueless as Kittamaquund, and caught finally, traditionally, by citizens' posse, brought to justice, to jail, to instant book and movie of the week.

Well. Yes. Excuse me.

We need to go back. We need a sign.

It's there, back at the beginning of the state, at Point Lookout, stuck into the sand near the public toilets, just beyond the chain-link fence protecting the lighthouse.

If we take the state at its word, as a seed containing the nation, then in that sign we can see the seed that contains both.

Inscribed on it are words from the diary of the aforementioned

Father Andrew White, written as he sailed past that pointing finger of the new world: "Having now arrived at the wished-for country," White wrote, "we allotted names according to circumstances."

It is a statement that encompasses us, both wonderful in its vision and terrible in its selective blindness. ". . . The wished-for country": the dream itself, a tabula rasa where the voyager could reinvent himself, liberated from the rigid and unequal divisions of the old world, allot names according to circumstances, as White did, ignoring that there were already names, derived from other sets of circumstances, fixed to the places he saw. He wished for transformation, but carried with him, as heavy as the English stones used as ballast in the hold of his ship, all the weight of the world he thought he'd left behind.

White's words limn the dream and then narrow it and begin its rot; they contain the paradoxical tension that still defines us. The first port of call in the Americas for the Maryland expedition was Barbados, and the first sight White saw in that hopefully misnamed new world was the mutilated corpse of a slave who had been hung on the dock. A victim himself of anti-Catholic persecution who would end up dying in chains, White—a name so laden with ironic portent that I wouldn't dare give it to a character in a novel— rejoiced. He saw the hanging as the work of Heaven: the slave was to have led a revolt of "the servants," who would have taken over the first English ship, White's ship, and sailed it along a different path of dreams, back to Africa instead of to the deserved gift of the river White would come to see before him at Point Lookout.

He was a man as complex and contradictory as the dream itself, as the wished-for country that grew from the dream. He was horrified at the subsequent exploitation and abuse of the Native Americans he found in Maryland; he loved his Piscataway. But what he loved about them was their willingness to be his, to see the world through his perceptions, to see in him not only a path to God but the godhead itself. "Since they had never seen such a large ship," he writes of the

Piscataway waiting at Point Lookout, "messengers were sent in all directions, who reported that a Canoe like an island had come with as many men as there were trees in the woods," attributing to those observers an awe White wanted them to have. Surely, he must have thought, we are blessed; surely everyone would like to jump on board such a miraculous vessel as we can build; surely our only motives are to bring you with us to the City of God, to us. Not knowing, or disregarding that he did know that his curious and apprehensive audience had already been exposed to and underawed by the British, whom they regarded at best as helpless infants who couldn't care for themselves, and at worst as cannibals, who when starving in Virginia because they spent all their time looking for gold had taken to murdering and eating the Piscataways' brother Algonquians; not seeing that in fitting them into his own vision, he, White, was gobbling them up himself, as voraciously as any cannibal.

"Never have I beheld a larger or more beautiful river," he wrote of the Potomac. "The Thames seems a mere rivulet in comparison with it. . . ." The new land seen and defined, as new lands must be seen and defined, in comparison to the old—though, reading those words, one can't help thinking of the opening of another narrative: Conrad's Marlow speculating to another little boatload of Englishmen floating on the Thames that once, "this too was a place of darkness," disassociating his nation from the Roman soldiers who brought civilization to it with the sword. They were only, after all, robbers, while what his countrymen brought to the heart of darkness shone with the pure light of good intention; Marlow being as white as White, confusing conquest with enlightenment, assuming that good intentions couldn't mask arrogance, greed, and thievery. "Fine groves of trees appear," White wrote, "not choked with briers or bushes and undergrowth, but growing at intervals as if planted by the hand of man, so that you can drive a four-horse carriage, whenever you choose, through the midst of the trees." Not imagining that the natives, that vaguely threatening red cloud following the ships along the bank, customarily burned out that underbrush with controlled fires in order to preserve and manage that forest and keep hunting lanes open for the flight of their arrows without destroying the habitat of their game—the herds of deer that another early Marylander, the indentured servant George Alsop, described as being "as numerous in this Province of Maryland as Cuckolds can be in London." Not imagining that a short time after White's arrival the tribes to whom he brought the light of civilization would be used up as a surrogate army in a trade war for beaver fur against the tribes the Virginians were also using up; that all of the old-growth hickories and oaks he so admired in those fine groves would be cut down and that the bay, which he saw teeming with every manner of fish and fowl, would, 369 years later, be sick with fisteria and fecal bacteria and runoff from uncontrolled overdevelopment, its oysters and crabs nearly gone from pollution and overfishing and the pure, naked greed that became synonymous with freedom, the word and the dream newspeaked to their basest definition. He did not see, for that matter, that the tobacco plantations his colony would grid over the Piscataway land would need the labor of African slaves to succeed financially, so that the state he would help found would later adopt as its official song a paean to the right to own other human beings, and would contribute a chief justice to the Supreme Court, Roger Taney, who would rule in 1857—the same year that Harriet Tubman would steal her own parents from an Eastern Shore plantation—that those so owned were "a subordinate and inferior class of beings . . . [who] had no rights a white man was bound to respect." This was a sentiment that brought Marylander Frederick Douglass's outcry: "What, to the American slave, is your Fourth of July? I answer: a day that reveals to him, more than all other days in the year, the gross injustice and cruelty to which he is the constant victim. To him, your celebration is a sham; your boasted liberty an unholy license;

your national greatness, swelling vanity . . . your shouts of liberty and equality, hollow mockery . . . a thin veil to cover up crimes which would disgrace a nation of savages." All ingredients in a national confusion over self-definition that would finally stain the fields of western Maryland red at Antietam, and plant a prisoner-of-war camp on that point White saw as the harbinger of the New World, where, right behind our sign, a black federal regiment, the spiritual sons of that hung Barbadian slave, would exact a terrible revenge on the flesh of their Confederate prisoners, a payback—and forth—that has yet to end.

"Having now arrived at the wished-for country," White wrote, and his words on that sign at the beginning of the state, at Point Lookout, contain the seeds of despair—and yet also of hope. They are precursors to Thomas Paine's words, a century and twoscore years later: "We have it in our power to begin the world over again . . . the birthday of a new world is at hand," for we know that the transforming liberation they yearn for, once named and put into the world, can no longer be controlled, and the dispossessed and enslaved who hear the idea of an inherent right to freedom expressed by a master struggling against a colonial power, shortly and surely must ask the question: but what about us? They remind us, White's words, of the necessity of vision: we can't create what we don't wish for, nor, until we articulate the ideal, can we see—and change—the ways we fall short of it; they remind us that we have not yet arrived.

The words contain the state and the nation. What White saw was not, and is not, the achieved country. It is the wished-for country.

MASSACHUSETTS

PAST PERFECT MASSACHUSETTS

Elizabeth Benedict

A parlor game for Freudians: if California were a region of the psyche, which would it be? The id. New York? The ego. Massachusetts? The superego.

Impulses associated with the states: California—adventure. New York—ambition. Massachusetts—renunciation.

The Beach Boys. Benny Goodman. Bach.

Beauty. Nerve. Brains.

On second thought, Massachusetts is brainy *and* beautiful, exquisitely so, from the hooked tip of Provincetown to the verdant heights of the Berkshires. It's easy to appreciate but dizzying to contemplate because of all it was and is and aspired to be. And because of all that has been written about it: its goodness, its fleeting greatness, its complicated failings. The writing is so vast and tormented, so filled with ambition, anguish, self-examination, and genius that it exists as a shadow identity, somehow essential to our experience of the state, whether we begin reading with *The Scarlet Letter*, *Couples*, or Robert Lowell's "The Quaker Graveyard in Nantucket." Boston and Cambridge have inspired so much literary scrutiny that it would be safe to conclude that they desire to be studied, that the unexamined city is not worth living in. Yet somewhere, beyond the literature, is the place itself. Maybe. The mind wanders not to a quintessential street corner—Sunset and Vine—or a central location—Times Square— but to the door of the library. Of course you won't be able to get into *the* library—Widener—without a Harvard ID, but the grand Boston Public, designed by Charles McKim in 1895, will probably do.

Massachusetts Bay Colony began as an idea of biblical proportion, as articulated in John Winthrop's sermon, "A Model of Christian Charity," which he delivered in 1630 aboard the ship that began the great migration from Old England to New. "For we must consider that we shall be as a city upon a hill," he intoned. "Justice and mercy" would prevail here, and "the eyes of all people are upon us, so that if we shall deal falsely with our God . . . we shall be made a story and a byword through the world." Eve ate the apple—we were only human, even after the ennobling voyage across the sea—and ever since, the state's scribes have been obsessed with the failure of the place to live up to its publicity. Early on, writers fretted over how much guilt they should feel over this. They clung to guilt for centuries, putting the emotion to its best use in fighting slavery. Guilt grew into anger and shame when Boston slipped from preeminence after the Civil War, when it became obvious that it would never achieve the greatness of New York or London.

Today, Massachusetts is not an historic relic like Venice, despite the meticulous preservation of its past: the restored Berkshire mansions; the miles of National Seashore; the twenty-thousand acres across the state permanently protected by the Trustees of Reservations (the country's first conservation group, founded in 1891); the village greens with their sparkling white Congregational churches; the grand houses of the shipping magnates in Salem, and those of the whaling captains on Nantucket and the Vineyard, with their widow's walks and shiny black shutters. In a museum on Nantucket are pieces of scrimshaw made by the sailors on those suicidal voyages while their wives waited for years at home. On the front of one we see an etching of a ship, and on the back, hidden from view—as the curators have displayed them—something pornographic. We think of the men as adventurous and stalwart, as people so distant from us that we cannot know their hearts, but they had to have been as full of longing and loneliness as our own.

This is what Massachusetts does, and I am not the only one to fall for it: it entices us to dwell in and romanticize the past, and, in some cases, to fling huge chunks of it overboard, leaving in their wake only the storybook myths. An example among many: in our minds, the glory of the abolitionists conveniently wipes out the state's history of slave owning and slave trading, outlawed only in 1788. The practices continued—to an extent still disputed—well into the early nineteenth century. Slavery did not originally take hold the way it did in the South largely because the Puritans' expectations of an agricultural economy, requiring thousands of hands to work the fields, were dashed once they arrived; the land was too rocky and inhospitable. The Puritans turned instead to the sea and made their fortunes salting cod, building ships, trading around the world, and eventually manufacturing, becoming "the codfish aristocracy" and the Boston Brahmins, who were recently given a wry requiem in Carolyn Cooke's short-story collection, *The Bostons*. In the title story, an aging father paints watercolors of the State House on Beacon Hill, and his grown daughter, who left husband and children to live with a woman in California, sends him a book, *New Lesbian Detective Stories*. He tries reading it but much prefers Thackeray.

It is something of a default position here: that the past is more seductive than the present, that old ways are the best. People and institutions have a tendency to cling, as though to a bad marriage, to creaky attitudes and policies when it would be wise and profitable to relinquish them. It's as though change requires a repudiation of the past, as though the Puritans are still in charge, and punishment—or,

God forbid, and perhaps more frightening, pleasure—is sure to follow. On the other hand, the communal fixation on the past makes it difficult for plunderers to have their way. Thus the battles over preservation and casinos—two often in the news—are ferocious and invigorating; you feel flung back to a time of heartier debate. To some admiring outsiders, the state still seems a bastion of enlightened liberalism, while to a good many out-of-state Republicans it is something of a joke, home to a bunch of San Francisco–style lefties. The illusion of enlightenment is kept alive by the presence of a hundred colleges and universities, by the influence of the People's Republic of Cambridge, and the Kennedys, and still, by McGovern's win here in 1972, the lone state to reject Richard Nixon for president. But the state's left leanings were only ever part of the story. Today they're an even smaller part, as our politics and politicians, like those everywhere, move dramatically to the right, in chilling lockstep.

In *Imagining Boston: A Literary Landscape*, Shaun O'Connell explores what he calls "the Bostonian habit of invidious distinctions: race, ethnic, and class," a habit inherited from our British colonizers. The Puritans hated everyone who wasn't one. When they became Yankees and Boston Brahmins, they hated the Irish, who arrived, fleeing famine, in the 1840s. The abolitionists supported blacks while they were enslaved and long after, but only 160 attended Harvard College between 1890 and 1940. By contrast, Jewish students were plentiful— too plentiful. Around 1918, the university declared "a Jewish problem." In 1922, when the freshman class was 22 percent Jewish, President A. Lawrence Lowell began to limit enrollment from the big-city public schools in the Northeast, code for "Jews." In the 1970s, Boston's racial and ethnic animus became ongoing national news when Judge W. Arthur Garrity, Jr. attempted to solve another problem by busing poor African-American kids from Roxbury to the schools of poor Irish-American kids in south Boston. All hell broke loose.

Today, things are murkier and generally more tolerant, with some glaring exceptions. There are people from seventy countries in the Cambridge public schools; 20 percent of the college and graduate students in the area's sixty schools are Asian-Americans; Boston, in the 2000 census, is now "majority minority," with 49.5 percent "non-Latino white," 25 percent non-Latino black, 14 percent Latino, and 8 percent Asian. In the past decade, the city's minority population rose about 10 percent. Yet the state itself is overwhelmingly white: 84.5 percent. The greater Boston metropolitan area—from the New Hampshire border down to Plymouth—is the third-whitest metropolitan area in the country, behind Pittsburgh and Minneapolis. The cities—Boston, Cambridge, Springfield—are the only places with significant minority populations, and the problems minorities face affect the poorest and most segregated, as well as the young professionals in Boston's workforce. If to white outsiders Massachusetts represents racial tolerance, black professionals in Boston and elsewhere know otherwise. The city is disturbingly well known for its inattention to hiring and promoting African-Americans. Although they go to college and graduate school in the area, the inhospitable business atmosphere encourages many to find work elsewhere.

Yankee industry and ingenuity are thriving in the state's three-hundred biotech companies, located mostly in the Cambridge-Worcester corridor—a fact that has inspired the slogan "Beantown is now Genetown." But the industry should be doing better, according to the Massachusetts Biotechnology Council, which in December 2002 released *MassBiotech 2010*, a major report that provides a fascinating window into the soul of the state at the start of the twenty-first century. The study warns that unless the biotech players—industry, academe, research institutes—and state government undergo what amounts to a personality and policy transformation, the state will lose its edge in the field to competitors in the West and South. The message is blunt: Hurry up and start doing what

California and North Carolina have been doing all along. Both have state biotech agencies that lure companies with incentives, promote life-sciences education to plump up the workforce, and foster productive relationships between industry, academe, and government—essential in this evolving, interdependent industry. In Massachusetts, there is no state biotech office and no apparent state awareness that California openness and Southern hospitality can have economic rewards. All players are on their own, even when a company needs to build a factory fast, to produce a drug the FDA has just approved. Many build out of state to avoid legal and bureaucratic obstacles just when the financial payoff for years of research begins sacrificing new jobs and tax revenue. Said one executive, "In Massachusetts, you never know what problem you'll run into."

One problem many researchers and businesspeople encounter is New England frostiness compounded by local arrogance: "The very strength of its dominant institutions sometimes makes it difficult for those institutions to work together," the study reports. "Is there something systemic in the culture and organization of Massachusetts institutions that inhibits the conversion of research richness into commercial power?" Does Macy's tell Gimbels? Does Harvard tell MIT? Apparently not.

Another high-stakes controversy in which the state's past is colliding with conflicting ideas of its future is taking place offshore. In a shallow, twenty-four-square-mile patch of Nantucket Sound called Horseshoe Shoals, four miles off the southern coast of Cape Cod, a company called Cape Wind Associates wants to build the country's first offshore wind farm, which the promoter's website describes coyly as a wind "park." The plan—several years from construction because many federal and state regulatory agencies must sign off on it—is to plant in the sound 130 turbines with three-pronged propellers and connect them to electric cables on the seafloor, pointing toward the Cape and islands. Each turbine would be 246 feet from the surface of the water to the top, except when the propeller blade stands straight up, pushing the turbine on 417 feet from the surface, the height of a forty-story building. Cape Wind claims the $700 million project is a clean alternative to fossil fuels and will produce enough electricity to power half a million homes. Pilots who fly small planes from Hyannis to the Vineyard and Nantucket aren't sure it's a great idea—FAA approval is necessary—and neither are the droves of activists concerned about fish, birds, fishing boats, sailboats, and the landscape. Every week brings new lawsuits, press conferences, plots, subplots—and plans from other companies to build more offshore wind farms from Massachusetts down to Virginia. I'm against the project, but it nevertheless seems to me a controversy worthy of the state's history, unlike the push for casinos, which is the same tawdry, tax-the-poor, money-grubbing scandal wherever it occurs. At issue on the Cape are serious questions about who controls the sea and the landscape and about where on earth, literally, we will get the energy to run our lives.

Speaking of water. Speaking of the sea. I lived for a time on Martha's Vineyard in the mid-1990s, before Bill Clinton became a regular and the island became a Hollywood hangout. Since then, the year-round population has gone up 500 percent; the real estate almost as much. The old ways might not always be the best, but they were cheaper, and you didn't have many day-trippers arriving with their motorcycle gangs or anorexic socialites who look like they just flew in from Palm Beach. One of my favorite places to bike to in the summer or to take my dog walking in the winter was Wasque Point on Chappaquiddick, a breathtaking beach on this tiny, one-paved-road peninsula, connected to the Vineyard by only a narrow sandbar and a three-car ferry. The point is a vast sandy beach where two bodies of water—the Atlantic Ocean and the calmer waters of Nantucket Sound—meet at a right angle. The water is often sapphire blue or a shade of turquoise, as though this were Florida. Nothing but deep blue water and sky-blue sky as far as you can see, and at your back, two-hundred acres of rolling dunes and pristine marshland, managed and protected by the Trustees of Reservations. What makes the beach especially dramatic is the right angle of the shoreline and the way the two bodies of water bow to each other as they hurtle toward land. The curling waves collide and kick up furious riptides and a gorgeous trail of phosphorescence.

The only house you can see from the beach is in the distance, on a bluff, a low-slung wood and glass beach house, or so it seems from here. You can see a wall of windows that face the water and, standing at the point, you share the same ocean view. An investment mogul—from out of state, it must be noted—bought the place and nine acres around it for $5 million in 2001, intending to build a 10,000-square-foot house. The local planning board said he couldn't; it was too big and out of character. (There are other big houses, but they're hidden in the woods. They don't mar every view of the shoreline.) When the mogul returned with a proposal for a 7,500-square-foot house and the threat of a lawsuit if he did not get his way, the board relented; many of his neighbors, still not pleased by the outcome, intend to change zoning laws for the future. Even though I have only been a walker on that stretch of beach, it saddens me to think that it is no longer a place where small is beautiful. A house in keeping with the shoreline would have been a victory for good taste, community, and the environment, a defeat for vulgarity, and a respectful nod to all that came before. Still, there are fiercer battles than this that need to be waged.

When I'm there I rarely think of it, but up the beach about a mile is the bridge for which Chappaquiddick is best known. Over the decades, thousands of tourists have come to look and have ripped pieces off—ripped off so much of it that the bridge had to be rebuilt several years ago. A woman whose name we didn't know beforehand was left to die, a man from the state's most famous family was never tried for the crime. And the rest, of course, is history.

MICHIGAN

NOT QUITE LEAVING MICHIGAN

Jim Harrison

ust because you go someplace doesn't mean you're actually
"there." The traveler, the visitor, the transient businessman
spin their fragile mental wheels, almost prayer wheels, trying to
truly locate themselves in alien cities and countrysides. A few
years back I wrote an essay on "dislocation" for the *Psychoanalytic Quarterly* in which the subject nearly exfoliated itself into the arena of the
somewhat surreal maps we make of the terrain in which we live,
which are finally less consoling than the Teutonic Rand McNally,
the topographical renditions known mostly to pilots and birds.

You're also not quite "there" when you're living in a place you no
longer wish to be. This is a metaphysical step well behind Dogen's
admonition that we must "find ourselves where we already are." I
effortlessly agree with this twelfth-century Zen genius and have
agreed with him for as long as we've owned our farm in northern
Michigan, thirty-three years, but I still found myself where I no
longer wished to stay. Leelanau County was changing faster than I
wanted it to change. I didn't want to become a powerless whiner
talking about the "old days" in a county that had gone in thirty
years from a basically agrarian and commercial fishing enclave to

an elaborate playground for the Republican rich. My farm was no longer a farm but a "property" and the fact that it had vastly multiplied in value was more melancholy than comforting.

When someone from Michigan wishes to tell the curious where they live, they hold up their right hand and repeat the saw that Michigan is shaped like a mitten, and then they point out with their left hand where they live. Leelanau County is the little finger. Our local American Legion is called the Little Finger Post. We are a peninsula surrounded by the waters of Lake Michigan and Grand Traverse Bay, a hilly country of surpassing beauty with a large stretch of waterfront protected by a National Lakeshore. When we moved to Leelanau County in the late sixties, vacant waterfront was sold for about three hundred dollars a foot. Recently a two-hundred-foot lot sold for twelve thousand a foot, bringing the total to well over two million dollars. Many of the hills I roamed and hunted, or lower areas where I followed paths to the lake to fish, are now occupied by McMansions where the often retired wealthy couples race between their seven bathrooms to make full use of their considerable investment. Thorstein Veblen's "conspicuous consumption" has become a euphemism.

Still, we might have stayed on in the considerable remaining beauty if both our daughters weren't in Montana, along with two grandchildren who are easier, moment by moment, to adore because they are being raised by someone else. Grandchildren are a beloved spectator sport in which you are a viewer rather than a referee.

The southern third of Michigan is heavily industrialized, though the population concentrations are surrounded by verdant farmland. The biggest cities, Detroit, Flint, and Grand Rapids, were always a bit muddy and confusing to an outlander, but nevertheless fascinating. Growing up in the north, the rumors of wages to be earned in these big cities were a magnet to country folk. When migrants from home returned from these cities on vacation they wore spiffy clothes and drove new cars. Back in the forties and fifties factory workers earned enough to send their children to college, something that hasn't been possible for decades. For those who stayed back home, the consolations of countryside, with forests, rivers, and lakes, seemed insufficient when you couldn't decently support your family. It still does.

The north, say the country upward from the base of the fingers within the mitten, had its own economic burgeoning in the seventies, eighties, and nineties, much of it fueled by tourism, small factories, workers retiring from the immense industries of the south. The only thing that prevented the sprawl from being uglier than it is was the presence of state and federal land, which makes up nearly half of the state's total acreage.

The problem with our instructive mitten is that it leaves out the Upper Peninsula, a grand stretch of land nearly three hundred miles long measured laterally, bordered on the south by the top of Lake Michigan, and on the north by the somewhat foreboding Lake Superior. This area is commonly left out of the mitten analogy because it has always been rather remote (a sign in the far west of the UP says DETROIT 600 MILES) and sparsely populated and it is rare indeed to meet someone from the Upper Peninsula, say, in New York or Los Angeles. I love this area and have had a cabin on a river near Lake Superior for more than twenty years, and as these years passed I began to spend so much time up there that my wife decided we had to find a more favorable area for a main residence. It has become gradually obvious to me that I favor the Upper Peninsula because the area replicates the atmosphere of my youth, before the population of the county more than doubled. Where else can I live where I can see a large timber wolf on the two-track leading to my cabin?

On the morning, however, of May seventeenth, I'm as petulant as a ten-year-old who can't go to the county fair this year because he has broken two dozen fresh eggs by throwing them against the silo. At mid-morning it is 35 degrees and the air is full of drizzle and snowflakes. Yesterday I found a patch of snow in a gully in the woods, which means it has been a cold spring indeed. How can I as an adult take weather personally? Easy. After an arduous week in New York on publishing business, plus several days in Ohio lecturing, I'm stopping at the cabin for a week on the way back to our new home state, Montana. I never miss this time of year, when I go into a large vacant area and walk among thousands of acres of flowering sugar plums, chokecherry, and dogwood, watch the arriving warblers, hawks, sandhill cranes, catch a few fish to eat.

This year there is not a single flower to be seen and yesterday the cold wind off Lake Superior was gusting to fifty knots, all of which serves to remind me that there are disadvantages to love, the foul climate being a form of especially aggressive PMS. You also have to pack in any interesting groceries as the closest good market is over a hundred miles distant. You end up with five jars of capers on the shelf for fear of being without. I highly value being lost in the woods, though not overnight, and there is ample opportunity for that. Being lost brings you to vivid attention and the imagination comes into full play when it seeks to view the terrain as a bird does. However, being lost is nearly unbearable in June at the height of bug season—mosquitoes, deerflies, blackflies, and others—when no amount of bug repellent will hold the insects fully at bay. I'm blind in my left eye and once had to stumble out of the woods holding the lid of my right eye open, so swollen was my face from insect bites. I shed my clothes and swam in the river that flows by the cabin, the cold water allowing my pretty face to recover.

The politics of Michigan as a whole are, like many states, a mere microcosm of the national arena, which is to say a mixture of Sunset Strip and the boxing world. In the past, of course, we were relentlessly warned against disproportionate powers of corporations and the rich, but now they are both totally shielded by a national ethic of greed for its own sake. Our governor of eight years, John Engler, has effectively destroyed the Department of Natural Resources, the only barrier to the endemic theocracy of land rape to be found more often in western states. It is interesting that the worst recent malefactors make much of the hokum of patriotism, religion, and family, whereas the robber barons of old didn't bother with costumery. In the history of Michigan in particular those who gave their working lives to the extractive businesses of logging and mining were allowed and encouraged to have full mythologies of conquest—to the point of heroism—having committed the often destructive work of the owners. Songs were sung but the money went elsewhere, especially in the Upper Peninsula. Oddly it was a moderate Republican, William Milliken, who built up a magnificent Department of Natural Resources, only to see his wisdom cast aside with a boggling cynicism.

As a left-winger from essentially populist farm families on both sides, my somewhat jaded anger has had a contemporary rejuvenescence in terms of my own geezer land ethic. I'm less likely to blame Engler, who is a mini-Bush, and Bush, who is a mini-Reagan. The earth herself is only an abstraction these men stride along on their way to a permanent top wherever that might be. They both remind one of mean-minded fraternity boys who will never get closer to nature than the usual denatured golf course. They are less men than emblematic clones of the culture that produced them. Neither of them as of yet has grandchildren to whom they owe a future beyond a stock portfolio, though their ignorance of history reflects itself against a future that is within them a vacuum, a tabula rasa in which they hope only to grease the wheels of the class for whom they toady themselves.

Of late I've been studying a relatively new academic discipline, called "Human Geography," for a new novel. Other recent works have entailed the study of anthropology and the nature of the human brain. In contrast to my mediocre college years the application of this modest new knowledge has been immediate. I would doubtlessly receive a low grade if tested on any subject other than my own imagination, though not lower than members of the U.S. Congress given a diagnostic test on American history. (World history is as out of the question as simple honesty.)

I immediately seized on the term "geopiety," which is used in Human Geography. It is easy enough to witness how people frame the reality of where they live—whether townships, counties, or states—in the most pleasant light to justify to themselves why they live there. I wish I had put in my journals the number of times on my travels I have heard locals describe their areas as "God's country," which is to suggest that he is likely not present in other areas.

Much is clearer to us when we watch the Republican or Democrat conventions, when state delegate votes are announced and the speakers extol their home states in that peculiar stentorian manner that politicians are so fond of. Often we receive the state mottos or even the mention of the state bird, and all states are invariably described as "great." Politics is, above all else, the art, theory, and practice of xenophobia. The occasional and apparent loathing of one state or region for another can be both amusing and appalling. Sometimes this is personal and nearly subconscious, say in the irrational antipathy many northern journalists felt for Jimmy Carter and Bill Clinton, as if all reason were abandoned when the target of inquest came from south of the Mason-Dixon line. Xenophobia is often implausibly simian, and rather than reading political texts we might better look for comprehension at the work of Jane Goodall or the more recent *In My Family Tree* by Sheila Siddle. To witness someone transcending xenophobia we must listen again to Woody Guthrie's "This Land Is My Land."

Michigan, my Michigan, the "winter-water-wonderland," as we call it. The paths of where we have lived our lives are ineradicable. The forests and lakes absorb the boy rather than vice-versa. Creatures are like that. The dozens of Michigan rivers I have fished continue to flow in my brain during a month in Paris, and I will doubtless hear the sounds of these beloved rivers on my deathbed. As a boy I was convinced that dogs, cats, cows, pigs, and horses were my true friends, and a love of Shakespeare and Dostoevsky, Mozart and Caravaggio does not replace this early companionship. The large black bear that visits my cabin bird feeder for a snack raised its own image in Arles last November when I followed a black dog past Roman ruins.

Meanwhile the paths that dominate our lives are the roads that lead back and forth to our livelihoods. Recently I dreaded a trip to New York but ended up having the best visit in decades because I stayed downtown rather than at the Carlyle, which had been my expense-account habit for twenty-five years. Earlier in life I had lived in the city as a woebegone beatnik, and also had a brief two years on the faculty of Stony Brook. We landed at LaGuardia on a clear, sunny May morning and I had the unexpected gut jolt, seeing the missing Twin Towers. On early mornings, I walked out my old haunts in the Village, which were no more the same as in the early sixties than my own home county in Michigan. For reasons not clear to me there was not a trace of unpleasantness. The world won't stay the same for me. Despite Heraclitus, you can't even step into the same river once. Poor young poets can no longer rent a place in the Village for forty bucks a month, but then, as my younger daughter, Anna, crossly reminded me, she and her schoolmates will never be able to live in the county they were raised in. I agreed, but then why can't they discover the Upper Peninsula? Nearly everyone is ground down by the same economic boot.

I'm keeping the cabin, though it will involve a 3,600-mile round-trip from Montana several times a year. I am quite unable to totally leave my home state. I asked Tom McGuane, a novelist and Montana rancher and friend since college, if I would hear our dreaded eastern mono-ethic catchwords, "healing, caregiver, closure" in Montana.

He thought not, but I would certainly hear "sustainable" and "megafauna." I sort of knew this, having fished in Montana nearly every year since 1968. When a newspaper reporter asked me why I'd made the move, I said because I liked "dirty cars, fat cows, and trains." Livingston owns a large railroad-repair shop and switchyard. Rich and poor live within blocks of each other and even greet each other on the street.

On a sunny Sunday morning in New York, I walked around Brooklyn with two young novelist friends, Colum McCann and Jeffrey Lent, then we proceeded on foot across the Brooklyn Bridge, the first time for me since I was nineteen and paying homage to Walt Whitman and Hart Crane. I could live here I thought, swept away by the splendor of it all, though for reasons of claustrophobia it would have to be in a one-room cabin in the middle of the bridge.

MINNESOTA

THROUGH ONE POET'S EYES

David Mura

innesota, in the popular national image, is still the land of Scandinavians and Lutherans. Perhaps no longer the farmer's daughter, but a more updated version, say Mary Tyler Moore—the down-to-earth gal next door who'd rather say gosh than dammit. Like Mary, whose innocent ways often seemed befuddled at worldliness or irony, Minnesotans are supposed to be down-to-earth, unpretentious, nonconfrontational.

Also a little repressed. After all, it's a cold place. A white place. Lots of snow. Lots of white people. As Chris Rock says, "Minnesota? The only black people there are Prince and Kirby Puckett." In a movie like *Fargo*, locals are pictured as still retaining a trace of Scandinavia in their accent. That's about as foreign as our image gets; no fleet of cabbies here who don't speak English.

Sometimes we get written up as one of the most livable places in the country. A well-educated workforce, a strong high-tech sector, relatively low unemployment. Low cost of living, reasonable housing prices. No hourlong commutes and clogged freeways, no smog, no rivers that might be set on fire. From time to time, there's some talk here of urban sprawl, but it's nothing like Atlanta; there's room here to build. The public education system still seems to work (though recently, as elsewhere, it's under siege). No vast urban ghettos, no White Flight.

We're called the Land of Ten Thousand—really more than forty-thousand—Lakes, and this too is part of the state's attraction. Ice fishing and hockey are big here, as are summer cabins. The landscape, as Sinclair Lewis pointed out, is not flat but rolling. More open fields and farms in the south, and vast forests as you move north. Though the official state bird is the loon, the unofficial is the mosquito. The winters are historically long, brutal, and cold. But the cold keeps the Twin Cities from becoming a Seattle, with its rising housing prices and signs to Californians telling them to go back where they came from. Recently, though, the winters have been surprisingly mild. "If there's going to be global warming," a friend jokes, "this is the best place to be."

In our politics we're seen as a liberal state. We're the only ones that voted for Mondale in Reagan's reelection. We're the land of the Happy Warrior, Hubert Humphrey, clean Gene McCarthy, the late Paul Wellstone—probably the furthest left of any senator in recent memory. In the latter's honor, Wellstone supporters recently started sporting the bumper sticker—WWWD: WHAT WOULD WELLSTONE DO?—which I'm sure drives the members of the Christian right here bonkers.

Some of these popular images are true. Some not. The cab drivers, for instance, are most likely to be Somali or Ethiopian; the last mayor of Minneapolis was a black woman, Sharon Sayles Belton. St. Paul recently elected the first Hmong legislator in America, State Senator Mee Moua. There are more Vietnamese restaurants here than Perkinses or Denny's. The Minneapolis school system is 60 percent students of color; the students come from homes with 150 first languages.

We do have a liberal tradition, but our next-to-last senator, Rod Grams, was a conservative Republican who fell in step more with Jesse Helms and the southern Republicans. Our current governor's also a Republican, one of those who sport the conservatism-with-a-kind-heart rhetoric, though his recent business and campaign scandals show him partaking of the usual smorgasbord set out by the rich. Our last governor was the bald ex-WWF wrestler and Independent Party member Jesse Ventura. If Mary Tyler Moore was often rattled by her gruff boss, Lou Grant, our current governor would have her racing for her Haldol. Jesse was the brief shining id to our state's overdeveloped superego.

We do sport the nation's highest rate of philanthropy, but what would straitlaced Mary do with the fact that our use of escort services is the highest in the Midwest? Or that we sport one of the nation's highest rates of gambling? So much for Lutheran repression. (Perhaps it's the winters.)

More and more, then, the traditional images of the state belie what's happening here. Otherwise, probably the last person you would get to write an article on Minnesota would be someone like me—a third-generation Japanese-American. You'd go get Garrison Keillor to tell you about Lake Wobegon.

I do have a sneaking suspicion that I was asked for the job because *The Nation* couldn't afford Keillor. That's OK. We Japanese-Americans have a long history of working for less.

I first came to Minnesota in 1974 to go to grad school in English. I'd gone to Grinnell College in Iowa, and a fellow student there was from Minneapolis. I noticed that his car had a cord and a plug hanging out of its front grille. What's that? I asked. Oh, he said, sometimes it gets so cold up there, we have to heat our engine blocks with electric heaters. How could someone live like that? I thought.

Little did I know I'd live my entire adult life here.

I went to the University of Minnesota because the only professors in my college English department who had enjoyed their grad school time had gone there. I carried with me the images from the poems of Robert Bly, whose book *Silence in the Snowy Fields* was the first

book of contemporary poetry I'd ever bought. Bly's poems pictured
a place of vast emptiness, a place so unpeopled that even the inhabitants felt as insubstantial as spirits. The poet seemed to find comfort
in this, in the loneliness the landscape evoked. A place for medita-
tion, quiet contemplation:

> I am driving; it is dusk; Minnesota.
> The stubble field catches the last growth of sun.
> The soybeans are breathing on all sides.
> Old men are sitting before their houses on car seats
> In the small towns. I am happy,
> The moon rising above the turkey sheds.

My favorite poet, James Wright, was also associated with Minnesota.
His poem about encountering horses along a highway near
Rochester had for many an almost legendary status (Rochester in
the poem was less the site of the world-famous Mayo Clinic and
more just another forlorn place on the prairies). His Twin Cities too
had a ghostly quality, populated by drunks and vagrants, whose
bodies might wash up under the city's bridges; by "tall Negro girls
from Chicago" who "know when the supposed patron / Is a plain-
clothesman"; by "legless beggars" and "Chippewa young men" who
fought and stabbed each other. In a place where "The Walker Art
Center crowd stare / At the Guthrie Theater" and the poor went
unnoticed except by the poet, Wright wrote that "There are men in
this city who labor dawn after dawn / To sell me my death":

> But I could not bear
> To allow my poor brother my body to die
> In Minneapolis.
> The old man Walt Whitman our countryman
> Is now in America our country

Dead.
But he was not buried in Minneapolis
At least.
And no more may I be
Please God.

Given such an epitaph for this city, I did not think when I first came here that I would stay. After all it was the place where another famous poet, John Berryman, had committed suicide by jumping off the Washington Avenue Bridge, which separated the two sides of the University of Minnesota campus. Berryman, who mixed immense erudition and scholarly ways with his own drunken version of the Dylan Thomas dance toward death, seemed also out of place here. For him, Minneapolis was characterized by such philistine phenomena as Lake Street, which he and Saul Bellow dubbed "the land of the used cars." It was as if a writer like Berryman (or Bellow, who was here briefly in the fifties) felt here as if they had been exiled to Siberia, to a vast wintry wasteland far from civilization.

During my years in grad school, I spent a good deal of time at a local rhythm and blues bar, The Cabooze. The patronage mixed working-class hippies with bikers. I was always the only Asian there; there were sometimes a few blacks, mainly men. I was just learning that the cities had a reputation as a mecca for black-white couples. Groups like John Hooker and James Brown would play there; on Tuesdays and Thursdays it was two for one, and everyone got plastered.

One night I met a blonde girl who had been in Berryman's class. She said she wore short skirts and sat in the front row until he noticed her. Later, in a jealous rage, he had lit one of his poems on fire in a trash can and broke his foot trying to stamp it out. He had wanted her absolute devotion, though of course he was married at the time. When he killed himself, she dropped out of school and went to Mexico.

In many ways it was in that bar that I first became connected to the city. I met there an Indian girl who took me through the bars on Franklin Avenue, home to one of the nation's largest urban Indian populations, and told me she wanted to show me her people. I met a young girl who had first run away from home at thirteen and was now seventeen and who, the night I had met her, had severed her finger by trying to open a beer bottle on the wall. I spent the night with her in the hospital waiting room, watching the gunshot and knife wounds come in. I thought then of Wright's young Chippewa men.

Like Wright, I tended to romanticize my loneliness, my sense of alienation. His darkness had been fueled by his alcoholism, mine by marijuana and by seeking out women in bars and by my sense that my race and the color of my skin marked me as an oddity and a nonentity. I didn't belong here, I wasn't blonde or Scandinavian or Irish Catholic or even black. Sometimes I'd go to a movie and look around and see no other Asians at all and wonder, What in the hell am I doing here?

After five years of grad school, I had seven incompletes. The graduate school director called me into his office one day and told me they were taking away my teaching assistantship and I should go away and try to finish up my incompletes. Then we could talk about my coming back.

I never went back.

What might seem surprising though is that although I had been kicked out of grad school, I chose to stay in Minnesota. Despite my alienation. Despite my feeling that this place was not my home.

The Twin Cities were the first place in the country where corporations instituted a 5 percent after-tax-profits rate of giving. This is in keeping with what I call the spirit of socialism that's part of the climate here. We're known for our strong social services and generous welfare system, qualities that conservatives here sometimes decry and that cause them to complain about attracting too many bad elements.

One effect of this spirit of philanthropy and social liberalism is that the Twin Cities are a national center for the arts. Artists and even arts organizations move here from the rest of the country because of the funding here. We support more theaters per capita than anywhere but New York City. Dancers from New York move here for the grants, the reasonable houses, and cheap performing spaces. There's a host of literary organizations and small presses; we even have the nation's only Hmong and Arab-American literary journals.

In 1979, just after I dropped out of—or rather was kicked out of—grad school, I received a grant from the local Bush Foundation for my poetry. I also received a smaller grant from the state arts board. I started working in the Writers-in-the-Schools program. In contrast to my poetic forebears, I began to see the state as a place supportive of writers and other artists. Gradually, it became clear I was going to stay.

When I went out-state for the Writers-in-the-Schools program, students and even teachers would ask me where I learned to speak English. They would sometimes remark on how I didn't speak with an accent. They would ask where I came from. Generally I tried with some patience to answer them, though I couldn't help but feel like they would never understand both how American I felt and how alien.

My friend, the black novelist Alexs Pate, says when he used to travel around Minnesota to teach in the Writers-in-the-Schools program he'd start getting images of *Deliverance*; as a black man he just felt safer in the city. In an out-state motel once, he found, instead of a Gideon's Bible in the dresser, a book titled *The Naked Rise of Communism*. There were animal heads on the walls. The owner of the motel's son was in the class Alexs taught, and after Alexs gave them an exercise, the boy refused to read out loud the poem he'd written. It seemed an act of defiance, and it increased Alexs's feeling that he was a weird exotic outsider. But by the end of the week, the boy handed

Alexs a bottle of pop and a poem that said, "To my friend Alexs. I'm glad I met you."

So, actually what occurred there was a different type of deliverance. Sometimes you can be surprised here.

In many ways, my own deliverance started even before I left grad school. One summer I was asked to teach a special section of freshman composition to Southeast Asian refugees. For me, the class was the first experience where my being Asian-American was a plus. I sensed the students felt more comfortable with me than if I had been white. After the class, I wrote a poem about a paper done by one of my Vietnamese students, who compared his saving of his brother from drowning in the Mekong when they were younger to his current inability to do anything for his brother who was now in prison:

> Now, through Saigon, your mother carries kettles of soup to sell
> at dawn.
> While malaria numbs your brothers' limbs, he shivers on a cot
> in prison.
> You write: "I wait for his death. Safe. Fat. World away." I red mark
> your English.
> There was a jungle you fought in. There's a scar above your wrist.
> A boy dives, splashes and, going down, clutches his stomach
> and twists.
> You're at the bus stop by Target. Snow still falling, a fine
> blown mist.
>
> (from "Huy Nguyen: Brothers, Drowning Cries")

In this poem, I discovered a way of writing about the local that was far different from that of Bly or Wright or Berryman. It was part of my discovery of my own voice as a Japanese-American and Asian-American, and a discovery that that voice too could be part of

Minnesota and America. It was a less private voice than my predecessors, in part because I could not separate the discovery of that voice from what was happening in the society around me, the shifts in populations and immigrants and migrations.

In the years since that first wave of Vietnamese and Cambodians came to Minnesota, we've had wave after wave of new immigrants—Hmong, Somali, Ethiopian, Bosnian, Tibetan, Mexican, along with Korean and Chinese adoptees. There are now significant Mexican populations in the southwest of the state in towns like Willmar and Asian populations in the northwest in Warroad. It's not quite California or New York, but almost. And in certain ways, because of the smaller population and geographic closeness, as well as the lack of long-standing racial enmities and the liberal social atmosphere of the state, there's much more interracial mixing here than elsewhere in the country: we rank fifth in the number of multiracial young people.

As much as any writer, the poet of this new Twin Cities may be the photographer Wing Young Huie. His book, *Lake Street USA*, shows how the street Berryman dubbed "the land of the used cars" has been transformed into a tapestry of the new America—multiracial, multiethnic, a complex mélange sorting itself out, strangers encountering strangers and somehow becoming familiar, if not friends. A young man in one of Huie's photos is a Hindu who was born in Surinam, moved to Brooklyn, and then, after his brother got shot, to Minneapolis: "Living in Minnesota has been the greatest. It's a great honor to be in a society with so many different cultures. At our school, you've got the Hmong Society, the Islam Society, the Hindu Society, and the Christian Society. We have a multicultural club where we try to sort out a lot of our cultural differences so we don't fight with each other."

At the same time, despite this growing urban diversity, the suburbs here are still mainly white, insular, and a growing source of Republican power. "I resent being demonized by those in the inner city who want me to pay for the projects dreamed up by leftist politicians," states former Republican mayor of Egan, Pat Awanda. "Suburban and rural people value freedom more and local control. We like our yards. We want a private yard on a cul-de-sac. We want our kids safe from crime."

The smugness of Awanda's statement is typical of a certain suburban mindset. She resents the criticism of city-dwellers, yet implies, that we don't value freedom or want our kids safe from crime. The idea that the preference for privacy over community might have its drawbacks or that some cannot afford such privacy seems beyond her. Nor does Awanda consider that suburban residents benefit from the culture and infrastructure of the city. As for demonizing, it's my humble guess that suburbanites like Awanda are more guilty of seeing demons than those of us in the cities.

I suppose things do look different from the suburbs. Certainly, the threat and presence of gangs continued to plague life in the Twin Cities. Still, we've made progress from a few years back when we were dubbed "Murderapolis." The reputation of the police here as "easier" than those in Chicago probably remains. Yet, as elsewhere in the country, charges of racial profiling abound. A Minneapolis Police Department survey indicated minority drivers were stopped more often than whites; St. Paul statistics indicate the same. My black artist friend Seitu tells of how he was riding his bicycle down Lake Street in Minneapolis and soon found himself slammed up against a police car because the police were looking for a bald black man in a T-shirt. Seitu looked up, spied a mural he'd painted, and pondered the absurdity of saying to the cop, "I'm not a criminal. I'm an artist. Look, that's my mural!"

Alexs talks about how when a policeman was killed in a pizza joint on Lake Street, he would go into a bar or a convenience store and the white bartender or clerk would look below the counter at the police drawing and then eye Alexs suspiciously. The frequency of this treatment caused him to write a poem about how, as a black man, he constantly feels guilty; every siren or wanted poster is meant for him. His struggle is to believe in his own innocence.

In contrast, white Minnesotans, like Awanda, believe firmly in their own innocence. Their racism is rarely of the in-your-face kind; it hasn't had to be, given the long-standing whiteness of the state. More typical is the white working-class couple who asked Syl Jones, a local black columnist, "no offense intended," "Why is it so many African-Americans speak jive and cause so much trouble?" Jones resisted the temptation to point out the couple's own grammatical errors, such as "don't need no." He too has learned Minnesota decency.

This insistence on white innocence also carries over to dealings with other groups of color. While some blame the state's high gambling rate on the Indian casinos, others want the state to start its own casinos. They see the reservation casinos as a plot to avenge indigenous losses. As a good liberal I happen to think they're a pretty neat plot. You take people's land, commit genocide upon them, stick them in reservations, rip away their kids and send them to B.I.A. schools where you beat them for speaking their language, and you might think you owed these people something. But some white Minnesotans can't figure out why the Indians get to do something the rest of us can't, whether it's gambling or special fishing rights. These whites weren't around when all those bad things happened; they just live on the results. They don't seem to realize that elsewhere in the world victims of genocide generally want to kill their victimizers in wars of reprisal, not offer them a good time and a chance to lose or even win some money.

Instead, the whites here look elsewhere in America, see how bad it is in other places, and believe there couldn't be discrimination here, in Minnesota. We're not Texas, they say—we're not New York.

Incidents like the black man chained to a car and dragged down a rural Texas road or the Diallo or Louima case could never happen here. If you're one of the handful of blacks or Asians or Mexican-Americans in rural Minnesota, you'll get insulted from time to time, but you probably aren't in any real danger. You can get a decent education—if you can stand the sense of alienation you'll inevitably feel—far better than in rural areas elsewhere in the country. And if, in a 1996 report, 37 percent of Minnesotans interviewed stated that blacks were "prone to violence" and 25 percent thought Indians were "lazy," it's still only a small minority who think like that.

In this, such apologists have a point. Seitu or Alexs stay here in part because they know things are worse in other cities. Alexs, for instance, grew up in Philly, where he says you could go blocks without seeing a white face; only government-paid white people ever entered his neighborhood. When he got here, he was amazed that he could see the sky, and he sensed he needed that. He felt he could breathe. The police here wouldn't bomb a whole city block like they did in Philly to destroy the radical black group MOVE. The severe segregation that takes place in cities like Philly or Chicago isn't present.

And despite the fact that the local regional theater, the Guthrie, put on its first play by an African-American playwright only a couple of years ago, the situation for artists of color here has its bright spots. In the local paper, the artist of the year was Louise Erdrich, who's part Chippewa and probably the most famous Indian author in the country. Of course, an award like that doesn't do much for the dropout rates of Indian students in our school systems, but it makes us feel good and decent. Besides, the Somalis seem to have sprouted up in what used to be the Indian neighborhoods. Maybe the indigenous are all disappearing. Except when they're taking our money at the casinos.

These days, at my children's school, I sometimes see people I used to know when I lived on the West Bank near the University of Minnesota, and went to the Cabooze, and spent too many nights of excess. Some of us have gone through treatment and therapy; Minnesota is, after all, the twelve-step capital of the nation (Kennedys and movie stars come out to Hazeldon to dry out and get their act together). Some of the men still sport long hair or ponytails; the women lack the well-polished looks of suburban soccer moms. The school is an open school, which means among other things that the kids call the teachers by their first names and they attend events in their siblings' classes and tutor younger students and have a freer reign of the building. The population of the school reflects the city's and state's changing demographics and image.

In my son's second-grade class last week, the assignment was to pick a hero and give a speech or presentation as that hero. My son, who is half Japanese-American and three-eighths WASP and one-eighth Jewish, chose Martin Luther King, Jr. His classmate Ishak—one parent white, one parent black—chose Thomas Jefferson. Ishak talked about the great care Jefferson took in writing the Declaration of Independence and recited the famous opening sentence about "all men are created equal." But at a certain point he also talked about how Jefferson had slaves. So, said Ishak, Jefferson was a great man who wrote this document about equality, which helped form our country, and yet he was also a slave-owner.

Afterward, I thought about how these presentations in a second-grade Minneapolis classroom were changing both our past and our future. If you talk to people older than fifty about Jefferson having slaves, they will often try to ameliorate that fact or talk about how political correctness has tarnished one of our great leaders. But in my son's second-grade classroom, Jefferson's greatness and contradictions are simply a fact of history. And they will accept this just as much as the fact that my son could identify with Martin Luther King, Jr., or a young white girl could identify with Kristi Yamaguchi.

It's no longer Mary Tyler Moore's Minnesota, nor Garrison Keillor's, nor Robert Bly's, nor even mine. I see the future here but I can barely keep up with it. All I know is that if I live out my years in Minneapolis, it will feel like home in a way neither I nor James Wright could ever have imagined.

MINNEAPOLIS PUBLIC

There are 150 first languages in our schools
and so many aliens even E.T. would go unnoticed,
though if your tongue moved one way in the land of your birth
it must move another now, awkward at first.

There are blacks here who've never been to Africa;
Africans who've never heard a Baptist prayer,
much less the solemn dirges of Lutherans
or how the artist formerly known is some sort of Prince.

In the anthology of American Buddhist poetry
you will find not one face of a Tibetan
but they are here with girls and boys named Tenzin
and one, my son's good friend, throws a hard mean spiral.

Esmir is not the name of a girl but a Bosnian
boy who crouches at a table and glues a lamp together
and later with my other son conspires on a book—"A Touch
of Rabies"—a heartbreaking tale of good dogs gone bad.

(Why tell a soul of the sieges that brought him here
or stories of the Dalai Lama or the temples destroyed
or troops of the warlords in the streets of Somalia,
the borders dividing death from safety if not evil and good?)

Say you're Egyptian or Haitian: Here you're singular,
not part of a Big Apple ghetto. If you're Chinese,
most likely you're adopted, or else your parents study
engineering at the U. And have I mentioned the Mexicans?

In *West Side Story* the rumble starts with Puerto Ricans
and working-class whites in a high school gym;
this year Maria's still Natalie Wood white to Jamaica's
half-black Anita and the Jets sport blacks, one Tibetan,

and my happy daughter who still doesn't question
such casting, or why *Bye Bye Birdie* last year
just might not be the choice of half the school
for a song and dance they could take on as their own.

Still at the spring school dance J-Lo and Ja Rule
set the awkward bump and grind of junior high girls
and the boys watch on the sidelines as boys that age do,
whether Bosnian, black, white, Somali, Tibetan.

I'm told we live in the Land of Great Lake Wobegon
where all the women are strong, the men good-looking,
and the children above average—and, I always add,
everyone's white. Hey, Tenzin, Nabil, go tell Garrison:

Not now. Not quite.

MISSISSIPPI

IDIOSYNCRATIC, INCOMPREHENSIBLE, AND AIR-CONDITIONED

Steven Barthelme

The other day we stopped by Sam's Club to pick up one of their rotisserie chickens, and two young butchers were standing back behind the counters shooting the breeze when we walked up. The nearer of the two guys, who looked to be Indian or Pakistani, asked if he could help us, and I said, "Well, we were wondering which of these"—I waved at the plastic boxes on stainless steel shelves under the heat lamps—"which is the most recent to arrive here." "They've all been set out within the last half-hour," the guy said. My wife and I looked at each other, examined the chickens, which all looked pretty savory, discussed a couple in detail, hesitated. The butcher stepped up, selected the last package on the upper row of plastic boxes, and lifted it slightly. "Carl," he said, "would be an excellent choice." We took Carl. This is Mississippi, 2003.

Another day last week, as we left the Home Depot parking lot, I noticed in the sky a bird, big and flying erratically. Close your eyes and imagine: Home Depot behind us, the main post office over there to the right, Eckerd's drug store to the left, other stores here and there, fifty-five SUVs coming, going all around, and up above, the bird, flying in its peculiar pattern. Suddenly it dropped straight down like a—it wasn't like a rock, it was faster than a rock, more like a bullet, say—and disappeared from view. There was probably an SUV in the way. So we pulled to a stop behind several of them in the left-turn lane there, and looked over to the Floyd's Formal Wear and Buckos Dry Cleaning parking lot where in the parking space next to a Ford Explosion stood some kind of small hawk, kite, or kestrel balanced on top of, and with his talons deep inside (it took a few seconds for the brain to focus this picture), some kind of very white victim bird; might've been a pigeon or a dove. Feathers scattered around there. You could see their eyes, the hawk with an irritated stare, for being gawked at, and the dying bird with a sort of bizarrely quiet, uncomprehending look. This is Mississippi, 2003.

The front page of the coast newspaper, the *Sun-Herald*, recently reported the plan for a new Hard Rock Hotel and Casino. It is to be built next door to the Beau Rivage, known locally as "the Beau," a junior cousin to the Bellagio in Las Vegas, opened in 1999 by Steve Wynn's old outfit and currently the fanciest of twelve casinos on the Mississippi coast. One day last month, I pulled out of another casino's parking lot at 5 AM, gazing across the street at a giant Catholic church looming up in the dawning light, wondering what there was to say about Mississippi in 2003, and it came to me. Schizophrenia.

Today the local paper's front page offers a photograph spreading across four of its seven columns. It is a picture of bare-shouldered women, a beautiful white one hugging a beautiful black one who has just become the first African-American to become Mississippi's "Miss Hospitality," and in the background other smiling women. There are tears, too. It's apparently a title of some consequence. I don't make anything of the various participants' apparent joy— their sincerity and insincerity about the same admixture as at the conclusion of all such pageants. In the Miss America competition the first black to be Miss Mississippi won in 1987, sixteen years ago. It's the Sunday newspaper.

The point of these four brief items is only that I don't have to look very hard to find them, and beyond that, the fabric of life here is as idiosyncratic, rich, painful, incomprehensible, and air-conditioned as any place else—but no more so than any place else. If you live in some other part of the United States and the Mississippi that you have in imagination is the clown place drawn in books and (mostly) movies, high and low, well, that's OK, and we hope y'all enjoy it. Just don't come down here looking for it.

Apologies to Faulkner, but today in Mississippi the past, where everything was race and race was everything, while still not dead, is finally past. This is not to say that the state has become a race-blind paradise, that men and women look at each other indifferent to skin color, or that any transaction takes place between people of different races in which ethnicity doesn't figure, or that in a few sections of the state, notably the Delta region, some of the tawdry habits of a hundred years ago don't remain in force. But, for the majority of the place, black people are finally in the game, and in to stay. Race counts, but only in the same way it does in the other forty-nine states.

So I don't have to begin an essay on Mississippi the way all previous essays on Mississippi begin, with a nervous and puzzling caveat suggesting that the state is an odd, sinister place so baffling that outsiders are hopelessly ill-equipped to think about it. To wit, Beaulah Ratliff, *The Nation*, 1922, "It is hard, perhaps impossible for a Northerner to understand Mississippi," or John R. Skates, *The Encyclopedia of Southern History*, 1979, "Mississippi, more even than other southern states, is the victim of a stereotype," or even V. S. Naipaul, *A Turn in the South*, 1989: "It was my wish, in Mississippi, to consider things from the white point of view, as far as that was possible for me. Someone in New York had told me that it wouldn't be easy." Ms. Ratliff goes on to describe a grotesque culture of whites dominating, disenfranchising, and sometimes lynching blacks; Professor Skates acknowledges, in his professorial way, that the stereotype contains much truth, "like most stereotypes"; and Naipaul inhabits whatever point of view he chooses, effortlessly, or so it seems. All Ratliff and Skates seem to mean is that the place is somehow different. Maybe it was. In the century just past, Mississippi certainly spent an awful lot of time, like an angry stepchild, proclaiming it so.

But it seems to me that the state can be pretty well understood in the light of two facts. Of thirty-four states in existence before the Civil War, Mississippi was by some measures the fifth wealthiest, a center of money, influence, and power; after the Civil War, and up to the present day, it has been about the poorest, a stubbornly rural place with a primitive agricultural economy. The second key notion is the racial makeup of the population: For a hundred years, between 1840 and 1940, blacks were the majority—60 percent of the people— in some counties outnumbering their former masters six or seven to one. As the whites were doing the counting, these numbers probably underrepresent the tilt. This doesn't excuse but it does make easier to comprehend the fierce and often criminal anxiety the white population felt. In ways that ranged from polite to barbaric and often twisting themselves into shapes verging on the schizophrenic in the process, Mississippi whites spent a hundred years preventing black citizens from being citizens. Since about 1970, that has faded. But the place is still poor.

To understand Mississippi, the first thing you might do is sit down to watch a dozen or so of the movies made in or about Mississippi in the past fifty years—*Mississippi Burning, This Property is Condemned, A Time to Kill, Crimes of the Heart*—awash with screen doors, oily fat boys with their shirttails hanging out, hysterical women, extra-scrawny dogs, pickups, petticoats, shacks, dirt roads and deppity sheriffs, buildings of all sorts with startlingly white columns out front, and oceans of y'alls and yessums. It might be set in the 1980s or 1990s, but everything looks like the '50s or '40s. The state stands before you on the steps of the "co'thouse," hitching up its ill-fitting pants, wiping its massive brow with a white linen handkerchief. Spittin', maybe.

Well, we're selling y'all that. That clown state that you have heard and seen so much of is our marketing concept. We seem to be able to sell almost boundless amounts of that stuff, your appetite unlimited. You'll buy it in magazine articles, cable TV specials, on NPR and PBS, in novels and in films, supercharged by Hollywood, as if the place were nothing more than a 48,000-square-mile Seashell & Curio Shoppe. But even in the spots where Mississippians have turned their towns into quaint little caricatures of what the rest of the country thinks of them—the red brick, white column town square of Oxford, where the University of Mississippi resides, complete with its own knockoff Louisiana Hayride radio show, staffed (apparently) by university students—it's now done with an entirely different sort of self-consciousness than that present in 1936 when the school changed its football team's name to "Rebels." Back then they were probably serious. Previously the nickname had been the Ole Miss "Flood." Nowadays this sort of self-definition is done with circumspection; they know it's a joke. They just don't know how small a joke it is, or how much they are trapped in it.

Because the rest of the country doesn't want to hear anything else from Mississippi. If a laptop and an Escalade and a copy of *USA Today* were to rudely thrust themselves into one of those movies they're always making out of John Grisham or Willie Morris books, bang! There goes the box office. "The image," Noel Polk writes, in his memoir *Outside the Southern Myth*, "can't seem to adjust itself to the reality, no matter how hard it tries," although outside of Polk's own book, it never seems to try very hard.

Meanwhile, after being kept out for more than a hundred years, today black students fill Mississippi classrooms. Much is made of the rise of private white academies, but in one recent year 85 percent of the state's white students were in the public schools. Integration is the rule, up to and including the big state colleges where the University of Southern Mississippi's undergraduate enrollment is 21 percent African-American, Mississippi State is at 16 percent, and even Ole Miss, where forty years ago James Meredith's matriculation led white folks to riot, has a black enrollment of about 11 percent. One might note the University of Texas (4 percent), UCLA or Berkeley (5 percent apiece) or New York University (8 percent). Mississippi has more black elected officials than any other state, and is second only to Georgia for African-American representatives in the U.S. Congress and state legislature, according to the 2001 *Statistical Abstract of the United States*. Mayors, local officials, and education board members are black men and women, as are a fair number of police and those deputy sheriffs the movies are so fond of. Interracial couples, while not common, cause no stir strolling through Wal-Mart.

All this doesn't make it paradise but it is remarkable in a state whose one idea between about 1865 and 1965 was to keep the black population in the agricultural labor force and out of the body politic, a goal implemented in large measure by preventing them from getting an education, and often achieved by violence and the threat of violence. It was, of course, a hundred-year hysteria, and tragic. The strategy was hatched in the Reconstruction period (later, in the South generally, called "the Mississippi Plan"), codified in the Constitution of 1890, and then helped along by Mississippi progressives like "White Chief" James K. Vardaman and Theodore Bilbo, who used racial fears as a ticket to power and then used their authority to break the hold of conservative "Bourbon" planters who had run the state before them. Once elected, Vardaman and Bilbo often pursued humane policies regarding prison reform, poor whites, child labor, usury laws, and the excesses of corporations and railroads, combining bigotry with progressivism.

The progressive impulse, exemplified in modern times by governors

William Winter (1980–84) and Ray Mabus (1988–92), goes back at least to those fans of Andrew Jackson, frontiersmen and small farmers, who settled much of the eastern half of the state, opposed the planter aristocracy that owned the western half, and who in the 1820s had sufficient strength to force the capital to be moved from Natchez, whereupon they renamed it Jackson. Historians suggest that had race not been such an issue, this struggle between west and east Mississippi, conservative planters versus Jacksonian poor whites, would have defined the state's politics.

For about twenty years at the beginning of the last century, Vardaman grew into an effective progressive leader. His political career ended in the U.S. Senate when his opposition to the nation's entry into World War I lost him cred back home. We like our wars in Mississippi, always have. Agrarian progressivism also had the unfortunate side effect of reinforcing the white citizens' anti-industrial attitudes about urban and rural life. Vardaman, 1907, quoted in William F. Holmes's biography: "I thank God that we have not great cities. I thank God that we have very few multimillionaires." We still don't have great cities, and the multimillionaires are minus one, now that Bernie Ebbers went down.

But for a hundred years, race trumped everything. The one hysterical idea—the elaborate and obsessive exclusion of the black population from the society around them—that white Mississippians embraced and that Vardaman, Bilbo, and others nourished required of the white population a self-selected isolation from the rest of the nation, an insularity that turned out to be nothing short of economically disastrous. That isolation, as much as the suppression of their black brothers and sisters, is what white Mississippians have slowly relinquished since the civil rights era.

Although race was a major reason for the state's alienation, and federal force the principal reason behind its relinquishing the Neanderthal treatment of its black population, Mississippi's return to the national community has been accomplished by commercial and economic means as well, midwifed by television. Broadcast reporting played a large role in the successes of the civil rights movement, exposing abuses to the rest of the country and to the world. At about the same time, television started showing the rest of the world and its wonders to more and more Mississippians, who, happily or unhappily, likely began craving those bottles of Pepsi-Cola and boxes of Tide and chrome-bejeweled Lincolns and Beatles records and Swanson Dinners, just like the citizens of all the other states. The stick and the carrot, delivered by TV. Somehow the old, "That's not the way we do it in Miss-re-sippi" didn't cut it anymore.

And so, smacked by the federal stick and lured by luridly advertised 1960s consumer goods, Mississippi finally relented to allow its black citizens to be citizens. Very late, the twentieth century sort of roared into Mississippi, ready to make money (overlooking, I suspect, in a great many cases that a great many Mississippians don't have much money).

Nonetheless, down here nowadays, while we still talk funny, just like you we go to the Eckerd's and the Rite-Aid and the Walgreens, and that's just for drugstores. There's a Home Depot over there and an Office Depot over that way, past the Gateway Store, and down there, a sad little Baskin-Robbins. On cable we're watching the Weather Channel and HBO and that Republican in drag shouting on *Hardball*. We microwave the bejesus out of practically everything, when we aren't eating Whoppers, Nachos Supreme, or Happy Meals. We buy more Toyotas than an Afghan warlord and SUVs by the truckload, lard up classrooms with computers shipped in by FedEx, with the same magical belief that the machines are surely so fancy they'll educate somebody. We've spent the last few years obsessed with and then forgetting (in order) OJ, Monica and Bill, Kosovo, Gary Condit, Florida, Osama, and Rummy, just like we were supposed to. You bet.

We fret about Kobe and WMD's and J-Lo. We hate ourselves while we do it. We're just like you.

Except we probably gamble more. It's our second-largest industry. Biloxi, Gulfport, and the other coast towns have been more or less taken over by casinos, with their hotels a dozen stories taller than anything else on the skyline, had there been a skyline prior to the casinos' arrival, which there wasn't. Other casinos grace Natchez and Vicksburg, better known for cotton and battlefields, and the biggest development in the state is the campus of casinos in Tunica County, in the Delta, below Memphis. In all, about thirty state casinos make $2.5 billion in revenue and pay $280 million worth of taxes as of 1999. One might think this would make some huge difference, but other than the new neon skyline, a lot of jobs, increased tourism and tax money, an explosion of pawn shops and payday-loan storefronts, and likely a local uptick within the nationwide uptick in bankruptcy filings, major effects haven't yet become visible. No doubt the absentee corporations that own most of the casinos are buying generous chunks of the state and local governments and a sprinkling of judges with campaign cash. Still, the clown Mississippi that exists in the American imagination doesn't sort well as the third-largest gambling spot in the country. There's history there, too: Gambling boats were putting out of Gulfport or Biloxi well before 1991, and a hundred years before that, in 1886, Natchez was first electrified because the casino needed lights.

What I know best of Mississippi are the people who pass through my classes, bearing no resemblance to the clowns in the movies. They are as complicated and mysterious and decent and often wonderful as any strangers anywhere. Oreathia, intense, obsessive, who wanted to make movies even though her father, a musician, wanted her to do something more practical. Diana, the Vicksburg daughter of generations of schoolteachers, who could write like an angel but took up photography; I suspect someday she'll wander back to the typewriter. Bradford, crazy for Kafka (in the German), probably the only student ever to get me to lose my temper in the middle of a class. Rose, forty-five or thereabouts, poorly schooled but thoughtful and acute in her quietly astonishing way, who thinks she can write books and, given the considerable luck every writer needs and some time, probably can. And Woody, small-town Mississippi kid who has about him a strange and sublime seriousness, taking his time, figuring out what he wants to do. On the first of the dozen recommendations I have cobbled up for him over the years, I finally gave up and wrote, "He's sort of like Gandhi." Three white, two black, none quaint. There have been many others.

I don't mean to suggest that it's all enlightenment and racial harmony and shopping malls and cyberculture down here. We have had a very long way to come. It ain't Vienna. Some nights there's junk on the parking lot-usually fried chicken bones, diapers. We've got wall-to-wall Wal-Marts. We have more churches than you have. And Mississippi still has plenty of mean little towns around. But, you know, I was in Carlisle, Pennsylvania, once, if you want to talk mean little towns. Still, we're not urbane. Hattiesburg is the third-biggest "city" in Mississippi, with 50,000 people. Open a Chili's or an Applebee's and you'll make money, but open an interesting restaurant and you'll probably go broke. But, there again, my favorite Austin restaurants were always going under, when I lived in Austin. Once a couple of prospective graduate students from New York and Florida (as best I recall) came here together to look the place over and reported that they had been driving down a street somewhere across town and almost ran over a chicken. Chickens! They were horrified and, of course, delighted. You can still find that clown place or something like it if you're intent on it. Lots of extra-scrawny dogs. Make offer.

MISSOURI

THE PROVINCIAL AND THE SKEPTIC: THE "SHOW ME" WORLD OF MISSOURI

Gerald Early

In the administrations of both George H. W. Bush and George W. Bush, Republican politicians from Missouri have had an important presence or, at least, have provided a nationally significant moment. On July 1, 1991, President George H. W. Bush nominated Clarence Thomas to replace Thurgood Marshall on the Supreme Court. John C. Danforth, senator from Missouri, for whom Thomas worked when Danforth was the attorney general of Missouri, sponsored Thomas's candidacy. (There is a double Missouri connection as Thomas, obviously, lived for a time in Missouri.) In 1977, when Danforth was elected senator, Thomas joined his staff in Washington, a move that led to his rise in Washington Republican circles under President Reagan, who saw him as a young, ambitious black conservative with possibilities. It is well documented how Danforth fiercely defended Thomas after his Supreme Court candidacy was attacked by various civil rights groups and particularly when Anita Hill testified that Thomas had sexually harassed her when they both worked at the EEOC. Indeed, in his book about shepherding Thomas's nomination through the Senate, *Resurrection*, Danforth expressed regret for the sharp nature of his attacks against Hill's character, which proved to be groundless. Danforth succeeded in getting Thomas through the process by a narrow Senate confirmation vote of fifty-two to forty-eight. But the battle was costly for him politically as, three years later, he left the Senate. It was well known at the time that Democrats and his political enemies were targeting him because of his role in the bruising Thomas confirmation hearings. Liberal women's groups in Missouri were poised to oppose Danforth and there was talk of liberal Harriet Woods of the St. Louis suburb of University City, who had served as lieutenant governor and had run for the Senate in 1982 (against Danforth) and 1986, mounting a campaign against him. Many felt that he did not run because of the Thomas confirmation but, from all indications in *Resurrection*, he may have become disillusioned with the brutal, no-holds-barred nature of partisan politics. When George W. Bush was nominated by the Republicans to be their presidential candidate in 2000, he thought for a time, how seriously is difficult to tell, of choosing Danforth as his vice president, perhaps in part for what he did in getting Thomas through the confirmation process for his father. Danforth had also led the politically sensitive investigation of what had become known in the press as the Waco incident, where the actions of FBI agents resulted in the fiery deaths of several members, including women and children, of a separatist religious cult called the Branch Davidians. In the end, Danforth, a moderate Republican and an Episcopalian minister, though respected throughout his party, was probably considered not conservative enough for Bush's taste. Danforth represented the kind of "blue-blood" Republicanism that Bush's father represented, so Bush may have felt that Danforth would not expand his base within the party. Moreover, Danforth had never been a part of Bush's inner circle. So goes one story of a Missouri politician and recent national politics.

Here's another: President George W. Bush selected John Ashcroft to serve as attorney general of the United States on December 22,

2000. The confirmation process was contentious, as the nomination was opposed by liberal Democrats and pro-choice, civil-liberties, and civil rights groups. If Danforth, the member of a prominent, high-achieving, old-money Missouri family, represented one strain of political conservatism, Ashcroft, as the gospel-singing son and grandson of Assemblies of God ministers, represented another, a mixture of socially conservative evangelical Christianity, an important and volatile new element in the Republican political mix, and the conservative political philosophy of tax cuts, welfare reform, and opposition to affirmative action. Reared in Springfield, Missouri, and a graduate of the University of Chicago Law School, Ashcroft became Missouri's attorney general in 1976, winning reelection to that post in 1980. He became governor of Missouri in 1984 and again in 1988. When Danforth retired from the Senate in 1994, Ashcroft ran in his place and won the seat. It was an odd turn of events in his reelection bid in 2000 that led to Ashcroft becoming the U.S. attorney general. His opponent for the Senate, Democratic governor Mel Carnahan, died in a plane crash near St. Louis three weeks before the election. It was impossible to have Carnahan's name removed from the ballot, and the interim governor chose Carnahan's widow to serve should Carnahan be elected. This, doubtless, helped to mobilize Carnahan supporters as well as intensify a sympathy vote that probably crossed party lines. Ashcroft, unable to campaign effectively at all in the closing weeks, lost the election to a dead man. Had he won the election, he would have been less likely to have been selected for attorney general, probably being more helpful to his party by being in the Senate; and, if he had been selected, he would have been less likely to have accepted it, probably preferring the Senate. His staunchly conservative credentials made him an ideal candidate for attorney general as a reward to the more conservative wing of the Republican party for having supported Bush in his tough fight over the Florida recount during November and December, when the outcome of the presidential election was in doubt. Since his confirmation, Ashcroft, who had originally intended to fight crime and pornography (he did a great deal to rid Missouri of pornography during his tenure as governor, an effort which, if nothing else, reduced the amount of sleaze a casual consumer was likely to encounter) while balancing the state's budget, has become more prominent on the issue of civil liberties than he might have because of the terrorist attacks against the United States on September 11, 2001. If George W. Bush is successful in achieving popular support for two terms in office, it will be, in some measure, due to the public's acceptance of Ashcroft's hard-line approach to dealing with civil-liberties matters in relation to national security since 9/11. Indeed, if Bush remains in office, it will mean, in part, that Ashcroft has succeeded in redefining national security in ways far more radical than anything even during the height of the cold war.

It might be thought from this that Missouri is a deeply conservative, or, from the liberal's perspective, even reactionary state that has produced nothing but varieties of conservative politicians and public figures. After all, the state's slogan, "Show Me," sounds like a combination of both the skeptic and the provincial, a sort of doubting Thomas who won't believe unless he can see the wounds. That might certainly give outsiders the impression that the state is something like a stick-in-the-mud, slow to change, resistant to innovation. This would not be true. For those who don't believe that conservatives can provide dynamic leadership, the state has had its share of powerful liberals. Strong Democratic, pro-union leaders such as Congressmen Dick Gephardt, who has run for president, and the retired Bill Clay, have been major liberal voices in the state. Former Democratic senator Thomas Eagleton, who was briefly George McGovern's running mate in 1972, has long been a major liberal presence as well. Moreover, the state has a liberal tradition dating back to Harry S. Truman, who was a county judge, then a U.S.

senator, a product of Kansas City machine boss Tom Pendergast, who learned his trade from his older brother, and who ran the politics of the westernmost part of the state for nearly forty years. Truman went on to become vice president under Roosevelt and, eventually, president, doing more to promote civil rights during his tenure as president than any other president in history except Lyndon Johnson. Stuart Symington was also one of the major national Democratic figures to emerge from Missouri; starting out as president of Emerson Electric, he was selected by Truman to serve as the first secretary of the Air Force in 1947. He was an important influence in helping to implement Truman's executive order 9981, issued in 1948, which integrated the military. He won a Senate seat in 1952 and served until 1976, becoming a leading expert on military affairs and foreign policy. He, too, was a staunch supporter of civil rights.

Several Missourians have had a considerable impact on popular culture. Most recently, of course, is rap star Nelly, from St. Louis. But in the realm of music, there was rock-and-roll inventor Chuck Berry, who was born and grew up in the Ville, the self-contained, high achieving black neighborhood of north St. Louis. Ragtime has deep roots in Missouri (it was born in Sedalia and St. Louis), with Tom Turpin and composer Scott Joplin having developed the art form there. And Kansas City was central in the development of swing music. Count Basie's orchestra, a reconfiguration of Bennie Moten's Blue Devils, came out of Kansas City with a particularly raucous style of playing that drew its influence from the black territory bands of Oklahoma, Kansas, and Texas. While many know of the success of the New York Yankees, fewer know that the major-league team with the second-greatest number of world championships is the St. Louis Cardinals, a storied franchise whose games are as well attended as the Yankees' in a far smaller market. St. Louis, for a considerable time in major-league history, was the most western and southern of all the teams. Kansas City did not get a major-league team until 1955, when the Athletics left Philadelphia to become the westernmost team briefly until Los Angeles and San Francisco acquired two New York teams, the Dodgers and the Giants, in 1958. And Atlanta did not get a major-league franchise until 1966 to become, until two Florida franchises joined the league, the southernmost team. St. Louis, for a time, was a frontier, as was the state of Missouri itself. Kansas City was the center of Negro League baseball. Indeed, the Negro Leagues were founded there by the great black pitcher and impresario Rube Foster in 1920; the Kansas City Monarchs, which produced people such as Buck O'Neill, the storyteller of Ken Burns's *Baseball* documentary, and Jackie Robinson, the first black in the twentieth century to play major-league baseball, became the most storied franchise in the history of those leagues. Today, Kansas City is where both the Negro Leagues Museum and the American Jazz Museum are located. And let us not forget the Spinks brothers—Leon and Michael—of the Pruit-Igoe housing project of St. Louis, both of whom won gold medals in the 1976 Olympics, where they became household names and went on to become champion professional boxers.

In literary culture, Missouri has produced a number of significant names, including T. S. Eliot, Kate Chopin, Tennessee Williams, and Samuel Clemens (Mark Twain), all born Missourians. Twain, doubtless, became the most celebrated author from Missouri, and two of his most famous books—*The Adventures of Tom Sawyer* and *The Adventures of Huckleberry Finn*—are set completely, or in part, in Missouri. Missouri, indeed, became so tied to Twain's fictional accounts of his growing up here that Hannibal, Missouri, where Twain was raised, is now a tourist attraction. William Wells Brown was born in Missouri and spent several of his formative years in St. Louis as a slave to a wealthy family. Brown eventually escaped from bondage and became one of the first black persons of letters in the United States. He wrote an autobiographical slave narrative in 1847 that is considered one of the classics of the genre (and, without question, the most humorous, as Brown was something of a trickster). He also became the first black playwright; the first black to publish a novel; and, more important, the first black to write a travel book, about his years in Europe. He was also one of the first blacks to write a general history of African-descended people, several years before George Washington Williams. Playwright Ntozake Shange's coming-of-age novel, *Betsey Brown*, recounts her childhood years in St. Louis. The most famous black writer from Missouri was Langston Hughes, born in Joplin, Missouri, who went on to live in Lawrence, Kansas, and Cleveland, Ohio, during his childhood, and who became a writer of international renown. Other important literary figures who were born or lived in Missouri include William Gass, Sara Teasdale, Howard Nemerov, Stanley Elkin, and children's writer Eugene Field.

In truth, Missouri's character is very much like its geography. It is a border state in more ways than one. Missouri is not quite a southern state. It was, indeed, a slave state and "officially" seceded from the Union on October 28 in a General Assembly vote at Neosho that was probably not legal. But Missouri had a Union governor as well as a so-called Confederate government and was torn by bloody guerrilla warfare, as it had a strong anti-slavery sentiment in its German population. Besides, Missouri was never southern in the way that Tennessee, Kentucky, and Maryland, other principal border states, were. Missouri lost its character as a western state, which it had had in the early nineteenth century, as the country continued to expand westward. It is considered midwestern by many, yet when one thinks of the Midwest, Missouri does not immediately come to mind; rather, states like Illinois, Ohio, Indiana, and Iowa do. Missouri partakes of a southern (slave) heritage, a western heritage, and a midwestern heritage—without being quite any of the elements that go into its makeup.

Missouri, like many other states, is a borderland in another way. The state is divided along the Interstate 70 corridor that traverses east to west, connecting the major cities of Missouri, from St. Louis in the east through Jefferson City (the state capital), Columbia (the location of the main campus of the state university system), Sedalia, and Kansas City in the west. (Kansas City is spread across two states, but most of the city is in Missouri. Indeed, in the 1990s, much to the chagrin of St. Louisans, Kansas City was declared the biggest city in population in the state, a position traditionally held by St. Louis.) There are other important cities not on the I-70 track, such as Springfield, which is connected by another interstate. But, by and large, the major urban arteries of the state are tied together or closely connected to I-70. The rest of the state is, by and large, rural. Sections of it, like the Bootheel, the southernmost part of eastern Missouri, are very rural and very poor, with significant high school dropout rates and the problems attendant with a poor, unskilled working population with little in the way of modern technological industries. The two major cities in the state, Kansas City and St. Louis, have their share of problems as well, not unlike those of other major cities. Both have virtually dysfunctional public school systems, which have hurt both cities' abilities to attract industry and to keep their middle-class populations from fleeing to the suburbs, eroding their tax bases. Missouri has had population increases every decade from the 1940s to the 1990s, but each decade has found the state with an increasingly smaller percentage of the nation's population as a whole. In short, Americans do not see Missouri as a desirable place to live, and certainly not its big cities. Some probably think, after the Times Beach disaster of the 1980s, where an entire town had to be abandoned because it was built on a dioxin waste site, that the state is nothing but a chemical dump. Others think Missouri is just some cultural flyover. By the 1990s, St. Louis city had a population of under 400,000. It has continued to fall. Kansas City has managed to increase its population, and by the 1990s, it was around 450,000, larger than St. Louis. But this meant that neither of Missouri's largest cities had a population of over 500,000. Both cities have seen their nonwhite populations increase—not just African-American but Asian and Hispanic—and perhaps this is where their futures lie.

The failure of the public schools is not the result of insufficient money, but rather of inadequate leadership, rampant politicization that has only further polemicized the public schools as an institution in American life, and the problems attendant upon dealing with a segment of the population that sees little value in education or that lacks the wherewithal to instill this value broadly for a variety of reasons, some of which are not pathological. Institutions designed to help the poor sometimes succeed in doing so, but more often they simply isolate the poor, confining them within the institutions' spheres and subjecting them to the institutions' power and whim; this as poverty itself ceases to be a political problem in the eyes of the public but rather a moral issue related to the character of the poor, which is automatically seen as inferior to the character of middle-class people. Some of this is intentional, some inadvertent. The change in American industries, with China, for instance, becoming the workshop of the world, has been particularly unkind to states like Missouri, which were largely shaped by nineteenth-century industrialization. The increasing reliance by the state on gambling and tourism for revenue does not bode well for the future, as neither are truly sound ways to rebuild or modernize an economy, subject as they are not only to immense competition from other states that probably have more to offer in both areas, but also to a range of whims, from weather to fluctuations in the national economy.

However, there is much that is hopeful about life in Missouri and much that is hopeful for the future of the state. It has a fine and diverse set of institutions of higher learning, from private universities like Washington University in St. Louis and the fine Jesuit school, St. Louis University, to a first-rate state system, a broad community-college system, and a collection of smaller schools like Webster University and Maryville University. Missouri has a vibrant community of artists, writers, and musicians, a fine array of cultural institutions, including one of the best zoos in the world and probably the most innovative and successful of all children's museums, The Magic House, and several strong industry headquarters, including Anheuser-Busch. It is also one of the nation's leading centers for research in the biological sciences. Missouri, moreover, has its share of lively political factions, both left and right, and more than its fair share of entrepreneurs and people with ideas and the passionate belief that what Missouri has and what Missouri is are worth preserving.

MONTANA

BETTER FEARED THAN IGNORED

Walter Kirn

T o understand Montana, first stop fearing it. I know, I know:
the militia, the Unabomber, and all those supposed Nazis
and white supremacists, heavily armed and camped out
among the pines. Just mention the state in a major coastal city and up
go the eyebrows: "You're from *where*?" In the popular mind, Montana
is rebel territory, the political forest primeval, the new Deep South.
It's the home of the bearded right-wing bogeyman, decked out in
camo and toting a Holy Bible. Cross these borders at your own risk.

In a way, it's a privilege to wear the big black hat and serve as America's
enemy within. Lord knows, for a state this big and dry and empty, any
publicity is good publicity. Maybe our new state motto ought to be
"Better Feared Than Ignored"—especially since our old one, "Oro y
Plato" (Silver and Gold) is meaningless. The mines are mostly closed
now, no longer viable, and the jobs are gone, too. All kinds of jobs are
gone. Logging jobs, ranching jobs, railroad jobs, the works. And if that
leaves the job of scaring people, fine. At least it's work.

If only it were so, though; if only Montana were what outsiders think
it is rather than what its residents know it is: poor. The capital of second
jobs performed in the shadow of second homes. A former company state

whose former company—the dread Anaconda Copper Company—left long ago with its money and its metal and its corrupt political influence and was never replaced, by anything. You can drive over six hundred miles across Montana and almost three hundred more from top to bottom and not find a single Fortune 500 headquarters, nor even a Fortune 1000 headquarters. We used to have one—the Montana Power Company, heroic generator of electricity, burner of coal, and operator of dams, famed for its modest rates and steady dividends—but in a series of strange financial maneuvers that the company's customers, shareholders, and employees still can't fully wrap their heads around, the stable utility somehow transformed itself (with the help of Wall Street's best and brightest, of course) into a tenuous high-tech phone company that immediately started to fail and then went bankrupt.

Montana's economy? Don't ask. There isn't one, for the most part. Consult your census. Close to last in per capita family income. Close to first in percentage of families living in poverty.

It's enough to make any state a nest of radicalism, on the right *and* the left, but not Montana, unfortunately. When Montana goes bust, it doesn't make a fuss; it heads to the tavern and waits for the next boom, electing business-as-usual Republicans while sustaining itself on small, exotic liberties such as the legal right to drink and drive and—until a couple of years ago—the right to do so without a posted speed limit. Hungry? Go into the yard and shoot a deer. Thirsty? A few of the rivers are still quite clean. Broke? There's a pawn shop on every other corner.

And a rich man from out of state on every mountainside. They've been coming, and building, for a while now, providing a needed economic buffer with their offers of miscellaneous lawn and garden chores and their insatiable hunger for having their huge log homes painted, chinked, and surrounded with pretty trout ponds.

In the state's conventionally scenic regions, where there's plenty of timber and interesting topography and, in nondrought years, a little bit of water—the western third of Montana, approximately—

the new boom has arrived in the form of wealthy refugees from congested California and the East Coast, but it's come without the customary high wages and rising government revenues. The swank new folks don't live here, they just play here, for the length of the growing season (barely three months) and a couple of weeks in the winter when the skiing's good. Since a lot of them own a sufficient number of acres to qualify for an agricultural rate, the property taxes they pay are laughably low, but since their young children (if they have young children, since a lot of them are retired people), don't go to school here, what's the problem?

For these folks, there is none. The fishing is still good (though it's not what it used to be, of course) and the golf, well, it's improving, thanks to them. One splendid new golf course, the Old Works, set between the impoverished former mining towns of Butte and Anaconda, is ingeniously situated atop a slag pile. Its sand traps are black; they're filled with cinders, raked smooth. And no matter which hole the duffer is teeing off from, he can look up and see the abandoned masonry smokestack whose copious fumes stunted trees for miles around and rained only God knows what into the rivers, which have washed it downstream to God knows where.

Behold the new dwellings: true castles upon a hill. It might have been better to build them lower down, where their costly rooflines wouldn't block the view, but that would obstruct the three-story picture windows that light up all pink and orange in the sunsets as if flashing a message to the peasants below: "You couldn't afford to build up here. We can." If there's water nearby, they build directly beside it, right on the floodplain. No zoning equals freedom.

And freedom, out here, is what it's all about. Freedom to farm, for example. In my home county, whose southern border touches Yellowstone National Park at the tip of a valley nicknamed Paradise (perhaps for the vast square footage of its new residences and the loveliness of the huge golf course being developed there), the total annual income from ranching and agriculture is a ten-million-dollar net loss. This leaves only two kinds of people working the land: affluent types who believe that cows and crops give their places a rustic, lived-in look that is worth paying for all by itself, and the bankrupt (or near to it). Both types take all the government subsidies they can get. These handouts are pure gravy for the first type and starvation rations for the second.

Unless they sell out. Unless they subdivide. I'd like to report that most do so unwillingly—that their love of open country is that intense—but it wouldn't be true, in my experience. A lot of landed bankrupts simply can't wait to dice up their unremunerative holdings into grassy pads for modular homes or larger tracts suitable for mansions, and who can blame them? It's hard to love the earth that's burying you. And even when you love it anyway, it's hard to let feelings overrule finances—particularly your children's finances.

I know a rancher. Every year he buys more cattle, feeds them and waters them, pumps them full of medicine, and then sells them at a loss to the out-of-state feedlots and packing concerns that run the whole game. When he sees his wallet's empty, he heads downtown to a thriving real estate agency and offers another hunk of land for sale—just enough to pay his bills. He doesn't know what he's up against, but he's certain he's up against something, so he guesses. Environmentalists top his list of enemies, those reintroducers of cattle-killing gray wolves and foes of one's God-given right to drain a spring creek in order to irrigate an alfalfa field. He doesn't much care for Canadians, either—they flood the market with cheap meat, he says. Or maybe the problem is atheists. He's a born-again Christian, my rancher friend, and he told me once, without a hint of humor, that God created rivers to water livestock and anyone who believes otherwise is opposing the will of Heaven. He loves the countryside, he says, and he claims that its beauty sustains his soul, yet a lot of his enemies are wild animals. Here's his prescription for running off problem beavers: toss used oil filters in the stream.

Montana, reads the popular bumper sticker, IS NOT A ZOO. It's a way of telling tourists that people need to make a living here doing things besides cleaning up motel rooms and guiding visiting doctors and lawyers on raft trips, and sometimes that living involves killing things. Still, it's tourism dollars that buy these bumper stickers, by and large. For the grumpier old Montanans this fact entails a great indignity: playing host to the very outsiders whom they suspect of fleecing them on a large scale. For most who work in tourism, however, the industry means crucial cash and—perhaps more importantly—human companionship. That's a scarce commodity in these parts, and the seasonal onslaught of rental cars and motor homes would be welcome if only as a balm for loneliness. Montanans are talented ad hoc socializers, making fast friends of footloose passers—through and not letting superficial differences of age and class and race get in the way of that. The image of the rigid, wary frontiersman is sheer baloney, only trotted out for tourists who expect no less. The Montanans I know are clingy, if anything. *Stay, don't go. We'll feed you. Please don't go.*

All this shifting around of land and people creates an atmosphere of transience. New settlers come for the scenery and fresh air and leave when they go broke, because you can't eat snowcapped peaks. A lot of movie stars have homes here, as you've no doubt read, but in most cases their caretakers and house sitters know the floor plans better than they do. If you hit the right town—say Bozeman or Missoula—at just the right time in the middle of the summer, the chances are good you'll see a famous journalist, an Oscar contender, and a CEO sitting side-by-side at the same lunch counter.

And then there are the writers. They're everywhere, in absurdly large numbers, and often they're permanent residents, drawn here and kept here by the modest housing prices, the lack of interruptions, the plentiful bar rooms, and—in the circular manner of such things—the presence of other writers. One reason Montana looms larger in the world than its tiny population warrants may be all the novels that are set here, from A. B. Guthrie's Western, *The Big Sky*, to romantic dreck such as *The Horse Whisperer*. In the early 1990s in my hometown of Livingston the Robert Redford–directed movie version of Norman Maclean's fine memoir, *A River Runs Through It*, touched off a real estate boom that's never subsided, even though many of the houses and ranchettes purchased during that first flush of enthusiasm have changed owners several times since then.

Did I mention the landscape, the vistas? I don't have to. Anyway, they're not part of the state. The state's a political, not a natural, entity. Its beauty preceded it. Let's hope it outlives it.

It's not what Montana is but what it isn't that holds old-timers and lures visitors. It isn't the rest of America—not yet, not quite. National restaurant franchises and chain stores that the rest of the country takes for granted don't exist here. Want a pair of Banana Republic khakis? Try Minneapolis or Seattle. One female friend of mine calls the state a "shopping-free zone" and laments that it's almost impossible to spend money here. (Which I think is good, since so few people are earning any.)

There's also a scarcity of rules—and of the petty officials who enforce them. Except in certain forward-thinking communities that represent the future, I suppose, you can smoke wherever you please. You can drink in your car, as I've said, and when your bladder's full no one will look askance at you for pulling off next to the highway and unzipping. Want to turn your back forty into a salvage yard? Go on ahead. The entirety of the dress code, even in the best restaurants, is just this: dress.

People here are responsible for themselves, especially in the rural outback—not because they're rugged individualists but because there's no one around to monitor them. The sheriff's departments and local police forces are spread so thin by poor funding and geography that they can't clamp down on anything. Nor are they particularly inclined to. A couple of years ago, on my farm, I set alight a twenty-foot-tall pile of rotting lumber, tree branches, and refuse that included several truck tires. I didn't have the free burn permit required, and the bonfire was set out of season, in any case. A pitch-black cyclone of toxic smoke rose up, visible for miles around. A half-hour later a fire truck appeared. Busted, I thought. Instead, the volunteer crew—who just happened to be passing by, they said, after putting out a nearby house fire—let me off with a couple of strict frowns and a warning to stay by the fire until it burned out, lest I ignite my whole pasture. Then they vanished.

Montana, where the honor system lives on, to the immense relief of the dishonorable. Some would call this irresponsible, but I find it gratifyingly humane.

As for the gun nuts, mad bombers, and survivalists of media legend—I suppose they're out there, but in no greater numbers than anywhere else and with no compelling reason to bother their neighbors, since they're generally left alone in their own fantasy worlds. The fabled militia is a joke. I attended one of its meetings once and the darkest statement I heard that night was one poor old fellow's hare-brained theory that the price scanners in supermarkets were secretly used to track the movements of citizens. Hell, he might have been right. No Nazi salutes, though, just a room of fifteen or twenty confused nonentities resentful about high taxes, rich politicians, and the need to buy a hunting license whenever they wished to bring home a little venison. They couldn't have organized a charge on the local minimart, let alone the U.S. government.

On the edges of old maps, where the known world broke up into terra incognita, cartographers used to draw sea monsters and dragons. That's Montana's function in the country now: to represent the slightly spooky unknown and substantiate the always alluring notion that parts of America remain untamed rather than just comparatively ungroomed. It's a lie, as we know, but we're glad to play it up in much the same spirit of those costumed "train robbers" who cuss and fire blanks to thrill the tourists. Anything to get a little attention. Anything to pay the mortgage. The winters are long and dark, the summers short, the mines inactive, the ranches in foreclosure, and the companies that used to rape the land seem to have lost interest and moved on.

Anything for a moment of excitement.

NEBRASKA

THE LAND THAT TIME FORGOT

Ron Hansen

I first think of the weather. Stunningly hot summer days, the July sun a furnace, grasshoppers chirring in the fields of alfalfa, and nothing moving, no one but me fool enough to be out, the shimmer of heat waves warping the farmhouse in the distance, and the asphalt road beneath my sneakers softening into tar. Or January and its zero cold stiffening my face on my predawn paper route, my gloves and galoshes not enough to protect fingers and toes that hurt as if hammered, and a fierce snow flying with the sting of pins as I slog forward through high drifts, twelve years old and near tears.

The hottest temperature ever recorded in Nebraska was 118 degrees, and the coldest, minus 47. And there's a wide range of climate even within the state, with flooding possible in the southeast while the parched west worries through weeks of drought. Our thunderstorms are the stuff of horror movies: lashing rain and a far-off flash of light in the heavens, then the scratchy sound of sailcloth tearing until the fifty-megaton bomb goes off and children scream all over the neighborhood.

Also, of course, there are tornadoes, more than two thousand of them in the last fifty years. Once an Omaha friend driving home from his office noticed the May afternoon becoming strangely cool and gloomy and he glanced into his rearview mirror. His initial impression was of a sepia cloud and the churning turmoil of hundreds of crows. And then he realized he was seeing the swaying funnel of a tornado and what he saw flying around in the whirlwind were not crows but, as he gently put it to me, "things." I have read aftermath articles about pigs in flight, about straw pounded through planks like ten-penny nails, about a dead woman found sitting stiffly upright in her front-porch rocker but a mile away from home, about a house destroyed except for the dining room wall with its ornately framed print of Leonardo da Vinci's *Last Supper*.

Nebraska, meaning "flat water," was a Plains Indian name for the swift, shallow, brown Platte River that streams eastward the length of the state, sistering what is now Interstate 80. The first settlers used to lament that the Platte was "too thin to plow and too thick to drink." Locals still maintain it's "a mile wide and an inch deep," and Mark Twain claimed the Platte would only become a respectable river if it were laid on its side. The geography that the Platte slides through was part of what was once called "the Great American Desert" when the Nebraska Territory included all the states between the Missouri River and the Rocky Mountains and from the fortieth parallel of southern Kansas northward to the Canadian border. When Nebraska became the thirty-seventh state in 1867, it was scaled down in size, but its area of seventy-seven thousand square miles is still gigantic by eastern standards, large enough to contain all of New England plus New Jersey. Wayfarers on the Oregon Trail who got through the wide emptiness used to congratulate themselves by saying, "I have seen the elephant."

More than a century ago a Nebraska geologist asserted, "Rainfall follows the plow," and statistics bore him out. Once European immigrants with nothing more to lose began cultivating the prairie of Nebraska, the Sudan of the first explorers gave way to some of

America's richest farmland: waving acres of corn, wheat, sorghum, soybeans, and sugar beets, or sandhill grasslands where most of the state's six million cattle feed. Hidden underneath that land is the Ogallala Aquifer, a huge underground reservoir roughly the size of California that was formed by geologic action eons ago. Wells needed to reach into the earth no more than fifty feet before they tapped into a pure water source that seemed everlasting. Windmills and irrigation have made such use of this great lake that now, with an annual farm income of six billion dollars, Nebraska trails only California and Texas in agricultural prosperity.

And it's rural in the extreme: only Alaska has less land devoted to metropolitan areas. So there's still a great vacancy in the dunes northwest of Kearney, with fewer than seven people per square mile. (Omaha, for example, has 150.) Which means in half the state you have six-man football teams, volunteer fire departments, houses that are left unlocked, two or more grades conjoined in the schools, weeklies that list the wedding presents the happy couple received, five-hundred-watt radio stations whose way of giving the news is to read aloud the front page. There the hired hands still ride horses. Some roads are scarcely more than Caterpillared cattle trails. Houses are starkly exposed on the topography, as in a painting by Edward Hopper. Rarely is there landscaping: with so much potential for loneliness, privacy is not a high priority. There you know the names and kin and histories of everyone you see. Once my brother-in-law surprised the sunrise occupants of a sandhills diner by wandering in and sitting alone at a booth. While he scanned the breakfast menu he could feel the men in feed caps and bib overalls staring at him until one finally strolled over and said, "We all want to know who you are and why you're here." No fear or warning was involved; it was sheer curiosity.

Ethnically, the heritage is primarily German, then Irish, then Scandinavian and English. In a population of 1,700,000—Philadelphia has as many people—only a little over 5 percent are Hispanic, 4 percent are African-American, 1 percent Asian, less than 1 percent American Indian. I was in high school before I first sampled Mexican food or had a Chinese dish that was not chop suey. I was ten years old when I first saw a Jew, a red-haired kid at a bowling alley, wearing jeans, a cowboy shirt, and a knitted yarmulke. A friend once insisted his town of sixteen thousand was not as insulated as some outsiders thought, declaring, "We even have a black family now."

Up-to-date as the state sometimes strives to be, there's still a land-that-time-forgot quality to much if it. I once drove through a small town on the Fourth of July and felt I had happened onto some Disneyland version of an America long gone: a white gazebo in the main square; girls in shorts writing their names in the twilight with sparklers; the old folks licking ice cream cones; a purple-costumed marching band just finished playing and the haggard members sitting on the street curbs, hugging their instruments, their high hats off, eating hot dogs and sipping Coca-Cola through straws; a grinning boy racing his Schwinn beside my car with an American flag flying from his red rear fender and balloons tied against his spokes in order to make a blatting motorcycle noise. It could have been a movie set for Thornton Wilder's *Our Town*.

Middle-American normalcy is still the main draw. Whenever I have asked people why they moved here from the East or West Coast, their initial reply is virtually always, "Well, it's a great place to raise kids." At last look, Nebraska was No. 1 in job growth, increasing 2.6 percent while the nation as a whole declined. Five Fortune 500 companies have their bases here. Wages are low—the state ranks forty-fifth in teacher salaries—but so is the cost of living. A full breakfast at Cecil's is $3.70. And reading real estate ads can be hallucinatory to those who've just moseyed in from overpriced regions: twelve-room mansion, $300K. Small wonder Realtors claim Nebraska has the highest percentage of home ownership in the nation. It also has America's cheapest coal and, thanks to a mixture of corn-derived ethanol, startlingly inexpensive gasoline. But the telling statistics have to do with the concerns of families. Ranked sixth among the fifty states in "livability," Nebraska is twelfth in books per capita, seventh in public libraries, fourth in community hospitals, third in percentage of government expenditures going to education, and first in the public high school graduation rate, at 91.9 percent. Nebraska's students score 100 points higher than the national average on the Scholastic Aptitude Test. And if they stay put, they tend to achieve an admirable senescence in Nebraska, which is ranked fifth in the percentage of the population older than eighty-five. (The snide may recall singer and sausage-maker Jimmy Dean's comment on those who forsook worldly pleasures for a more healthy lifestyle: "You may not live to be a hundred, but it'll feel like it.")

The old can-do spirit is alive and well here. With no available wood or stone for housing, the pioneers chopped blocks of sod and called it marble; heated and cooked with cow manure and called it Nebraska coal. In civic response to the area's treelessness, Nebraskans sowed fast-growing, fast-spreading cottonwoods, invented the spring rite of Arbor Day, produced near Thedford America's largest hand-planted timberland, and created in Omaha the Lied Jungle, the world's largest indoor rain forest. Cyclical flooding losses have been curtailed by the most extensive system of flood-mitigation projects in the country. The architectural wonder of its Art Deco state capitol building was paid for as it was constructed, without the aid of bonds or sales and income taxes, levies that were still a generation off.

South of Omaha is Offutt Air Force Base, home of the United States Strategic Command, the national control center for the Navy's submarine-launched Polaris missiles, the Air Force's bombers, and the intercontinental ballistic missiles hidden in silos, as well as "warfighter" space operations, warning systems, intelligence assessments, and global strategic planning. Arguably the most significant military installation in the world and the subject of great wrangling in Congress and among the military services, Offutt has managed to maintain a strikingly low profile in the community; there's hardly a word of it in the nightly news. This is no Fort Benning or Cape Canaveral; it's the picture of laconic restraint and muscular, just-doing-my-job-ma'am dutifulness, which perfectly correlates to the personality of its home state.

Characteristic of Nebraskans are sincerity, independence, friendliness, stoicism, piety, and caution. Conservative values are predominant, good citizenship is honored, the Armed Forces have no problem recruiting. The percentage of registered voters is twelve points higher than the U.S. norm. Independent Republican George W. Norris, who represented Nebraska in Congress for forty years, promoted the state's one-house, unicameral legislature, and because of that Nebraska ranks last in the nation in its number of state politicians. I have never met anyone who did not consider that a good thing. Although the statewide vote generally tilts Republican in presidential elections, there's a surprising disinclination to vote along party lines—the state legislature is at least nominally nonpartisan—and there's even a contradictory, nuisance tendency to split the vote, with a governor of one party and a lieutenant governor or attorney general of the opposition.

Owing to its position on the map—it's slightly north of the geographical center of the nation—Nebraska commands attention in a way that more outlying states do not. But the general notion seems to be that it's a dull, deadly, *Children of the Corn* kind of place, each steely-eyed and taciturn face concealing a fiend with a rifle. Theodore Sorensen, the head speechwriter for President Kennedy, once dismissed his home state as "a place to get away from and a place to die." Even those who have not gotten away sometimes convey the same impression. Omaha is the mecca of the state, the flourishing, hilly, spottily cosmopolitan city where people honeymoon, have their larks, celebrate high school graduation, and find jobs or objects they can't get elsewhere; yet there's a bumper sticker that reads: OMAHA— WHERE THE WEST BEGINS AND THE EAST JUST SORT OF PETERS OUT. And when the *Omaha World-Herald* ran an article about the local ballet troupe, its headline was: NYC DANCER FINDS OMAHA AS GOOD A PLACE AS ANY. The idea for many is to never single yourself out or get too big for your britches, but to accept your measliness and stolidly accomplish your chores.

The grand exception to that is the majesty of Big Red football. Since 1970 the University of Nebraska varsity has won five national championships, and in the years 1993 to 1997 the football team won sixty times, including three unbeaten and untied seasons, for the finest five-year record in NCAA history. Memorial Stadium in Lincoln, which can accommodate more than eighty thousand fans— making it on football Saturdays Nebraska's third-largest city—has had 255 consecutive sellouts, another NCAA record. And the list goes on. City streets can be without traffic when a game is played. Elderly women in retirement homes are rooted in front of television sets. Red jerseys, jackets, seat cushions, memorabilia, and the other stuff of fandom are everywhere, no matter the season. Nebraska football is not just the primary feature of sports pages, not just the common religion and language of the state, but the overriding id of the psyche. I have seen people who have never even thought of higher education become sick with desolation when the university's football team loses, wild with exaltation when they win.

Still, when I think of Nebraska I first think of its climate and wide, green cornfields, the shuddering windbreaks that shield a farmhouse and barn, skies that are blue as a jay. Sixty percent of its days are sunny. Well above average. And each season has its intimations of paradise. Cloudless October days when it's just cool enough to hint at a sweater and giant harvesters roll through the fields of sorghum while the operator tunes his Walkman to the Cornhusker football game. Or the first soft snow of December, the elm tree branches mittened in white and the flakes hanging above you like God just shook the paperweight. Warming afternoons in March, shrubs burgeoning pinkly with their new buds, water quietly trickling beneath the final holdouts of ice, a baseball smacking a glove somewhere. August nights when the twirling sprinklers have made their crawl of the yard and the pale moon is rising, but it's just so pleasant out it's a shame to go inside, and the sultry air is sweet with the tang of mown bluegrass, a smell that seems to heal the lungs with each inhalation.

NEVADA

LEAVING AMERICA: STATE LINE, NEVADA

Marc Cooper

A s a young boy in the fifties and throughout my adolescence into the sixties, I would always feel the giddy anticipation build as soon as my parents' car would finish gassing up in the dusty California desert town of Baker, two-thirds of the way from LA to Las Vegas.

From the parking lot of the Bun Boy restaurant, there was a grueling forty-minute ride uphill toward Clark Mountain and the Nevada border, often with summer temperatures above 110 and with the attendant concerns of radiator boil-over.

Then, at the summit of 4,700 feet, the road flattening out, we'd glide through the flyspeck town of Mountain Pass, then, still in California, and making a sharp descending curve right at the turnoff for Nipton, we'd be confronted with an awesome, sweeping view of the oceanic desert to our east. The panorama from atop that pass unfolded as a wall of purplish-brown mountains with rose-ochre skirts to our right, rippling mahogany hills to our left, and straight in front of us, the sandy desert flats of pastel beiges, tangerine, and pink stretching through Ivanpah Valley and then ever deeper into Nevada. The black stripe of Interstate 15 slashed right through its heart. And on the hottest of summer days the smell of the bubbling, sticky asphalt would pour right into the cab of our red Plymouth Valiant.

This was the fabled "Baker Stretch"—the last, lonely, fifty-mile leg into Las Vegas. The view was essentially unpopulated desert. Vegas itself lurked behind another set of mountains, and there was no suggestion of its presence except, of course, at night, when the unrivaled battery of lights along the Strip faintly silhouetted the dark mountains with an otherworldly atomic-like glow.

But from atop the summit of the stretch, no more than ten miles away on the looming horizon, was one small clump of civilization— at least, of a sort. The minuscule border settlement of State Line, Nevada, was little more than a two-pump gas station, a wooden windmill, a ramshackle dozen motel rooms, one reddish neon sign, and a mom-and-pop convenience store plunked down in the middle of nowhere, still forty miles shy of pulsating Las Vegas Boulevard.

Unremarkable was State Line, by every measure, except for its single row of noisy vintage slot machines. In today's America, with gambling legal in nearly every state and Indian casinos as common as 7-11s, slot machines are themselves nowadays nearly as familiar as ATMs (though the money flow is reversed). But forty years ago, those one-armed bandits exercised a near-totemic pull.

Indeed, our family stopovers in State Line had a ritualistic, almost baptismal quality. My father would purchase a ten-dollar roll of silver dollars (talismen that seemed to circulate nowhere in America except in Nevada casinos). And given the close confines of the State Line "casino," even as a minor, I could get damn close to the action. Close enough to decipher the spinning triple reels of oranges, pears, cherries, and plums. The kerplunk of the dollars into the machine, the click-lock of the handle coming down and snapping back, the ensuing whir and the infrequent clatter of more coins dropping into the metal retainers below were all unmistakable signals to me that—having arrived in State Line—we had not only crossed the border of California, but we had, at least temporarily, departed from America. And from its daily strictures and norms. Standing at the slots, my father was no longer a steel salesman, my mother no longer president of the local PTA. For those moments, at least, they were of a much more exotic species. They were gamblers. And they were gambling in the only place on the continent where there was no risk of jail.

The classic attraction that this state, and certainly Las Vegas, has exercised on outsiders, is precisely that it's legal to be illegal in Nevada. And though even as a youngster I knew that the country's only legal bordellos were a short drive from State Line in the hamlet of Pahrump and that the glittering Vegas casinos run by their mobster bosses were only a half hour away, just watching the slot machine reels spin was an exhilarating sort of devilish sinfulness for an eleven-year-old from the LA suburbs. For millions of weary road travellers, I'm sure that State Line was no more than a blur in the rush toward a weekend at the Desert Inn or the Stardust. But for me, it was the gateway to all that was elsewhere forbidden, or tainted, or suspect.

The origins of State Line reside in legend. One version has it that it came into being as State Line Station, a lone water tank along the tracks of Senator William Clark's San Pedro, Los Angeles, and Salt Lake Railroad (one of the major engines of southern Nevada's development). What we do know is that sometime in the 1920s, a grouchy miner named "Whiskey Pete" McIntyre set up shop, offering gas and hootch to road-worn Angelenos making their Vegas pilgrimages. McIntyre died of miners' lung in 1993 and is said to be buried standing up by the roadside.

Around the time I first came to State Line, in the early 1950s, a Los Angeles–based gambler, Ernie Primm, took it over. The owner of poker-card clubs in the LA 'burbs, Primm paid only $15,000 for four hundred acres of desert around State Line and acquired another four hundred acres under the Federal Land Grant Act. He snookered the feds into the deal by complying with the act and actually planting fields of barley around his slot machines.

McIntyre and Primm were but two among legions of risk-takers, gamblers, thieves, and outcasts who built this state, long before anyone had ever heard of Bugsy Siegel. Throughout its history, one region or another has been dominant in Nevada. Orginally the Virginia City area dominated as the Comstock lode was unearthed. At the turn of the century, power shifted to south-central and eastern Nevada as the Tonopah and Goldfield mines offered their booty. And for most of our lifetimes, that power and dominance has irrevocably shifted to southern Nevada and specifically to Las Vegas.

But in each and every case, it was the gamblers and outlaws who did the bulk of building this desert world. More than any state in the union, Nevada was constructed not so much by those searching for America, as by those yearning to break free of it. Imagine the gamble taken by fur traders and explorers like Jedediah Smith in 1826 and John Fremont in 1844 when they nudged into the unforgiving and uncharted desert of what is now modern Las Vegas, making first contacts with the Paiutes.

At what is now the corner of Las Vegas Boulevard and Washington Avenue, in 1855 became Fort Mormon after Brigham Young sent thirty of his acolytes to set up permanent shop as the first white settlers in the Las Vegas Valley. But talk about outcasts. The persecuted Mormons' main purpose was, according to historians Sally Denton and Roger Morris, "to mine local metals for bullets and weapons needed for their growing resistance to U.S. rule." Their missionary work, however, was a flop. To the horror of their Mormon saviors, the Paiutes were not only indulgingly tolerant of some egregious gender bending, but by some accounts, they were also . . . well . . . degenerate gamblers. The authors, Ed Reid and Ovid Demaris, of the classic Vegas exposé, *The*

Green Felt Jungle, described the Paiutes, who were prone to stealing the Mormons' corn, as spending vast hours of the day "rolling bones and colored sticks in the brown sand, the true ancestors of the modern Vegans." After only two years, the original Las Vegas Mormons gave up and returned to Utah. (Nonetheless, remnants of the original fort still survive in the shadows of the Vegas mega-resorts, and Mormon political influence remains formidable throughout the state.)

Though the original attempt to settle the southern Vegas valley collapsed, other parts of the state boomed as another wave of gamblers and speculators poured in from across the nation—this time in the guise of prospectors and miners. As they swung their picks and axes, this new crop of American self-exiles would sing:

> What was your name in the States?
> Oh, what was your name in the States?
> Was it Thompson, or Johnson, or Bates?
> Did you murder your wife and fly for your life?
> Say, what was your name in the States?

By the turn of the century, capitalist buccaneers—if not outright gamblers—like Clark, Stanford, and Crocker had built a transcontinental railroad putting Las Vegas formally back on the map as a way station. Colorfully named gambling saloons like the Gem, the Double-O, and the Star, along with the plush Arizona Club bordello, mushroomed in the notorious two-street-long Block 16. As locomotives pulled in for three hours of loading and unloading, sun-baked travellers would lustily pluck their own forbidden pleasures of poker and sex from among the offerings of what eventually became a full-blown red-light district in the heart of downtown Vegas.

The success of Block 16, the notion of Las Vegas and Nevada as an oasis of naughty respite from quotidian modern regimentation, was irresistibly infectious as the young and sparsely populated state's marketing-and-development strategy. By 1927, divorce in Nevada, always a relaxed affair, became simply the easiest anywhere. Four years later, as construction of Hoover Dam was getting underway, bringing thousands of Depression-battered workers into the Vegas area, gambling was legalized statewide.

"Nevada has always been a company state," says historian Michael Green of what would be Nevada's tectonic shift from a mining to a gambling- and entertainment-based economy. "In 1931 we merely changed companies."

No sooner was the ink dry on the bill legalizing gambling, than the sharpies, professional grifters, and gangsters from across America started caravaning toward the New Jerusalem of Nevada. In that same year, Guy McAfee, a corrupt LAPD vice squad captain, opened the first gambling joint on desolate Highway 91 a few miles south of Las Vegas and dubbed his roadhouse the Pair-O-Dice Club. This nearly forgotten hustler and husband of a Hollywood madam was, much more than Bugsy Siegel, the first Vegas visionary. It was he who first dared to call that wind-whipped stretch of dark highway "The Strip"—deliriously envisioning it as a future twin to his hometown's twinkling strip of nightclubs and dinner clubs, on Sunset Boulevard. McAfee had called it right, and in spades.

The rest of the story we know from the movies. Bugsy, Meyer Lansky, Tony Carnero, Morris "Moe" Dalitz, Jake The Barber, Frank "Lefty" Rosenthal, Tony "The Ant" Spilotro, Benny Binion, and so many others came and fulfilled—thanks in some cases to the leaven of Teamsters pension funding—that solemn promise that young Michael Corleone made to his gal pal Kate as he proposed marriage: "Kate," he said, "In five years the Corleone family will be legal."

If not quite fully legal, Mob-run Las Vegas certainly was respected, tolerated, and highly profitable. Profitable enough that by the mid-seventies the real professionals—Corporate America—moved in and eventually pushed the messy amateurs of the Mafia out. Or, if you prefer, merged with and absorbed them.

But as Las Vegas's center of gravity shifted from mavericks and mobsters to mainstream MBAs, as Sin City burgeoned into the most visited resort in the country, outside the circle of its blinding light, the rest of America was going through its own radical transformation. Family farms foundered. The Rust Belt snapped. The battering winds of globalization uprooted the factories and mills of the heartland and scattered them from Mexico to Southeast Asia. Unionized jobs gave way to temps and contingency workers. In one company town after another, a century-old social contract was shredded as insurance was revoked, pensions rolled back, and factory gates shuttered. Eventually, socking away the nest egg in what once was thought to be an ironclad 401K made about as much sense as letting it all ride on one spin of the roulette wheel.

By the 1990s, the more acute social scientists detected a curious pattern of human migration. What had been the decades-old steady flow of Americans into Las Vegas began to wildly accelerate. The population of Las Vegas had doubled in the decade of the 1980s and then doubled again over the next ten years. No metropolitan area in America was growing at anywhere near the pace of Vegas.

This generation of immigrants, however, was different in many ways from its predecessors. Sure, there would always be a handful of trimmers, fugitives, and shake-down artists looking to launder themselves in the Vegas sun. But most of the six thousand a month who were now crowding into Las Vegas were refugees from an America where everyday life had become too much of a gamble. Where either the Reagan recession of '81, the Bush slump of 1990, or the bubble-burst of a decade later had left them as devastated as blackjack players who have lost it all on dead 16 to the dealer's 21. The only risk they were interested in now was the off-chance that Vegas—of all places—could provide the normalcy, the security, the certainty, that once anchored their lives, or at least their dreams. Given the options, it wasn't a bad bet.

For Sin City had dramatically morphed into Disneyland in the Desert. Around it flourishes a densely unionized service economy. Immigrant maids can make $12 an hour. White-haired grandmothers with Culinary Union pins on their halter straps bag a grand a week as cocktail waitresses. Former factory workers with nimble hands retool as blackjack dealers for maybe twice as much. Their children have a shot at breaking into the bustling state university. A family home can still be purchased for little more than the down payment on an LA or San Francisco residence. Del Webb and others have conjured up some of the largest, most antiseptic, ordered, comfortable, and affordable planned residential communities seen anywhere.

For some enthusiastic observers, Las Vegas has become nothing less than the New Detroit. Which is perhaps a bit of an overstatement as, unlike Motor City, Las Vegas produces nothing tangible, only industrial-sized measures of hope and despair. On the other hand, the balance still tips decidedly in favor of hope. The next century of Nevada's history is in the hands not of those fleeing America, but of those trying to recover it.

I invite doubters to revisit what was once that sleazy stopover of State Line, forty miles short of Vegas. In 1977, Ernie Primm paved over Whiskey Pete's old gas station and convenience store with its aging slot machines and constructed a state-of-the-art Vegas-class casino in their place. Primm died before he could see his town grow two more megacasinos, including a mammoth-sized medieval-themed reincarnation of Whiskey Pete's. Today, a space-age monorail arches over the interstate and links the two sides of the town that together boast more than 2,500 hotel rooms, 100 gaming tables, and nearly five-thousand slot machines. In front of Buffalo Bill's resort and casino, the 209-foot-high Desperado roller coaster darts up and down day and night. From its top, you can see the glint of the modular prefabs where five hundred of the town's three thousand workers live, and you can gawk at the beach-sized parking lot in front of the 100-store designer-outlet shopping mall. The lot's eastern flank is anchored by one of the most-trafficked McDonald's franchises in the world. The two new gas stations in town are estimated to pump twelve million gallons of gas a year. All three casino-resorts are now the property of the MGM Mirage gaming corporation, and together they generate about $200 million a year in net revenue.

A half-dozen years ago, State Line's name was officially changed to Primm, honoring the family that built it. The roller coaster is about the only desperado left in town.

NEW HAMPSHIRE

A DEFACED OLD MAN

Donald Hall

On a Saturday afternoon in May, a newspaper telephoned to ask for a quote on the demise of New Hampshire's Old Man of the Mountains. The stony profile in the White Mountains that had become the state's logo was dead at 100,000 years of natural causes, defaced during the night by rains and erosion. It was the first I had heard of it, and it should not have been a surprise. Even when I first saw it, seventy years ago, the Old Man's prognathous physiognomy had been supported by human agency, by cables and steel clamps. Every summer my parents drove me past it. Growing up, I read Nathaniel Hawthorne's short story, "The Great Stone Face," and became aware of Daniel Webster's allusion, and Emerson's. Responding to the reporter, I came up with nothing quotable, but I speculated on the response of our new governor. (I suggested that Craig Benson might want to replace the granite with something in epoxy resin.) A few weeks later, on the way to the Frost Place in Franconia—a shrine to the stony poet at his old house north of the Notch—I observed a caved-in pie-face under the old improbable forehead. I was surprised to feel melancholy over the disappearance. Like Webster and Emerson and everyone else, I had made the Old Man allegorical, especially in collapse. Did the Old

Man let go because of the election of Craig Benson? It seems doubtful, considering earlier governors.

Governor Benson was elected when Bush II was elected—although New Hampshire had shown small enthusiasm for Bush; McCain beat him by nineteen points in the Republican primary. New Hampshire would have gone to Gore if Gore had received the votes cast for Nader. Benson replaced Jeanne Shaheen, a Democrat, who served three terms as governor, then ran for the Senate against Sununu II, and lost. Colonists may have defeated the hereditary English king but the descendants still go in for families. Sununu II's fellow U.S. senator is Judd Gregg—Gregg II: his father Hugh was governor, like Sununu II's father. Young Sununu takes his name and his conservatism from his father, but seems slicker—without his father's arrogance or cheerful egotism. A couple of years ago I bumped into the former governor on an airplane, who recognized me not by my name but by his ownership: "You were my poet laureate."

Craig Benson brings to the governor's office a CEO's manners. He avoids consultation with legislators. He holds gubernatorial meetings in a room without chairs; apparently, encounters are briefer when no one can sit down. He brings this practice from Cabletron Systems—which he co-founded and ran—a computer-systems company that he sold before it went *splat*. He governs Newhampshiretron because he is rich. He spent many millions of his own dollars to buy the governorship, mounting a tedious assault of television ads running on Massachusetts and New Hampshire stations—narrowly winning the primary over less affluent, more qualified, and equally conservative opposition. His Democratic opponent in the election was Mark Fernald, and it was no contest—because Fernald ran as a proponent of a state income tax. New Hampshire remains the only state with neither an income tax nor a sales tax. Fernald's advocacy was honest, fair, equitable—and guaranteed Benson's election. It was also a quixotic advocacy, because the Republican House in New Hampshire would never pass an income tax, whatever a governor wanted. Governor Benson had one message in his campaign: no new taxes. It was impossible to discern any other idea.

In the same state of New Hampshire, the Episcopalian Church elected as bishop a gay man named V. Gene Robinson. Separate votes of the clergy and the laity supported Robinson. The appointment sits uneasily on the agenda of the national Episcopal Church, which eventually voted this summer to confirm. That conservative New Hampshire elected a gay bishop has caused consternation. When newspapers all over the country reported that New Hampshire elected the first gay bishop in the history of the Episcopalian Church, the reaction was universal: "New Hampshire" had to be a reporting error for "Vermont."

Doubtless the Episcopalians who voted for a gay bishop had earlier voted for the gubernatorial candidate who proposed an income tax. Still, New Hampshire is not so monolithic in its conservatism as folks think. New Hampshire's politics have frequently favored the mildly eccentric over the bland standard-issue, thus McCain over Bush. Reporters and analysts speak of New Hampshire's retail politics, as opposed to wholesale. The improbable and unattractive Craig Benson's victory was unsettling because it was delivered by money and marketing, rather than by living-room chit-chat, handshaking at picnics, and Rotary Club speeches.

Meantime across the river is Vermont, whose former governor runs against Bush II and the war. At the moment in the New Hampshire polls Howard Dean runs second to Senator Kerry, but Dean may be closing in fast. The two states make a famous contrast. Vermont endorses same-sex civil unions, and New Hampshire makes eighteen-year-old women get parental consent for abortions.

Even the grass is greener. When I drive up Interstate 89 to Norwich, the contrast of borders is extraordinary. On the New Hampshire side of the bridge sprawl acres of car dealerships and fast-food joints, motels and mattress stores, wholesale clubs and Borders Books— pavement, nothing green, a gray jungle of commerce hectic and noisy with signs. On the other side of the Connecticut River, green hills undulate among small towns without malls, with trees and grass and streams, white churches and town halls. The contrast, however, is not a result of Vermont good taste. Vermont is greener because it costs more to shop there. Vermont has a sales tax.

New Hampshire was settled by people who escaped the Common-wealth of Massachusetts in the pursuit of liberty—people for whom independence was more important than community. The state has always been populated by a good proportion of mavericks. Eccen-tricity is honored. The farmer who used to cut my hay, half-retired, has taken to raising elk. Selling elkburger is not a way to get rich, but its oddity is something for neighbors to brag about. "Fellow over there breeds elk for slaughter." Conversations at the PO and the minimart— the minimart replaces the general store, except in Vermont where the authentic general stores are compulsory—often celebrate weirdness. "Did you hear what Windy Phelps said, over to Danbury?"

Independence or eccentricity is political and social, not just anec-dotal. My great-grandfather, who fought in the Civil War, was a Copperhead who loathed Lincoln but joined the Army to stick with his neighbors. After the war he extended his loathing to all Republi-cans, a politics he passed on to his children. His son, my grandfather, born in 1875, became a New Dealer, an extoller of Roosevelt. Because politics was local, and you voted for the man, his Republican neigh-bors elected him to the New Hampshire House.

New Hampshire's legislature is vast—424 legislators—because you should know the people you vote for. At Town Meeting you not only know them all, you yell at them and vote them down. Town Meeting is once a year. Otherwise you stay home and milk your cows. Well, you used to. People in Derry and Salem, New Hampshire's Boston suburbs (the Sununus come from Salem), milk very few cows, and the population of New Hampshire has altered more than its politics has.

Portions of the new population are tax exiles from Massachusetts. If they get their salaries from Boston, they pay Massachusetts income tax, but no sales tax where they shop, and liquor is cheap because of the state-run liquor monopoly. Even cigarettes are cheaper than in neighboring states. This year the New Hampshire House, trying to arrive at a budget, wanted to add tax to tobacco, but Governor Benson—*no new taxes*—threatened to veto it, and the proposal collapsed.

The persisting citizenry of old New Hampshire—neither suburbanites nor retirees from Connecticut—are the descendants of millworkers and farmers, and they are anti-government more than anti-tax. If they are more or less libertarian, they are not converts to the contemporary Libertarian party, but rehearse an archaic political template of eighteenth-century liberty. Such a tone survives social change and changes in population, as if it had become the air we breathe. Local independence and eccentricity remain values to this citizenry. In the unsuburban countryside, zoning is difficult: "Fellow owns his land, fellow can do what he wants with it." When the fellow by legal fiction turns out to be a corporation, watch your ass. The template does not notice that society has changed, and thus the ethics of almost-anarchic liberty turns into the politics of entitlement, riches, and accumulation. New Hampshire's distrust of government leaves it at the mercy of government by the rich.

In high summer more cars than ever carried tourists through Franconia Notch, where road signs still pointed to the Old Man of the Mountains. Governor Benson had done what all governors do when they don't know what to do: he appointed a commission to decide how to memorialize or replicate the vacated profile. The governor made it clear that no taxes would support the commission or its project. Meantime a poll revealed that New Hampshire's citizenry overwhelmingly rejected notions of a Styrofoam impostor.

New Jersey

On Mediocrity's Cutting Edge

Luc Sante

New Jersey, a smallish state with an insistent, almost typographical shape—an ampersand—has for three centuries had the mingled good and bad luck to be the neutral conjunction between New York City and Philadelphia. If it were a country it would be a sort of Belgium, constantly run over by armies surging or retreating from one center of power to the other. Instead it became a domestic colony, employed as vegetable patch, factory lot, depot, dumping ground, and eventually spare bedroom for the great cities on either side. Its nickname, "The Garden State," is a nice way of acknowledging this servile condition. It doesn't grow much for the market anymore anyway; agribusiness probably has single-crop spreads in Texas that are bigger. The only two significant rural regions left in the state are the pie slice of the Appalachian Range in the extreme northwest and the ineffable Pine Barrens in the south, both of them saved from subdivision by their topographical inhospitality. The rest is mostly suburb.

It does have cities, almost all of them beset, aggrieved, half-ruined, embodying the idea of city in the sense of demographic density but not in that of power, prosperity, or even pleasures of the flesh. Most arrived at this condition as industry tumbled in the latter half of the past century; earlier they had been hard-edged, unglamorous communities of strivers. Newark, Jersey City, Elizabeth, Bayonne, Paterson, Camden, Trenton. The first has had some intermittent, fleeting success in positioning itself as a subsidiary Gotham; the second has become a catch basin for lower-Manhattan overflow. They also retain their share of misery, however, and misery is most of what you find in the other cities, not excepting the state capital. If the American middle class continues to expand its numbers and stomach, it will eventually find a way of refashioning and inhabiting former factory cities, but for the time being they are useless except for housing the poor, badly. They have inferior building stock, vast and unrecyclable vacated plants, empty lots of poisoned soil, and populations that have never recovered from the loss of security—if, indeed, they ever knew such a thing. Seemingly everyone who can do so has bolted to the suburbs, which lie all around, just beyond the highway belt. Oh, and there is also Atlantic City, in which a froth of imitation high life sits atop a heap of misery. The misery is real enough, but the casino fringe is less a place than a drug or a manic episode. It is a feeble knockoff of Vegas, which is itself a three-dimensional metaphor you can almost put your arm through. Atlantic City is tethered to New Jersey, but it really seems to drift five miles offshore.

The predominant look of New Jersey these days is pale if not pastel, ostensibly cheerful, ornamented with gratuitous knobs and fanlights, manufactured in such a way that clapboard is indistinguishable from fiberglass—the happy meeting of postmodernism and heritage-themed zoning codes. A couple of decades ago the latter asserted themselves in the state by coating diners in ersatz brickface and carriage lamps, the former by turning out dry-cleaning establishments and ten thousand bars with plural names (Mumbles, Fumbles, Stumbles) that were apparently made of beaverboard and aluminum and featured French-mansardish roof extensions that all but scraped the ground. But that was adolescence. Now, with maturity, the suburban style of New Jersey has attained a purposeful, militant blandness, the kind you associate with plainclothes security personnel at Disney parks. The "welcome" signs, artfully disposed, make it clear that hospitality is merely an allusive flavor; they are in no wise meant to be taken literally. The past, similarly, is a reference without a referent—all you need to know is that some humans, now dead, invented the principles of quaintness. And nature is a commodity that, while valuable, is yet in a primitive state of development. It will be a better thing all around when bioengineering has refined the landscape so that people no longer need to coax proper behavior from its component parts. Someday you will be able to unscrew your trees, rotate your hedges, and shampoo your lawn.

Such suburban commonplaces exist across the nation, of course, but as potent as they may be in California, say, that state also has mountains and deserts, extremes of weather, remote settlements at the ends of roads. New Jersey, with its accommodating temperate flatness and closeness of scale, was virtually designed to be a suburb. Accommodation was the operative quality. The elements rolled out the carpet for exploitation in the first place, and then successive generations of rural aldermen and freeholders happily submitted their townships to the shredder. They traded their placid neighborly four-corners and pastoral outlands to the shopping-mall and condo-complex bulldozers in exchange for golfing vacations in Bermuda. But what self-preserving trustee wouldn't do the same? New Jersey has always been all about location; North Dakotans can only gnash their teeth in envy. And people have to live somewhere, don't they, there being so many more of them than there were yesterday. Among the numerous consequences of such accommodation is the eradication of historical identity. This tract-house suburb began life as a utopian agricultural commune, that one as a religious sect's earthly fortress; today the only evidence of these origins resides on the unvisited shelves of the local historical society. Of course, the way such origins have been turned into tourism fodder in places where the architectural heritage is more abundant suggests that the loss may not be so great after all.

Bereft of history, though—and, yes, New Jersey does boast of a dozen George Washington sites, as well as the more apposite traces of Thomas Edison—the state's identity is pretty thin. Like a Belgium, New Jersey has long been the butt of jokes and complaints, a convenient kick-me for its more powerful neighbors. Hoboken and Ho-Ho-Kus, or at least their names, have served as the mythic Nowheresville in urban smart talk for generations. The state's name was shorthand for "soulless commuter dump" back when Long Island was still overwhelmingly rural. And the Jersey driver remains a prominent folk devil all over the Northeast: bumptious, heedless, hostile, and barely competent. The epithets chart a subtle change in perception of the state, from dull, square outland to parking lot for middle-class transients. The New Jerseyan is generally seen as the embodiment of upwardly mobile rootlessness and material self-satisfaction. He or she may have grown up in Oklahoma or Idaho, or even abroad, but has shed every trace of accent and custom somewhere on the climb, and now marks time in a factory-fresh jumbo house made of two-by-fours and gypsum and Tyvek and filled with gadgetry, on a street with no sidewalks and planted with saplings, while awaiting a corporate transfer to some interchangeable burg on the other coast. Whole swaths of the state are held together only by school sports and property-tax outrage. If you parachute into one of these places without a global positioning device you will be more lost than if you landed on the steppes.

It remains true that if you navigate around the gated communities and behind the corporate campuses, you will come upon remnants of a former New Jersey. There are still tomato fields and cranberry bogs here and there, and old Italians babying their back-yard fig trees in urban neighborhoods that have so far managed to avoid detection by the hip dollar and its agents. There are still rogue bars, many of them along highways demoted by the interstate system, and now and then you'll see a local diner that is still prima-rily made of sheet metal and caters to a clientele constitutionally similar to the one it served forty years ago. There are still factories in the state, with attendant industrial housing precincts, even if every year more of them are admitted to the ranks of the dead. The Pine Barrens continue their mysterious ways, and down there you can still shoot skeet behind somebody's barn and canoe down swampish rivers far from any road. Immigrant communities, some of them new, maintain their churches and groceries in obscure byways on the fringes of cities. It is also true that the curvilinear streets of neosub-urbs can shelter the most unlikely assemblages of citizens behind the apparent uniformity of their extruded facades. Some places, after all, readily admit that they are but containing vessels; as long as the inhabitants keep their doors shut and their lawns manicured they are free to worship shrubs and paint themselves blue if that's what floats their boat.

New Jersey, a conveniently flat and temperate piece of real estate situated between two great cities, one of them possessing capital-of-the-world pretensions, has long served as a laboratory for testing upgrades and streamlinings of middle-class life. The success of these innovations has ensured their application around the country and in the more prosperous countries in the rest of the world. It is thus pos-sible to see the spirit of New Jersey in a great many places as you travel. When you come upon a grouping of large tract houses, or of low-rise apartments masquerading as large tract houses, that is her-alded by a signboard bearing a title ("Lark's Crest Estates"; "The Vil-lage at Hunter's Ridge"), you are seeing New Jersey, even if you happen to be in Colorado. When you enter a venerable rustic inn that has lately come under new management, and notice that the reproduction antiques in the foyer are labeled with instructions for purchasing duplicates, and that the desk personnel sport matching blazers, hands-free telephone headsets, and friendly smiles under impenetrably dead eyes, you have come into New Jersey, even if the hostelry is situated in Europe. When you opt for the latest techno-logical innovation, the biggest car, the smallest portable device, the most all-encompassing home-entertainment system, not from any specific need but simply because you want the best, you yourself have become a New Jerseyan, even if you have never set foot in that state. It is not so much that any of these modes of living or conducting business was necessarily pioneered in New Jersey itself—California does have a lot to answer for—but that no state is as exemplified and ruled by them. New Jersey, an old state with many fascinating his-torical byways and a considerable fund of lore and legend, is the image of the future, assuming that the future is assigned a value of perhaps fifteen minutes.

NEW MEXICO

THE LAND OF ENCHANTMENT

Tony Hillerman

E ach month, *New Mexico* magazine publishes new evidence
that our state—the fifth largest—remains invisible to our
fellow Americans. This feature, "One of Our Fifty Is
Missing," prints items provided by its readers.

Some examples:

A University of New Mexico dean reports an inquiry from the
University of Florida: will a transferring student need a visa?

A salesman home from Maryland reports that a TV newscast
there showed Texas abutting Arizona on its weather map.

A New York antique restorer asks a Santa Fe gallery if he needs a
"green card" from the Immigration Service to work in New Mexico.

A Chicago equipment company rejects an order for gaskets from
Farmington, explaining it doesn't ship out of the United States.

An Albuquerque sportswriter calls New York seeking a Winter
Olympics press pass. He's told that he'll have to get that through his
country's delegation headquarters in Mexico City.

The significance of this is the joy with which New Mexicans report
being missing. We call our state "The Land of Enchantment," and our
capital (Santa Fe) "The City Different." We'd love to believe that we,

and the high, dry, and mostly empty landscape we occupy, warrant the titles. Our peaks are the homes of mystical beings: Turquoise Girl of the Navajos, Spider Grandmother of the Tewas, the War Gods of the peaceful Pueblo tribes, and the Mountain Spirits of the Apaches. Our canyons and cliffs are marked with the sacred symbols of Anasazi priests. The beauty and silence that surround us offer no riches, but they do enchant. Enchantment makes one different. New Mexicans like being different.

My encyclopedia says nothing of this. It describes our population (a bit less than two million) as "sparse." We are a mix of communities: the nineteen Indian pueblos who got here first; then the Navajos and Apaches who probably showed up in the fifteenth century; Spanish colonists who arrived a hundred years later; more recent immigrants who trickled in after 1850 when the United States took the area from Mexico; and a diverse recent influx. Two huge national laboratories (Los Alamos and Sandia) and the high-tech companies they attracted gave the state a frosting of doctoral degrees. My encyclopedia says this forms "an unusually multicultural society unlike that of any other state."

Even the original Spanish culture has been divided. Those whose family names dot our map consider themselves Hispanics and the Iberian Peninsula their ancestral homeland. Newer arrivals from Mexico, Central America, and South America consider themselves "Chicano" and link their culture to the Maya, Aztec, Toltec, and other civilizations that flourished before the Spanish conquest. They tend to hold the Spanish, and all other Europeans, in low esteem.

Scholars from Spanish universities who visited New World colonies in the 1950s to find out what had happened to their language found that its evolution had been about normal up through South America to the Rio Grande. Our "Chicanos" speak modern Spanish, but among the Hispanics of New Mexico's northern mountains, the scholars heard the voice of Cervantes and of classical Spain with modern developments dealt with by modifying English words (a truck became *la trucke*). A popular book, *Come Se Dice Big Mac in Espanol*, deals with this problem—the answer being "Mac Grande."

Nor is the non-Spanish population as easy to label as it once was. In the old days it was defined by a popular "chisti."

"Election day. African-American at a polling place is asked the standard election-day question:

'How much they paying for votes?'

'I don't know,' says the African-American. 'They haven't got to us Anglos yet.' "

As late as the mid-1950s, an Anglo was anyone who was neither Hispanic nor Indian. It included Chinese, Jews, Arabs, members of our Sikh community, etc., as well as Anglo-Saxon types. But now the drive to establish Balkanizing "diversification" among Americans is producing new labels. "People of color" for example, to lump non-Nordics, or "Tejanos" and "Hollywoods" as pejorative class categories. ("Tejano" is New Mexican for Texan, the ancient enemy, and "Hollywoods" are the "ricos" who crowd the hills around Santa Fe and Taos with expensive summer homes.)

New Mexico's political base has also changed, but manages to remain a sort of lonely liberal lighthouse in the conservative Mountain West. Being on the Union side in the Civil War and traditionally hostile to Texans (Democrats), we came into statehood solidly Republican. But the Republicans elected with statehood were the progressive sort. With Franklin Roosevelt and the New Deal we went solidly Democrat and remain so by party registration. However, our Democratic majority tends to vote for liberal-to-moderate Republicans, and we are one of the few mountain states that hasn't yet moved to the right on social issues.

In the 1930s, long before political gays elsewhere were emerging from the closet, our senator, Bronson Cutting, was denounced by the Democrats for his sexual leanings and accused of "keeping a harem of Harvard boys" in his Washington office. The senator published the homophobic speech on the front page of the *Santa Fe New Mexican*, with neither denial nor comment, and won the election. Our last Republican governor campaigned on a bicycle and pushed legislation to legalize marijuana. Only Oregon has shown similar signs of sanity on this issue.

Old-family Anglo names are less common in our state. When the westward migration flood of "manifest destiny" happened, there was little to attract it to New Mexico. Our immense oil, natural gas, coal, copper, potash, and uranium deposits were mostly invisible until the twentieth century. And our previous rulers, King Philip of Spain and the various Mexican governments, had imposed policies that handicapped exploitation.

What does a colonizer do about Indians if they object to him stealing their land? The French married them. Lord Amherst suggested to King George III a more economical tactic. Since the Indians were extremely sensitive to smallpox and doted on woven wool blankets, collecting such blankets from smallpox pest houses and presenting them to the tribes seemed an economical solution. The British history books do not report whether this plan was actually used, but tribes in the original thirteen colonies quickly faded away.

Out west, the Spanish colonists ran into a problem. The Franciscan priests accompanying the Spanish invasion complained to King Philip about the military killing off folks who might soon be Christians—and his new subjects. A Royal Commission considered this and ruled that the Indians were *gente de razon*. As "reasonable people" they should be converted to Christianity and treated as fellow citizens. Royal grants were issued certifying ownership of the lands to the pueblos, and with the land, the rights in perpetuity to the water they were using.

When Mexico freed itself from Spain, it maintained these rights. When we took the West from Mexico, it insisted that a clause in the treaty continue these guarantees. The Senate approved the plan. The

U.S. property-tax system (alien to Mexico) provided a way for Anglos to wrest much of the real estate from Hispanic grant owners, but Pueblo Indian land and water rights remained intact. In 2002, they were posing a huge financial problem to Albuquerque, which is required to meet downstream water-purity standards for the Isleta Indians.

I suspect some of the above will surprise a good many readers whose American-history lessons focus more on pilgrims and the original thirteen colonies. They might also be surprised to know that the Spanish of New Mexico raised a substantial fund to help finance the war of the British colonists against George III. And amazed to know the Indians actually won a war out here—organizing the scattered pueblos into an alliance whose warriors captured Santa Fe in 1680, and drove the Spanish out of the entire territory. After they were reconquered in 1692, the Pueblo tribes and the Spanish joined forces to fight the Navajos and, later, the Comanches. Odd as it sounds, the Hispanic villages, under a law that allowed only soldiers to have guns, armed themselves by buying rifles from the Comanches at a spring trading event held at Ranchos de Taos. The Hispanics would swap blankets, bridles, metal pots and pans, etc., to the Comanches for rifles—and as ransom for the prisoners the Comanches had taken in the previous summer's raids.

New Mexico is almost square, including 121,598 square miles of mountains, mesas, river basins, and prairie, over which are scattered as many citizens as reside in Houston. West from Texas to Arizona: 351 miles. South from Colorado to Mexico: 391 miles. Our mean elevation is 5,700 feet. Our lowest point is Red Bluff Reservoir, in our southeast corner, which, at 2,342 feet, is higher than the highest place in a good many states. Wheeler Peak, 13,131 feet, is our highest point. Appropriately for our invisible state, it is also mostly invisible—being so surrounded by mountains almost as high that few New Mexicans have noticed it.

New Mexico was left roughly in its current form about twenty-five million years ago in a planetary upheaval geologists call the Laramide Revolution. We tilted from northwest to southeast, with this tilt complicated by volcanic bubbling. In the southeast, eruptions pushed Sierra Blanca twelve thousand feet into the sky (providing an ideal place for a ski lodge, gambling casino, and summer resort, where the Mescalero Apaches now play host to Texans fleeing heat in the flatlands). Another eruption formed Mount Taylor—the sacred Turquoise Mountain of the Navajos—whose snowy winter peak Albuquerque sees seventy-five miles to the west. Ship Rock emerged at about the same time to tower like a gigantic Gothic cathedral over its namesake Navajo town.

Geographers place us at the southern end of the Colorado Plateau, with our Sangre de Cristo (Blood of Christ) Mountains and a plethora of smaller ranges forming the last gasp of the Rocky Mountains. Except for our southeast corner, there's no place in New Mexico where mountains aren't visible. They range in title from the Animas to the Bears, Big Burros, Little Burros, and Broke Offs, down through the alphabet to the Zunis. On my map, seventy-three of these ranges are big enough to warrant a name, and among them are 310 peaks high enough for labeling. Eighty-five of these are at least two miles high and seven reach above thirteen thousand feet.

Volcanism produces most mountains, but New Mexico, of course, has notable exceptions. "Rifting" produced Sandia Peak, which shades Albuquerque from the morning sun, and the Sacramentos and Organs, pushed skyward when the earth's crust between them sank and became the Tularosa Basin.

On Sandia Mountain's ridge, a bit under eleven thousand feet, one finds neither volcanic ash nor magma. One finds limestone and bits of fossils from the bottom of an ancient ocean. Geologists say this was caused by the sinking of a strip of the earth's crust to a level almost a mile below the present Rio Grande Valley. That produced pressure, pushing up Sandia Mountain and the Manzanos.

New Mexico is aptly known as "The Land of Little Rain." This aridity causes us to cluster along our rivers, and rivers that carry enough water to supply towns are few—principally the Rio Grande, the Chama, the San Juan, and the Gila. Snowmelt runoff from mountains can restock underground reservoirs for small towns here and there, but major populations are tied to water. That means big, quiet, empty places are easy to find.

You can stand atop Sandia Mountain at night and see the lights of more than half of the state's population. Directly below is the sprawl of Albuquerque, with a necklace of satellite towns up and down the Rio Grande. Behind you fifty miles is the twinkle of Santa Fe. A little to the right in the Jemez Mountains is Los Alamos. Between and beyond these spots of light is undiluted, uncontaminated emptiness, lit only by the dazzle of a trillion stars. An oddity often mentioned by visitors from the flatlands is the nature here of lights at night. Our cities tend to twinkle rather than glow. Physicists say this has two causes. One is altitude: air loses one-thirtieth of its density with each nine hundred feet above sea level. Thus, Santa Feans breathe air about one-fourth thinner than folks in Boston or Portland. It is rich in hydrogen, poor in oxygen and carbon dioxide, and thereby more transparent. The second cause is extremely low humidity.

Cause one means visitors unused to high altitudes must cut their martini consumption sharply until their lungs adjust. Cause two means soda crackers remain crisp and dry, and so do our complexions. Combined, they take the diffusion out of light, make our sky a darker shade of blue, and, to borrow a poet's phrase, "on a clear day you can see forever."

Precipitation in Albuquerque is about nine inches a year. When the wet clouds come, they tend to hang over the mountains. Since we lie in the "prevailing westerlies" weather zone, most of these drift in from the west, giving us what remains of their Pacific Ocean moisture after dropping much of it on the mountains they cross en route.

And most of them arrive in what we call, with sardonic irony, the monsoon season. In good years it begins in July and continues into September. The prayers of the ski-lodge operators become fervent in early November, and sometimes are answered with late-November snowstorms. After a good winter, snowpack in the state's highest ridges has been measured up to eight feet deep. Snowmelt, not rainfall, keeps our rivers running.

We rarely enjoy those slow persistent rains brought to America's fertile midlands out of the Gulf of Mexico. The Navajos call them "female" because they are productive of corn crops, grass, and all good things. The much more common "male rains" of summer come from towering thunderheads. When surface humidity is low, their rain is only *vigore*, a promising-looking deluge that evaporates before it reaches the earth. Otherwise they produce huge, cold drops often mixed with hail or "popcorn snow." These "male" rains typically last only a few minutes. If they linger, flash floods roar down our arroyos.

The songwriter who wrote that popular "Springtime in the Rockies" song clearly had never been in the Rockies in springtime—a season of cold, dusty winds. Nor do other notions about weather hold in New Mexico. We rank at the bottom of the fifty in rainfall and right at the top in both "observed lightning strikes" and "deaths per capita caused by lightning." New Mexico boasts of having the loudest and driest rainstorms.

Given that, it shouldn't be surprising that the sand of our White Sands National Park isn't actually sand. It's gypsum, washed down adjoining mountains for untold eons into what was once a lake and blown endlessly into towering drifts. Pick a moonlit night, drive out into this universe of dunes, climb one, and exercise your senses. Except for the sounds of your own heart thumping, the silence is total and eerie. You will smell only the rare aroma of totally pure air. You will see no sign of light, except moon and stars and the light reflected from the snowy peaks of the Sacramentos. If your imagination is working, you can make yourself the only human left on a deserted planet.

While the mountains divide us geographically, psychologically we are divided by what we call "La Bajada." That "descent" is the great lava-topped mesa wall that New Mexicans climb to get from Albuquerque to Santa Fe, from the lower, milder, easier, richer middle of the state to the colder, more mountainous, harder high country. The Rio Grande cuts through that plateau and thus the territory above is "Rio Arriba" and the land below "Rio Abajo."

Before Mexico won its independence from European control, the highlands above La Bajada were the extreme northern frontier of the immense Spanish Empire. The families who settled there were the heroes—typical frontiersmen of American history. They were the independent-minded folks of the seventeenth century. When the war of liberation drove the French from Mexico and the new government closed Catholic churches and seminaries, these frontier families resisted, keeping the faith alive in little family chapels and the *morados* of a brotherhood modeled after the "Brothers of the Light" in Spain. When the U.S. Army of Occupation arrived at the close of the Mexican War, it ran into the same independent spirit in the highlands. The village of Taos and the adjoining Taos Indian Pueblo resisted and the battle provided America with a remarkable reminder of the cost of war. At the entrace of the pueblo stands what's left of the walls of the pueblo's old church. The Indian-Hispanic villagers took refuge there. Our army knocked a hole in the adobe church wall, put the barrel of a cannon in it, and blazed away, killing those inside and burning the church. Male survivors were rounded up and hauled in a wagon to temporary gallows in Taos Plaza for a wholesale hanging—done by driving the wagon out from under them after the nooses had been secured. So far, the National Park Service hasn't gotten around to putting up historical markers about either the ruined church or the wholesale hangings.

In New Mexico, such ineptitude in the business of historical sites is common. The burial place of the most famous of our numerous badmen, William Bonney (aka Billy the Kid), is well marked in Lincoln County, where he was the principal gunman on the losing side of the Lincoln County War. There the grave is marked by two tombstones. The first marker was stolen; it was replaced by a second one, also stolen. Then, after a large, unstealable third stone was put in place, the first stone was returned by the repentant thief to stand beside stone three. Making this a truly New Mexico affair, Billy the Kid is actually buried far to the north. He was interred at the edge of Santa Fe's Rosario Cemetery. The grave was overlooked in a highway realignment, and Billy is now driven over by Santa Fe traffic.

Lew Wallace, our territorial governor after the Civil War, summed up our nature. "Things that work everywhere else don't work in New Mexico," said Wallace, thereby giving us our unofficial motto. The cynicism in that remark might be explained by the circumstances when he wrote it. The governor was trying to finish *Ben-Hur*, his epic novel, while dealing with Bonney and the Lincoln County War. Bonney had promised to shoot Wallace, and the governor was writing his novel with the window shades pulled down in the governor's mansion.

That mansion, correctly called the Palace of the Governors, provided my own "One of Our Fifty Is Missing" incident. The tour bus showing Philadelphia to a bunch of New Mexicans passed one of its many famous historical sites. We were told that the one to our right was "the oldest public building in continuous use in the United States." Our tutor had just said that William Penn had arrived here with his grant from England's King Charles II to found the town in 1682, which she obviously considered early. However, King Philip of Spain had authorized "The City of the Holy Faith of Saint Francis of Assisi" in 1610, and the Palace of the Governors has been in continuous use since then. Why do I mention this? Because the New Mexico tourists did some winking and grinning, but no one wanted to issue the correction.

Our secret remained safe. New Mexico is still missing.

NEW YORK
(NEW YORK CITY)
SEEING THROUGH THE RUINS

Marshall Berman

Why, when things are broken, do they always seem
like more than when they're together?
—Thomas Berger, *Crazy in Berlin*

New York City is vulnerable. To anyone who lived through the attacks of September 11, 2001, the city's vulnerability is so obvious, it seems silly to mention it. But it wasn't obvious to my generation, the kids who grew up in New York after "The Good War." We took it for granted that *we* were vulnerable, but we couldn't imagine that *the city* could be vulnerable, too. That was something we had to learn, and we learned it, at least I think we learned it, in the last third of the last century.

I began to see the city's vulnerability in the late 1960s, when I came back here in 1967 after several years away. My neighborhood was the Upper West Side, and somehow I hadn't heard about the heroin epidemic that was tearing up Broadway. The gutters were full of syringes; on the sidewalks, the living casualties lurched at you, though more often they crumbled into themselves. Exploding with need, they got crazily violent. I had seen plenty of violence already, growing up in the Bronx in the *West Side Story* years, and I had been mugged and robbed and knocked around. But that was stuff teenagers did to each other; the Fordham Baldies and the Savage Skulls had mostly left adults alone. Late-1960s urban violence had no structure, apart from the junkie's one endless need, and no limits. A woman in my building left her key in the front door, and there were two brutal robberies within ten minutes. As it happened, the guy was frothing at the mouth and carrying too much stuff to outrun the cops, but they told us there was no way that catching this guy would stop the next one. The point was, the city was full of people running around out of control. There were defenses that all of us needed to learn fast. As a lifelong New Yorker, I was pretty blasé; I couldn't believe there was anything significant about city life that I didn't already know. I found out I was wrong.

It took years to learn how to defend against the next catastrophe: fires. The fires burst out mainly in poor minority neighborhoods all over town, but ethnically and economically mixed neighborhoods like the West Side were afflicted as well. For years, midnight fires ate up not only buildings but whole blocks, often block after block. Then we found out that, even as big parts of the city were burning down, their firehouses were being closed. In fact, all over the city, a collapse of public services was going on. This turned out to be one of the signs of the city's developing "fiscal crisis," which led New York to the edge of bankruptcy. After a year-long cliffhang, federal loans helped the city meet its payrolls, and the new Emergency Financial Control Board (EFCB) balanced the budget and got the city back into the credit markets. But the cost was crippling layoffs and draconian service cuts. Hundreds of thousands of people lost jobs, homes, pensions. Year after year, streets, subways, bridges, public buildings broke and did not get fixed.

One of the EFCB's commissioners confessed that they had balanced the budget "on the backs of the poor." But somehow they got the poor to trust them, to see them as beleaguered honest citizens rather than crooks and hacks of class war. In the poorest neighborhoods more than anywhere, people flaunted T-shirts that proclaimed I ♥ NY.

As the 1970s ended, there was a sense of relief in the air, a feeling that the city was recovering at last. Ironically, the 1980s brought a whole new wave of disasters: masses of homeless people, spread out right there on the streets and in the subways, filling up every empty public space, and leading the city fathers to rack their brains to find ways to cut down public space; the AIDS epidemic, something completely different, nearly surreal, in the annals of sexual disease; and crack cocaine, the first killer drug to crack the mass market, lift violence to new heights, and jump-start the spiral of horrors all over again. Through all these happenings, dozens of ordinary nice neighborhoods, like the one I grew up in, metamorphosed into gigantic, twisted, grotesque ruins. Diverse populations brought up to lead pallid but peaceful lives found themselves engulfed in pathologies, ending in unending early death. The phone's ring late at night became a cry of dread.

Have I left anything out? I'm sure I've left out plenty, but this is a pretty good start. It was as if disintegration became not an absence, a lack of integration, but a presence, an active force, a new principle of integration. A very wide assortment of New Yorkers came to feel like characters in *King Lear*: the feeling that life had grown so bad, it couldn't be worse, was a guarantee that "this is not the worst," and that down the road, whether or not there still was a road, life *would* get worse. And yet, and yet, even as this protracted horror show destroyed the city, somehow it energized its citizens; the force that killed New Yorkers made them more alive. As things got worse, more energy was focused on just trying to survive the day and the night; much of the thrill of being here now came to be *Look! We have come through!*

It wasn't like that when I was a kid. Not that there wasn't plenty of conflict and struggle, but it had a different form. When I was growing up in the Bronx fifty years ago, after the good war, at the start of the cold war, it looked like the basic human conflict was between the magnificent buildings downtown and a lot of yearning, desiring, imagining, questing selves, across some bridge or tunnel, so near but yet so far. I had only a vague idea of what went on inside ("business"?), but the buildings and the skyline seemed magical and eternal, and the greatest bliss I could imagine was to make it there (my grandmother asked, what was this crude English, "make it"?), and to be recognized by other people as a man who had made it. I grew up on New York film noirs, though it wasn't till I was a grown-up that I saw that this was a particular sort of movie with its own special history, rather than, as I had at first believed, simple reality. For a time my primal fantasy was like the first scene of *Force of Evil*, where John Garfield swaggers into a skyscraper lobby, and takes the elevator to the top; as he moves, he startles a carful of people who look like they were born at the top. However, anybody could see just from the big buildings' shapes that very few people would ever reach the top, and even fewer would last long up there. It didn't seem so hard to figure out the way things were. The great mass of us would never get anywhere near the towers; or if we did, we wouldn't be allowed inside; or, if we ever did get in, whatever thrills we might get, whatever we might give, we could count on getting kicked out before we were ready to go. I knew that was the tragedy of New York, long before I knew the word.

That story was what I heard when I heard them tell Willy Loman he didn't belong on the elevator; and when I saw the Jewish and black boys on CCNY's basketball "dream team," national champions once and nearly twice, disgraced for shaving points—I felt those kids were being set up, but how could they have caved in? Hadn't they seen *Force of Evil* or *Body and Soul*? And when my father got caught up in the garment center's wheels within wheels, and he suddenly died; and when my hero John Garfield himself, soon after starring in *Force of Evil,* got thrown down from the top of the movie business and crushed by the cultural cold war. Was all this the same old story, the normal working of "the system"? I swore I would spend my life working for a better story, and for a better system. (I'm still working.) But I couldn't stop loving those cloud-capped towers and that metropolis. There were real reasons to be mad and to demand a better world. But the radiance of downtown and the luminosity of the towers were real, too, and a better world would open up the thrill of "making it" to everyone.

When I came back in 1967, I came as an assistant professor at CCNY. I had dreamed for years of a job in this place. I imagined myself as a sort of late addition to Nat Holman's "dream team," using my mind's power to recoup CCNY's honor, and my father's, and John Garfield's, and New York's, and searching for a way for us to fling our brilliance and our soulfulness in America's face. But I was swamped, my late-1960s self was swamped, by an array of troubles I hadn't foreseen. I was attuned to an unending struggle between people who were soft and vulnerable and a city that was grand but hard and implacable. I was a veteran of this struggle, and pretty sure I could prepare students to wage it on their own. What I wasn't prepared for, but had to learn fast, was the precariousness and vulnerability of the city itself.

The spring of my first year at CCNY, soon after Martin Luther King was killed, buildings around the college started burning down. At first it was only a few, on the side streets between Amsterdam and Broadway, where I liked to walk on sunny days on my way home from school. The first fires were small, just an apartment or an upper floor, or one side of a building at a time. Streets that were jammed, with boys playing ball and girls jumping rope and hopscotch, mothers with babies, old men at cards or dominoes, began to thin out. Kids I'd met as part of stickball teams became solitaries throwing rubber balls against walls—and now, suddenly, there were lots of unattended walls and empty lots, great playspaces but hardly any players. When I came back to school in the fall, several densely packed rows of houses were gone, streets suddenly bathed in sunlight. It was ghastly, over the next couple of years, to see crowded streets thin out and noisy ones quiet down. Some of the same people were still there, but the kids, even as they grew, grew paler: were they more undernourished, or just more worried? Sometimes I would try to engage people in conversation. I'd ask, "What happened?" People would point all around and say, "The fires, the fires," and shake their hands to signify they couldn't understand.

Where did people go? Often to nearby housing projects, to double up with family or friends. Without the projects, the neighborhood would have been totally destroyed. It was only thanks to these projects, opened in the early 1960s, that it was continuing to exist at all. And the change in Washington, from the Johnson to the Nixon presidency, marked a great shift in urban policy that made it pretty clear that cities wouldn't be getting any more money to build housing for people like the people who were being burnt out. When I tried to talk with people at CCNY about this, no one knew what to say. Until well into the 1970s, the mass media weren't yet saying anything. I myself didn't know what to say, except "My God!"

If buildings around CCNY were crashing down around me, many of my kids inside were crashing from within. City College used to have a beautiful campus, the South Campus, an old nineteenth-century convent with redbrick buildings and a bell tower nestled in lovely groves of trees. Just when I arrived, the college administration was trying to tear down one of those groves to build a parking lot. (Our college president: "The issue is not trees. The issue is order." That was how authorities talked in 1967.) Kids saw the equipment rolling in, left their classes, and sat down in front of the bulldozers. I joined a faculty group in their defense. I felt instantly at home with these kids, most of them just a couple of years younger than me, mostly Jewish boys and girls from scruffy Bronx and Brooklyn neighborhoods like my own. They hung out in the South Campus Cafeteria, one of the most magical spaces I've ever been in. (It gets a nice plug in an early Woody Allen film.) The cafeteria kids were wiseguys, but serious. Their parents had been and often still were leftists of various sorts, and they felt radical activity as a family obligation. But they went further than their parents in experimenting with themselves. They had a way of talking about their lives, I remember I called it radical innocence: they would try something wild; if it didn't work out, next time they'd try something else. As they sat with their feet on the tables or stood on food lines or worked on their homework (sometimes it was homework for me), they concocted hilarious black-comic riffs about their bad trips, beatings (wanna see my scars?), abortions, suicide attempts. Lenny Bruce, Richard Pryor, Lily Tomlin, would have been at home here. Everybody loved "Howl":

> I saw the best minds of my generation destroyed by madness,
>   starving hysterical naked,
> dragging themselves through the negro streets at dawn looking for
>   an angry fix . . . .

I loved "Howl" myself. But I knew that Allen Ginsberg had developed a powerful sense of self *before* he began his experiments on himself. So had I, I realized: if I dug sex and drugs and rock and roll, it was for the sake of happiness, for the satisfaction of a self I already knew. But many of the cafeteria kids were somewhere else: they leaped into crazy love, into deadly drugs—remember, this was heroin's heyday—into bizarre religious and political cults that crushed their members' selves, at a point in their lives when their selves weren't yet defined, and they were helpless to resist. One boy wrote a paper on *Easy Rider* for me: he said he and his friends were committed "to go as far as we can go." The trouble was, most of them didn't yet have the inner ballast to keep them on the road. I said they "weren't ready"; I said, they were "too young"—and in the instant I said it, I felt myself, barely out of my twenties, *geworfen* into middle age. By 1971 or so, I, too, was seeing some of the best minds of my generation destroyed by madness: kids I had known as smart, sweet, radical acid-heads only yesterday had morphed into filthy, angry junkies panhandling on St. Mark's Place today; others were scuffling "underground" on the mall on upper Broadway, or deep in the bowels of Bellevue, or dead. I couldn't stand it; I became prematurely mature, a kind of hippie square, saying things I never dreamed I'd say, things like *Stop! Don't do it! Get out! Get clean! Go home!* Eventually, after much *tsuris*, many of these kids came out the other end, and became distinguished citizens; a couple are my friends today. But I still miss that brilliant lost generation of would-be Philippe Petits, so brave as they scaled the towers without stopping to learn to climb, without even knowing for sure which way was down.

As the 1970s unfolded, it turned out that the troubles I had seen in and around CCNY were just tips of titanic icebergs. Gradually I learned what deep trouble New York was in. It was caught up in a long wave of what economists came to call Deindustrialization. In the late 1960s and early 1970s, deindustrial progress destroyed millions of manufacturing jobs, hundreds of thousands of them in New York, mostly connected with the garment industry. People working themselves to death morphed into people dying for work. The towers downtown still offered plenty of work for *other* people, hypothetical people with education and (increasingly) computer skills, but the ground was cut out from under many of the real people who were here. New York's workforce in the 1970s needed federal help more desperately than it had at any time since the Depression, but at just this Nixonian moment, federal help dried up and disappeared.

In the 1970s and 1980s, New York's greatest spectacles were its ruins. Gradually it emerged how they had come to be. All around the town, landlords of old buildings were having more trouble than ever with tenants who were ever more unemployed. Meanwhile, as many old, shabby buildings began to cave in, they found themselves redlined by banks—"redline," a crucial word in the self-awareness of the 1970s—so that, if they were located on the wrong side of the line, they couldn't get loans to fix up the buildings. Somewhere along the line they came to believe that their buildings were worth more dead than alive. The result was a tremendous, protracted boom in arson, with much destruction of life. All through the 1970s, it happened simultaneously in dozens of neighborhoods. But the biggest explosion was in the

South Bronx, not far from where I grew up. At the start of the 1980s I was finishing a book on what it means to be modern, but I felt I couldn't finish until I had gone back to where I came from. So I went back—the building I grew up in was still there and still lived in, but the whole block across the street had burned and crumbled into ruins, and then started to sink into the swamp that the whole neighborhood was built on. In 1979, 1980, 1981, I spent many lonely afternoons wandering through the Bronx's ruins. Some of the wanderers I met came from countries that not so long ago had had formidable ruins of their own. I met a couple of young architects from Glasgow, searching for a site for a submerged plaza with a giant monumental column to be built out of rubble. Their drawings were beautiful, but as they said, if there were any chance of their structure being built, there would be no need for it to be built. (Looking back, I can see how their vision prefigured some of the recent brilliant ideas for Ground Zero.) I met a German art critic who told me that when her friends came to visit, they were totally indifferent to the sights she loved in New York, but implored her, "Where is the South Bronx? Take me to the burning buildings. I want a lover from the ruins."

We couldn't believe the enormity of these ruins. They went on and on, for block after block, mile after mile. Some blocks seemed almost intact; but look around the corner, and there was no corner. It was uncanny! I remembered, from college, the Enlightenment aesthetics of "the Sublime"—Shaftesbury, Piranesi, Hubert Robert, Burke, Kant, Schiller, et al.—the kind of beauty that springs from extreme contrasts and evokes horror and dread. Would some architectural or aesthetic society give the Bronx a gold medal for sublimity? The uncanniest part, I thought, was the people who were still there, painting their houses, taking their kids to school, fixing their cars on the street—at least, one man told me, they didn't have to worry about parking spaces anymore—not screaming or foaming at the mouth, as I was sure I would have done, but talking straight and being nice to strangers and working hard to keep life together.

The fire years created a whole new vocabulary and iconography. As all survivors of 9/11 know, urban ruins make great visuals. There were years of tabloid headlines, magazine covers, TV documentaries in many languages entitled something like THE BRONX IS BURNING! A new urban picturesque emerged out of horizons lit by lurid flames, montages of buildings in different stages of disintegration, shards of beds, tables, TV sets, debris of real people's lives that might have been our own. For many years the *Times* carried a box, always on page 2 or 3 of the Metro Section, that listed "Buildings Destroyed" the previous day or night. (I and many people I knew always turned to this box first, even before the baseball scores: was "our" old building still there?) In October 1976, during the World Series, cameramen working from the Goodyear Blimp got a view from above that showed the Yankee Stadium at one end of the frame, and flames from a burning building at the other. Announcer Howard Cosell exploded with rage, and thundered: "What's wrong with those people? Why are they doing this to themselves?" Cosell, a native of Newark, should have known better. Blaming the victims became the cliché, repeated endlessly on the news. The saddest part, I thought, was when the victims—who themselves depended on TV for their news—bought the cliché and blamed themselves. Thus, for years, any day or night, on the local news, you could see a tattered family in tears in front of their smoking building, gathering the few possessions not burned up, and asking, like Job, "What did we do wrong?" The man with the mike would say, with great solemnity, "We don't know, Mr. Vargas, we just don't know."

The real ravaging of the Bronx had begun back in the 1950s, when Robert Moses drilled his Cross-Bronx Expressway right through its center, destroying some of the most crowded (but intact) neighborhoods in the city, displacing thousands of people from their homes. The CBE was (and still is) a wound in the Bronx's heart, but it made the Bronx very easy to get out of.

Many thousands moved along the highway's route, to the suburbs of Long Island, New Jersey, Westchester, but commuted to the city by car every day. The Bronx borough president developed a lingering sympathy for these commuters. Why, he asked, should they have to look at ruins? (He didn't add that the Bronx's ruins might be gravestones of their own earlier lives.) His office ordered painted decals, of different shapes and sizes, which portrayed a Potemkin Village of pastoral urban scenes on top of the shattered windows and facades. Alas, when these scenes were displayed at life size, they resembled the graphics in *Fun with Dick and Jane*, and the commuters were not amused. Meanwhile, some guerrilla graffitists scaled the ruined facades, and painted over the decals with messages like "This is a Lie," "This is a Fraud," and "This is a Ruin." People cracked jokes about "the borough president's new clothes," which took on new resonance a couple of years later when he went to prison for bribery. It was nice to see that life in the Bronx, impoverished in so many ways, was rich in irony.

How would respectable society deal with the ruins? In the early 1960s, when poor city neighborhoods started getting wrecked, news reports often portrayed residents saying that now the rulers of America would have to rebuild the slums in a better way. By the end of the decade, it was clear what a delusion—what a touching delusion— this had been. Late in the 1960s, the RAND Corporation, the Defense Department's research center, opened up an urban subsidiary. In the early Nixon years, governments at every level were cutting social services, but all of them were uneasy about charges of racism. It then became an intellectual problem to find a formula for service cuts that didn't look blatantly racist. RAND's idea was to base all service policy on gains or losses in population. In neighborhoods that were losing people, cities would have a supposedly color-blind way to cut. In neighborhoods losing lots of people, the cuts could be wholesale. The Bronx seems to have been one place this formula was tested: in the years the South Bronx was burning down, and people were fleeing the fires, the Bronx lost a third of its fire services. *Touché!*

This sounds outrageous now. But it was peanuts compared with the one really grand idea that emerged from the Bronx's ruins: Roger Starr's "Planned Shrinkage." At different times, Starr was New York's housing commissioner and the *Times'* main editorial writer on urban affairs. His 1976 plan, quoted below from a *Times* front-page story, has the ring of a directive from General Waste-more-land in Vietnam. In neighborhoods certified bad, Starr said, the city should cut all transportation links, turn off the water and electricity, make daily life literally impossible, and move people out. He explained:

> We should . . . stop the rural Puerto Ricans and blacks from living in the city . . . [and] reverse the role of the city. . . . It can no longer be the place of opportunity. . . . Our urban system is based on the theory of taking the peasant and turning him into an industrial worker. Now there are no industrial jobs. Why not keep him a peasant?

The *Times* covered this, but pointedly did not endorse it. It was so *blatant!* Many readers simply recoiled in horror. Others, perhaps more sophisticated, concluded that it must mean more than meets the eye: maybe Starr was writing a kind of neo-Swift "modest proposal" that was meant as a reductio ad absurdum of social planning? To be read this way was an ironic fate for a writer who always declared his hatred for irony. In any case, the "Planned Shrinkage" scandal closed the books on bureaucratic plans for wholesale population transfer. The meaner sectors of the ruling class may even have profited from the affair: they learned there were plenty of ways to insult and injure the poor, without actually getting rid of them.

I've been talking about the Bronx so much not only because of my childhood and its enduring charm, but because its misfortunes exploded shortly before the crisis of New York as a whole. Observers of the Bronx's troubles, including many New Yorkers, developed an elaborate vocabulary of deflection and denial that very soon would be used against New York itself. "What's wrong with these people? Why are they doing this to themselves?" Magic words like these transform victims of misery and misfortune into perverse perpetrators of malice. Social scientists got millions of dollars in grants, from foundations and federal agencies, to explore the character defects of poor people from the Bronx that led them—here was another dehumanizing cliché of those days—"to foul their own nest." No one found an answer, maybe because there's really no way to imagine hundreds of thousands of people burning down their homes and getting themselves and their children killed. The mayor's Arson Task Force, probably New York's most thoroughly New Left government agency, and an unlikely ally, the insurance industry, proposed to change the questions, and to shift focus from the tenants to the landlords. The giant insurance companies, which had bought up Bronx insurance pools in the pastoral early 1960s, suffered enormous losses there in the 1970s. Lloyd's of London alone was said to have lost sixty million pounds. Finally, in the early 1980s, the big companies resolved together to stop paying claims on tenement fires. All at once, as if by magic, tenement fires ceased. In the last year of payoffs, the Bronx lost about 1,300 buildings to fire. In the first year without payoffs, it lost 12. In the second year, it lost 3. Isn't it nice when, as happens every now and then, very complex human questions have very simple answers? And when the answers keep poor people in their homes, not put out in the street?

The defamation of the Bronx helped to create a language for the much more extensive and profound defamation of New York. As the city's finances plummeted and its credit evaporated, it began to seem at least possible that it could go bankrupt. I, and most people I knew, found this scary. If the city's whole existence were in the hands of a judge or panel of judges in bankruptcy court, responsible to no one, who knew what might happen? They could simply dissolve any of the city's public institutions and auction off or redistribute any of its assets.

Some people with whom I had recently gotten arrested, over Vietnam, said New York should take a chance and go bankrupt voluntarily. After all, life was so bad already, how much worse could it get? I felt depressed that my friends didn't realize how much worse life could get.

When the crisis was very acute, I had a dream, and I've had it again with minor variations through the years. It's laid out like a television news spot in which "the Colonel," a southern congressman, is asking the folks in his district what they think about bailing out New York. While the dream story is going on, a voice-over says, "THIS EVENT REALLY HAPPENED." The story has a distinctive "look": it resembles those 1930s or 1940s films, mostly by Warner's, about political murder and menace in the South. "The Colonel" wears a white suit and a sombrero, has a big belly and beady eyes, long white hair and elaborate mustaches, and sounds like Fred Allen's Senator Claghorn. He gives a long speech about "Jew York's—I mean New York's" depravity. Then "the Colonel" says, "So what I want to know, I want you folks to tell me, about New York, about that city, way up there, Should it live or should it die?" As he asks, he smiles (in closeup) in an insinuating way. Now the voice-over cuts in, and notes that although the event really happened, it is a "pseudo-event," *not* real, in that the people have probably been choreographed, rehearsed, and paid off. They jump to their feet, grin obscenely at each other like crowd members in a lynch-mob photo, then they clench their fists, bulge out their eyes, and shout in unison: "DIE! DIE! DIE! DIE! DIE!" I know it's (probably) not real, but still I'm terrified, and I wake up screaming.

A number of bailout plans gradually materialized, establishing something like the EFCB, enabling the city to borrow enough money to pay its bills, at outrageous interest rates, with federal guarantees. But many commentators and politicians said the plans weren't punitive enough; they aimed to restore New York to some sort of normal life, rather than destroy its capacity for life. For a year or more, it was hard to pick up the paper or turn on the TV without hearing those menacing notes: "New York has lived a sinful life, shouldn't it be made to pay for its sins?" or maybe "New York is a dirty, noisy, smelly, nasty, degenerate place, a blot on America, and now America has the power to sweep it up and throw it down the drain once and for all." Just like the voices in my head! So it went.

The climax of these anathemas was the FORD TO CITY: DROP DEAD speech. In this speech, the president said he was going to veto any congressional bill to bail out New York, because he didn't see how the fate of New York was of any concern to the American people. I heard the speech on a cab radio, coming home from the airport; I remember how Ford's combination of ponderous awkwardness and blasé insensitivity blew my mind. The West Indian driver and I traded obscenities—his were fresher, I thought—but after we'd cursed Ford out, we both felt listless and depressed. My heart leapt when I saw the *Daily News* front page next day, FORD TO CITY: DROP DEAD. I thought, This is why New York exists: to tell the truth like a wiseguy. And I thought, Whatever those creeps do to us, at least we won't go quietly. Next day's front page featured Mayor Abe Beame in front of City Hall, looking both wounded and defiant, displaying the page to the world. Ironically, FORD TO CITY was not only a great headline, but a superb consciousness-raiser. It helped people everywhere see how New York could be both magnificent and precarious, both a great beast of Babylon and an endangered species. And it helped the city get the help it needed.

I never really doubted it. I figured the Babbitts in the GOP could never beat the billionaires; the billionaires might be greedy, but they weren't stupid; they could be counted on to grasp how all markets were integrated, and how the act of crushing the biggest city in the country could bring down the whole national economy, including trillions of dollars of their own investment capital. These guys were the money center of the GOP, as well as of the world; I was sure that in their normal backroom way they'd get the word to the White House, and when they did the White House would cave. I did my best to help my students see this and maybe relax a little. But emotionally I was racked with pain and helpless rage. I hadn't much respect for the people who hated New York, and who I knew would hate me if they knew me; still, it hurt to be hated. I knew that, till this blew over, we would have to sit still—like, not spit in their faces—while the creeps in Congress and the media swaggered around and told us how it served us right to suffer, and how their innate purity and virtue were polluted by the pack of grubby mongrels and sex maniacs and dope fiends and un-Americans who were us. And I knew something else, which I'd learned when I'd done that ultra–New York thing, gone into therapy: I learned that the punitive sadists who ran down New York and people like me were not just "out there," in the White House and in the world, but in my head as well, a persistent part of me, and that I was going to have to learn not only to get through their assaults, but to confront my own inner police and to learn to bail out myself.

I wanted so much to bring those corrupt Captain Americas down! But I knew for our city's sake we had to lay low and resist not evil with evil, at least for awhile. Still, I thought, maybe, like the great anonymous *News* headline writer, we could find our own ways to say DROP DEAD. If I look back on myself as a writer, I see that, in the year or two of the fiscal crisis, I wrote the two angriest pieces I've ever written in my life. Both were attacks on titanic figures, one I hated (Robert Moses), one I loved (Erik Erikson). Both these guys were Jews who built ultra-American heroic careers on denials of their Jewishness. Both articles explode off the page with an energy I wish I could sustain today. Now don't get me wrong, I don't want to take back anything I wrote thirty years ago; but *oy*, I was so *nasty*! My mother's voice: When you know you're right, you don't have to be nasty. Really? . . . I don't know mum. . . . But maybe I wouldn't have felt a need for such heavy artillery if I hadn't felt like a citizen of a city under heavy siege.

Meanwhile, inside the walls, the city's high school and college kids—some of my CCNY kids with them—were going through an outburst of creative energy, and inventing a whole new thing, a thing called hip-hop. Today, hip-hop is the basic idiom of American popular culture. But twenty years ago no one could tell how long it would go on, or whether it would be seen or heard or noticed by anybody out of town. Its most distinctive expressions were rap music, break dancing, and graffiti painting. The vortex where all these activities converged and whirled together was the subway. Now it is vital to know that the New York subway system in the 1970s was in a state of extreme decay, probably drearier and scarier than at any time in its history. It perfectly embodied the cliché of the modern city as "a grind." This was the point where a generation of kids began. They filled its grim cars with dazzling color, and its gray spaces with musical structure, dancer's grace, wiseguy irreverence, and life stories—remember, this is rap's primal identity, a medium for life stories—and a sense of exuberance and adventure. I was delighted; I felt hip-hop gave New York just the kind of energy we needed to survive the crap that was being dumped on us.

However, there were plenty of New Yorkers who not only couldn't identify with hip-hop in any way at all, but who felt that its graffiti, rap, and dance were themselves the crap that was being dumped on us. It wasn't just that they didn't like it: they foamed at the mouth. Try to imagine a college or university soirée, with people who had got through the 1960s with their minds more or less intact. Conversation would flow, and I would remark that I liked some rap or piece of graffiti art; or maybe I would say something to distinguish some from others. Suddenly traffic would stop, and middle-aged deans and professors would start to curse like drunken sailors, or shriek like the Duchess in *Alice in Wonderland*. Once I even heard a famous sociologist, a lifelong liberal cold warrior, say he envied the USSR, because it had no public defenders or Bill of Rights, and the state could just grab kids like these off the streets and throw them into labor camps *en bloc.*

Twenty years later, I still don't get it: What drove these defenders of civilized moderation into barbaric frenzy? What made people I knew and trusted in real life metamorphose into shadowy menacing figures from my dreams? It was a moment when thousands of our poor and minority kids, instead of blowing their lives standing on street corners, harassing people and getting high, had become reflective and active and disciplined and were actually *doing* something. Why couldn't more grownups get the message? Maybe this was another symptom of civic collapse: so many people with good heads seemed to lose their heads.

> Don't push me 'cause I'm close to the edge,
> Trying not to lose my head. *Hah!*
>
> It's like a jungle sometimes
> It makes me wonder
> How I keep from going under. (*Huhh huh huh huhh*)

This was the choral refrain of "The Message," by Grandmaster Flash and the Furious Five, the first international rap hit, released in 1982. The album cover is set on a South Bronx (or maybe South Bronxesque) corner, the kind of place that you can see was claustrophobically dense just yesterday, and that is weirdly empty today. Their image evokes the Persuasions' late-1960s album, *Street Corner Society*, except that, after years of disintegration, the corner has no street. "The Message" is an instant classic of urban realism, linked in spiritual pathos to older classics like *Maggie: A Girl of the Streets* and *Call It Sleep*. The narrative is a guided tour of the neighborhood-as-horror-show. It features junkies, pushers, whores, pimps, hit men, all sweet homeboys and homegirls just a little while ago. At the end, the survivors are taken away by the cops; only the beat goes on. The rapper, Mellie Mel, confronts a dear friend, now a handsome corpse: How could he get himself killed? "You lived so fast and died so young." He is increasingly desperate to understand: is there any way his friends could have kept from "going under"?

Is there any way *he* can keep from going under? New Yorkers (like the rappers themselves) may see a subtext of civic allegory in his question: is there any way *the city* can keep from going under? The prospects look bleak. And yet, and yet, the rapper can't help but see:

> They pushed a girl in front of a train,
> Took her to a doctor, sewed her arm on again.
> Stabbed a man right through the heart,
> Gave him a transplant and a brand new start.

(The voice-over might say: "These events really happened." I remember them; I even remember the names.) Here's the message: sometimes, somehow—we don't know how, but somehow—it's possible to emerge from the vortex of horror and violence with "a brand new start"! You can come from ruins, yet not yourself be ruined. You can get close to the edge, but then get back to the center. Social disintegration and existential desperation can be sources of life and creative energy. A city can collapse, and yet can get "a brand new start." Our first hit rappers know something that Hegel said modern men and women had to learn: they know how to "look the negative in the face and live with it." They have looked the ruins in the face, and they have lived with them, and they have come through. Now they can see and feel their way to new life.

I can remember when I first heard "The Message" blaring from a West Harlem record shop, in the Reagan summer of 1982. Right away I was thrilled. It wasn't so long ago that I'd lost a kid (*Marc Berman, 1975–1980*); I'd been pretty low. Was I moving my limbs again? Now these kids from the city's most horrendous ruins had created a masterpiece that looked the negative in the face and lived with it, and still dreamed of coming through. I thought, if they could dream this, then damn it, we were going to come through. I knew New York still had plenty of sorrow ahead. There were homeless families all over the streets and in the subways. A dear friend of mine had just died of AIDS—and I don't think it had even been named AIDS. (I know I can look up the name date; forgive me if I don't.) I couldn't even conceive of crack, our late-1980s twist of fate. But I knew our *via dolorosa* had a long way to run. Still, of all the forms of suffering, I thought, the worst is where your imagination shuts down. Once you can imagine getting out of the hole you're in, even if you can't imagine how, the worst is past.

I was starting to notice things. I read that New York's population, after dropping sharply for a decade, was growing again. Once more, new immigrants were coming. Many were said to be squatting in the ruins. Was I ready to go up to the Bronx again and look around? In other recent ruins, people had cleared away the rubble, planted lovely gardens, created plazas and amphitheaters, reinvented ancient Greece and Latin America, or else turned disasters into new fusions of the country with the city. (And yet, before I knew it, many of these ruins would be "real estate" again: Mayor Giuliani would put them up for sale to developers; Bette Midler would protect them from the market by exploiting her market power, buying up millions of dollars worth of gardens and turning them over to a public trust. The mayor called it Subversive Marxism.) All around the town, people from I didn't know where were selling foods I'd never seen from carts and trucks on the street—did I dare to try some? I'd gone to some Mets games, and I was getting to know the Number 7, which ran from Times Square to Shea Stadium and Main Street Flushing. The 7 offered an amazing feeling of connecting to the whole world, a different country or continent opening out at every stop, with breathtaking visions of the skyline bringing it all together. I wondered how I had missed this train all my life; wasn't it there all along? That summer, too, for the first time ever, the subways had air conditioning that worked, and rubber wheels that made it quiet, so you could have a real conversation in a moving car. If New Yorkers could talk, who knew what else might happen? When I heard "The Message," I felt it was post-collapse New York's way of saying "We Shall Overcome," and I believed, Yes, we can, we will.

New York
(Long Island)
The Fish-Shaped Riddle

Tom Gogola

I t was the first day of the flounder season and I was fishing on a Montauk party boat, in the early spring of 1996. I dropped my bait among strangers in the stern as we drifted across Montauk Harbor in a stiff northwest breeze. After a while I started talking to a late-middle-aged black man about surf-fishing along the south shore of western Long Island—he had apparently been a pioneer of some sort—and then he pointed out a young man in a clamming skiff, a hundred-odd yards off our port side, raking the mud in the cold March morning. As it turned out, he was the man's son; before long, the captain started talking about clamming, and then we all whistled with respect and joked about the tough lot of the commercial fisherman. My new acquaintance Percy lived in Montauk full-time now but told me that he had rented here for many years before finally being *allowed* to buy a house in the isolated village, located at the furth'st-flung end of Long Island's southern fork. Into the 1970s, the "golden rule" of Montauk was that you didn't sell to blacks, but eventually, he explained, "the only color that mattered was *green*."

On the way in, we sipped strong coffee and talked about music. As it turned out, Percy was Percy Heath, pioneering bassist for the Modern Jazz Quartet.

Unfortunately, there's nothing unusual about the practice of racial "steering" in Long Island, whose suburbs are the most segregated in the United States. Take note: *in* Long Island—Nassau and Suffolk counties only. Therein lies the source of the island's confused provinciality, the wellspring from which much of its awkward identity is carved: you can be *on* Long Island but not necessarily *in* it. Paumonok (its Algonquin name, and what Walt Whitman called it) is indeed a fish-shaped riddle—an enigma wrapped in plastic siding.

The island tries, desperately at times, to define itself as separate from the great Gotham to the west, even as it shares geographic, not to mention dialectical, space with Kings and Queens counties. As the cramped pan-ethnic jumble of the city begins its block-by-block segue into the half-conscious dream of an idyll deep in the suburban remove, at a few key asphalt seams around the Queens–Nassau border (the Cross-Island Expressway being the most evident), a culture of shallow yet obstinate individualism takes hold. The insular Irish-Catholic enclave of Floral Park in Nassau couldn't be any more different from the international frenzy of Flushing, Queens—yet they are mere miles apart. The problem for the island is that New York City is as different from it as it is different from the rest of the country—except that in this case, you can't escape it. The jobs are in the city, the culture is in the city, the terrorists are in the city.

And so, the island has adopted a pigheaded posture in relation to the city, organizing itself for maximum deniability—we are not them. From a tactical perspective, the infrastructure itself makes for excellent color separation—the Long Island Expressway, the railroad lines, the scores of north-south routes, the strategically located strip malls play a key role in delineating the multitudinous borders within which the various shades have been arranged: blacks to Brentwood, browns to Central Islip, whites to Selden, and so on.

Still, the old "sameness of sprawl" myth endures among ill-informed urban sophisticates, as does the media-fueled notion that this low-slung heap of variegated glacial deposit is a silly, greedy, hopeless place—the women are a bunch of vain, whiny, gum-snapping dingbat shopaholics bloated on K-Mart merch; the men are vain, antic, goombah hammerheads bloated on Big Gulps from yon 7-11 (there's one in every driveway, it seems). In truth, only some islanders are like that—a plurality, at best.

Nevertheless, it's a place where, sadly, breast cancer and Lyme disease are practically rites of passage, where a numbing parade of bunkerlike blocks of U-Store-It facilities blend into equally long racks of flimsy condos, which blend in turn into your classic pizza-videodrugstoredelicardshophairsalon strip malls. Affordable housing is an oxymoron, the groundwater is going kaput, xenophobia is rampant, and overdevelopment even more so, the Hamptons are doomed, the drive-ins are all gone, road rage rules, Hempstead is the new Harlem, they're naming a federal courthouse after Alphonse D'Amato (!), they're freaking out about gangs (Bloods especially) yet the hometown Pagans motorcycle gang rarely engenders the same fear and loathing, and the idiotic "wiggers" of the "Strong Island" movement faded out a few years ago.

Property taxes are consistently the highest in the nation; about a billion dollars is raised annually, and *for what*? You can't hang a clothesline in Southampton for putatively aesthetic reasons, and your house can't have two front doors in some Nassau villages, the mother-daughter, rooming-house implications being too "city" for the self-identified sleepytown hicks from Hicksville to bear. And what kind of place is this where they name beaches for Robert Moses and malls for Walt Whitman?

But *that's* not *even* the worst of it!

Have you ever heard the way many of them *tawk*? A couple of years ago I was seeing a woman, a blue-blooded Texas academic who, by her own admission, spoke with an accent whose linguistic locii fell somewhere between "a valley girl and a pig farmer" (for the record,

I found her breathy drawl to be irresistibly sexy). Anyway, we were on the LIRR heading east one afternoon, and a wave of classically big-haired island broads—oh, but they definitely qualified as *broads*—came rushing up the aisle, babbling excitedly about something or other as they worked their way through the car. Tex shot me a quizzical look and asked, "Why are they *talking like that?*" And this, from a woman who, besides the aforementioned accent, wasn't wearing her hearing aid that day!

Why, indeed? It may be a simple matter of overcompensation in the face of a whopping inferiority complex, itself grounded in a fear of everything that New York—a crime-ridden cesspool of moral degeneracy, after all—represents. And so, you get this weird tic of the tongue, passed down from generation to generation—an embarrassingly gloopy bastardization of classic Brooklynese. In a sense, the tautology runs that if you *tawk* too much like a *New Yawka*, then you might as well be in a gang. Gangs are filled with "animals" from the city, and this isn't the city, so stop *tawking* like you're in it, or else . . . you're an animal. And so, something soft and awful emerges—distinct to be sure: a grating, paint-peeling baby*tawk*.

Arguably, the most appalling example is the way the word "more" is often pronounced in Long Island. The *maw-wa* you hear, "I want *maw-wa* . . . give me *maw-wa* . . . I told *Mawk* [that would be 'Mark'] I'm not gonna see him no *maw-wa*," the easier it is to believe that the island is nothing more than the nation's vestigial organ: a useless, 125-mile-long appendix to the continental landmass, fluttering in the sea and poisoned to the popping point.

Ah, but poisoned with what? The Mexicans or the shopping malls?

One's perspective on that is the key to unlocking the riddle of *Lawnguyland*; in reality, gauging tolerance is a house-by-house endeavor, and the island isn't without its soft spot for the underdog, for the obvious reason that it is one. Besides, the highways can never conspire to keep the polyglot completely at bay, and, more to the point, the imperatives of the global economy have demands all their own.

In my hometown of Farmingville, located in the vast suburban blur of central Suffolk County, Mexican migrant workers now live fifteen to a house right down the street from the Gogola homestead; they trundle up Waverly Avenue to Horseblock Road each day to get picked up for day work; landscapers, farmers, and various tradesmen arrive and pile them into their pickups and head, generally, to points east. A few workers have been beaten up by the local goon squads, but most of the anti-Mexican animus is launched from self-appointed guardians of area real estate values. The most out-front of the anti-immigration lot calls itself Sachem Quality of Life, which uses the imprimatur of my high school alma mater—Sachem is one of the largest suburban school districts in the country, and histori-cally has been overwhelmingly white—to call for immediate INS blitzkriegs on the offendingly overcrowded households (lately also in the guise of "national security").

For the record, those property values have actually risen, on average, since the latest "invasion" began some ten years ago, and will continue to do so for all eternity—the market suffers from pri-apism: once it's up, it stays up. Once you dispense with that non-starter, and take into account that the Mexicans are, by and large, a Catholic, hard-working, family-oriented lot, and toil at jobs that no one else on the island *wants to do*, what's left of the anti-Mexican argu-ment? Oh, they're *brooding*? Wouldn't you brood, too?

"But they don't speak English."

And what language, exactly, is it that *you* are speaking, Mr. *Maw-wa*?

You do have to wonder what Long Island's patron pagan, Walt Whitman, would make of all this intolerance, how the infinite span of his diversified, songful embrace would bear up under the twenty-first-century island.

Not very well, is my guess. In Whitman's time, the island was rough, remote, agrarian, seafaring, rum-running, and wide open. It was an inspiring, and perhaps a mystical, place, and you didn't have to—though it was the quickest sure bet, as Whitman knew—take to the coastline to experience transcendent joy. Ol' Walt wasn't around to see the great postwar transformation that beset the island, when his famous "interlocking similitudes" would be tested by, among other transforming moments, Levittown and its disconnects. Even with the benefit of hindsight, it's hard to argue against providing housing for returning WWII vets—until you factor in the "golden rule" by which Levittown, like Montauk, abided: no blacks.

Hell, one could argue that the entire island—the *in* portion—lived by the golden rule at one time. The first few decades of the twentieth century saw a tradition of puritanic insularity, dating to the pre–Revolutionary War period, morph into something far more insidious: the xenophobes put on the robes. By the 1920s, *Newsday* reports, roughly one in eight Long Islanders was a member of the Ku Klux Klan—that's twenty-five-thousand hoods, probably more than all the Bloods, Pagans, and Strong Islanders added up (but who's counting?). By the 1930s, the prohibitionist, Protestant Klan was on the outs, only to be replaced by a fresh batch of haters, in the form of beer-swilling German-American Bundsmen.

It's incredible to think that there were, at one time, streets in Long Island named for infamous Nazis, Hitler included, but 'tis true. In the heyday of the mostly Catholic bund, thousands would regularly gather at Camp Siegfried, a community located on a small lake in the heart of the Yaphank pine barrens, to offer hearty *seig heils* to Hitler and his plans for a thousand-year Reich. Germany's invasion of Poland in 1939 spelled the end of the Siegfried colony, and while the subdivision still exists, Joseph Goebbels Street has since been renamed.

At least it can be said for the Siegfried neighborhood that it is one of the few places on Long Island where the woods surround the subdivision and not vice versa. For those of us who grew up in the vast, low-slung central subdivisions, without the ready benefit of an ineffable shoreline to inspire, identity formation begins with the particulars of one's own suburb, the inexact similitudes therein, especially as defined by the ever-shrinking interzones of flora-'n'-fauna separating one tract from the next. The interzones are key to understanding the suburban experience, since every kid who went to the end of the dead-end road and into the woods was not only laying the foundational elements of future nostalgia, but was, perhaps, planting the seeds of future discontent.

Of course, anyone who grew up in the suburbs is nostalgic about their own subdivision—drive through a neighborhood not your own and it can seem totally indistinct, menacingly bloodless, *Stepford Wives* territory—but even if you know all the stories behind all the doors and give voice to the torrent of memory that comes whenever you visit the old neighborhood, it's really the woods that get one to pining for the past: all the houses are still there, mutated though they may be by add-ons and strange landscaping schema, but the woods are probably gone.

Across the street from my house there was a town park that was mostly wooded, and it's still there; behind the park was a huge patch of interzone woods that was developed by the late eighties—those "backwoods" exist only in memory. There were all kinds of crazy-looking boulders and kettle holes back there, and my pals and I would make underground forts out of the latter feature—kettle holes are big round holes that were created when the receding Wisconsin Glacier would tear a boulder from the earth. We'd drag plywood over the four-thousand-year-old ditch and hunker down inside with candles, cadged provisions, and, naturally, porn; I can still smell the sassafras roots dangling from the walls of these preadolescent playhouses, and fondly recall ogling those unforgettable images in mid-seventies-era *Oui* magazine. *Leaves of Grass* didn't tempt me until many years later—after they'd paved my paradise and put up a cul-de-sac.

Fortunately, there is growing recognition among islanders that all this development might not be such a great idea, after all—despite the benefits it brings for the legions of tradesmen who live and work here. Circumstances have dictated that the interconnected issues of affordable housing and the environment must be tackled in new, creative ways. Thus, the principles, if not the practices, of "smart growth" have taken root (developing brownfields instead of potato fields, for example). Long Islanders, by and large, do not support the Earth First!–style tactics that have been deployed on several occasions—most notably when subdivisions have encroached on the pine barrens, under which lie the island's groundwater supply—but they will mobilize for candidates with solid pro-environment agendas, provided they're not too namby-pamby about it, provided they can see the dark humor in bumper stickers that read, PIPING PLOVER: TASTES LIKE CHICKEN. In the 2002 congressional midterms, Southampton College provost Tim Bishop eked out an extremely narrow victory against GOP incumbent Felix Grucci—one of only three races nationwide that year where a Republican congressman was unseated. The race was, to put it mildly, ugly, as Grucci tried to portray Bishop as a pro-rape, Osama-coddling menace; his tactics, fortunately, backfired—but only barely.

It was late in the summer of 2002 and I was working as a mate on a party boat out of Montauk that specializes in catching fluke, porgies, sea bass, and striped bass. We were out on a night bass fishing trip with about twenty anglers aboard, and the fishing was, as we say, "a pick." The fish weren't flying over the rails, but there were enough being caught to keep everyone focused. My job as first mate was to set the customers up with rods and reels, give fishing lessons where needed, untangle lines, offer encouragement, bait hooks for squeamish sorts (we used live eels for bait). When they'd hook into a bass, I'd gaff it for them, haul it into the boat, and give a hearty, oftentimes bloody handshake or backslap to the angler.

I had been working on the boat all summer, on both the day and night trips, and had come to love the work. Each day, the rails were filled with anglers from all over the tri-state region, a fair percentage of whom were vacationing families drawn from the place-names given by the thirteen Algonquin tribes of Long Island—Manhasset, Patchogue, Massapequa, and so on. We had them all: 9/11 firemen, cops, construction workers, unionists, stockbrokers, musicians, a bowling-alley manager, chefs, lawyers, layabouts, and on one unforgettable evening, a duo of hot bisexual Russian masseuses who offered to take me to Le Cirque 2000 sometime. Oh, Tatanya, where art thou?

The funny thing is, the more time I spent on the boat, the *maw-wa* my own Long Island accent reemerged—I stopped bothering to try and nip it in the bud—and the more I realized that there is plenty of succor among those soccer moms I'd come to scorn in my urban years. I had no problem with those friendly fellows from the trades, so long as they refrained from outright racist comments; they were here to relax, catch fish, and chug Buds while celebrating the inevitable decline of Saddam Hussein. At a certain point, I gave in to the temptation of Whitman's all-embrace—and that's when the tips started to get really good!

On this trip we had two groups in the mix—a quintet of Korean men from Flushing fishing in the port bow and a pod of seven or eight white suburbanites occupying the stern.

As the night wore on, the fishing slowed, so I grabbed a pole and started to jig for squid. The Koreans took note of this and asked if I might catch a few for them—of course. I coaxed a few of the ink-stained wretches from the pellucid waters and one of the Koreans proceeded to prepare the squid for immediate consumption—cutting out the cartilage, cleaning the ink out, peeling the skin off—and then he and his friends took to the cabin, broke out a jar of hot sauce, some hot peppers, some chopsticks, and dug right in. As I walked by, they gestured to me—did I want to join them? They gave me a set of chopsticks, and we enjoyed the crunchy, incredibly fresh feast together.

"Have you ever tried raw bluefish cheeks?" I asked. They hadn't. Oh, but you must. We'd caught a few of those brutarians that night, so, the next thing I knew, the bunch of us were standing around the fillet table while I carved the cheeks out—they were a hit. Then we decided to go hog-wild, and I grabbed one of their bass and started to cut it up for sashimi.

This activity had not gone unnoticed by the group in the stern, and they made no bones about expressing their disdain—their disgust—for this display of Asian gluttony. What was amazing, and sort of hilarious, was that they were actually *threatened*, and felt they had to stand up for their own culinary culture. One of them shot a hostile look at the grinning Koreans and said, with undue defiance, "We're going to bring the barbecue next time, and cook up some hamburgers and hot dogs."

I stood there at the fillet table with a big knife in my hand, lips smeared red from the hot sauce, a length of squid dangling out of my mouth, and laughed in his face. Didn't make a tip; didn't care.

New York (Upstate)

Burden of Romance

JoAnn Wypijewski

New York is spare, is lush, is desperate, is mad with the memory of better days, raw as an Adirondack winter, gentle as a Great Lakes leafy summer, cruel as the clank of its prison doors. It is old or young and in bonds, young and heading out; is searching, is drunk, is bunkered in the suburbs of dying cities, stubborn in the patchwork of disappearing farms, hopeful as a booster's plastered smile, stirring as its landscapes in survival. It exhausts its sloganeers, this anxious breeder of "destinations," attic of obsolete treasure, graveyard of revival schemes: "The Empire State" of an empire cracking up.

Other states trail it in almost every category of development. But those that are poorest or sickest or dirtiest or worst-schooled have at least the reassurance of history's low expectations, and the reward of investors who find virtue in backwardness. Once first in everything, New York has only New York—the city, with its outriding commuter towns and oceanside extensions—to confound its profile of decline, and about the city, "Upstate" is ambivalent. Round about last call in the mid-heeled bars of Buffalo, Rochester, Syracuse, Albany, patrons who in another setting might complain, unjustly, that their taxes are the city's life support will link arms and kick high, bellowing with Frank Sinatra: "Aaaand, if I can make it there, I'm gonna make it anywhere . . ."

In the low-heeled bars they just drink. Eleven in the morning, 2:30 in the afternoon, the stools are warm, the next Bud set up before the last one is half-gone. There might be fizz in the conversation, but more likely fizzle. Who cares? There's booze and cigarettes, and hours away from the thousand-pound weight of idleness, the bone-cold house, too costly to heat past 55 in winter, the freeze-dried marriage or the reproach of undone tasks. On one recent Christmas Eve afternoon it seemed the city of Troy, near Albany, had split for the mall and left the drunks in charge. All matted hair and soft silly smiles, they patrolled downtown streets, greeting through-travelers with the news that the diners were all closed but the bars weren't, pawing their food-flecked shirtfronts as they vied to explain some dubious emergency to a fire crew and contorted to keep from falling.

Consolation through drink is hardly novel. In their "Castorland Journal" of the 1790s, Simon Desjardins and Pierre Pharoux, French aristocrats touring the Mohawk River Valley and the frontier west of the Adirondacks to Lake Ontario, punctuate their survey of the region's lakes and streams, romantic escarpments and cascades, immense trees (then briskly falling under the settler's ax), extreme weather, and swarms of biting blackfly with accounts of a rascally populace, exacting tribute in their fragrant taverns, bribable with a draught of gin or cask of rum and nimble enough to get the better of the deal from the aggrieved French. A century later the neighborhoods of immigrants whose labor powered the cities were likely to have a bar on every block. Communal institutions, they were as vital as churches or relief missions in advancing industrialism by mitigating its brutalities. Another hundred years plus, what is remarkable is not the drunkenness but the void. The images stay with anyone who has traveled observantly through Upstate cities.

Inner-city suburban-style homes with attached garage but no place to buy a quart of milk on Buffalo's Sycamore Street, erstwhile commercial thoroughfare of the black and Polish communities; no place to buy much of anything besides drugs farther down, past the lawns, where addresses are useless because so are most of the buildings, and where at night the only things rolling down this long, wide boulevard are a lone car and a guy in a wheelchair.

Monuments of restoration in Utica, the movie palace, the train terminal, the Hotel Utica, magnificent, but nearby, deer roam in vacant lots where houses were bulldozed by the block because, even for a dollar the city couldn't find buyers.

Downtown Amsterdam, 10:30 P.M., the still of the main street undisturbed except by blowing papers and raccoons.

Children may welcome this return of the wild. Animals are quite charming, absenting ticks and rabies, and Bambi on the front lawn beats a plaster replica when shrubbery is a parent's worry. With a hundred years more, grown-ups may learn to live with it. But those alive today must manage through transition, between a past too fresh to forget and a future as yet unfathomed. The Norma Desmond of states, New York burdens its people with romance.

It erects no markers to typhus, TB, or infant death, nor to Indian die-off, white-man massacre, maroon capture, child labor, or the many-stranded scourge on women. The towns built on textiles no more remind their citizens of whence the cotton came than New York City teaches its about the source of its mercantile wealth. Those built on steel and railroads protect generations from the knowledge that soot choked their grandfathers' lungs, that an ingot was sometimes all their grandmothers got for burial after a steel accident. In the farmlands, the pastoral memory does not admit publicly of the loneliness and inbreeding and brutish hard work, nor about hunger, indentured labor or even such quaint details as the eighteenth-century innkeeper's habit of changing sheets but once a week, on Sunday, and woe to the traveler arriving Saturday. No Civil War draft riots, no civil rights race riots, no Harriet Tubman and Underground Railroad, no Niagara Movement or Ansonia Conference, no workers' battles won or lost, receive their proper study by the masses. Women's suffrage—Seneca Falls. Bible communism and free love—Oneida. Bible communism and abstinence—Mount Lebanon/Shaker Village. Mormonism—Palmyra and the Hill Cumorah. All are mere marks on a motorist's map, the state's children kept ignorant of the potent mix of courage, revolt, liberty, repression, experimentalism and from-my-god-to-thee madness that is their legacy.

Instead, Upstate gorges on faded grandeur. In a sense, it always has. Recall Troy. Troy got its name in a tavern. It was early 1789; the English were bridling at the submergence of their identity to that of the Dutch, who had laid claim to the spot, and what would become the state, in the 1600s after swindling the Indians. They were all Americans now, so the whole village, at least as many as cared, went down to the bar and, exalted by the grog, threw off the cumbersome, old-countryish "Van der Heyden's Ferry" and embraced the name of antiquity's lost cause. Word of this traveled, and soon New York sprouted Hector, Helena, Homer, Ilion, and Paris—as well as Albion, Athens, Attica, Aurora, Carthage, Cato, Cicero, Corinth, Etna, Euclid, Hannibal, Ionia, Ithaca, Macedon, Manlius, Medina, Minerva, Minoa, Ovid, Plato, Pompey, Rome, Scipio Center (and -ville), Seneca Falls (and Castle and Hill), Vestal, Virgil, Utica, and, just off the Union Turnpike in Queens, Utopia.

It was the age of Neoclassicism, and if today such names require a healthy sense of the absurd, there was something more than alcohol or a touching wish for refinement behind the European settlers' anticipation of greatness. Ninety-two of the Revolution's 308 battles had taken place in the state, the greatest concentration of fighting. Transport had favored war as it soon would commerce. Troy sits at the junction of the Mohawk and Hudson rivers, these two forming a perpendicular natural highway through the state and to the sea. In the War of 1812 the city shipped arms, supplies, and, most famous, beef (stamped "U.S." by Troy meatpacker Samuel Wilson, the original "Uncle Sam") to American troops. By 1825 it was the southern terminus for the Champlain Canals to Canada and, more important, the eastern terminus for the Erie Canal, which, extending west to Buffalo and the Great Lakes, provided the country's only sea-level route from the Atlantic to the West.

The cities that flourished along this corridor, and the outlying farms and resource lands that fed them, made New York the richest and most populous—hence "Empire"—state. Before the Hudson Valley settled into the purely picturesque, it produced more bricks than anywhere in the world, and had many of the busiest foundries and docks in the country. Until Andrew Carnegie established his mills at Pittsburgh, Troy was the steel center of America. Thomas Edison set up what would become General Electric and had the country's first industrial research lab in nearby Schenectady, which, being a locomotive center as well, proclaimed itself "the city that lights and hauls the world." In Amsterdam, the hosiery and knit-goods factories alone accounted for 3.4 percent of the national GDP going into the 1950s. In Buffalo, the combination of steelmaking, flour-milling, meatpacking, lake-shipping, railroading and power-harnessing at Niagara Falls fostered both delusions (the city as a second Paris) and rational assumptions about progress that persisted into the 1960s.

As the twentieth century began, New York State was first in the country in manufacturing and in vegetables, second in fruits, second in hay and maple sugar, first in oysters, high in fish, dairy, and hops, first in salt, first in gypsum and sandstone, in magnetites and millstones, first in black marble, near the top in limestone, granite, and natural-cement rock, first in finance, printing, publishing, photographic materials, millionaires and union sentiment.

It moved so fast, being first, that it rarely paused to think it could ever be anything else. No one thought much about Willis Carrier's curious invention of 1902, for instance. The air conditioner could be imagined as revolutionary for the future of manufacturing and urban growth only if the South could be imagined as something more than a terror-land and source of black workers massing north in the Great Migration. In Carrier's hometown of Syracuse, as in the neighborhoods around Buffalo Forge where he did his fundamental research, most white workers must have regarded the South as an irrelevancy until, decades later, their plants and then their children started moving there. Mr. Carrier's invention may not be the signal factor in the state's decline, but it is the most piquant.

Three years into the twenty-first century the business school of Canisius College in Buffalo issued an economic assessment of the region that applies as well to most of the state: "The trend is obvious and ominous, what we produce in Western New York is becoming less and less desirable to the rest of the world."

Throughout the 1990s boom, as wealth amassed in New York City and its suburbs, it seemed the fortunes of city and state were finally, irrevocably uncoupled. In every year of that prosperous decade, growth in personal income in New York State lagged behind the nation as a whole, the city's fabulous gains, statistically speaking, never being enough to offset losses in the rest of the state. Then the stock bubble burst, the Twin Towers collapsed, and even the William Morris Agency, icon of Manhattan's image machine, is leaving town. "We are all New Yorkers now": For the first time in years many of the state's people actually mean it. Everyone reads the bad news. City and state are financial wrecks, and neither appears capable of rescuing the other. In Albany, state politics are sclerotic where not corrupt, a club with three bosses, bereft of energy or invention. Yet there is money here, and everyone knows that too. Each limping Upstate city overlooks suburbs with "good schools," smug consumers, and defenses against incursions of "the city," also known as black and brown people. Those who scrape together a rural living or resist retirement from the farm despite the spike in real estate and the crash in milk watch in wonder as the land around them is stripped and rolled for jumbo homes—"damn rookeries," in the phrase of a crusty North Country man. "What do these people do out here? Nobody knows. They come to lay their eggs and hatch their chicks, far enough from anywhere so there are no niggers, no spics, just a bunch of pumpkins from the hills, but at least we're white."

The buying and building, like New York City's surface vitality and loud-living rich, have a frantic quality. Amid the gathering gloom the economics of hope takes many forms, and is now so regnant that "Excelsior" might as well be replaced as the state motto by the slogan of Mets fans: "Ya gotta believe!" In New York City, boosters are betting on the Olympics; in Syracuse, on building the biggest mall in America, DestiNY USA, and shoring up the lake/cesspool Onondaga for condo development. In Newburgh they've built a river walk and a dock for cruises on the Hudson, hoping pleasure-seekers won't be deterred as they drive past the winos and drug deals and emptiness of Broadway to get there. The river's tonier towns, Cold Spring and Garrison; the ones with recent makeovers, Beacon and Hudson; the ones like Kingston crafting an un-mall identity—they are hoping the day-trippers and antiquers, the country-householders and refugees from the art world, keep spending. The resort towns of the Adirondacks, suddenly refreshed by New Yorkers' fear of flying, are hoping that lingers. In the Appalachia of Jamestown, a place so hard, poor people take comfort that at least they're not in Newburgh, hopes for tourist development rest on the cult of home-girl Lucille Ball; in the old Lake Erie steel town of Lackawanna, on the cult of a hero almost no one knows.

Petitions in Lackawanna's rococo Our Lady of Victory basilica urge visitors to join in entreating the Vatican to put Father Nelson Baker on the path to sainthood. Baker built the basilica and a network of charitable facilities, and his edification is the town planners' second development priority, after the usual incentive-laden light-industry Empire Zone projects. New York has other saints. Auriesville, where Isaac Jogues and two holy Christian martyrs were dispatched by the Iroquois in 1642, is best known for the hillside cross formed by trees recognizable to travelers on the New York State Thruway between Utica and Albany. These three were the first North American martyrs, canonized in 1925, yet Internet sites list not a single motel or bed-and-breakfast in the town. Nearby in Fonda, votaries of Blessed Kateri Tekakwitha, "Lily of the Mohawks," who survived smallpox and, "in the midst of scenes of carnage, debauchery, and idolatrous frenzy. . . lived a life of remarkable virtue" until her death in 1680, had to wait three-hundred years just for her beatification, and still lobby for sainthood. Perhaps Lackawanna's relative bonhomie and indeed endurance, after losing 70 percent of its tax base when the steel mills closed in the 1980s, will one day be attributed as miracles to Father Baker. Like Fonda, the town is betting long term.

Who is to say it's a bad bet when other towns seek rescue in blackjack, roulette, and many a more businesslike, though no less highstakes, revival scheme? A few years ago state and local politicians promised long tax holidays and $100 million in incentives for Adelphia to set up in downtown Buffalo. They called it "prudent" but were operating on faith rather than knowledge of the company's bona fides, and when Adelphia imploded in scandal, it was as if they'd been had on a bluff. Now gambling has been blessed by Albany, and there is something perversely satisfying in the fact that the state that mythified the Indian and lighted the forest of American romanceseeking via James Fenimore Cooper should correct the record with Indian casinos. Every town with a tribe nearby knows someone angling for a deal, from Akwesasne at the Canadian border to the Catskills borscht belt to the Niagra frontier. And what an epidemic of sentiment that has arisen among the people! What a surge in respect from the white man, and in recovered memories of Native heritage now that it might be fungible! Somewhere in Niagara Falls there is a portrait of the Jesuit Hennepin, first white man to record his sighting of this seventh wonder of the world. More an adventurer than missionary at heart, Hennepin didn't bother about "saving" the Indians—that would come later—though in the painting they have acolytes' expressions. Now the Christians of Niagara Falls pray the Seneca Nation will save them, or at least transform their storefronts into something, anything but the weird gallery of graffiti and dead flies that they've become. The first casino there opened in December 2002. In time, St. Mary's of the Cataracts around the corner may post meeting notices for Gamblers Anonymous along with AA, but these days it has added two masses, and in the collection baskets dollars mix with chips.

I have always lived in New York State, and I suppose it is true with places as with people that first you fall in love, and then you like what you love. To anyone with freedom here, there is yet beauty amid the ruins, and I think I have sensed it most profoundly in concrete and water. Maybe because in Buffalo a ritual of childhood was going to "watch the boats" with my grandfather, my favorite place in that city—and thus toward the top in all the state—is just over the iron bridge at the corner of South and Alabama streets, where asphalt, rail track, and the Buffalo River conjoin in the service of two immense concrete silos. Grain elevators were invented here when the mills needed an efficient way to store grain that came on barges from the Midwest. Intrinsically monumental, they were cheap to erect, designed to last, and are too expensive to demolish now that most of them are idle. They punctuate the city like great exclamation marks, accidental totems of modernism, more stirring and durable than the International Style buildings of Gropius and Le Corbusier, which they inspired. Even derelict at the edge of Lake Erie, they are not sad. Like the lake and the people, they tough it out, and are among the surprises of time.

I swam in Lake Erie when I was young, feeling lucky to have been born in New York and not Kansas or Utah or some other blocky, landlocked state. I did not know, growing up, that it wasn't normal to feel sticky after swimming in freshwater. I played joyously in the waves, watchful to avoid the fish with dusky scales and milky eyes that floated by. The lake had died so that steel might live. Bethlehem Steel poured molten slag into the lake, remade the shoreline that way. There was a beach right next door, though we bathed much farther away. I remember riding on the high bridge that arced above the steelworks. Whatever it was in reality, in memory it was like skating on the rim of hell. Furnaces cutting ghoulish silhouettes against the sulfur sky; fire from the stacks; fire streaming into the lake; monstrous, thrilling, and, I assumed, perpetual. I was wrong. For the old folks in their lawn chairs and the youths entwined at sunset beside the lake in downtown Buffalo today, it is just as well. Some loves are too awful to regret.

For others, regret is too weak a word. I used to swim in the New York City water supply once I grew up and moved to Manhattan. Always illegal, this is impossible since 9/11. I would catch sun on the rocks of the Croton reservoirs, picnic in view of the Catskills on the pebbly shore of the vast Ashokan, glide through crisp water that tasted almost as it would from my kitchen tap, and marvel at the unenforced obedience of the masses who denied themselves such pleasures. I never saw another swimmer save the friend I'd brought along and the fish. They say the Adirondack lakes are just as clean but they are cold; the Finger Lakes just as beautiful but they are popular. In all the state I have discovered only one more blissful pond, and it is posted PRIVATE. The lake of the Harriman heirs, crystal fresh, it is ringed by cottages that are rarely occupied, interrupted by a boat-house whose rooftop once trilled with partygoers and glittered in the pretty splash of Chinese lanterns. The state's grand families, too, have adjusted to the era of lowered expectations, and, on the Harriman estate, to the din of thruway traffic hurrying along just below.

I used to suppose, while floating in a reservoir, that someone dead now must have regretted the flooding of the dry land. Someone else must have mourned the diversion of one-tenth of Niagara Falls' volume for the world's first power plant. No one alive has seen the falls as Hennepin's Indian guides did. Nor the Steuben Hills as those French aristocrats did; even they were too late. We drive the state's loveliest roads—near the gorges of Ithaca, through the misty morning hills en route to Cooperstown and the Baseball Hall of Fame, across the broad fields in Schoharie County, and up around the little rises where strange descendants of the clannish hillfolk, the Floughters, dart into view and disappear like wild things. We call it "the country" and don't think too much that it once was covered with hemlock forest, that the Adirondacks are isolated, "unspoiled" only in relative terms, that, as Marx wrote, "the nature that pre-ceded human history no longer exists anywhere."

No such indifference attends a tour of the cities, whose pasts are inscribed in their presents without the consolation of progress. Anyone can see that the methadone clinic used to be a bank, and the flea market a factory, and the revival church a movie house. Upbeat "new use" projects abound, converting industrial sites into apart-ments or gallery space or restaurants. Buffalo's downtown, dismem-bered over decades by catastrophic political decisions at the state and local level, comes alive at night in a way it didn't just ten years ago; largely because of the vision of one club owner who found a way out of no way, this long-segregated city at least entertains itself interra-cially. But as an old friend once said of medical efforts to treat his ailing body, "it's just patch-patch-patch." Decline is inescapable, and worse than decline, the poverty of imagination.

The natural, then artificial, highway that linked the cities for commerce; the overall scheme of sustenance, growth, and recreation that bound city to countryside to waterfront and made the state a coherent economic unit—those are obsolete or shattered. Only one thing beyond sentiment and state lines unites the place, and that is the worst thing. The only highway that gives tangible meaning to Upstate for Downstate, to country for city and vice versa is the one that carries New York's children to prison.

In a reversal of the historic pattern of commerce in the state, the goods, as it were, move mostly from downstate up. One weekday morning in a typical Bronx courtroom, the city taps the only natural resource it has, a stream of young people, mostly men, mostly black and Latino, mostly there on nonviolent drug charges, and designates them for shipment north. One Sunday afternoon in a typical diner in Elmira or Attica or Ossining or too many towns to mention, the local trade is augmented by mothers, wives, or girlfriends who have taken the long trip up and, heavy-lidded, await the return bus home. The city supplies 70 percent of the state's prisoners; Upstate, 90 percent of its prison cells. The one gets relief from its surplus population; the other, a reason for being. One ordinary day in Albany, any day the legislature is in session, small-town officials lobby for prison business. As Henry Rausch, the mayor of Coxsackie, south of Albany, told filmmaker Tracy Huling in *Yes, in My Backyard,* "The more beds we have over there, the more inmate population, the more water they're going to use, and the more sewer services they're going to use and the more jobs are going to be needed . . . .You politick for it— that's what you do."

Rausch, whose day job is in prison food service, neglected to mention that the more prisoners a town has, the higher its population count in the census, hence the bigger its portion of state and federal aid, and the greater its political clout. The town of Malone, high in the North Country, twenty miles from the Canadian border, has three prisons including the new 1,500-bed supermax Upstate Correctional Facility. Most of the latter's inmates are there because they were caught doing drugs in looser joints. Prisoners make up one-third of Malone's population. A local banker told a Department of Corrections magazine, "It's frightening to think what the economy around here would be like" without the prisons. More so in nearby Dannemora, where prisoners outnumber free people.

"This way at least the kids don't have to leave home," older people in the prison towns will say. Their kids remain close because others' kids are far away. Two-thirds of the state's prisons are more than a three-hour drive from New York City. On September 11, 2001, there was pandemonium at the women's prison in Albion, where the majority of inmates were helpless for news of their loved ones, four hundred miles away. Statistics on the prison economy can make a soul quake. Since 1973, when the state passed ironhanded drug laws, the population behind bars has gone from 12,500 to 67,000. Seventy-five percent of them have no high school diploma. Their minders are barely more educated, and at a starting salary of just over $25,000, they aren't paid to be. Public universities have been starved, losing 29 percent of their funding between 1988 and 1998, while prison spending increased by 76 percent, though there too college programs have been eliminated. It costs the state $2 billion a year to run its prisons, but even in budget crunching times, as is incarceration the state's only large-scale economic strategy, too much depends on it for politicians to abandon it now. Since the early 1980s, the state has added 46,000 prison beds, almost all them upstate, and it employs 30,000 people there. By way of comparison, since 1990, some 43,000 fewer people are employed in farming, fishing, hunting, and mining. In the rural towns, the ambitious and the educated still leave home, while their peers study violence as a way of life. "We're doing time too," a prison guard at a maximum-security facility told investigators from the Correctional Association of New York.

The state has yet to exploit its prisons for tourism. Somehow the domestic equivalent of military subjugation is hard to wrap in glory. The city of Auburn advertises itself as the home of Harriet Tubman, and its region of the Finger Lakes as one that is as scenically splendid as it is historically rich. That this region was one of the most energetic centers of nineteenth-century antislavery activity is slowly being reclaimed. That it also gave us the cell block; that Auburn State Prison, circa 1817, became the model for America's punitive architecture; that its prisoners built the home of the country's first formal death house, Sing Sing on the Hudson, and now, in a state once notable for furniture manufacturing, make furniture for 17–42 cents an hour—about such things, there is a discreet silence.

Perhaps one day, when New York has long shed its Empire State pretensions and imagined itself into a more gracious condition, some heritage-trail planner will lay out its inconvenient history beside the many-times-told stories of its greatness—if not for commerce then at least to help its people understand how, as the twentieth century slouched into the twenty-first, their state became everything it once abhorred.

NORTH CAROLINA

I'm a Tarheel Born, I'm a Tarheel Bred, and When I Die, I'm a Tarheel Dead

Jill McCorkle

These days I am a person with two homes. I have my native North Carolina, and I now have Massachusetts, home to my children. In my mind, the utopian place is a merger of these two, the liberal politics of Massachusetts with the land and open friendliness of North Carolina. Both states have a wealth of history. Both have the Atlantic Ocean as well as mountains. Still I think that "home" most often remains what we knew in childhood, the place that shaped us into who we are. My home will always be the wide, sandy white Carolina beaches and the endless stretch of flat tobacco fields surrounding my home county. The image in my mind is one stripped of all that the past thirty or forty years have brought to the area. Often, I am as homesick for a time as I am for the place, and yet enough of it remains the same—the history, the land, the people—that when I return, all the old feelings and my senses about the area rush back into place.

North Carolina is the eleventh most populous state in the country. People are drawn to the climate—mild winters, four seasons—and they are drawn to the geography, from the coast to the Blue Ridge/Appalachian mountains with farmland and golf courses sandwiched between the two. People are drawn to the booming industry of Research Triangle Park and to the academic institutions of UNC–Chapel Hill, Duke University, North Carolina State, and Wake Forest University. These institutions also conjure images of Atlantic Coast Conference athletics and the prestigious list of celebrities (Michael Jordan and Mia Hamm to name two) that we can claim. In recent years, the movie industry has found its way to Wilmington, North Carolina, where locals routinely spot stars in restaurants and on the beaches, and line up to serve as extras. Golfers have always made a pilgrimage to the world-renowned courses of Pinehurst. We have Biltmore Palace—summer home to the Vanderbilts—a major tourist attraction and movie site to many films, most memorably Peter Sellers's wonderful *Being There*. The palace and grounds are extraordinary—architectural and botanical wonders, complete with a working vineyard. People flock to see the outer banks and Ocracoke, drawn to the tranquil unspoiled beauty as well as to the tales of pirates and shipwrecks along what is known as the graveyard of the Atlantic. Bald Head Island is a perfect bit of land with a fascinating history all its own. This is where Theodosia Burr (daughter of Aaron) disappeared en route to New York. Many think she was taken by pirates; hers is a story prominent among those of local ghosts, as is the famous Maco Light—supposedly rail-road engineer Joe Baldwin swinging his lantern in search of his head—near Wilmington. Bald Head Island boasts one of the largest sea-turtle conservancies as well as a lighthouse that has weathered many hurricanes over the years. The maritime forest offers tropical foliage that is not found north of this coastal region. And, like most good things—like the research triangle and the Piedmont triad (Greensboro, Winston-Salem, High Point) regions—the best-kept secrets are out. The magazine *Coastal Living* built two incredible spec homes on Bald Head, and the *New Yorker* routinely advertises the lovely retirement communities of the Carolinas. For years Carolina cities have been listed as top places to live and several of our high schools (Chapel Hill and Charlotte) were listed by *Newsweek* as among the best in the country.

The tobacco industry, though not what it was in the past, still accounts for the livelihood of one in eleven workers. Cotton, soybeans, corn, peanuts, and wheat are produced, as well as livestock. Perhaps nothing in recent years painted such a portrait of the state's resources as the disastrous losses of both crops and livestock caused by Hurricane Floyd in 1999, and Hugo and Fran before it ('89 and '96, respectively). In my childhood the grown-ups always referred to Hurricane Hazel, a storm that hit in 1954 and completely changed the face of the North Carolina coast. People would refer to something as before Hazel or after Hazel. The same timelines now exist for Hugo and especially Floyd, a devastation that hurt the state both emotionally and economically, but that also proved once again the real attraction of "The Old North State" a steadfast and loyal sense of camaraderie and good-neighborly behavior. In the aftermath of these terrific storms, there was an outpouring of human interest stories on how people came together. The story goes that the nickname "Tarheel" came not only from the state's production of pitch, but because of the steadfast loyalty of the Carolina troops. It was said that they stuck like they had tar on their heels, and Robert E. Lee was rumored to have said: "God bless the Tarheel boys."

Even though my town, Lumberton, was right in the middle of a county that had one of the highest crime and poverty rates, it also had an old-fashioned downtown area where trucks parked in the summer and farmers sold melons or boiled peanuts in little, damp brown sacks. Children rode bikes to and from the movie theaters where you were allowed to sit from one show right into the next. The candy counter had big jars of dill pickles and those fat Charms suckers that only cost a nickel and could last through an entire show. It cost 50 cents to get in, and the lush red-velvet curtains were drawn closed and reopened with each new showing, beginning with a couple of trailers but mostly preludes of cartoons. There was a sign on a restroom near the candy counter that said "colored." I was quite young with this memory, but it was a powerful one and along with it are various facts and tidbits I was told or overheard. There had at one time also been separate entrances. The movie balcony was divided between the black people and the Indian people. Our county has a Native American population—the Lumbees—a tribe of people many believe to be descended from the Lost Colony of Roanoke Island.

I remember one Sunday after church standing in a hot line of people that snaked through the old high school building (where my parents went to school and I went to middle school—an old red-brick building that no longer stands) to take a sugar cube with our polio vaccine. I remember someone my mother knew and worked with—a black woman—saying that Dr. King would insist they use brown sugar if he were here. People laughed. It was a good and friendly memory, but I also remember tensions breaking out in other places, a school in the county where a race riot left one dead. I remember children too young to have formed political opinions, clamoring for the likes of George Wallace. When I look back on that, I find it chilling, not unlike how I feel when I glimpse old footage of Nazi youth, or any other situation where children parrot the ugliness of the grown-up world. Better memories are of the old bathroom in that same red-brick building, where sixth-grade girls shed their bulky winter coats (rarely needed anyway but especially not with the big radiators whistling and bucking with heat) and danced while singing songs by the Jackson Five and comparing such important differences as why white girls shaved their legs and asking politely to touch the others' hair—the big haloed afros of the time and the silky straight parted-down-the-middle style. In my mind this was where the real peace talks happened. It felt like an open threshold.

Now with the recent changing of the guards—Jesse Helms no longer senator, the Strom Thurmonds and George Wallaces and Lester Maddoxes a thing of the past—there was a hope that things were further along. I'm talking about thirty-four years passing, and yet it still rears its head with Confederate flags flying and separate proms. I am always relieved when it is *not* happening in North Carolina, and yet, the fact remains that within our country, the promise that was made all those years ago continues to teeter and wobble. When people think "racist," they look to the South because this is what history dictates they do, and yet, this is not an issue limited to the South by any means. If anything, my southern childhood gave me a glimpse of people living and working together; for the most part, it was an integrated society, which is not the case in many cities and suburbs across the country. Economics has and will always be the greatest divider of people.

I look to those living in North Carolina, like my niece and nephew—both college-age—and I see in them the open mindedness that I would hope to find. Certainly it is a mindset fostered by places like Chapel Hill, a place Jesse Helms once said should have a fence built around it and called the state zoo. (A quote recited often and proudly by many!) But this is Bible Belt country, and though many strides have been made, there is still a firm line of conservative thinking. I saw this while teaching in the 1980s at the university there. The students were not as politically liberal in their thinking as they were when I was a student a decade earlier. A short story about abortion or mixed-race relationships still fostered heated debate. Young women adamantly declared that they absolutely were not feminists. "I shave under my arms," one might say. Or "I like boys, I do!" I would quote Rebecca West who wrote in 1913: "I myself have never been able to find out precisely what a feminist is: I only know that people call me a feminist whenever I express sentiments that differentiate me from a doormat." After class, many days, I would go away wondering what on earth had happened. Society was moving along in one direction and then . . . *Wham!* While I wasn't looking it took giant steps backward. I then taught in New England and found many of the students' opinions to be similar—I was disappointed by the whole but also relieved that it wasn't a southern thing. It was a national thing. It was Wall Street's "greed is good" mentality along with the "me me me" decade. *And* thankfully, it was only a percentage of the population. Maybe this wasn't exactly the future my childhood promised me, but we were still moving in the right direction. Weren't we? And then I read something like an essay by novelist Lee Smith, where she talks about all the different people who have come together to form the backbone of a Carrboro, North Carolina restaurant and many businesses like it—different races, different backgrounds, different sexual orientations—and I believe that we are indeed moving in the right direction. And I hear a speech delivered by the writer Allan Gurganus, who brought a huge crowd of people to their feet as he described the changing South, how we could hold onto our rich history and still move forward in a progressive and open way, and I know that yes, that's the right direction. I watch with great interest the courage of the Fayetteville, North Carolina, paper, which chose to run an announcement of a same-sex marriage. The fallout was enormous. Their stride into a new realm, keeping pace with New York and Vermont, was again an affirmation of movement in the right direction. When I hear of such moments I can't help but picture the Bible Belt; it's still there, cinching the waistline of the South, but there's a new style, a new fabric. I believe the belt is going to have to continue stretching and breathing as it accommodates the changing shape of things.

North Carolina is a state with a long history of survival, those heels dug in like they had tar on them. It is a state still filled with promise and hope. But take someone away from "The Old North State," and conversation reflecting upon what they miss will immediately turn to barbecue and hush puppies and Calabash-style seafood. People miss "beach music" groups like the Tams and Maurice Williams and the Zodiacs and the Fantastic Shakers, serenading generations of shaggers (the shag is a dance). You sing a few bars of James Taylor's "Carolina in My Mind," the chosen anthem of misplaced Carolinians. You might sing "Tom Dooley"—the old folk tune that tells the true story of Tom Dula and a bit of the North Carolina folklore. Or you might quote a bit of "The Tar Heel Toast": "Here's to the land of the long leaf pine, the summer land where the sun doth shine, where the weak grow strong and the strong grow great, here's to 'down home,' the Old North State!" And if that doesn't satisfy the urge, there is always: "I'm a Tarheel born, I'm a Tarheel bred, and when I die, I'm a Tarheel dead." It doesn't get much simpler than that.

NORTH DAKOTA

NORTH DAKOTA AND THE PROBLEM OF BELIEF

Larry Watson

When Rand McNally left part of North Dakota out of one of its atlases in 1989, it may simply have been reflecting what is a psychic reality for a good many Americans for whom the state barely exists. Eric Sevareid called his home state "a large rectangular blank in the national consciousness." But while doubt might have a great deal working in its favor, with faith, the right kind of faith, it is possible to believe in North Dakota.

I'm guilty of skepticism myself, and I was born in North Dakota (in Rugby, the geographical center of North America), grew up there (in Bismarck, the state's capital), and attended one of the state universities (in Grand Forks). Yet once I moved out of the state, I began to distrust my memories of my years there. Could the summer storms truly have been that fierce? Could the drifts have piled up that high? Surely it wasn't possible that blowing snow prevented us from seeing the end of our driveway? But North Dakota kindly served up a few reminders. On one visit back to the state, a blizzard stopped us at Fargo, and nothing but luck enabled us to find the street that would take us to the motel—blowing snow obscured not only the intersection but the traffic light telling us when we could turn. A few years later, I was reminded that, yes, it was possible for drifts to stack up to my six-foot height—in summer. Hailstones fell for more than an hour, and when they stopped, windows were broken, trees shredded, and roofs unshingled. People shoveled hail from their sidewalks, and snowplows were required to clear streets. Our car was exposed to the storm, and afterward was so pock-marked it looked as though it had had acne in its youth. The car has since been repaired, but fortunately we took enough photographs to convince us when our memories grow uncertain.

Those extremes of weather (121 degrees and minus 60 are the state records, both set in 1936—a spread few states can match or would care to) are among the reasons why so few people have experiences with the state. And the experiences they do have are apt to be fleeting. Interstate 94 bisects the state, 340 miles of excellent highway over fairly flat terrain (White Butte at 3,506 feet above sea level is the state's high point and the Red River at 750 feet its low) with a 70-mph speed limit helping to hasten travelers through on their way to Yellowstone Park or the Mall of America. If Middle America is flyover country, North Dakota is your classic drive-thru.

But perhaps North Dakota hasn't lodged very securely in the American psyche because it simply hasn't been around long enough to have much of a history (allowing, of course, for a view of history that has to do with the presence of white people who keep the kinds of records that interest other white people). North Dakota became a state in 1889, the same year that Charlie Chaplin and Adolf Hitler were born. The other "North" state—Carolina—had already been a state for a hundred years. The Washington monument, Brooklyn Bridge, and Statue of Liberty were all in place. In 1889 the Giants were playing baseball in New York, and the White Stockings in Chicago. A church in my Milwaukee neighborhood had been welcoming congregants for almost twenty years.

It probably doesn't help that transients are responsible for much of

North Dakota's history. Lewis and Clark spent the winter of 1804–1805 (I know—*winter!*) at Fort Mandan, near what is now Washburn, North Dakota. When they left, they were accompanied—and immeasurably aided—by a young woman who served as an interpreter and guide as they moved west. But Sacajawea was probably no more native to the region than Lewis and Clark. She was a Shoshone, from what is now Montana, but she had been captured in a raiding party by the Hidatsa, brought to their village, and eventually traded to a French fur trader. George Armstrong Custer stayed longer than Lewis and Clark, but when he left in the summer of 1876, there was no question of his ever returning. Custer commanded Fort Abraham Lincoln for three years, and according to many accounts, he and his wife Libbie loved life on the plains. As did Theodore Roosevelt, who first visited the Dakota Badlands in 1883. His statement, "I would never have been president if it were not for my experiences in North Dakota," is always taken as a compliment and is no doubt how Roosevelt intended it. But his Elkhorn Ranch was a financial failure, and trying to raise cattle in western Dakota, a country plagued by grasshoppers, drought, and winters that could last half the year, might have made a return to East Coast politics seem like a less formidable way of life. The badlands defeated more than one would-be entrepreneur. The Marquis de Mores, a French aristocrat, thought a fortune could be made with a meatpacking plant in western Dakota. The marquis founded a town, built his plant, set up a freight business, and settled into his twenty-six-room chateau. In 1884 Medora (named after the marquis's wife) was booming. By 1889 the town was deserted (it has since been restored), and the marquis and his family gone. Sitting Bull spent the last years of his life on the Standing Rock Reservation in what is now North Dakota, and after his death in 1890 was buried in Fort Yates, North Dakota. For a while . . . in 1953, South Dakotans sneaked across the border and stole Sitting Bull's remains. And perhaps South Dakota has the stronger claim, considering they built the grander monument to the man. It's odd, however, that a dispute would arise over the bones of someone who in life was often depicted as a villain and was feared throughout much of the Dakota Territory.

But while these outsiders came to North Dakota and brought it— and themselves—a measure of fame, native-born notables have often had to go outside the state's borders to gain the acclaim that made them known beyond those borders. Maxwell Anderson, Warren Christopher, Angie Dickinson, Phil Jackson, Louis L'Amour, Peggy Lee, Roger Maris, Eric Sevareid, and Lawrence Welk—all North Dakota born but not a lifelong resident among them. Novelist Larry Woiwode left but came back. Throughout his life, poet Tom McGrath had trouble staying in North Dakota but also had trouble staying away.

Of course leaving is as North Dakotan as lutefisk (cod soaked in lye—a culinary crime perpetrated by people of Norwegian ancestry), and today the state's young people carry on the migratory tradition. They leave mostly for jobs, and the places they mostly leave are farms and small towns. The state is forty-eighth in population, and more than half of the approximately 634,000 citizens reside in only five counties (of the state's fifty-three). Only four states lost population from 2000 to 2001, and North Dakota was one of them. If projections prove accurate, its decline will continue.

Persevering, however, is also North Dakotan. My maternal grandparents emigrated from Norway and Sweden, and homesteaded in central North Dakota, and though it was the twentieth century, it was still life on the frontier with its requisite portions of struggle and sorrow. They lost two sons within a year's time, and the 1930s buried much of the region under dust and debt, yet when my grandparents sold the farm it was not with a sense of desperation or defeat. They were proud of what they had done to start and sustain a rural community, a country church and school (both gone now), but they knew their youngest children would have more opportunities in the city (Fargo). It would never have occurred to my grandparents to blame the land or the weather or the times for the difficulties of their lives.

Contradiction, inconsistency, anomaly—these trouble the mind of the would-be believer, and North Dakota, like any state, abounds in paradox. The eastern part of the state is midwestern, and the soil of the Red River Valley incredibly fertile. Cross the Missouri, however, and you're in the West, the Great Plains, cattle country, droughty and sparse. After the process of confiscating the land from the original Americans was largely complete—Arikara, Assiniboin, Chippewa, Hidatsa, Mandan, and Sioux had resided in the region for centuries—the state took its name from the Lakota (Sioux) word for "friend." Home to one of the largest powwows in the United States, North Dakota also has more golf courses per capita than any other state. This state so associated with rural life has the majority of its citizens living in a few cities. Anyone standing out on the boundless prairie under the topless sky might feel, within an instant's span, insignificant *and* important. North Dakota proclaims itself "The Peace Garden State," in honor of the gardens shared with Canada, yet was once a major nuclear power. Along the state's northern tier, hundreds of missiles once waited in underground silos (a term used unironically, as far I can tell) for a phone to ring and two people to turn a key simultaneously. A state almost as treeless as the site of the British Open features a tree in full leaf on the state seal. In the 1980s, a pair of Rutgers University professors advanced their "Buffalo Commons" land-use theory and aroused the ire of many North Dakotans. But Frank and Deborah Popper never suggested that steps be taken to deliberately depopulate the state. They simply said that the attempts, lasting well over a century, to turn the Great Plains into farmland were certain to fail, and that the best use of the region might be to allow it to revert to its presettled condition. North Dakotans were indignant, yet they continued to leave the state voluntarily, making the Poppers look more and more prescient with each passing decade. The American bison has a brighter future on the northern plains than a recent college graduate.

Theodore Roosevelt called the state's beauty "mystic," an odd choice of word to describe a landscape to which the adjective "boring" has frequently been attached. But my Dakota ancestors, like many others, believed there were few sins greater than pretension or boastfulness, and North Dakota is often appropriately modest about revealing its charms. The two most otherworldly beautiful natural sights I've ever seen were in North Dakota. The first occurred when winter hoarfrost transformed Bismarck into an enchanted city, and every outdoor surface was furred in white and every twig and grass blade bristled with silver filings. On the second occasion, we left Bismarck after dark, driving east, and a full moon rose over the prairie, turning the road to gold and allowing every coulee and draw to shadow itself in blue. Are these scenes likely to occur again? Certainly, but they aren't available on demand, and, like Shangri-La and Brigadoon, are apt to be especially elusive for those who seek them with the improper spirit. Anyone can be awed by a mountain range or a seascape; it takes a discerning eye to appreciate North Dakota's subtle ornamentation.

An article in the *New York Times Magazine* about the emptying out of the Great Plains wounded North Dakotans by asking, "Is North Dakota necessary?" But little in life is necessary—not Coltrane or cold beer, yet who wants to live without them? It is certain that diminution of one kind or another awaits all of us; we might need North Dakota because it serves the same purpose as Frost's oven bird—it teaches us what to make of a diminished thing.

Even absent any cultural validation—no television series is set in North Dakota, no fad emanates from there—it is still possible to believe in North Dakota, but what is probably required is the kind of faith that religion asks of its followers—the ability to believe in the absence of evidence. So North Dakotans continue to value community even when its communities are vanishing. They prize neighborliness though few want to visit their neighborhood. They find beauty where others see emptiness. They treasure a history that's barely registered beyond the state's borders. They trust that life is unlikely to go better elsewhere. I don't have that kind of faith. I once did, but I don't any more. The loss is mine.

Ohio

Predominance

Kiki DeLancey

O hio is driving around the outer belt. The sky turning dark
is gray, then for an instant beautiful blue, and in that
instant the trailing red lights, reflected in triplicate across
the icy lanes, and the blue dash a glint too reflected on the bottom of
the coated windshield, becomes the moment that matters. The car
was cold at first and back in the parking lot the driver had turned the
heater knob to red, and sliding down the ramp three minutes later
had spun the blower control to max. The car was hot now, and the
driver beginning to sweat, but that was an unconscious thing. For
this moment the only thing in the driver's realm of awareness was
the color blue, dark and beautiful, with the red lights and the
reflected white gleaming lights sliding across it, and out past the
perimeter, beyond conscious awareness, the unacknowledged but
dominant sense of the ring of surrounding trees.

It was strange how brief this moment always was. In the earlier
grayness everything was all of the gray. That was the daily manifest
of virtual reality, everything all of the gray and seemingly insignificant. In the black night that followed and insinuated its blindness
until morning, the perimeter narrowed to a tunnel, an unguarded

breastwork, and the car was reduced to a distinct and lonely object shooting isolated toward a destination. The deep blueness was beauty, though, and the perimeter of trees then a groomed and visible expression of the moment's perimeter. The taillights and moving reflective rear bumpers of the many autos entwined into a moving pattern that was the reason for that moment's duration, for the whole outer belt and its foundations and structures, and for the jobs that purposed the outer belt, and the gross spiraling plats that had predicated its construction. Then the moment was so beautiful, and not only the red lights beautiful in their sliding, and the glints of white and the deep blue atmosphere. The moment was beautiful itself, the being in that transfixed light and existence. Then everyone was in that moment: the driver of the car and everything in view. Self-projection ended. At work, hunching over a counter or desk, the bored mind crept and wandered. At home, relaxing or eating in the ill-colored rooms, there was radio, or television, or a newspaper, anything. The moment was so sharp in beauty as to seem the reason, while it lasted, for all of the hunching, the waiting, and the clacking, and for those overheated and dull hours of dim sprawling. It lasted thirty seconds or forty-five seconds. It never lasted any longer. After that, blue became night, and lusterless.

Ohio equally is that place above the river on the slope of the big hills where no road is, and no house. Only a person who had toiled up through the ivies, or who had flown to that spot, could be looking down to the south, along the Ohio side of the river, and see the familiar shape of the land, the same unchanged curve of the banks and curving treetops spread there as always. Houses and bridges, trestles, partially clog the line of the bank. Wires cross the flat water. Its flat edges accommodate a variety of corrugated warehouses and tall blue metal chutes. Still the chrysoprase-colored water's course is unmistakably unchanged. Old lithographs and tintypes, preserved, present the same view. It's no feat at all to see the exact image of the ancient in the still-resisting contours, stripped in the mind of the temporary appurtenances so hurriedly shoved into place, and less of one to imagine it in the future day when rust or economics or law have removed these ruins, removing these contours back to their old unadorned countenance.

Ohio mostly is the familiar country. It's country of fields and woods. These are so like faces, not friendly or hostile faces but overwhelmingly familiar, and always dun or yellowing or green, bordered with slim lines of fence or high grass, growing or blowing fallow, and spread with trees. The trees predominate. Chopped and regrown, harvested or hacked, then always reappearing. They do always irresistibly reappear a mile away or ten, or ten feet. They've never flagged or failed. Centuries of milling haven't removed them. They must be bigger than that. Shrub, scrub, hardwoods, or valueless: they predominate. Houses cobbled together arose. Roads were dug and shored up and paved, fields tilled and fenced. This has been going on for hundreds of years, but as actions they don't seem to matter in the scheme of Ohio. Along the streets of towns, along the broad roads that pull in to the cities, and among the streets of the cities, in the curves of the interchanges and in sudden huge blocks between major city streets, but mostly and predominantly on all of the body of the state, rooted and occupying the vast bulk of the actual land area, on the vast square mileage of it—even with all of the enormous fields, the multiplying vineyards and the productive quarries, still covering almost all of it—and always in view and approaching. The cities, areawise, are really only dots, even with their spread and sprawl and urbanity. Their streets cross miles, their malls and strips acres and their office towers blocks: all of these are minute in the broad square fact of the breast of Ohio's lands. The farms and fields are a big part of that huge space, and always the little towns, the small human villages, part tree and part little field and part human shelter and necessity; but mostly it's composed of tree lots. They cover miles, bisected by roads at times, wetted with ponds and rivers, but uninterrupted in many places for miles. They cover entire counties, southern Ohio counties, eastern ones, those along the river and turning up through the west; through most of the counties, in fact, even much of the flattest central ones. You go away from the highway, even along the highway, and there they are. That hasn't yet been significantly altered.

It has to be said that it's also the elevator: the descent in the elevator. It's a long way down. Not so long if you look at it as feet, 200 or 240 feet, but it's long enough in its distance from air and from light, long in the distance posed between the unconscious normal and the acute knowledge of each movement underground and of each drawn breath. The strangeness of this is immense, and it always has been. To have rock and aquifer as your ceiling, and roadway and town as your roof is no stranger now than it had been one hundred or two hundred years ago. The earth and its core are your footbed. The rock's face is the face you look into. It looks back from complete darkness, dark too and wet and rough. The earth is as hard, the coal is as black and the water is as bitter as miners found them three hundred years ago. The strangeness is in the continuing primitive nature of nature: the rudeness of energy's bond to physical matter. That matter is still chiseled, pried, and drilled from earth's hold. It's lifted physically by conveyor and car, to burn in fire, to be made into fire, the same old fire, in this day when the visible virtual is the omnipresent presence. Voice and sound are transfigured into light— rapture of soul and spirit into eternal optic fiber. Words great or ignominious become strings of numbers, while color and form are digitized and queued into the representation of color and form. It's democratization of the real. Jackson Pollock done as 0011101011 is not so strange as looking into the kindled orange fire. This is the same fire, same in shape and color as the fire that caught the edges of burning chunks in Franklin's stove, a Renaissance hearth, and an ancient ringed pit. Our eyes looking into the fire are the same, too. They have the same meaty curves, bright whites, and ineffable blacks and blues. That the clean American, the polished and primed modern, still relies on the physical use of fire is amazing. The coal is literally clawed up out of the soil and placed into a fire, and so the smoke, chemicals, carbon, and ash are still necessary, and the yellow reflection in the irises blue or black would be the same, if they were allowed entry past the fences and power-plant gates.

The elevators jerk into motion, taking the booted, coveralled men down. They continue to go down.

Then there's the sweet part of it all: I think the secret sweet heart, that most of the people have sometimes intimated but don't fully believe. It's the trip from home to work, and from work in that half-empty store or small office to the town's diner, and from the house to the school three blocks away, and sometimes a few streets farther to the church or to the doctor's office or the dentist's, and from any of these places to the short strip on the state route where grocery, discount store, and fast-food place have been staged. In a small town these trips take place throughout life on five or six streets, maybe ten or a score, over and over. The street names stay unchanged. The building facades are virtually always unaltered, and even the edges of the old curbs and the plane of the sidewalks and narrow grass borders all unchanged and unforgotten through years. In a place where real property is neither particularly valuable nor worthless, things are maintained but unaltered. Streets are resurfaced but not extended.

The journeys along them are made by foot in childhood, when it's most like a journey, through water and into culverts and over grass. Adulthood provides cars to bear us, but always through the same streets: Sixth Street, Seventh Street, Maple Street, and Market Street. It's the long-term repetition that counts for something. You realize that early and value it eventually. Nothing can ever count for more.

Trips, in both directions, along these streets, and the accumulation of impressions of these buildings, and their shapes and the tones of their shadows and of their bricks, the light in leaves or dropped down through branches against them, all on the same retina again and again; and the sidewalk, and the selfsame cracks crossed for twenty years, for thirty years, for forty years, for fifty years, and still being crossed; and the pale grass, not the same blades but blades of the same fiber and stock and their bleached winter poorness and again their summer rectitude; the little slope of the yard, and the two stony steps of conglomerated pebbles up to the flat of the little grass yard; the damp, brown-tinged shade of that porch; those people's overgrown lilac that bends the chain-link fence and never blooms. Over years these things and their scent and their nature impress themselves on the cornea, and on the character. There's no way but by seeing them and making that journey.

And always lined with trees. That's what you have to remember. The person who lives in a town in Ohio is affected by them, because they predominate. They are predominant. In some towns these trees are so numerous and so large that living among them is very much like living in a forest. If you look, you can see that the trees greatly outnumber the houses. The houses are one part of the scene. The big tree canopy, green and full of light or in winter a thin lattice, covers. Here, you don't have to wait for evening. You don't have to look for red taillights slipping in reflection across black ice, because the moment of beauty is ongoing. This is a heavily populated and long-industrialized state. I'm not saying no one's tried to spoil it, but they haven't succeeded.

Oklahoma

A Brand-New State

Elizabeth Seay

There's a place in downtown Oklahoma City where the past seems to unbury itself: a bronze head and torso emerge from the pavement, arms pushing a huge sphere up two sloping tracks. When I was last there, one clear Sunday morning, the statue had no placard, but I noticed a group of people hanging around, and I asked one of them, an unassuming, skinny, fifty-year-old white guy in jeans, if he knew anything about the piece.

"Yeah," he said. "I'm the sculptor." An urban-renewal group had asked him to commemorate the black community that grew here, around the railroads and freight yards in the heart of the city, in the early years of the twentieth century. During the boom times, there were hospitals, schools, libraries, newspapers, and a vibrant community that launched both Charlie Christian's jazz and Ralph Ellison's modernism. The community also fought for civil rights before the term was invented, taking campaigns on voting rights and segregation to the Supreme Court in the 1920s. So the statue, most obviously representing the muscle that built the railroad, also celebrated intellectual brawn and moral force.

But I also sensed a wry commentary: the sculpture, of course, was meant to recall Sisyphus, the mythical man who was punished in Hades by having to repeatedly roll a huge stone up a hill, only to have it roll down again. And Sisyphus never wins. The neighborhood that the statue commemorated had disappeared, leaving this cryptic monument as the only tribute. (I wondered whether this acknowledgment of the past reflected a renewed commitment to racial equality or was simply a shrewd gesture, part of Oklahoma's relentless quest to be modern, part of the "everything's up-to-date in Kansas City" vibe. Now, being up-to-date would mean including a sop to the past, a dollop of political consciousness in the urban-redevelopment plan.)

We stood for a while in the plain, sunny space. There were few people that morning in what's billed as "Oklahoma City's newest dining and entertainment district," and it felt to me, with the wind loud in my ears, like the spacious grassland from which the city sprang in a series of "land runs" in the 1890s. The land runs are the primary legend of Oklahoma; in them, the last pioneers of America—the frontier officially closed that same decade—drove carriages, rode horses, hung off an advancing train, and literally ran to stake out plots of land. Here, where I stood, Oklahoma City was developed, shrank, and developed again. Now, as we recalled the razed community, there was a promise and regret in the air, and the moment felt like Oklahoma to me.

Many places have a kind of rejected history, a curious, closed door or a road not taken, that continues to define them. Often, it is a memory of an external enemy. (The South: the North; England: France; Texas: Mexico—and the United States.) Sometimes, it is an internal enemy. For Oklahoma, it is a series of erased alternatives, societies as utopian as America itself that washed over the land and then ebbed out of view. Oklahoma is a cleared landscape, and what was cleared continues to haunt it.

Odd that such a young state—the forty-sixth, founded in 1907—

should even have much of a past. But of course the land is far older than the state. It was settled by Native Americans driven from the South in the nineteenth-century, and traversed by unbounded tribes for millennia before that. The tribes that were "removed" from the South came unwillingly, in wintry marches over various "trails of tears" that killed thousands. But once in the new territory, they saw the opportunity to run their own nations. They created constitutions, judiciaries, and legislatures, published newspapers in their own languages ,and even convened a constitutional convention for a pan-Indian state that would be called "Sequoyah" after the man who invented the Cherokee syllabary.

Meanwhile, the territory—terra incognita on most maps, lacking mountains, mines, and myths—seemed a blank slate for other racial projects. It became a destination for white settlers—farmers, fortune-seekers, and dispossessed southerners, with their own roughneck dreams of free land in a new territory, mythologized in the land runs. Railroads gained crossing rights, and settlers pushed in. Indians were once again "removed," only this time through the resettlement of other defeated tribes in their territories; the division of reservations into individual plots (a nineteenth-century forerunner of privatization); and the removal of Native culture and language through boarding schools that taught children white ways.

Meanwhile, after the Civil War, tens of thousands of African-Americans came from the South, drawn by black entrepreneurs' circulars promising unprecedented freedom in an all-black state. Joining the freed slaves of the Indians, they founded as many as thirty black towns all over the state. The black towns—part haven from white exclusion, part angry rejoinder—echoed white towns' gestures with signs on their doors like: WHITE MAN, IF YOU CAN READ, YOU BETTER RUN. The black towns rose and declined with the fortunes of farming life. Outside the towns, the black sections of urban areas like Oklahoma City, Tulsa, and Muskogee flourished.

They represent for many people "as close for a black man to being free and independent as America ever got," says Currie Ballard, a historian at historically black Langston University.

But Jim Crow laws, adopted as soon as Oklahoma became a state, limited blacks' lives. A flurry of statutes made Oklahoma City the home of the segregated telephone booth, among other legal milestones. White supremacy spread. Cherokees had their own Klan chapters. The worst racial violence occurred in 1921, when whites burned down Greenwood, the black section of Tulsa, in a riot that destroyed 34 city blocks—1,115 houses, 24 grocery stores, 8 doctor's offices—and killed as many as 300 people. Oklahoma started as what writer Scott Malcomson calls "a laboratory of separatism"—settled by Indians, blacks, and whites, each group with dreams of its own brand-new state. The result: armed factions, separate-while-unequal diversity, and a snarling multiculturalism.

Now, Oklahoma has evolved into an entity much like its northern neighbors, striving to attract and retain corporate headquarters, a would-be New Jersey of the South, lined with highways where commuters head home from work each night, briefcases on the passenger seat, waiting in traffic, and read memos balanced on their steering wheels as the traffic piles up. Oklahoma City is not so different from Kansas City. People live in tract houses, buy arugula and Britney Spears CDs, and name their daughters Madison, Hannah, or Emily. The stories of the past are overlooked, undiscussed, and not taught in schools. Students don't learn about blacks who fought against lynching or the cultural wealth of the Indians. The story of the Tulsa riots went unacknowledged for decades.

Indians—now about 11 percent of the population—live a separate existence, only lightly represented in business or local lawmaking. About twenty-four Native American languages are left, many spoken by only a handful of elders. Indians exist in public life mainly as a series of gestures—in iconography like the Osage shield and the crossed peace pipes on the flag, the NATIVE AMERICA motto on the license plate, and the name Oklahoma itself, coined by a Choctaw to mean "red man's land." Smiling Indians in feathered headdresses advertise the state on posters. Roadside shops sell arrowheads; dolls in fake buckskin; bolos of massive, mottled turquoise, ranging from the color of sky to grass, as if to remind you of the Comanches' single word for green and blue; night lights shaped like Kokopelli, the wild-haired humpbacked flute player drawn from southwestern myths; and beaded earrings spelling out words like "Noel."

Yet, even now, these lost potential societies, the black and the Indian state, shadow and provoke Oklahoma. The races continue to live and go to school in separate communities. Now, Tulsa's African-Americans are pressing for reparations, and they have gained an official acknowledgment, but the state denies bearing the level of responsibility that would require it to offer any compensation to survivors. The harsh past fuels racial distrust and separatism; raises debates over the debts of the past; provokes the kind of cynicism toward public life that permits corruption; and underlies the fears that make Oklahoma's incarceration rate among the highest in the nation.

At the same time, the past creates a poignant idea of potentiality that seeps through the writing of the state, from the pure pastoral of the musical *Oklahoma*, with its hope for "a brand-new state," to Will Rogers's line: "We spoiled the best territory in the world to make a state." Ralph Ellison dedicated a book of essays, *Going to the Territory*, to a friend with the following words: "my friend who knows that the territory is an ideal place ever to be sought, ever to be missed, but always there." These are territories of hope, reflecting the idea that in recent memory there was an empty, grassy place that was open to anyone, sunswept and soft-aired. (Here, at the edge of the Plains, the humid southern heat and the dry Dakota winds, when they're not forming tornadoes, make a balmy blend.)

I am all too familiar with the argument that there is no point in dwelling on the past. Growing up in cultured, corporate Tulsa, I learned the narrative of progress. My grandparents were swept in during one of the booms, one of Tulsa's efforts to become a "headquarters town," as my father put it, so I grew up in a Tulsa of greenswards and loggias. There are others—like the Tulsa of Muskogee Creek hymns at the Haikey chapel and the Tulsa of raw, sprawling subdivisions, megachurches, and minivans with antiabortion bumper stickers. But mine was the Tulsa of downtown buildings that tried to be something, Art Deco skyscrapers, and the tall, metal-clad tower by Minoru Yamasaki that resembled his greater work, the World Trade Center. This was Unitarian Tulsa, Philharmonic Tulsa, Planned Parenthood Tulsa, "Little Dallas" Tulsa, Tulsa of Porsches and art-house theaters where foreign films would play for a day or two, Tulsa of smooth, green lawns, where maids in white uniforms stood waiting for the bus back to their part of town. If street names say something about a town's aspirations, it is significant that so many of Tulsa's streets recall respectable northern cities—Utica, Peoria, and Sandusky (though their names, like Sandusky, meaning "cold" or "pure water" in the Wyandot language, carry tribal echoes, too). In the long Oklahoma struggle between "progress" and "backwardness," in which each side takes turns on the side of kindness, Tulsa is the home of progress.

And yet Tulsa also has a mysterious subtext, a disjunctive quality emanating from low-voiced conversations and the foreign, Indian names on the map. As a child, I knew nothing about the destruction of Greenwood, but I knew I could walk outside my neighborhood and visit the Perryman graveyard, an overgrown, unkempt corner lot with about fifty decrepit tombstones that spoke of a forgotten history. The Perrymans, a well-off, mixed-blood Creek family who came to Oklahoma in the 1820s, ran a ranch on some of the tribal lands. It all passed out of Perryman hands quickly after the Creek lands were allotted—including the place that would become my neighborhood. Most of Tulsa lay over the old reservation.

Past the Perrymans' graveyard, if I headed west, the land would begin to drop toward the Arkansas River, where the Public Utility Co. of Tulsa glowed and quivered like a steamship on the far bank and the oil refineries threw an infernal pink onto the smoke. On the eroded banks of the river, people found the arrowheads of the Osage, the Wichita, and other tribes that hunted there before the Creeks arrived. Down on the lowest banks, there was oily shale, and you could pick up a piece and flake off the top layer, baring a darker, older slice with the sheen of new skin. The sheen was oil: fossil fuel, the dormant dead, ready to be turned to fire.

Growing up, I came to sense the past as an archaeological reality: we lived here, but our lawns went scarcely a foot deep. The layer of basements went deeper, and the roots of trees kept going, but mixed in with it all were the remains of the dead, the dung of the Perrymans' cattle, and the Osage arrowheads. If I skimmed the grass from the lawns, this history would appear. But if a land deed rests on a shady sale from an Indian, if a child finds a white robe in a grandparent's closet—what is to be done? We were eastward-directed, disdainful of all signs of the old Oklahoma; we reflected Oklahoma's discomfort with its own past.

But what if . . . history is not over; the past continues to reweave itself through the fabric of the present; what if you get chance after chance? Lost communities informed my thoughts as I walked by Oklahoma City's downtown memorials. But I had other business there: I was visiting a Pawnee powwow in a downtown convention center.

A powwow is a riddle of identity. What's most striking about it is not how "exotic" it is but how Oklahoman it is—conservative, close-knit, religious, patriotic, supportive of the U.S. military. Indeed, powwows were created by the peculiar conditions of refugee life in

Oklahoma—along with the peyote church and the fry bread made from flour rations handed out by the government. While powwows could be traced back to Native American ceremonial dances that were part of preparations for hunting and raiding, that life disappeared when Indians moved to the Oklahoma reservations. It was only in the early 1900s, when tribes moved to revive the old dances—inspired in part by the fact that Anglos were already hiring old Indians to dance for them—that the modern powwow really took shape.

Always bring your own lawn chair to a powwow. The space of it is a communal circle, where the drummers sit in a knot and dancers go round, and the outer ring is defined by people sitting in their folding chairs, often a few rows deep. Having come to this powwow without a chair, I was stuck in social limbo, wandering around the arena. It was my first clue to the inner logic of the event.

As I stood and watched, an elder from the Sac and Fox tribe gave a benediction in his language; flags were paraded by a group of veterans from U.S. wars; and the arena slowly filled up with bright colors and flying feathers as dancers arrived. I had been to other powwows, but this one had patriotic blends I had never seen: one dancer wore a headdress of navy and white feathers with a red-and-white spangled headband. A doll sold in the stands wore a blue dress with flag stars on it; a Kiowa man wore a gold-spangled suit, with red Boy Scout kerchief and white headband. The Pawnees have a long relationship with the U.S. government, having served as Army scouts, and depict a U.S. flag in the corner of their flag.

I watched people help each other get dressed: a sixteen-year-old in jeans combed and braided the hair of her mother, who sat in a chair, wrapped in a shawl of fake buckskin. Behind them stood a boy tending a baby. And above it all, the emcee's gentle rap drifted out over the microphone, easing people from dance to dance. "Make it happen, dancers, make it happen," he said; I had read that the emcee's role was to provide "narrative continuity" for the event. Along with his patter and the constant, hypnotic drumming, I could hear the muted clanging of headdresses with mirrors hanging from them, high cowbells, little jingle bells, and tin-can spangles. Half a dozen little girls rattled by, chasing each other in jingle-dress costumes.

This powwow was meant to honor Youngbird, a traditional drum group that had been nominated for a Grammy and was trying to raise money to travel to the show. Members of Youngbird walked around selling raffle tickets, hair slicked back into ponytails, wearing fresh, dark, baggy jeans and plaid shirts that made them look like the coordinated boy bands popular at that moment. The members themselves were Oklahoma hybrids. The one I knew, Brian Frejo, a Pawnee-Seminole, also had a hip-hop crew called Culture Shock Camp and was trying to use the powwow drum as a hook in his hip-hop.

A little later, Youngbird went out on the floor, and the young men went into a daze of drumming, singing with their eyes closed and hitting with great power. They were surrounded by singers, then by people with Camcorders, and then by a whole circle of onlookers and dancers. An announcer thanked them and hoped they would "bring the award back home to the great state of Oklahoma, the Pawnee tribe, and the Youngbird family"—group nestled within group.

As I watched the casual unfolding of the event, with drummers following invisible cues from each other, I thought of the early meetings of American Indians and Europeans. From the 1600s on, reports of the Indians' freedom from rulers' sway, as well as the absence of hereditary distinctions, stimulated the Europeans to ponder the possibilities and limits of democracy. Here, the circling and the informal, egalitarian structure brought to life the traditions of older communal societies that predated the white presence in America. "Giveaways" informally dipersed community wealth with gestures like a blanket covered with $20 bills, and families built relationships by dedicating songs to individual people.

"We're proud of this girl," the announcer said at one point, pointing to a thin nine-year-old standing on the sidelines. "She's in third grade. Prayers have been said for her to go through high school and college and get a good job."

"*Aho!*" some guy yelled, in a pan-Indian cry of agreement. People seemed to forget about the sterility of the arena, the giant roll-up doors, the concrete floors, the wheeled bleachers, old popcorn on the floor, and industrial garbage cans.

Many visitors say powwows seem "inauthentic," by which they mean: no natural fibers, lots of dyed feathers, the scene as garishly colored as a jar of gumballs. Indians don't live up to outsiders' expectations—or they do too well, creating what academics call "post-Indian simulations"—their regalia no more functional than the urban cowboy's ten-gallon hat.

And yet powwows have their own authenticity. Unlike meticulous re-creations of the Stone Age, powwows are part of these hybrid communities' life. The rituals evolved in part for whites but then were reabsorbed into the community, like an oyster taking a foreign object, absorbing it, turning it into something else. Back and forth: people took sacred feathers, colored them navy and white, and reincorporated them into a headdress.

I noticed, too, the lawn chairs that made up the ring. Some were the old-fashioned aluminum kind with webbing; others were modern polyester chairs with cup holders. More often than not, they were personalized: painted, covered with quilting, or piled with needlepoint cushions; one was a red OU Sooners chair; another was upholstered with bright-striped Indian blankets, and another draped in shawls; one was fitted with flowered slipcovers, and another was simply a metal folding chair with the name "Whitewolf" written in Magic Marker on the back.

I had never been to a powwow where people didn't sit on these portable chairs, a modern adaptation—and a familiar gesture. These were the same lawn chairs that people used elsewhere in Oklahoma for fishing or camping or suntanning. At $6.99 apiece, lawn chairs are all-American; they are egalitarian, down-home, and unpretentious; everyone uses them to set up a temporary community in a public space, whether it's a football tailgate or a gospel revival or a pops concert by a brass band or a Fourth of July fireworks celebration. The circle of lawn chairs struck me as a way of claiming the place for the evening.

Such gestures have particular resonance in Oklahoma, where land has always been something you claimed casually; no one felt it was a homeland; no one had been here for long. The land run required settlers only to exist on the land, to stake it out and stay, in order to make it theirs. On this night, the Pawnees were holding the land for the floating world of their own communal system, their lawn-chair democracy.

Here was a kind of mixing that Oklahoma rarely acknowledged. It was a living structure of history, a rare example of an alternative past existing alongside the present. And, while it solved no questions about the past, it represented a culture that Oklahoma didn't have to memorialize—only, for once, to sustain.

That was the night, and in the morning, it would be over, and I would be walking through the bright, wide avenues of Oklahoma City, looking at memorials.

OREGON

A CONTRARY UNIT

Joanne B. Mulcahy

*Languages, though not necessarily synonymous with distinct cultures,
express a bond between people and place that offers perhaps the closest
human counterpart to the adaptive "fit" of genetically distinct salmon
stocks to their ancestral coastal streams.*
—*The Rainforests of Home: An Atlas of People and Place*

They named themselves as they stood, one by one, survivors
of nations within our state: Burns Paiute, Coquille, Klamath, the Cow Creek Band of Umpqua, and five separate
groups of Confederated Tribes—Grand Ronde; Warm Springs; Siletz;
Umatilla; and Coos, Lower Umpqua, and Siuslaw. Beaded regalia
shimmered under the lights of the Portland Convention Center,
newly opened in 1990. Smatterings of Sahaptin and Chinook mixed
with English as Oregon's nine federally recognized tribes processed
through the hall. Their presence refuted the 1950s attempt to assimilate American Indians by terminating their tribal status. Of the 106
tribes and bands terminated nationally, 62 had been native to Oregon.
They called themselves "The First Oregonians."

My friend Eva names herself this way: Genoveva Castellanoz—
Mexicana, Latina, *curandera* (healer), Catholic, traditional artist, and
finally, with a hint of pride in her voice, Oregonian. Born in Guanajuato and raised in Texas, she arrived in Nyssa on the Oregon–Idaho
border as a young bride at eighteen. The families of her nine children
now encircle Eva as she heals the sick from migrant camps and
teaches Latino arts to local gang members. Surveying the vast

sugar-beet fields surrounding Nyssa, she says, "This was my daddy's dream. He came here as a *bracero* to make a home. I want to be part of it—the realization of that dream." The 1940s *bracero* program brought Mexican laborers north to fill labor shortages during World War II, presaging the steady stream of Hispanic workers who now make up 8 percent of Oregon's population.

Sabah, Carmen, Fatime, Mabi, and Valeriana gather once a month for a sewing circle run by Portland's Immigrant and Refugee Community Organization. Spanish blends with Pashtun, Arabic, French, and English as women in chadors, dashikis, and jeans admire one another's handwork. A microcosm of the nearly ten thousand refugees and immigrants arriving every year, they come together to preserve essential parts of their cultures.

Hope and Harold McLaughlin moved from Colorado to a farm near Enterprise in eastern Oregon's Wallowa Mountains. They embody pioneer resourcefulness, utilizing everything: rags and scraps for Hope's quilts and rugs, scarce water to irrigate their acreage, bits of lumber for Harold's tables and picture frames.

All are Oregonians, seeking to fit language and culture to place. I met many of them traversing the state, first as a folklorist seeking local arts, then as a writer teaching workshops. Despite the seeming uniformity of an 86 percent white and English-speaking population, we are distinct. Our ancestral streams are many and growing. In Portland's schools, loudspeakers blare announcements in Russian, Spanish, and Vietnamese. In what was a predominantly Caucasian Willamette Valley, one in four residents now claims a racial identity other than white.

As a folklorist, I listen to stories. What I've heard is what unites us: passionate commitment to a place sacred to its indigenous inhabitants, an "Eden" to the first white settlers. What I've heard is what divides us: fear that we lack bounty enough for so many cultures, doubt that we'll find a lingua franca amid the growing Babel.

I came to Oregon in the 1970s, a wanderer from the east. In my early twenties, I fell in love with a fisherman, then with the drenched rain forests, headlands, and estuaries of the Oregon Coast. The holy triumvirate of fishing, logging, and farming ruled the economy then. Trawlers and crabbers dotted the craggy coastline; gargantuan logging trucks thundered by on my first drive from the Portland airport to the ocean. Much in the Willamette Valley echoed the New England of my family's heritage: simple clapboard houses with wraparound porches, miles of dairy farms, and Eastern monikers like Portland. The Maine namesake replaced "Stumptown" after an 1851 coin toss that might have yielded Boston. Green prairies rising to buttes, groves of hazelnuts, the snow cap of Mount Hood gleaming on the horizon—my first views evoked the mythic descriptions of the early white settlers. Local folklore records the story of a man who died and went to heaven only to discover people there chained and guarded. They were, Saint Peter explained, Oregonians yearning to go back.

How does one claim a place as home? I remember an old man in Baker City who stopped playing his fiddle mid-tune to tell me he hoped to die an Oregonian. I found his statement quaint; after all, he'd only come from Idaho. Then I heard similar stories from others; finally, it was my story, too, when I realized I'd never leave Oregon.

Like zealous converts everywhere, our attachment is deep. The land beguiles us: a three-hundred-mile coast zoned against private development, central Oregon's juniper and sage desert and painted hills, the azure basin of Crater Lake, the cliffs and chasms of the Columbia River Gorge, and eastern Oregon's rim-rock canyons and migratory-bird refuges. The people welcome, exhibiting the fabled friendliness outsiders always note, despite Governor Tom McCall's famous 1971 exhortation to visitors to please not stay. We're proud of the state's environmental record, embodied and mythologized in the 1971 first mandatory bottle-deposit law. We're traditional, attached to old-fashioned celebrations like Portland's ninety-six-year-old Rose Festival, complete with the Queen of

Rosaria and her court, and we're progressive, organizing for some of the country's largest antiwar demonstrations during Vietnam, the 1991 Gulf War, and the recent war in Iraq. Even when the "we" breaks down and old divisions gape, a shared contrariness surfaces. Consider the decision on physician-assisted suicide. Even those who voted against the referendum can claim the vote as typically Oregonian.

I live in Portland now. Poised at the confluence of the Willamette and Columbia rivers, our largest city's famed livability garners descriptions of a small-town feel. We boast 9,400 green acres, including Forest Park, the largest urban wilderness in the country; extensive light-rail and bike-path systems; a stunning Chinese classical garden; the largest independent bookstore in the world, Powell's City of Books; a thriving arts scene; and remarkably diverse architecture including an icon of postmodernism, Michael Graves's Portland Building. In 1985, the building's facade gained *Portlandia*, the sculpture of a crouching woman holding a trident. She traveled via barge along the Columbia River, then flatbed truck through the city. Locals lined the streets in welcome, hands outstretched to touch her pounded copper before she ascended to a third-story perch. Bent at the knees, *Portlandia* measures thirty-six feet tall, but were she to rise, she'd tower at fifty feet.

We may need her erect posture at this particular juncture, someone to stand tall enough to propel us from the mire of 8 percent unemployment; one of the highest rates of hunger in the nation (5.2–6.2 percent, depending on the survey); among the lowest allocations of spending for the arts (one study lists us fifty-second, behind Guam and American Samoa); an inability to fund the innovative and nationally lauded Oregon Health Plan; and a consistent refusal to institute a sales tax, despite an educational funding crisis spurred by a 1990 referendum that rolled back the support base of property taxes.

What happened in Eden? Local and global forces have driven many from The Garden. High-tech companies, service jobs, and tourism edged out resource-based industries; automation and the decline of unions forced wage cutbacks. High-tech's own descent followed, busting the 1990s gold rush. Jobs elsewhere lure newly minted teachers; loggers and fishermen must reinvent themselves. In rural areas, economic choices are uneven and sometimes unsavory. Witness eastern Oregon's Umatilla County, where growth rests on Wal-Mart, a state prison, and a chemical-weapons incinerator.

Our passion for the land may be shared; not so our vision of its husbandry. In the 1980s loggers clashed with environmentalists over the endangered spotted owl in the Willamette Valley's old-growth forests. In 2002, water wars erupted in southern Oregon. Farmers and the Klamath Indians sparred when the U.S. Bureau of Reclamation diverted irrigation water to endangered suckerfish held sacred by the tribe. Along the coast, 3,437,200 hectares form part of the largest contiguous coastal temperate rain forest in the world. Dense ecosystems that sustained human communities for five millennia still survive. But just barely. Development has claimed 44 percent, threatening salmon and watersheds.

Was Eden ever real? Or did our shaky economy simply expose the myth of plenty and opportunity for all? Surely Oregon was less than Edenic for African-Americans who arrived as cowboys and railroad workers in the nineteenth century or to the shipyards during World War II. They faced racist laws including a ban on interracial marriage until 1951. Plenty eluded the Chinese who confronted the 1880s depression, exclusionary laws, and violence. Opportunity had a different cast for the family of a Japanese-American woman in a workshop I taught in Hood River. While others described a deep sense of community, she detailed displacement, internment camps, and lingering shame.

As Oregon's economic woes deepened, rifts formed between self-defined "real" Oregonians and "others." Xenophobia and hate crimes surged after 9/11. Attacks against Arab-Americans and Sikhs escalated; DIE JEW and swastikas appeared on the gates of Portland's

Shaarie Torah cemetery. Each incident recalled earlier waves of fear. In 1992, the Oregon Citizens' Alliance introduced Ballot Measure 9 to limit gay rights. That fall, I traveled south to Springfield, conservative sister city to liberal Eugene, where Earth First and Grateful Dead stickers flourish. My NO ON 9 bumper-stickered car was filled with woodcarvings from an art exhibit to return to a retired logger. At his house, we talked about everything but politics. As I rose to leave, he nodded toward my car. "Can't we just let people live their lives?"

We could, but we haven't—at least not the tribes terminated, the gays and lesbians excluded, or the ethnic and religious populations threatened. We might learn from the embedded fault lines in our history. The Spanish ventured north first, reaching the southern coast as early as 1542. The British followed, vying with the French Canadians and Americans, who triumphed with the creation of the Oregon Territory in 1848, then statehood in 1859. The contests' prizes were many: the mythic trade route between Atlantic and Pacific, furs for Asian trade, souls to convert, and always, land. In 1823, the U.S. Supreme Court's "doctrine of the right of discovery" ruled that Indians, as nomads, didn't own the land. The predictable logic of displacement followed: free land to white immigrants, negotiated but unratified treaties, the reservation system, and the repression of indigenous traditions and languages.

Like people everywhere, we find myth more alluring than history. Our story of Eden is not false but partial—it fits if you're the right sort of person at the right historical moment.

There are places in Oregon that feel to me like ancestral songlines. Several times a year I visit Menucha, a retreat center in the Columbia River Gorge. Standing on an overlook above the river, I listen for a train whistle that catapults me back to the small Vermont town where I spent childhood summers. Grief rises at the memory of leaving soil soaked in family history; a surge of affection follows for the home I've found. Perhaps this is what all immigrants feel: nostalgia for the abandoned place, renewed passion for the chosen one. The open spirit of Oregon birthed me as a writer, nourished my language and culture. Knowing that this sense of possibility has not been equally extended to others chastens the comfort of my connection here.

Can we find a language of inclusion? Is restitution of past wrongs possible? I might have asked someone from the farmworkers' organization, the Human Dignity Coalition, Basic Rights Oregon or a host of other social-change organizations. But imagining the future evokes the past, triggering a still-searing memory from The First Oregonians Conference. At the close of the gathering, one elder stood to tearfully acknowledge the tribes' first reunion since the nineteenth century. She urged those assembled to address the past but move beyond it. Her optimism stunned me. The near decimation of language and culture, the loss of land, the brutal fact of tribal termination—how could they recover?

On my last trip to the coast, I veered off Highway 18 just past the turnoff for the Grand Ronde Tribes' Spirit Mountain Casino. At the tribe's Educational Complex, Tony Johnson's class was winding down for the day. His black ponytail hung to one side as Tony velcroed shut tiny shoes and hunted stray lunch boxes. Isabelle, the newest participant in this language-immersion program, lingered for one more story from an illustrated book. She pointed to a mouse's long tail to explain the words "yutskat up^{h}uch" pasted over the English text. Her face brightened as she chattered away in what most assume is a dead language—Chinook wawa to indigenous tribes, Chinook Jargon to the French, English, and Americans who added loan words to this Northwest Creole. Words for objects unknown to local Indians such as "fork" found form through relationship—"opitsah yakha sikh"—"friend to the knife." The language is built on compounds—a grammar of connection. The need for communication across difference was also the Jargon's genesis, Tony explained. "The tribes created the creole long before outsiders arrived. When Indians speaking different languages married outside their tribe, they needed a new language. They invented Chinook wawa." He paused for a moment, clear eyes focused on a distant point—the past, perhaps the future. "To whites, the Jargon was for trade. But to us, Chinook wawa is a language of love and relationship."

Watching Isabelle wrap her arms around Tony's legs, I glimpsed why he passed up a graduate fellowship in linguistics to teach here. Born in Washington to the Chinook tribe, he is to my mind a real Oregonian: committed to something larger than himself, to this place, these children, and a unique way of speaking and knowing that might otherwise pass from the earth.

Two hundred years ago, different languages thrived at the mouth of every Oregon river—Chinookan, Sahaptin, Molallan, Cayusan, Lutuamian, Kalapuyan-Takelman, Alsean, and Siuslawan among them. Liz Woody, a poet from the Warm Springs Reservation, tells of hearing stories from her maternal uncle about the days when multiple languages and tribes prospered. Different worldviews and scarce resources threatened their unity, too. Perhaps they seemed as different to one another as the newest Afghani refugee seems to her Mexican neighbor, as foreign as some of my fellow Portlanders seem to me when they vote against taxes for health care and school funding. But the earliest tribes understood that survival depended on mutual respect, on language that connected, and on sharing wealth in ceremonies such as the huckleberry feast.

A few months ago, I journeyed to Enterprise to visit with Hope and Harold McLaughlin. Harold waited to display his portable wooden tables, multiplying since he retired from farming at age eighty-six last year. As we talked, Harold burst out, "We're so different! I wonder why we're friends?" Hope surveyed him with affection and incredulity before pronouncing, "Because we're so different."

Our differences shouldn't threaten equitable distribution. In piecing together strained resources, we have models: the inventiveness of the early pioneers, the huckleberry feast. Restoration beckons —of watersheds and salmon, of jobs for displaced workers, of the dignity of excluded peoples and their cultures. In learning to communicate, we might look to the creoles born of our multilingual past. Perhaps there lies the root of a language of relationship, a contemporary Chinook Jargon reaching across our divides.

PENNSYLVANIA

Kathryn Davis

When I was girl of sixteen, more innocent and fanciful than any sixteen-year-old girl would dream of being these dreary days, after we all got herded across the bridge into the twenty-first century, there were two places in my natal city of Philadelphia where I particularly loved to go. One was high atop City Hall, where you could stand in the open air at the enormous feet of the statue of William Penn; the other was deep inside the Franklin Institute, where you could take a walk through the enormous chambers of a talking, beating heart.

William Penn and Benjamin Franklin: you might say that these two men, in combination, represent some essential character of the state of Pennsylvania, a peculiar admixture of sobriety and imagination, of gravity and wit. William Penn was a devout Quaker, a staunch advocate of religious freedom and a lover of nature, who made friends with the Native tribes and learned their language. Benjamin Franklin, on the other hand, was a sharp-tongued intellectual, the enormously charming and politically astute cosmopolite who gave us *Poor Richard's Almanac* and bifocal lenses and the glass harmonica. Even at John Story Jenks Elementary School, which I attended from 1951 (when I first encountered the grim practice of napping on a mat on the floor in Miss Patterson's kindergarten) until 1957 (when I sat rapt in Mr. Fine's sixth-grade classroom listening to *The Ride of the Valkyries*), the fundamental difference between these two heroes of Pennsylvania history was abundantly obvious.

William Penn was a very good man, a man of vision and integrity, a man the Leni-Lenape liked so much they gave him a belt made of wampum. Usually he wore a ridiculous-looking hat and enormous shoe buckles, both of which you had to include in your drawings of him. He was an earnest man and, hence, boring. Whereas, though Benjamin Franklin wasn't a bad man, he tended to say things like, "Fish and visitors smell after three days." He had little patience with the pietism of the Quakers, and couldn't stand William Penn's son Thomas, who was, truly, a villain. You didn't usually draw pictures of Benjamin Franklin, but if you did, you might show him adventurously flying a kite during a thunderstorm or sitting by a Franklin stove. When the thirteen independent colonies began organizing to act in unison, Franklin served as their ambassador to France, where the women went wild for him and wore coonskin hats called "The Insurgent" in his honor. Thomas Jefferson, who succeeded him, said he was a tough act to follow.

Does a state consist of its statesmen?

William Penn and Benjamin Franklin. Sobriety and humor; gravity and heart. The Pennsylvania landscape, "never wild nor terrible . . . neither garish nor odd." Brandywine Meadows, Paradise Valley. Wilkes-Barre, on the Susquehanna River in Lackawanna Township, where the Russians, Slovaks, and Irish came to dig black diamonds from the earth, and where my father regularly disappeared for days at a time back when he was still on the road, footloose and fancy free, selling televisions and dishwashers. The Mummer's Day Parade, on the first day of every new year, when hundreds of grown men would deck themselves out in sequins and feathers and dance down Market Street, playing banjos and glockenspiels, singing "Oh, dem golden slippers." The philosopher's stone, tossed into the Wissahickon Creek immediately after the death of the mystic Johann Kelpius, at which point the stone exploded, and for a time thereafter flashes of lightning and peals like unto thunder came out of the water. Pennsylvania has always appealed to mystics of one stripe or another. The Swedenborgians built their cathedral in Bryn Athyn. Maybe it's easier to be a mystic if the landscape around you isn't too extravagant. Edgar Allan Poe also lived in Pennsylvania for a while, during which time he wrote "The Murders in the Rue Morgue."

To get to either the statue or the heart I would take the Reading Railroad from Wyndmoor to Center City, usually in the company of my friend Amy, who not only had been inflicted with hair every bit as unstylishly kinky as mine, but who also shared my appetite for adventure (that is to say, escaping suburbia), and who also happened to be my companion at the weekend work camp sponsored by the Society of Friends where my heart was broken by a Congregationalist minister from New Haven, Connecticut, who told me that my desire to help the poor black people of the Philadelphia ghetto came from a smug and condescending place Jesus would never have approved of.

The honest desire to do good is a large part of William Penn's legacy to the state whose name he permitted his own name to be subsumed within, as long as its sylvan beauty was also included; that legacy is tempered by Franklin's coolly appraising mind and gaze.

When William Penn first arrived in this country he mistook the Leni-Lenape for Jews. "Their eye is little and black," he wrote. "A man would think himself in Dukes-place or Berry-street in London when he seeth them." He thought their language was like Hebrew, one word serving in place of three. The Leni-Lenape revered Penn: he kept his promises and treated them with respect. Their friendship, they pledged, would endure "as long as the sun will shine and the rivers flow with water." But fifteen years after Penn's death his villainous son, Thomas, decided to redefine the boundaries of what came to be called the Walking Purchase, in which the Leni-Lenape had agreed to deed Penn as much land as a man could cover in a leisurely three-day walk. After a day and a half Penn the elder came to a halt somewhere in what is now Bucks County, having concluded that he had more than enough land. But Thomas advertised for runners, one of whom made it deep into the Poconos, and relations between the two groups were never the same again.

It was a short walk from Reading Terminal to City Hall, though you had to ignore the Reading Terminal Market on your way out, where farmers from Lancaster County would try to sell you an entire baby pig with black holes where its eyes had once been, or lacy sheets of tripe, or eggs specked with chicken shit, or a shoofly pie made with molasses and lard. That smell of the abattoir, that smell of meat, not quite rotting but on the verge, combined with the smell of engine exhaust and urine—when I was a girl of sixteen, that was the smell of freedom.

Amy and I would head west on Market Street for three blocks, where we'd enter City Hall through the central courtyard and take the elevator to the top of the tower. Construction of the building, a massive structure in the late French Renaissance style, began in 1870 and dragged on for a third of a century. City Hall is located at the intersection of Broad and Market streets, Philadelphia's main north-south and east-west thoroughfares; the statue of William Penn, which weighs twenty-six tons (including that hat and those buckles), was hoisted into place in 1894, the same year Thomas Eakins delivered his lecture "The Differential Action of Certain Muscles Passing More Than One Joint" at the Academy of Natural Sciences, and electric trolleys made their first appearance on Chelten Avenue.

Until 1987 a "gentleman's agreement" had decreed that nothing in the Philadelphia skyline was allowed to rise higher than William Penn. From his feet you could see the whole world: up Broad Street to the north, past the dark red brick of the Pennsylvania Academy of the Fine Arts, where Eakins famously lost his job after yanking the loincloth off a male model, and where I would one day attend school; or south to the Italian market, where mountains of unpaired high-heeled shoes presented a fairy-tale challenge to the hapless buyer, and farther south to neighborhoods where little girls from the suburbs weren't ever supposed to set foot. You could look west on Market Street past the orthopedic shoe store where my friend Peggy used to buy special shoes for her daughter who was born pigeon-toed but is now perfectly fine; and over the Schuylkill River to the University of Pennsylvania; you could look down Market Street to the east, past the Crystal Tearoom at Wanamaker's where my mother used to take me and my sister for bisque tortoni after shopping for Easter hats in the days before we betrayed her by turning from cute little girls into disagreeable and not especially attractive teenagers, and all the way to Independence Hall, where Benjamin Franklin helped draft a new nation's constitution. "What kind of a government have you given us?" a woman is reported to have asked him. "A Republic, madam, if you can keep it," he is said to have replied. If you looked really hard you could see all the way to the banks of the Delaware River, where William Penn first set foot on the land he'd been granted by Charles II, in settlement of a debt to his father. The first day of every January Penn was required to pay the king or his heirs two beaver skins and the fifth part of all gold and silver found in the province, though Pennsylvania's mineral wealth, as it turned out, ran more to lead, zinc, feldspar, nickel, and copper. And, of course, coal.

When you stood perched there at Penn's feet, you felt like you could see to the ends of the earth. The prospect was entirely outward, far-reaching, exploratory—your eyes traveling through space, registering landmarks, taking it all in but not to deeply analyze or brood upon unduly. You were like a bird, one of the city's million pigeons, that most boring of birds, predictably drawn to those most boring of buildings, the great gray structures in which a populace conducts its civic affairs. You were a pigeon but aspiring to the condition of those birds about which one early European visitor to Pennsylvania wrote:

> It is impossible to overpraise their beautiful colors and their lovely songs. First of all there are yellow birds with black wings; secondly red birds with black wings; thirdly, completely yellow birds; fourthly, starlings, bigger than ours, blue all over with red heads; fifthly, brilliant red ones with plumes on their heads; sixthly, entirely blue ones; seventhly, white ones with black wings; eighthly, multi-colored ones; ninthly, grass-green ones, with red heads; tenthly, there is a pied species colored black and white. These birds can imitate the song and the whistling of all other birds . . . but the most marvelous bird of all, not only in Pennsylvania but perhaps in the entire world, is a little bird rarely to be seen. This little bird is not even the size of a May bug. It is not bigger than a gold-crested wren. It glitters like gold, and it sips nothing but honey out of flowers, and that is why it is known as the sugar-bird.

Of course before there was William Penn, or Thomas Eakins, or Miss Patterson, or the Leni-Lenape, or even before there were the grass-green birds with red heads or sugar-birds, there was the raw material that was to become Pennsylvania, and that would, in its own indifferent way, determine the character of the state it was to become. The oldest part of Pennsylvania is the Piedmont Plateau, composed of rocks that became dry land at the beginning of the Paleozoic era, 540 million years ago. To the west of this landmass a huge inland sea extended into what is now Ohio, where the Paleozoic strata, which would become the famous coal beds of western and central Pennsylvania, were deposited. At some point a huge upheaval running from northwest to southeast buckled and folded the beds of the bay, like a big tablecloth, making mountains. The glaciers came relatively late and left behind plants otherwise native to the far north in the bogs of the northern counties. Leatherleaf and Labrador tea.

Eventually it would get boring, up there at Penn's feet, high above the city. People aren't birds, nor are they gods. There is just so much spectating a person can do, just so much taking in of the landscape from a bird's-eye view, just so much imagining of oneself into this place or that—into that squalid little tenement the train passed after leaving Wayne Junction where you'd live in sin with the handsome senior who kept condoms in his wallet, for example, or (a different reverie entirely) inside the twelfth-century French cloister, which was itself inside the Philadelphia Museum of Art, where you could kneel on a prie-dieu like a pure and holy twelfth-century nun when the guards weren't looking. Too much reverie and you're taken over by the kind of weariness bred of prolonged dissociation from the things of this world that can't be seen, by a frantic impatience with compass points and facts, by a wild desire to at long last get down to the bottom of things.

From William Penn's feet, Amy and I would take the elevator back down to street level, where we'd walk in a northwesterly direction, up Benjamin Franklin Parkway to Logan Circle and to the Franklin Institute, where, in addition to the Hall of Prime Movers, the Hall of Aviation, the Fels Planetarium, and the thirty-foot statue of Benjamin Franklin, was the giant heart.

The moment you entered the heart, you heard it beating—*ba-bum, ba-bum, ba-bum*—and it was as if you were inside your own heart, which was mysteriously, simultaneously, inside you. The sound of the beating was loud and hypnotic. "I am the left ventricle," the heart would say. "I receive the blood from the auricles and pump it into the arteries." Or something along these lines—I never really paid attention to what the heart was saying, since the point of walking through it was not to acquire facts but just to *be* there, astonishingly, inside a heart.

Usually, in those days, no one else was in the heart, though there were always signs that others had been there before you: graffiti on the walls, chiefly of the Sally-loves-Jimmy variety inside a cartoon heart, as well as lots of balled-up trash on the floors. The heart wasn't especially well kept. Compared to the Fels Planetarium it was obviously low priority. In fact it was pretty depressing, but we couldn't seem to get enough of it.

I don't think of myself as a Pennsylvanian. No artist owes that sort of fealty to a political jurisdiction. But there are parts of the landscape of my youth that have entered into my soul, becoming part of everything I write.

From the bright prospect of a world viewed at a distance, filled with facts and place names and with endless possibility, to the litter-infarcted passageways of an outsize model of a hidden organ. From the hopeful outward gaze of Willam Penn to the less attractive precincts at the heart of things. This is what it means to inhabit a state, I think. To *be in a state*, really.

PUERTO RICO

CHANGES WITHIN A NAME

Rosario Ferré

THE TAKEOVER

In 1898, when U.S. troops landed in Puerto Rico, we had been a colony of Spain for almost four hundred years. San Juan was bombed in May by Admiral Sampson's fleet and after that the land operations of the campaign lasted two weeks. The Americans suffered four deaths and forty-seven wounded. The Spaniards endured only slightly more casualties.

The island passed from Spain to the United States on October 18, 1898. That day companies A, B, E, G, K, L, and M of the eleventh Infantry Regiment marched into San Juan armed with bayonets and carrying musical instruments. The soldiers stood in pairs and at attention at each corner of the main entrances to the old city, as two artillery divisions of the Fifth Regiment marched toward El Morro Castle. The key to the castle was ceremoniously handed over to the American captain. Henry Reed by the Spanish artillery captain Angel Rivero. At noon the canons of El Morro Fort and San Cristóbal Fort boomed out forty-five times (one shot for each of the forty-five states of the union) as the Stars and Stripes were hoisted over all of San Juan's public buildings, including the governor's palace. The town squares and streets were packed with people, but silence reigned. There was no applause, no hurrahs, while in the inland towns such as Ponce and Mayagüez, there had been joyous celebrations and welcoming committees.

Why the contrast between *la capital* and *la isla*, the island's capital and its towns?

In San Juan people were both cautious and afraid; the capital was the seat of the Spanish government, and sympathy for Spain ran high among many citizens. Hope, curiosity, apprehension gripped the population. The very character of the fortified city, sheltered by its massive walls and forts, had developed from the need for protection against *el Inglés*, as English pirates were called. Now the English language was in control of their destiny.

Puerto Rico at the time was sorely in need of social and economic reform. The island was deeply divided between rich and poor, educated and illiterate, white and black. The *criollo* well-to-do who were not Spanish citizens were eager to rid themselves of Spanish hegemony.

In Ponce and Mayagüez a considerable part of the population was of French, German, and Corsican descent, and had little or no sympathy for Spain. Left to their own resources by the empire for centuries, they had prospered far from the Spanish bureaucratic center of government in San Juan and were hampered by Spain's authoritative control. *El campo*, the hinterland, was poor, and had much to gain. In 1898 there were no public elementary schools and 98 percent of the population was illiterate.

Thus Puerto Ricans welcomed the arrival of the United States on the island for different and even opposing reasons—the educated classes in San Juan, silent behind their louvered doors, saw it as an opportunity to make a surgical cut with Spain and take political power for themselves; the masses, milling in the streets of the towns, understood it as a chance to become part of a political system which, for the first time in their four-hundred years of history, could secure them democratic rights.

The takeover was accomplished during a ceremony held in the "Throne Room" of La Fortaleza, the governor's palace, whereby the sovereignty of the island was officially handed over to the American military command by the Spanish Estado Mayor.

A photograph of the event, published in Paul Miller's *Historia de Puerto Rico* (1922), is symbolic of the role Puerto Rico played in this eerie drama, in which few died, no great battles ensued, and the silence of suspense reigned in the streets. General John R. Brooke (the future governor) sits elbow to elbow with General Frederick Grant (the son of General and former President U. S. Grant). Generals Sheridan and Gordon, and Commodore Schley, dressed in navy wool gala uniforms with their white-gloved hands resting on their sabers, are seated around the right side of the table. General Ricardo Ortega (the Spanish governor) and his generals, wearing wrinkled cotton drill uniforms and devoid of arms, sit slumped in their chairs on the left side of the table, faces thin and drawn, gloveless hands lying open on their thighs. Behind the table covered with orderly documents and wearing civilian clothes stand the only two Puerto Ricans in the picture: Manuel del Valle Atiles and Manuel Paniagua, wearing elegant jackets and ties, both of them translators. Witnesses to how their island was being passed from the Spaniards to the Americans, Atiles and Paniagua were facilitators of communication between two very different cultures, interpreters of both English and Spanish. They stand behind the assembled group, one on each side of a map of Puerto Rico exhibited on the wall of the Throne Room, and seem to be presenting the scene, captured on film for future generations.

But these translators' neutral, sophisticated gaze is more than that. It makes them active subjects, instead of identifying them with the passive, humiliated prey that, at that very moment, was being handed over by the declining empire to the ascending one. Like the camera's detached and minutely precise lens, their passivity is only apparent, as if in fact they knew they were the real protagonists of the drama that was being played before them.

What could have justified this pride, this self-assurance in the translators, Atiles and Paniagua? A translator is often one who interprets, deciphers, and sheds light on a situation at hand. To be a translator is not to be passive and everyone who is bilingual is, by necessity, a translator. Puerto Rico's bilingualism, in 1898, was already situating it at the vanguard of the twenty-first century. Atiles and Paniagua knew that the Americans couldn't speak Spanish and that the Spaniards couldn't speak English, and this put them in a privileged position. It's as if they had foreseen that the takeover of the Spanish-speaking territory would one day contribute to changing the course of American history.

FROM ISLA DE SAN JUAN BAUTISTA TO ISLA DE PUERTO RICO

Since the fifteenth century, when Christopher Columbus landed in Puerto Rico, we have undergone numerous transformations, as evidenced by our changing name. In the past four-hundred years we have gone from "Isla de San Juan Bautista" (in the late fifteenth and early sixteenth centuries) to "Isla de Puerto Rico" (in the sixteenth to the end of the nineteenth century), to "Porto Rico" (in the first half of the twentieth century), and back again to "Puerto Rico" for the past fifty years.

The name "San Juan Bautista" was given to us by Queen Isabel la Católica in 1492 and is represented by the lamb on our national coat of arms. It conferred on us a peaceful aura, which has persisted for four-hundred years. As a colony and later a commonwealth we have never had our own army, or declared our own war. But that peaceful aura is deceptive. Today Puerto Rico has one of the highest crime rates in the nation and battlefields are rife on the island, as drug trafficking, carjacking, and looting claim thousands of lives a year.

For three-hundred years pirates besieged our coasts, and they became a fierce theater of war. Because of the capital's imposing forts, San Juan Bautista became the stopover point where the gold and silver ingots from the fabulous Peruvian mines were deposited by the Spanish fleet. Spanish galleons dispatched from Seville came to pick up the ingots and take them to Spain. Renowned pirates, among them Sir Francis Drake in 1595, George Clifford, Count of Cumberland in 1598, the Dutch Boudewijn Hendrickzoon in 1625, and Sir Ralph Abercromby in 1797, repeatedly laid siege to the island. With the exception of Cumberland's short-lived success (not long after conquering the city his troops were decimated by dysentery, and he had to abandon it) they were all turned away. In any case, this persistent siege was the reason our name changed, from peaceful San Juan Bautista to Puerto Rico, the rich port.

The overwhelming presence of gold in the underground chambers of La Fortaleza and El Morro Fort undoubtedly contributed to making the social scene in San Juan very formal and stratified. José Campeche, Puerto Rico's most important eighteenth-century painter, depicts people dressed in Spanish finery, so that they that resemble Goya's characters. Houses were elegant, with ceilings twenty feet high, spacious rooms, and lovely inner courtyards. Floors were made of marble tiles, windows opened out to the bay where Spanish galleons were constantly sailing to and from Europe, bringing constables, generals, bishops, and governors to administer the city.

The countryside was settled mostly by runaway slaves from neighboring islands who knew that, once in Puerto Rico, they would become free (Spanish law made this a requisite for slaves not born on Spanish soil). Renegade soldiers, deserting sailors, convicts, and all kinds of runaways who abandoned ship as they sailed down the island's coasts also joined our citizenry as the centuries progressed. The newly arrived settlers outside the capital's walls established a smuggling economy with the Lesser Antilles that thrived for hundreds of years.

As we were the smallest and least-populated landmass of the Major Antilles, Spain ignored us, occupied with the bustling affairs of Cuba and Santo Domingo. Since the sixteenth century, when the gold mines of Puerto Rico were quickly exhausted, an economy of subsistence was established on the island, which could be compared to a rustic paradise. At the beginning of the nineteenth century the interior enjoyed a relatively leisured existence, thanks to the fertility of the soil, the rich herds of cattle smuggled by the settlers, and the thriving illegal commerce. Nonetheless, the amount of land was limited; the island is only a hundred miles long and thirty-five miles across, and a lot of it is dramatically mountainous and difficult to cultivate. The haciendas were never as vast as those of Cuba; the landed bourgeoisie never so staggeringly rich as they were in Louisiana.

As historian Angel López Cantos has pointed out, Puerto Rican farmlands were very fertile, but the *hacendado* was never wealthy enough to have masses of slaves cultivating them. More often than not, he would take off his fine clothes, harness his oxen, and till the land next to his serfs. A good deal of the island's history, in short, was defined by a mythical richness it never possessed, but held "in store" for others (as was the case of the bullion held in La Fortaleza's storerooms), or by the fecundity of a land that was hoped would compensate for limited extent. This situation led us to flaunt our name, "Puerto Rico," like a resplendent costume at a ball.

FROM PUERTO TO PORTO

When the Americans arrived in 1898, "Puerto Rico" became officially "Porto Rico." Porto Rico appeared on all written, legal documents. English speakers couldn't manage the "u-e" diphthong, and the sound was consolidated into "o," as in the Portuguese "Porto." Since English was declared the official language of the island and all official communication transpired in English, we began to call ourselves by that name also. "Porto Rico" was *un disparate*, nonsense that didn't mean anything. In calling ourselves Porto Ricans we were parroting the Americans who thought they had newly discovered us, when in fact our culture was two hundred years old at the time of Plymouth Rock. We saw ourselves as others saw us.

The literal translation of Puerto Rico no longer applied soon after the Americans arrived, because we descended into one of the worst economic crises of our history. The Spanish-American War, the subsequent change of hegemony, and the devastation of San Ciriaco, the hurricane that struck the island in 1899, plunged us into a maelstrom of poverty and recession.

During the first forty-eight years of American presence on the island we remained under the tutelage of the War Department and later the Department of the Interior. All government officials were Americans, named by the president of the United States. This fostered a growing resentment and disillusionment in the system, because now that we were finally part of a democratic nation, we were being denied the right to govern ourselves or to participate in the process. The struggle for self-government became a pitched battle: as an unincorporated territory we were unable to run for local public office except as candidates to the Puerto Rican House of Representatives.

The political situation did not benefit us economically, since once we became part of the United States we lost our European markets for coffee and sugar. In spite of the American flag, the island remained overwhelmingly poor.

Puerto Ricans were very different from Americans. We were short and had frail constitutions due to undernourishment. We were dark-skinned, a racially mixed nation. We died young of dozens of tropical illnesses: tapeworms, sprue, malaria, bilharzias, and smallpox, practically unknown on the mainland. A very important part of our difference was that we spoke Spanish. We began to flaunt our singularities as weapons against assimilation by *el otro, el americano del norte*, even though, after 1917, we had a common citizenship.

As the century progressed, our struggle for self-definition intensified. There were violent nationalist uprisings, especially in the thirties during the Great Depression. We were American citizens without democratic rights, and perhaps not having those rights served the purpose of reminding us we were different. And then we were sent to Korea and Vietnam, where we had to put our lives on the line like everyone else in the States. Blood gave validity to our American citizenship.

It took another thirty years until we were able to elect our own governor: in 1948 Luis Muñoz Marín was the first elected Puerto Rican to occupy La Fortaleza. Thanks to Governor Muñoz's initiative, in 1952 Puerto Rico held a constitutional convention that resulted in the ratification of our Constitution (after its approval by Congress) by the U.S. Congress.

Then, during the second half of the century, something unexpected happened. Puerto Ricans pulled themselves up by their shoestrings ("Operation Bootstrap" Governor Muñoz Marín called it), and we were no longer so poor. In 1997 our per capita income was $8,500, compared to $5,000 in Latin America. We ate Tastee Freeze ice cream, swallowed vitamins galore, and were no longer undernourished, frail, or short. Today we eat Kentucky Fried Chicken, Taco Bell, and Burger King Whoppers as well as *arroz con pollo*, *pastels* and *lechón asao.* Many of us access the Internet and are computer-literate. With the arrival of the postmodern age the other has faded more and more from the screen, except in one respect: language.

When Luis Muñoz Marín was elected governor of the island, a new cultural nationalism and pride in the Spanish language brought attention once more to the matter of our name. "Porto Rico" was scratched out of official documents and "Puerto Rico" was reinstated. The correct pronunciation of "Puerto Rico" became an insignia of nationality, an unfailing way for us to identify ourselves. Today our identity still springs from the fact that we are a port city, indeed, a port island. But it also comes from the fact that we continue to speak Spanish.

Fifty years ago, when I was thirteen, I was sent to study at a boarding school in the States. We were still "Porto Rico" then, and my parents wanted me to learn how to speak English without an accent so that no one would be able to guess that I was "Porto Rican." I never managed to camouflage my origins, and my accent is still Puerto Rican, but I did learn English well enough to become a bilingual writer.

Snakes are two-tongued, but bifid talk is rare; snakes prefer to strike before they communicate. My two-tongued ability proved to be an advantage, but in the Puerto Rico of today it has come with risks. One never simply learns a language. One internalizes part of the traits of the people who speak it, and may assimilate some of their attitudes. Once a language is known, the speaker can think in a different way, can look at the world from an alternate perspective. It's impossible to learn Spanish without becoming part Spaniard, to learn German without becoming part German. But in today's world this isn't necessarily equivalent to betrayal. La Malinche, the Aztec princess who was Hernán Cortés's mistress, is the classic example of how translation and betrayal are difficult to keep separate. But interpretation and reconciliation of divergent points of view are the skills of the sophisticated, and they are indispensable in the twenty-first century. Thus the importance of the historic photograph of "The Takeover": Atiles and Paniagua, the first Puerto Rican factotums, the first official translators, are our role models, and since then we have been unable to trust ourselves.

At the beginning of the century, when Anglo hegemony was thrust upon Puerto Ricans by the United States, and English was made mandatory in all schools, we reacted hostilely against the imposed language, and this resentment has still not healed. As a result, much animosity is felt by Puerto Ricans against those native-born who write in English for any reason whatsoever. Even speaking

English can elicit anger: when conversing in a mixed group, Puerto Ricans immediately switch to Spanish, often leaving visitors out of the conversation.

A large portion of our population today is bilingual as well as bicultural, but "Spanish-only" is the politically correct attitude shared by most writers and members of the intellectual community. This is understandable in light of the experience of other territories that have evolved into statehood. In Hawaii, as in Arizona and New Mexico, native languages and cultural identities were almost totally annihilated due to massive immigration and to the pressure of the dominating Anglo culture.

As a Puerto Rican writer, I share in my intellectual community's preoccupation with the threat to our language and culture. If we ever become a state of the union, we would have to be a Spanish-speaking state that retains its culture and traditions. American citizenship would have to continue to be grafted onto Puerto Rican nationality, as it is today. Before what began in Puerto Rico in 1917, when Puerto Ricans were made to be Spanish-speaking American citizens, can come to fruition, many questions must be answered. Will America evolve into a bilingual nation in which cultural differences are respected? Can the United States accept as a state a territory that speaks Spanish, and hangs on to its cultural identity as on a raft in mid-ocean? Or will the United States refuse to accept the risk of fragmentation?

Every four years we have overwhelmingly reaffirmed our desire to remain part of the United States, and we retain our American citizenship when we vote at the polls (less than 5 percent traditionally vote for independence). At the same time a discourse favoring more and more autonomy for the island has evolved into an ever-increasing crescendo. This situation is contradictory—American citizenship and independence cancel each other out—but it doesn't seem to bother people. As in some religious fundamentalisms, salvation of the national ethos is promised through a sacrifice that could be suicidal but at the same time leads to paradise.

How has the concept of an "independent state of the union" come about? America, when viewed from Puerto Rican shores, is the land of virtual reality, where everything is possible. Massive publicity campaigns promote conflicting policies, presenting them as equally necessary. For example, government agencies support measures that help control forest fires but hurt the environment, and simultaneously measures that support the environment, such as defending the habitats of endangered species. Puerto Rico's "American Dream" is to be a state in the United States and simultaneously to remain autonomous from the United States.

Puerto Ricans have great faith in the U.S. constitution, and are still confident their conflicts will be resolved. In 1999 during the last plebiscite held on the island, the government offered voters four alternatives: commonwealth, statehood, independence, and none of the above. The country voted overwhelmingly for none of the above, which could be interpreted as equivalent to all of the above.

In spite of the picturesque baroque that reigns on the island's political scene, one thing remains clear: to write in English in Puerto Rico today is a perilous endeavor. "If you write like them it's because you want to be like them and therefore are not like us" is the implicit message from the "Spanish-only" sympathizers. That the them and the us refer to one common American citizenship doesn't seem to bother anyone. The possibility that one may write in English so citizens of the same country may understand one another is seldom considered.

To translate my own work and write in English was an important decision for me. It has permitted me to reach communities outside the island that would have been unreachable otherwise, and my books have been published in France, Italy, Germany, Holland, and Greece. When Americans read my books, they have a better understanding of how Puerto Rico contributes to its cultural diversity.

And those of Puerto Rican descent who had Spanish taken away from them can read about their culture and their language, and perhaps recuperate it.

I write in English as well as in Spanish because I believe in freedom of choice; because I refuse to be coerced by either the English-only or the Spanish-only fundamentalist movements at home or on the mainland. To live astride two cultures has become an ethical cause for me.

Fifty years after I first traveled to the States, my Puerto Rican sense of identity feels much stronger. I take great care to pronounce the name of my country as "Puerto Rico," differentiating the "u" from the "e" and rolling my "r's" against my teeth as clearly as I can, in case anyone should be confused and think I come from "Porto Rico," a place that doesn't exist. And my American identity is strengthened because my writing is an expression of freedom of speech.

I, too, share in the modern American Dream. Spanish, which we thought lay buried and forgotten, has begun to reappear like ghost-writing. In New Mexico, California, Arizona, Florida, it was inscribed in America's subconscious in invisible ink. As wave after wave of immigrants bring the rich, resounding words with them, they wash over the memory of the old words, making the language more vibrant than ever.

RHODE ISLAND

NEW ENGLAND'S COZY NEIGHBORHOOD

Scott MacKay

At the Democratic National Convention in Chicago in 1996, the Rhode Island and Texas delegations bunked at the same hotel. The Texans were amazed that all of the Rhode Island delegates were on a first-name basis; the Rhode Islanders shrugged retort was, "Hey, most of us are related."

It would take 200 Rhode Islands to fill Texas, but why would anyone want to? In the neighborhood we call Rhode Island, everyone knows everyone else. Or knows somebody who does. This means the person who lives next door cares whether you are sick or well, alive or dead. This neighbor also remembers what you ate for dinner, noticed the strange car in the driveway yesterday, and knows what your brother is really like—she dated him before she married your cousin.

Outsiders wonder why there is a Rhode Island. A million people all crammed into the smallest state, a place you can drive across in forty-five minutes without breaking the scarcely obeyed speed limits.

To understand why this watery sliver of New England, a place bereft of natural resources, hardly big enough to be a county anywhere else, qualifies as a state, we take you back to the first white settler.

There is a Rhode Island because Roger Williams, father of the doctrine of separation of church and state, couldn't get along with the seventeenth–century Puritan theocrats who ran Massachusetts.

Williams was banished from Massachusetts for heresy. He and his band of renegades settled in 1636 at the head of Narragansett Bay in a place he named Providence. Williams was that rare preacher who wanted his flock to interpret God for themselves.

"Forced worship stinks in God's nostrils," said Williams. "No man should be molested for his conscience."

The colony became a magnet for dissenters of all stripes and evolved into a place which tolerated just about anything and anybody—Quakers, Jews, Antinomians, Ranters, agnostics and other refugees and riffraff flocked to Rhode Island. "The sewer of New England," and the "fag end of creation" is the way the orthodox Cotton Mather described the upstart colony.

Horror author and Providence native H. P. Lovecraft would later write that Rhode Island was the, "Universal haven of the odd, the free and the dissenting."

Williams even got along with the Native Americans, but subsequent white settlers were not so benign, infecting them with European diseases, stealing their land, and enslaving and slaughtering them.

Born in rebellion, Rhode Island evolved into Rogues' Island—a place that encouraged shattering the rules in politics and stretching the notion of what was proper in business.

"Rhode Island was the most liberal, the most entrepreneurial and the most modern" of the eighteenth–century colonies, writes historian Gordon Wood.

Slavery didn't gain much traction in Rhode Island, but once the slaves became commodities, the colony's marine traders saw their opportunity. About two-thirds of American slaves were transported on Rhode Island ships, most of them through the ports of Providence, Newport, and Bristol. Rhode Island rum was traded for slaves in Africa, the slaves were carted to the West Indies, where the ships were loaded with molasses, a byproduct of sugar refining, which was brought back to the colony to be distilled into more rum. An enterprising Bristol family, the De Wolfs, continued to transport slaves into the 1820s, long after the 1808 end of the legal slave trade.

It is a Rhode Island axiom that only the state's best families can trace their lineage back to the colony's original rumrunners and slave traders.

The huge profits slaving generated attracted even the most prominent families, such as the Browns of Providence, benefactors for whom the Ivy League university is named.

Slaving did create tension, even within the Brown clan. John Brown defended it until his death but his brother Moses Brown became a Quaker and started Providence's first abolitionist society. Some of the same families who profited from slaving in the eighteenth century became abolitionist ministers in the nineteenth.

Rhode Islanders have always lived by their wits and wiles. The profits of the great sea-trading fortunes were plowed into the textile industry. America's Industrial Revolution started in 1790 in Pawtucket, when Samuel Slater replicated from memory British textile machinery and developed the young country's first factory.

The state also became home to child labor—about a dozen children worked in Slater's first mill. Hundreds of mills sprouted up along the state's rivers, and by the time of the Civil War, Rhode Island was a prosperous industrial center.

Between the Civil War and World War II, Rhode Island attracted thousands of immigrants, first from Ireland and French Canada, and later from Italy and Portugal. It was this wave of newcomers who would forge the twentieth century in the state. The first generation huddled into wood–frame triple–deckers in the city's ethnic enclaves, but their sons and daughters would not so meekly abide the mind-numbing clatter of a cotton mill or jewelry factory.

A 1905 state census showed that Rhode Island was the first U.S. state with a Roman Catholic majority, but these immigrants wouldn't flex their muscles for another generation. They would organize labor unions and vote Democratic, eventually supplanting the Yankee political elite in the 1930s. These immigrants eyed each other and the Yankees warily. The Irish took over the Democratic Party and developed a machine in Providence, allied with the nascent labor union movement.

As the mostly Roman Catholic immigrants encroached, the native Protestants put all sorts of barriers in the road to democracy. A property qualification was enacted for voting, and one of the country's most malapportioned legislatures, anchored in rotten rural boroughs, kept power in the hands of the Yankees long after they were a numerical minority.

The state refined its reputation for political corruption. "An honest voter is one who stays bought," was the motto of Charles "Boss" Brayton, who ran a Republican Party controlled by the mill barons and the Yankee elite.

After muckraker Lincoln Steffens declared that Rhode Island was "a state for sale—and cheap," Brayton bristled.

"The Republican Party shouldn't be blamed for the present state of affairs," said Brayton. "The Democrats are just as bad, or would be, if they had the money." Corruption in Rhode Island was no worse than in other states, Brayton insisted. "Because Rhode Island is small you can see things better; that's what makes the difference."

Control of state government by Brayton and his gang kept Rhode Island firmly in the hands of the Yankee elite and mill owners. Rhode Island developed into one of the most tolerant states for child labor in factories and school–based homework. Even by 1910, only 48 percent of the state's school–age children were in classrooms; the minimum work age was not raised to fifteen until 1923.

The Gilded Age Robber Barons made their summer homes in

Newport, where the Vanderbilts, Astors, and Belmonts built the grand mansions that aped the royal palaces of Europe.

By the turn of the twentieth century, Providence was known as the most prosperous city in America. The city throbbed with industrial energy; Providence was a Silicon Valley of the Machine Age, a center for machine tools and steam engines, metal fabrication and rubber products, textiles and jewelry.

Its companies set the standards for the world: Gorham Silver, Corliss Steam Engines, Brown and Sharpe Manufacturing (the machine tool king), Nicholson File, and American Screw Company.

No one was much concerned about the heavy metals dumped into the rivers or the smokestacks that polluted the air with coal smoke and stained the colonial architecture.

The ancient Indian—named rivers—the Mohassuck and the Woonasquatucket—that coursed through the city's downtown area on their way to Narragansett Bay were putrid cesspools. The industrial elite's answer was to cover them with an ever—widening bridge. Two devastating hurricanes, in 1938 and 1954, walled the city from its waterfront heritage due to the construction of an ugly hurrican barrier. In the 1960s highway ramps further separated the city from the water.

The city's politics were controlled by an Irish Democratic machine. The lubricant was jobs and city contracts. Become mayor, and you got rich, your family got rich, and all of your friends got jobs.

It was enough for the political machine to keep running. Providence, thankfully, never embraced such good-government notions as tearing down "slum" neighborhoods in the name of urban renewal. White ethnic neighborhoods had too many votes to level; the only Providence section that fell victim to the developers' bulldozers was a historically black area. The wood—frame Victorian and Queen Anne wonders were standing when the historic—preservation movement awoke in the 1960s.

At midcentury, Rhode Island had gained a reputation as a place run—and not well—by labor union leaders, priests, party bosses, and the underworld. Providence was once the Mafia capital of New England. A friend of Frank Sinatra's named Raymond L. S. Patriarca headed a ruthless organized crime organization run out of Federal Hill—once a teeming Italian immigrant neighborhood, today given over to restaurants with valet parking.

When in 1962 Patriarca's son, Raymond "Junior" Patriarca, was having difficulty changing a course at the University of Rhode Island, dad called the governor's office for help. The FBI was listening and the call was dutifully taped. Rhode Island has always been a theme-park for Feds and reporters.

In today's homogenized world, Rhode Island's distinctiveness lies in its parochial political culture, fingernails-on-the-chalkboard accent and such gustatory quirks as coffee milk, quahogs, and johnnycakes.

Factories have emptied, sacrificed to the unremitting search for cheap labor, first to the American South and then to the Third World. Generations trekked to work at brick or granite mills, but nothing much of consequence is manufactured in the state now. The empty mills stand as mocking reminders of what once was.

Today's economy is tethered to separating tourists from their dollars, educating the young, or tending to the sick and elderly.

The biggest bank, Fleet, moved its headquarters to Boston several years ago. The state's newspaper, the *Providence Journal*, once the tribune of the Yankee overclass, was sold to Texans.

Rhode Islanders are neither rich nor poor; income figures put us in the mushy middle of American economic life.

Newport society today is an eccentric summer sideshow of the pedigreed rich. Occasionally one of these Bailey's Beach offspring marries into European nobility, and there is an overdone wedding peopled by grown men named Chip or Trip and women who answer to Muffy or Missy. Most of the old mansions are museums.

Rhode Island and Providence live in the long shadow of Massachusetts and Boston. We have Brown; they have Harvard. We have the minor-league Pawtucket Red Sox and Providence Bruins; they have the major league Red Sox, Bruins, Celtics, and Patriots. They have the Kennedy with clout, Senator Ted Kennedy; We have his son, Congressman Patrick Kennedy, better known for assaulting an airport security agent in Los Angeles than for any legislation in Washington.

Providence's train station brims with Boston commuters on weekday morning. One in seven Rhode Islanders earns his or her paycheck in Massachusetts and locals gripe that all the good jobs are in Boston. The ambitious young flee the day they earn their degrees.

This shadow and Rhode Island's size merge in an inferiority complex that puzzles newcomers but is embedded in the psyche of natives. Rhode Island, particularly its government, can't get anything right—as if bribes and unending DMV lines were conceived here.

What's left are rueful underachievers and those yoked to the state by family or tradition. Newcomers, particularly the well-off and those from New York and New Jersey, initially become enamored of the ocean, the unhurried pace of life, and the startling discovery of an open parking space at noon in downtown Providence.

Many of these newly arrived learn to shrug their shoulders at the political chicanery, even if they wince when their children start dropping their r's and referring to the water cooler as a "bubbla."

In time the newcomers begin to tell the locals how to live, educate their children, cleanse their politics. This leads to inevitable clashes, much grist for the local press and palaver for the talk–radio shows. Life goes on. The natives notice these folks hardly ever return to New York or New Jersey.

After September 11, the local joke was that it is nice to live some-where insignificant, where things should be fine unless the frozen lemonade or saltwater taffy industries become terrorist targets.

Rhode Island still has the largest proportion of Roman Catholics of any state. Nowadays many Catholics take their religion à la carte: They attend Mass and get married under one of the state's many vaulted church ceilings but swallow birth-control pills more readily than church teachings.

Rogues' Island lives too, encapsulated in the career of former Providence Mayor Vincent A. Cianci Jr., convicted of racketeering-conspiracy charges last year for running City Hall as a corrupt enterprise.

Cianci was the author of the city's rebirth as a tourist destination and a retail and arts center. But the FBI dug up evidence that the new Providence was run the old way—with cash bribes at City Hall. Cianci is serving a five–year sentence at the federal prison in Fort Dix, New Jersey, as he awaits his appeal.

Cianci was elected six times as mayor. Running as a Republican, he smashed the Irish Democratic machine and in 1978 became the first Italian–American mayor. A federal investigation netted twenty-two people in various City Hall corruption schemes, including extortion and bribery.

No FBI agent got Cianci. He got himself. Cianci was forced from office in 1984 after a felony-assault conviction on charges that he beat his estranged wife's lover with a lit cigarette and a fireplace log.

Cianci made an improbable comeback as an independent in 1990, winning a three-way race with the slogan, "He never stopped caring about Providence."

A relentless cheerleader for his city, Cianci took advantage of the boom years of the 1990s to forge a spiffed-up downtown for Providence. The city uncovered its downtown rivers, attracted a $500-million mall, and drew tourists to fancy bistros, art galleries, and cultural events.

But Cianci also presided over a pay-to-play and you-gotta-know-a-guy culture at City Hall that got him and his associates into trouble. His chief of staff, taking a bribe on an FBI undercover tape, was also convicted.

Rhode Island continued its tradition of tolerance by electing David Cicilline, who is openly gay, as the city's new mayor.

At the dawn of a new century, Rhode Island's hollowed-out cities have attracted a new energy in the form of yet another wave of immigrants, this time from the dusty, poor back roads of Latin America. The 2000 Census showed that Latinos are now the largest minority group. Providence's neighborhoods, abandoned by middle-class white ethnics, are being remade by a new generation of immigrants. Stroll down Broad on Providence's South Side and remember the names of businesses that live only in memory and family lore: Cohen's Market, Prescott's Drug Company, Moran's Bakery, Hanley's Tap, McNeil's Children's Shop, Celona's Pharmacy.

Walk that street today and see housed in the same buildings: Sanchez Market, Hernandez Liquors, El Malecon Restaurant.

Despite the searing poverty of Providence's inner city, these hope-driven new–immigrant risk–takers are remaking the culture of a place founded four centuries ago by Roger Williams and his band of dreamers and dissidents.

South Carolina

What the Rivers Know

MariJo Moore

From a distance, the mammoth rolls of hay adorning the field look like buffaloes. These reels of fodder deceive my eyes only because hard rain disfigured them before the farmer could gather his harvest. It often rains intensely here in the South; the importance of hard rains cannot be measured, only witnessed in the movement of the waterways.

There are more than eleven thousand miles of flowing water in South Carolina. The chilly mountain streams and the black coffee—colored rivers are the skeleton of this land, and rain keeps the flesh intact. Even when humankind tries to control, change, pollute, or dislodge, rain continues to fall, offering hope to the waterways, and to all manner of life depending on them.

South Carolina's three main river systems—curving from the northwest to the southeast—begin with their heads on the eastern slopes of the Blue Ridge Mountains in North Carolina. The Santee, with a watershed covering nearly 40 percent of the state, is the largest water system. The ACE (Ashepoo, Combahee, and Edisto rivers) Basin, which is a system of autonomous rivers, arises in the costal plains. The Pee Dee, which drains the northeastern part of the state, flows almost two hundred miles from the North Carolina state line to the Atlantic.

Yunwi Gunahita, the Long Man, is what we Cherokee call a river. A giant with his head in the foothills of the mountains and his feet far down in the lowlands. Flowing, always flowing toward his goal, and speaking in a language only those who listen to the spiritual silence of the universe can understand. Those who understand the stillness behind time.

Native populations such as the Cherokee, Waccamaw, Waxhaws, Wappoo, Savannah, Hook, Etiwan, and Catawba—just to mention a few of the nations—once filled this area, as did the buffaloes. Thousands of these original inhabitants, along with their tribal histories, stories, and languages, are today nonexistent due to pandemics of disease, weapons, pestilence, religious pressures, and racism brought by European contact, acculturation, and total annihilation. Of course, various indigenous peoples of this area did survive; their descendants are testimony to this. Trying to keep ancestral traditions intact while living in contemporary society is a challenge many deal with on a day-to-day basis.

Modernity accentuated by the still living past is how I describe South Carolina in 2003. The puzzlement of the permanent and the changing, the eternal and the transient, is the theme of existence. Electricity, technology, factories, highways, and people: lightning, rivers, trees, blue skies, and people. No longer just indigenous inhabitants: people from all over the world now call South Carolina home.

From the BMW auto plant in Spartanburg, to the bustling capital city of Columbia, to the magical charm of Charleston, thousands of South Carolinians dwell here. Do they ever wonder how it used to be? Do they ever contemplate, as I often do, what the rivers know? What knowledge is squeezed into their banks, hidden in their muddy bottoms, swirling in their eddies, imprinted upon the boulders situated instinctively like ancestral ornaments along their bodies? What do the rivers remember?

Long before numerous Indian nations were totally destroyed; before Carolina was named for King Charles I of England, in 1629 (Carolina is a Latin form of Charles); before the word *South* was added in 1730 when North and South Carolina became separate colonies; before white indentured servants; before African slavery; before colonial victories in the Battles of Kings Mountain and Cowpens were turning points of the Revolutionary War in the South; before South Carolina was the first state to secede from the Union in December 1860; before Confederate troops fired the first shot of the Civil War when they attacked Fort Sumter in Charleston Harbor on April 12, 1861; before civil rights, the rivers were here, listening, gathering, and flowing. Watching the world outside their banks change.

The Pee Dee, the Wateree, the Edisto, the Waccamaw, the Ashepoo, the Catawba, and the Santee rivers remember the Native peoples of long ago from whence came their names. They recall the children swimming and laughing, and the women gathering water in pottery fashioned from clay all along the banks. They retain recollections of the men burning out fallen trees to make canoes, and all the people engaging in ceremonious prayers, songs, and dances. They recall corn, potatoes, and other crops planted in the dark alluvial soil. The Broad River, which was an early boundary between the Catawba and Cherokee Indians, must have images of the Cherokees performing the sacred ritual of "going to water" that ensured healings, purification, and providential balance. The rivers remember all of this, and more. They remember when a world of spiritual harmony became disrupted by a world of greedy power fueled by progress.

South Carolina, the smallest state in the Deep South region, is a significant manufacturing state, and one of the leaders of the country in the manufacture of textiles. Also important in farming, South Carolina raises one of the largest tobacco crops in the United States. Indigo, cotton, rice, and sugarcane have been other crops of significance through the years. After the first colony was settled in South Carolina, it was soon discovered that African slaves were less costly in the long run than five-year contracts of white indentured servants. Not only were the blacks cheaper to clothe, feed, and house, but the owners had complete control over their lives.

Since slaves from more than two dozen ethnic groups and forty different languages were brought to South Carolina and forced together on plantations, it became necessary to craft a common language in order to communicate with each other. The Gullah language, created from similar African words combined with Elizabethan English, began as Pidgin English but, when used by the next generation of native-born blacks, became a creole language. (This process of combining different languages is called "creolization.") Some historians believe the term Gullah is derived from Angola, the name of the West African country, which was called "N'Gulla" by slave traders of the early 1800s. After emancipation, white landowners left their barrier-island plantations, isolating newly freed slaves who became known as the Gullah people. The West African cultural tradition of weaving sweet-grass baskets has survived along the bottomland rivers of South Carolina due to the generous growth of sweet grass, bulrush, and pine needles. Today's highly valued coil baskets made by Gullah artisans are sold just as the older generations of Africans were sold as slaves. But now, the Gullah people prosper from the sales.

At the same time the crops helped to feed and clothe the first settlers of South Carolina, blood often fed the land and offered red coating to the rivers. The Stono and Edisto rivers remember an early autumn morning in 1739, when a group of blacks broke into a store at the Stono Bridge and murdered the owners. Stealing ammunition, they murdered whites and burned down their houses and barns along the main road heading south. By late afternoon, when they stopped to rest on the banks of the Edisto, there were nearly one hundred in the renegade band of blacks. Because the whites had more men and guns, the band was eventually suppressed, but not before the deaths of over seventy-five black and white South Carolinians.

Although many of the slaves eventually found solace in Christianity and were sometimes baptized in the rivers, the slaves brought from the Congo-Angola region sought to retain their traditional Bakongo religion. They believed in Nzambi, a great deity from whom came the powers of good and evil. Men and women with special spiritual gifts could command these powers and connect with the spirits of the dead. Ceremonies were performed at night, near water, which was the obstacle between life and death. The river is where the sun went every night, signifying a cycle of life, death, and rebirth. Shards of Bakongo pottery marked by circles and x's, symbols of their beliefs, have been found in the rivers. These bits and pieces are significant reminders of the long-gone ceremonies.

By the 1760s, several townships, all accessible to navigable rivers, had been settled in South Carolina. The townships Purrysburg and Hillsborough, which settled respectively along the Savannah River and Little River, were French: Purrysburg settled by French Swiss and Hillsborough by French Huguenots. Orangeburg on the North Edisto River, Londonborough on Hard Labor Creek, and Saxe-Gotha on the Congaree River were German; Amelia, near the juncture of the Congaree River with the Santee River, and New Windsor on the Savannah River, were about one-half German; Williamsburg on the Black River and Kingston on the Waccamaw River were Scots-Irish; Boonesborough on Long Cane Creek was Irish; and Queensborough and the Welsh Tract on the Great Pee Dee River were English. After the American Revolution, many South Carolinians of European ancestry began marrying into ethnic groups other than their own. Of course, countless children of mixed races continued to be born as European men and women shared their beds with the West African slaves and Native Americans. Sometimes willingly and sometimes not.

The predominant idea that only whites owned slaves is not correct. The color line sometimes blurred when green money was the main focal point. American Indians and African-Americans participated in this greedy venture as well. In 1702, at the instigation of the traders in Charleston, the Chickasaws enslaved over five-hundred Choctaws for sale. Although the Indian slaves did not bring as much as the black slaves (the Africans who had been taken out of their homeland were deemed more helpless and less likely to escape), they were still in demand due to the idea that enslaving the Indian "savages" would help to refine them.

There were also American Indians who owned black slaves, particularly among the so-called Five Civilized Tribes. The Cherokees, Creeks, Chickasaws, and Choctaws practiced slavery while the Seminoles chose to adopt African-Americans into their tribe. When these tribes were removed from the southeastern part of the United States to what is now known as Oklahoma during the 1830s, their slaves went with them. Of course, not all members of these tribes owned slaves. However, it is estimated that at least 1,600 Cherokee slaves made the trip to Indian Territory on the infamous Trail of Tears in 1838.

William Ellison, a black (ex-slave) cotton-gin maker of the Sumter district, capitalized on the cotton boom and used his profits to purchase land and black slaves. By 1860, he owned more than sixty slaves, which was more slaves that any black slaveholder in South Carolina, and more than 90 percent of the entire nation's white slaveholders.

When this state was the first to secede, its leaders promised that there would be no war. The Savannah, Congaree, and many other rivers now know that the war was obviously inevitable. Although the rivers got a taste of Union blood, by the time the war ended, they had gotten their fill of Confederate blood too.

Of course, emancipation did not soothe racial tensions in the South. The rivers witnessed lynching and other senseless acts of murder in an episodic fate that seemed as unavoidable as the war between the states had been. Since this war, the rivers have witnessed much: Reconstruction; KKK; Jim Crow laws; mills; factories; employment; unemployment; railroads; steamers; interstates; civil rights; national monuments; state parks; minimum wage; the renowned rock group Hootie and the Blowfish; the first female admitted to the historically male military academy, the Citadel; increased populations in the up-country, low country, and the middle country; people moving here from as far away as Asia and as near as Mexico; old laws abolished, new laws established; old buildings torn down and skyscrapers taking their place; as well as various progressive discords and changes too numerous to mention. Other wars have taken, and continue to take, their toll on South Carolinians as their men and women are sent to lands they had never dreamed of. Ironically, blacks, Indians, and whites have fought side by side, defending a country over which their ancestors had once killed each other. Perhaps paradox is the one great certainty of life.

Rationalizing past recriminations does not destroy them. Nor can it ease the pain felt in the present. But time passes, sometimes quickly, sometimes slowly. Occurrences are forgotten and become debris that sinks to the bottom, dredged up only when similar circumstances cause them to float to the top of life's desire to explain itself. Yes, things change, ideals change, politicians die, babies are born, and the rivers flood. The horror of 9/11 in New York City unpredictably adds another element to the world South Carolinians inhabit. Terrorism is a word that has taken precedence over bigotry. A word that doesn't acknowledge color, race, sex, or endowment. A word that makes one stop and reflect on what could be as well as what has been.

There is no way to present the "now" of South Carolina without considering the past and contemplating the future. The ceremonious rivers join the happenings of the past and present to make them reminiscences of the eternal. Rivers are full of memories, and as they continuously surge through today, tomorrow, and the day after, they will witness even more happenings and eventually turn them into oceanic narratives.

Alongside all the history, modernity, failures, successes, comings and goings, extinctions, industries, expansion, and diversion in South Carolina, there is a special silence to be found here. An ancient silence, which is stronger than any human inventions or human destructions. This silence is in the whitecaps of the Atlantic bivouacking St. Helena and Hilton Head islands, in the colorful dawn creeping into cities such as Greenville and Florence, in the moonlight shining on the dark country roads, in the clouds circling the highest peak of Mount Sassafras, in the storming hard rains, in the misshapen rolls of hay, and in the hearts of the people who quiet their souls enough to listen to their spirits. They remember the ones who are now resting in this silence, and acknowledge the ones who are yet to be born from this silence. They are the ones who understand and can never forget what the rivers know.

SOUTH DAKOTA

THE LONG MILE

Kathleen Norris

It is no use flying to South Dakota. The long miles—1,700 to Rapid City from Manhattan; a little more than 900 from Chicago; 1,000 from Dallas; 1,300 from Los Angeles, 1,200 from Seattle—are best traveled by foot, bicycle, or automobile. For you are on a pilgrimage to a place where "miles from anywhere" takes on new meaning, a place as landlocked as it is possible to be in North America.

In a world gone mad for virtual reality, South Dakota is a gritty reassertion of the real. It takes real time to get here, and real time to travel across the vastness of the state. My home in Lemmon is four-hundred miles north and west from the state's largest city, Sioux Falls, and more than half the route is on a two-lane blacktop. There is seldom much traffic—one of the peculiar luxuries we enjoy—but summer storms or winter blizzards can turn the trip into a two-or three-day affair.

South Dakotans grow adept at giving geography lessons. When a book publicist in Boston scheduling a tour asked if it would be possible for me to do readings in Sioux Falls and Rapid City on the same day, I asked her if she could consult a map. The cities are some 350 miles apart, along I-90, the interstate that crosses southern South Dakota. Psychologically, the distance is even greater. You leave behind the comfortable spaces of the Midwest, with lush cornfields and tree-lined roads. After crossing the Missouri near Chamberlain, you enter the West River. Trees become scarce, and the experience of being exposed under a limitless sky may spook you. South Dakota writer Dan O'Brien once wrote, "When you get the feeling that the whole world can see you but no one is watching, you have come to the grasslands of North America."

The very ground under your feet has changed, no longer the rich loam of the Midwest's glacial moraine—the glacier stopped at the Missouri River—but the thinner soil of a prehistoric seabed. You cross mile upon mile of spare, rolling land with the occasional upsweep of a butte. Were you to climb one, you might find fossils of a mollusk or shark, or perhaps a live rattlesnake. Were you to travel due north, you would pass through a sparsely populated land of sagebrush and grass, all the way through North Dakota into Saskatchewan. This is the region *Newsweek* once dubbed the American outback, a no-man's-land between the gentle hills of the Midwest and the glamour of the Rocky Mountains.

Continuing west on I-90, you reach Cactus Flat, where you have the option of taking a loop through the Buffalo Gap National Grassland and the Badlands National Park, a stunning example of the geology of erosion. On exiting the badlands you find the oasis of Wall, South Dakota, where Wall Drug, famous for advertising in the *Village Voice* and *Paris Match*, is worth a visit, if only for the postcard room. Rapid City is fifty miles west, at the edge of the mountainous outcropping of the Black Hills (*Paha Sapa* in Lakota). Harney Peak, at 7,242 feet, is the highest point between the Alps and the Rockies.

As a transition point between Midwest and West, South Dakota remains only vaguely defined in the nation's consciousness. Even within the state, cultural identity is confused. South Dakotans east of the Missouri have more in common with Iowans and Minnesotans than with residents of western South Dakota, who are more likely to have rodeo clubs in their high schools and gun racks in their pickup trucks. Many believe that when the Dakota Territory was divided into North and South Dakota in 1889, it would have made more sense to have created an East and West Dakota instead. Others point out that despite a tenacious mythology of independence, South Dakota's western region has long been a colony of the federal government. Without the income from Social Security, the Veterans Administration, and the Department of Agriculture, the economy of western South Dakota would be on a par with that of many Third World countries.

In his history of the state, the writer John R. Milton suggests that "the key word for South Dakota is extremes. What happens to extremes is that they come together, and the result is a kind of tension." Perhaps that explains our contradictory political behavior; South Dakota tends to select safely Republican governors and send maverick Democratic senators to Washington; George McGovern, James Abourezk, Tom Daschle. In presidential elections, the state has voted Republican for many years.

But if South Dakota is famous for anything, it's our extremes of climate. I have experienced, in a single year, a temperature range of 155 degrees, from 115 degrees above zero to nearly 40 degrees below. In the past decade, excessive rains in the eastern half of the state have made new ponds of glacial depressions, while the west has suffered from drought. The state has been described as "The Sunshine State" and "The Blizzard State," and both monikers are based on fact. "The Windy State" would also be accurate. South Dakota is a natural for solar and wind energy, but that would require a capital expenditure that has not been forthcoming.

One reason is that in a culture in which demographics rule, South Dakota barely exists. From a marketing perspective, there is no one here, only 762,000 souls (roughly the population of San Francisco) spread out over seventy-six-thousand square miles. Well over half of South Dakota's population resides in the far eastern region of the state. In satellite photographs taken of America at night, Chicago and Minneapolis are large bursts of light, and one can discern a faint glow from Fargo and Sioux Falls. After that, there is a huge oval of darkness: the place I have called home for the past twenty-nine years.

I write from the diaspora now, and while I maintain a home in South Dakota, and return for a brief time each summer, it has become impossible for me to live there. The reasons are simple: my husband's health dictates that he live closer to medical attention (in Lemmon, we are 130 miles from a large hospital; roughly the distance between New York City and Albany) and in a climate in which it is easier for him to breathe. But mine is just one of the many thousands of stories of people who love South Dakota, but have been forced to leave. History books report that the "Great Dakota Boom" that began in 1879 with the first major influx of white settlers was followed by the "Great Dakota Bust" at the end of the 1880s, brought on by severe drought and a depressed national economy. The boom-and-bust pattern continues to this day.

In the 1900 U.S. census, the population of Perkins County is listed as zero, which reflects the fact that the area was used primarily as a summer hunting ground by Indians who returned in the winter to more permanent, sheltered encampments in the Black Hills, Montana, and North Dakota's Killdeer Mountains. An influx of settlers followed the construction of a railroad line, and my town of Lemmon was founded in 1907. Incentives from the railroads and the U.S. government, cheap travel, and free land for those willing to work up a claim caused the county's population to swell to more than 11,000 by 1910. The would-be farmers soon found that, contrary to the belief of agrarian boosters, rain did not "follow the plow." Unrealistic expectations of the living to be made off a few acres of land, droughts, severe winters, and a grasshopper plague drove out many settlers. The 1920 census recorded a drop to 7,900, and a trend was established that continues to this day. Over the past forty years the county has lost 44 percent of its population. In the early 1970s when my husband and I first moved to Lemmon, the county held 4,800 people. Just 3,300 live there now, far outnumbered by the antelope, deer, and cattle.

South Dakota has sometimes been the canary in the coal mine when it comes to national economic downturn. By the time the nation awoke to the Great Depression of the 1930s, it was old news to South Dakotans, whose hard times had begun in the previous decade. A similar thing happened in the 1980s: the "farm crisis" that struck at the beginning of the decade had become a national crisis by 1987. But as America's economy boomed in the 1990s, the farm economy worsened, and more and more families left the land, despite anticorporate farming laws in both Dakotas intended to protect small farmers. Dating from the 1920s, when the Dakotas were a hotbed of radical populism, the laws make it illegal for corporations to own farms or ranches in either state, except for family corporations with at least one member actively involved in the operation. Other vestiges from the populist era include a state-run cement plant in South Dakota and laws making it difficult to foreclose on a farm. But for most of the past century, the number of farms in South Dakota has dropped steadily, from 83,300 in 1935 to 31,280 in 1997. For a hundred years, South Dakota has been a place to be from, a place young families must leave in order to make a living. At a reading in Seattle in 1995, when I asked people with roots in the Dakotas to raise their hands, they constituted nearly half of my audience.

There are, of course, many South Dakotas. There is prehistoric South Dakota, revealed in the petrified wood and grasses of the Lemmon area, and in digs that uncover whole tyrannosauruses. South Dakota even has a state dinosaur, the triceratops. There is corporate South Dakota, which got a major boost when Citibank was drawn to Sioux Falls in the early 1980s, attracted by new state usury laws that placed no limits on the credit-card interest it could charge. The state still advertises in such periodicals as the Northwest Airline's magazine *WorldTraveler*, promoting South Dakota as a place with a reliable workforce (and little union labor) and no corporate or individual income tax.

There is the South Dakota of the wealthy hunters who pass through airports every fall, with huge crates of expensive dogs and guns. They come looking to bag pheasant, deer, or antelope, and increasingly they or their corporations are buying up distressed ranches and turning them into exclusive hunting preserves. There is the South Dakota of the families who come every summer to see Mount Rushmore, ride the water slide at the naturally heated Evans Plunge in Hot Springs, and take in the Passion Play in Spearfish, whose lead actor is advertised as a "world-famous Christus portrayer." As in tourist economies everywhere, the visitor's dollars are eagerly welcomed, even as the dependence on them engenders a measure of resentment. My husband and I were once stranded by a spring blizzard in Wall, just a few weeks before the influx of the RV people. At a bar near our motel, a drunk approached my husband and asked, in a vaguely threatening tone, "Where ya from?" "Lemmon," he replied, and the man announced, loudly, and with apparent satisfaction, "Right! I knew you weren't no fuckin' tourist!"

There is gambling South Dakota where, since the early 1990s, American Legion Posts, taverns, gas stations, and restaurants have harbored video lottery machines. The largest share of the money collected goes to the state for public education. The natural beauty of the Black Hills, first prostituted by the gold rush that began in 1874, an event that mobilized the Sioux and led to Custer's defeat at the Little Bighorn two years later, succumbed again to humanity's crasser instincts when casinos began replacing grocery, hardware, and clothing stores in Lead and Deadwood. Gamblers now come from all over the world to play blackjack and poker, and visit a sanitized version of Saloon Number Ten in Deadwood, where Wild Bill Hickok met his end. Even in winter, chartered buses in Rapid City fill up with German tourists willing to risk the icy mountain roads for a taste of the romance of the Wild West.

There is the complex South Dakota of the Sioux Nation, with its eight reservations: the Lake Traverse or Sisseton in the northeast corner, Yankton in the southeast, Crow Creek and Lower Brule in the south-central area, Rosebud and Pine Ridge in the southwest, and Cheyenne River and Standing Rock constituting the entire north-central portion of the state. In some western towns, such as Timber Lake, on the border of Standing Rock, a significant number of families are interracial. But there is a sense in which Indians and whites in South Dakota "live apart together," to quote David Allan Evans, a longtime resident and South Dakota State professor.

Several reservation counties have poverty rates of more than 30 percent, and Shannon County, home to Pine Ridge, has consistently ranked as one of the poorest counties in the nation. In 1999 its poverty rate was 36.4 percent with a median household income of $21,000. In Minnehaha County, by comparison, which includes Sioux Falls, the median household income was roughly twice that, and the poverty rate was under 8 percent.

One significant development of recent years is that the Indian population of South Dakota is growing. The birthrate on the reservations far surpasses that of the white population, and Indians weary of urban life are beginning to return home from such cities as Minneapolis and Denver. Some are bringing business experience and entrepreneurial dreams. The Cheyenne River tribe has developed a profitable buffalo-ranching operation, and there are other signs of economic life in Indian country, not all of it related to casinos.

There is a delicious irony in the idea that western South Dakota may be returning to the Indians and the buffalo herds. My one concern is that, given the history of our nation's treatment of its Native population, such a place would be all too easy for an increasingly urban America to ignore. Even today, most have little idea of the devastation wrought by deregulation on the rural populace. Where few people live, public services—transportation, utilities, mail, hospitals—are increasingly at risk. Private corporations stay away, because there's no profit to be had. My county is typical of those west of the ninety-eighth meridian identified by demographer Deborah Popper as being vulnerable to decline. As young people leave, the population that remains is increasingly aged and poor. Frank Popper once told me that a Manhattan with the population density of Perkins County —a little more than one person per square mile—would contain fewer than fifty people. The Poppers' concept of a "Buffalo Commons," which so intrigues and angers South Dakotans, may simply reflect our reality in the twenty-first century. If nothing else, we may come closer to answering the question of how many people the western plains can sustain. The boosters who thought Perkins County could support eleven-thousand in 1910 were obviously wrong. But what is a reasonable number, one that we, and the land, can live with?

To be fair, I must also point out that there is a South Dakota that is growing. Between 1990 and 2000, when my county lost 15 percent of its population, Brandon, a community just east of Sioux Falls, had a population increase of 60 percent. Other towns along I-29, near the state's eastern border, saw lesser but still substantial increases. If the trend continues, as expected, it won't be long before the Sioux Falls area alone will contain a full quarter of South Dakota's people. This will effectively disenfranchise the voters of the western half of the state. There are signs of this already. Referendums that are strongly opposed in the west are passed because of support in the east. In the hotly contested 2002 Senate race between Democrat Tim Johnson and Republican John Thune, the counties along the state's western border were a solid block for Thune, along with the sparsely populated counties in the center of the state. What won the race for Johnson was the Indian vote and the vote of eastern South Dakota.

The South Dakota where I have lived for more than half my life, where my roots go three generations deep, is something of an anomaly in today's America. It remains a place where Caucasians are a clear majority, where nearly 98 percent of the residents were born in America, and only 6 percent report speaking a language other than English at home. But my beloved West River is a place of diminished expectations and fear for the future. The ranchers and merchants who managed to hang on through the severe decline of the past twenty years were nearly done in by the drought of 2002, the worst in a century. The rains that came this past spring mean that they will remain, at least for a time.

Why do they bother to stay, particularly since many have college degrees and marketable skills? It's hard to give up a place where you can walk at sunrise accompanied only by the sounds of wind and meadowlarks. Where a sense of connection comes from knowing the life story of everyone you encounter: the banker, the clerk at the grocery store, the semi driver hauling cattle to market. Where a sense of trust still prevails, sustained by a low crime rate, and one of the lowest murder rates in the nation.

The last summer I spent in South Dakota, I had a large squash and pumpkin patch, with sunflowers that grew well over six feet tall. In my other, smaller garden, I tended my grandmother's perennials— columbines and day-lilies—and grew nasturtiums for salad, and a good crop of basil, chervil, sorrel, tarragon, and lettuce. One nasty hailstorm in August pummeled everything to the ground. The morning after, I mourned, realizing that my loss was nothing compared to that of sunflower farmers, who had lost much of their cash crop. My squash was gone, but the pumpkins survived the loss of their protective leaves, and ripened as they were, palm-sized or slightly larger. At Halloween, I gave them away to neighborhood children. I fully expected to be back the next summer to try again, but it was not to be.

My new home is also an old home, Honolulu, where I grew up, and where my parents have resided for the past forty years. Hawaii is a semitropical paradise, but Honolulu is also a noisy, if pleasant, city. I miss the quiet of South Dakota, especially in the summer and early fall. I miss the eerie, stark beauty of grassland under a full moon, with herds of antelope ghostlike at the side of the road. I miss the night sky revealing far more stars than urban dwellers ever see. Standing in my backyard in Lemmon, I can see all seven of the Pleiades. From my lanai in my neighborhood of Makiki, I can detect a few planets and constellations, but the pink lights of the Royal Hawaiian's hotel in Waikiki are brighter. The crest of Diamond Head pokes above the tops of the buildings.

I am slowly becoming an island person again, counting the days until the humid south winds will depart and I can welcome the trades again, and I appreciate the irony of having moved from a region of America that feels like a remote desert island, where cell phones still don't work, to a city in the most physically isolated island chain in the world, where cell phones work just fine. Isolation, it seems, is very much in the mind. In the time it would take me to get from Lemmon to the nearest airport, in Bismarck, North Dakota, I can be more than halfway from Honolulu to the West Coast.

Tennessee

Tennessean by Birth

Nikki Giovanni

I'm a native Tennessean. I was born there. During the age of
segregation. When you couldn't go to the same amusement
park. Or the same movie theater. When the white guys would
cruise up and down the streets and call out to you. When the black
guys were afraid of being lynched. But we went to church each
Sunday. And we sang a precious song. And we found a way not to
survive. Anything can survive. But to thrive. And believe. And hope.

I'm a native Tennessean. I was born there. But I was only two months
old when my mother and father moved my sister and me to Cincinnati. During the age of segregation. When Dow Drugstore wouldn't
serve us. When neighborhoods were red-lined. But at least Mommy
could get a job teaching. And Daddy could get a job behind a desk. And
after all if you are a college graduate that is the least you can expect.
Though the Pullman Porters took us south each summer. And
watched over us with an unfair faith. And got us from there and here.

I'm from Knoxville. I was born there. In the only state in rebellion.
That didn't have to undergo Reconstruction. In the volunteer state

that sent as many for one side as another. In an area where if I just have to have a car breakdown I would prefer any holler to any city neighborhood. But there was no work. And no way. And the "chronic angers" that flared would chase us to Ohio. We were not Liza crossing the river. Just four people . . . two in love and two who were loved . . . who needed to put to rest the rage.

But the rage stayed. And someone had to go. I chose me. But I was born there. So the going was a coming. I am a native Tennessean.

I take no joy in Davy Crockett. Nor Jim Bowie. They were wrong to be at the Alamo. They were wrong to fight for the theft. I love James Agee. I loved *Thunder Road* though I, a native Tennessean, was not allowed to play a bit part when the crew came to town to film the movie. Ingrid Bergman and Anthony Quinn came to take *A Walk in the Spring Rain*. And despite it all I like Andrew Jackson. At least he knew the big guys were wrong.

I'm a native Tennessean. I graduated Fisk University in Nashville. I know that the freedmen paid for that school. Nobody gave them anything. Pennies and nickels and prayer and determination. The freedmen paid for it. And many others. I know the American Missionary Society took the money the Jubilee Singers made to save Fisk and used it for other purposes. I know the American Missionary Society was wrong. I was educated by the singers of those songs. I love those songs. How could I not love Nashville? How could I not love Dinah Shore who invited the Jubilee Singers to sing at the Grand Ole Opry then had to hear the rumors. She sang on. Sang until she saw the USA in her Chevrolet. Ummmompt! I once saw her on a plane. I was going to the cabin. She was in first class. I said: "Hey." She smiled and said "Hey" back. When I got Georgia on my mind I rode the Chattanooga Choo-Choo to Lookout Mountain. I saw Memphis and was enchanted. From the mighty Mississippi gracefully turning all red to Beale Street beats at midnight. All those blues from so many bloods. Decided to turn my blues to Memphis gold. W. C. Handy. Bobby Blue Bland. B. B. King. The late great Johnny Ace. Stax and stacks of music. American music. The Athens of the South held Tennessee music. But Memphis put the tears to the lonely. And crossed over. Everybody wants to rock to my rhythm. I am Memphis. I heard the shots that took Martin. I know who killed the King.

I'm a native Tennessean. I know what it is to be free. I am singing the country blues. I am whittling a wooden doll. I am underground mining coal. I am running moonshine. I am a white boy with a banjo. Native to west Africa. I am a black boy with a twang. Native to the hills. I am smart. I am cool. I am unafraid. I am free. Yeah. I am a native Tennessean.

TEXAS

TEXAS ON EVERYTHING

Molly Ivins

W ell, sheesh. I don't know whether to warn you that because George Dubya Bush is president the whole damn country is about to be turned into Texas (a singularly horrible fate; as the country song has it, "Lubbock on Everythang") or if I should try to stand up for us and convince the rest of the country we're not all that insane.

Truth is, I've spent much of my life trying, unsuccessfully, to explode the myths about Texas. One attempts to explain—with all goodwill, historical evidence, nasty statistics, and just a bow of recognition to our racism—that Texas is not *The Alamo* starring John Wayne. We're not *Giant*, we ain't a John Ford Western. The first real Texan I ever saw on TV was Boomhauer, the guy who's always drinking beer and you can't understand a word he says, on *King of the Hill*.

So, how come trying to explode myths about Texas always winds up reinforcing them? After all these years, I do not think it is my fault—the fact is, it's a damned peculiar place. Given all the horseshit, there's bound to be a pony in here somewhere. Just by trying to be honest about it, one accidentally underlines its sheer strangeness.

Here's the deal on Texas. It's big. So big there's about five distinct and different places here, separated from one another geologically, topologically, botanically, ethnically, culturally, and climatically. Hence our boring habit of specifying east, west, and south Texas, plus the Panhandle and the Hill Country. East Texas is 50 percent black and more like the Old South than the Old South is anymore. West Texas is, more or less, like *Giant*, except, like everyplace else in the state, it has an incurable tendency toward the tacky, and all the cowboys are brown. South Texas is 80 percent Hispanic and a weird amalgam of cultures. You get names now like Shannon Rodriguez, Hannah Gonzalez, and Tiffany Ruiz. Even the Anglos speak English with a Spanish accent. The Panhandle, which sticks up to damn-near Kansas, is High Plains, like one of those square states, Nebraska or the Dakotas, except more brown folks. The Hill Country, smack dab in the middle, resembles nothing else in the state.

Plus, plopped on top of all this, we have three huge cities, all among the ten largest in the country. Houston is Los Angeles with the climate of Calcutta, Dallas is Dutch (clean, orderly, and conformist), while San Antonio is Monterey North. Many years ago I wrote of this state: "The reason the sky is bigger here is because there aren't any trees. The reason folks here eat grits is because they ain't got no taste. Cowboys mostly stink and it's hot, oh God, is it hot. . . . Texas is a mosaic of cultures, which overlap in several parts of the state, with the darker layers on the bottom. The cultures are black, Chicano, Southern, freak, suburban, and shitkicker. (Shitkicker is dominant.) They are all rotten for women." All that's changed in thirty years is that suburban is now dominant, shitkicker isn't so ugly as it once was, and the freaks are now Goths or something. So it could be argued we're becoming more civilized.

In fact, it was always easy to argue that: Texas has symphony orchestras and great universities and perfect jewels of art museums (mostly in Fort Worth, of all places). It has lots of people who birdwatch, write Ph.D. theses on esoteric subjects, and speak French, for chrissake. But what still makes Texas Texas is that it's ignorant, cantankerous, and ridiculously friendly. Texas is still resistant to Howard Johnson's, interstate highways, and some forms of phoniness. It is the place least likely to become a replica of everyplace else. It's authentically both awful, comic, and weirdly charming all at the same time.

Culturally, Texans rather resemble both Alaskans (hunt, fish, hate government) and Australians (drink beer, hate snobs). "They said it was Texas kulcher, but it was only railroad gin" goes an old song by Johnny Winter. The food is quite good—Mexican, barbecue, chili, shrimp, and chicken-fried steak, an acquired taste. The music is country, blues, folk, mariachi, rockabilly, and everything else you can think of. Mexican music—*norteno, ranchero*—is poised to "cross over," as black music did in the 1950s.

If you want to understand George W. Bush—unlike his daddy, an unfortunate example of a truly Texas-identified citizen—you have to stretch your imagination around a weird Texas amalgam: religion, anti-intellectualism, and machismo. All big, deep strains here, but still an odd combination. Then add that Bush is just another li'l upper-class white boy out trying to prove he's tough.

The politics are probably the weirdest thing about Texas. The state has gone from one-party Democrat to one-party Republican in thirty years. Lyndon said when he signed the Civil Rights Act in 1964 that it cost the Democrats the South for two generations. Right on both counts. We like to think we're "past race" in Texas, but of course east Texas remains an ugly, glaring exception. After James Byrd, Jr. was dragged to death near Jasper, only one white politician attended his funeral—U.S. senator Kay Bailey Hutchison. Dubya, then governor, put the kibosh on the anti–hate crimes bill named in his memory. (The deal-breaker for Bush was including gays and lesbians. At a meeting last year of the Texas Civil Liberties Union board, vicious hate crimes against gays in both Dallas and Houston were discussed. I asked the board member from Midland if they'd been having any trouble with gay-bashing out there. "Hell, honey," she said, with that disastrous frankness one can grow so fond of, "there's not a gay in Midland would come out of the closet for fear people would think they're a Democrat." Among the various strains of Texas right-wingism (it is factually incorrect to call it conservatism) is some leftover loony Bircherism, now morphed into militias, country-club economic conservatism à la George Bush *père*, and the usual batty antigovernment strain. Of course, Texas grew on the tender mercies of the federal government—rural electrification, dams, generations of master pork-barrel politicians and vast subsidies to the oil and gas industry. But that has never interfered with Texans' touching but entirely erroneous belief that this is the Frontier, and that in the Old West every man pulled his own weight and depended on no one else. The myth of rugged individualism continues to afflict a generation raised entirely in suburbs with names like the Flowering Forest Hills of Lubbock.

The Populist movement was born in the Texas Hill Country, as genuinely democratic an uprising as this country has ever known. It produced legendary politicians for generations, including Ralph Yarborough, Sam Rayburn, Lyndon, and even into the nineties with Agriculture Commissioner Jim Hightower. I think it is not gone, but only sleeping.

Texans retain an exaggerated sense of state identification, routinely identifying themselves when abroad as Texans, rather than Americans or from the United States. That aggravated provincialism has three sources. First, the state is so big (though not as big as Alaska, as they are sure to remind us) that it can take a couple of days' hard travel just to get the hell out of it. Second, we reinforce the sense of difference by requiring kids to study Texas history, including its ten years as an independent country. In state colleges, the course in Texas government is mandatory. Third, even national advertising campaigns pitch brands with a Texas accent here and certain products, like the pickup truck, are almost invariably sold with a Texas pitch. (Makes sense, with four times as many pickup drivers here as elsewhere.)

The founding myth is the Alamo. I was raised on the Revised Standard Version, which holds that while it was stupid of Travis and the gang to be there at all (Sam Houston told them to get the hell out), it was still an amazing last stand. Stephen Harrigan in *The Gates of the Alamo* is closer to reality, but even he admits in the end there was something romantic and even noble about the episode, rather like having served in the Abraham Lincoln Brigade during the Spanish Civil War.

According to the demographers at Texas A&M (itself a source of much Texas lore), Texas will become "majority minority" in 2008. Unfortunately, we won't see it in the voting patterns for at least a generation, and by then the Republicans will have the state so tied up by redistricting (currently the subject of a massive standoff in the legislature), it's unlikely to shift for another generation beyond that. The Christian Right is heavily dominant in the Texas Republican party. It was the genius of Karl Rove/George W. Bush to straddle the divide between the Christian Right and the country-club conservatives, which is actually a significant class split. The politics of resentment play a large role in the Christian Right: fundamentalists are perfectly aware that they are held in contempt by "the intellectuals." (In 1898 William Brann of Waco observed, "The trouble with our Texas Baptists is that we do not hold them under water long enough." He was shot to death by an irate Baptist.) In Texas, "intellectual" is often used as a synonym for "snob": George W. Bush perfectly exemplifies that attitude.

Here in the National Laboratory for Bad Government, we have an antiquated and regressive tax structure—high property, high sales, no income tax. We consistently rank near the bottom of every measure of social service, education, and quality of life (leading to one of our state mottoes, "Thank God for Mississippi"). Yet the state is incredibly rich in more than natural resources. The economy is now fully diversified, so plunges in the oil market can no longer throw the state into the bust cycle.

It is widely believed in Texas that the highest purpose of government is to create "a healthy bidness climate." The legislature is so dominated by special interests that the gallery where the lobbyists sit is called "the owners' box." The consequences of unregulated capitalism and of special interests being able to buy government through campaign contributions are more evident here because Texas is "first and worst" in this area. That Enron was a Texas company is no accident: Texas was also ground zero in the savings-and-loan scandal, is continually the site of major rip-offs by the insurance industry, and has a rich history of gigantic chicanery going way back. Leland Beatty calls Enron "Billie Sol Estes Goes to College." Economists call it "control fraud" when a corporation is rotten from the head down. I sometimes think Texas government is a case of control fraud too.

We are currently saddled with a right-wing-ideologue sugar daddy, James Leininger out of San Antonio, who gives immense campaign contributions and wants school vouchers, abstinence education, and the like in return. The result is a crew of breathtakingly right-wing legislators. This session, Representative Debbie Riddle of Houston said during a hearing, "Where did this idea come from that everybody deserves free education, free medical care, free whatever? It comes from Moscow, from Russia. It comes straight out of the pit of hell."

Texans for Lawsuit Reform, aka the bidness lobby, is a major player and has effectively eviscerated the judiciary with a two-pronged attack. While round after round of "tort reform" was shoved through the legislature, closing off access to the courts and protecting corporations from liability for their misdeeds, Karl Rove was busy electing all nine state supreme court justices. So even if you should somehow manage to get into court, you are faced with a bench noted for its canine fidelity to corporate special interests.

Here's how we make progress in Texas. Two summers ago, Governor Goodhair Perry (the man has a head of hair every Texan can be proud of, regardless of party) appointed an Enron executive to the Public Utilities Commission. The next day, Governor Goodhair got a $25,000 check from Ken Lay. Some thought there might be a connection. The guv was forced to hold a press conference at which he explained the whole thing was "totally coincidental." So that was a big relief. We don't have a sunshine law in Texas: it's more like a "partly cloudy law," but even here a major state appointee has to fill out a bunch of forms that are then public record. When the governor's office put out the forms on the Enron guy, members of the press, that alert guardian watchdog of democracy, noticed that number 17 looked funny. The governor's office had whited out the answers to question 17. A sophisticated cover-up.

Turns out 17 is the question about any unfortunate involvement with law enforcement. The alert guardian watchdogs were on the trail. We soon uncovered a couple of minor traffic violations and the following item. While out hunting a few years earlier, the Enron guy accidentally shot a whooping crane. Then he accidentally buried it, and as a result had to pay a $15,000 fine under what is known in Texas as the In Danger Species Act. We print this. A state full of sympathetic hunters reacted with, "Hell, anybody could accidentally shoot a whooper." But the press stayed on the story and was able to report the guy shot the whooper while on a goose hunt. Now the whooper is a large bird, runs up to five feet tall. The goose—short. Now we have a state full of hunters saying, "Hell, if this boy is too dumb to tell a whooper from a goose, maybe he shouldn't be regulatin' public utilities." He was forced to resign.

As Willie Nelson sings, if we couldn't laugh, we would all go insane. This is our redeeming social value and perhaps our one gift to progressives outside our borders. We do laugh. We have no choice. We have to have fun while trying to stave off the forces of darkness because we hardly ever win so it's the only fun we get to have. We find beer and imagination helpful. The Billion Bubba March, the Spam-O-Rama, the time we mooned the Klan, being embedded with the troops at the Holiday Inn in Ardmore, Oklahoma, singing "I Am Just an Asshole from El Paso" with Kinky Friedman and the Texas Jewboys, and "Up Against the Wall You Redneck Mother" with Ray Wylie Hubbard laughing at the loonies in the Lege—does it get better than this? The late Bill Kugle of Athens is buried in the Texas State Cemetery. On the front of his stone are listed his service in the Marines in World War II, his years in the legislature, other titles and honors. On the back of the stone is, "He never voted for a Republican and never had much to do with them either."

We have lost some great freedom fighters in Texas during the past year. Billie Carr, the great Houston political organizer (you'd've loved her: she got invited to the White House during the middle of the Monica mess, sashayed through the receiving line, looked Bill Clinton in the eye and said, "You dumb son of a bitch"), always said she wanted her funeral to be like her whole life in politics: it should start half an hour late, she wanted a balanced delegation of pall-bearers—one black, one brown, two women—she wanted an open casket, and a name tag stuck over her left tit that said, "Hi there! My name is Billie Carr." We did it all for her.

At the funeral of Malcolm McGregor, the beloved legislator and bibliophile from El Paso, we heard "The Eyes of Texas" and the Aggie War Hymn played on the bagpipes. At the service for Maury Maverick, Jr., of San Antonio, at his request, J. Frank Dobie's poem "The Mustangs" was read by the poet Naomi Shihab Nye. The last stanza is:

So sometimes yet, in the realities of silence and solitude,
For a few people unhampered a while by things,
The mustangs walk out with dawn, stand high, then
Sweep away, wild with sheer life, and free, free, free—
Free of all confines of time and flesh.

Utah

A Landscape of Extreme Views

Terry Tempest Williams

The truck looked like an American flag on wheels. As I got closer, it became clear it was a roving billboard for the radical Right that had parked itself across from the mailboxes in Castle Valley, a small desert hamlet in southeastern Utah surrounded by red-rock mesas and spires. REMEMBER RUBY RIDGE, WACO, AND OKLAHOMA CITY, it read on one side of the truck in large red letters. The trailer, painted black with white lettering, was reserved for the United Nations: GET THE UNITED NATIONS OUT OF AMERICA; and on the other side it read, SUPPORT UTAH'S UNORGANIZED MILITIA. Across the windshield of the red-white-and-blue truck, in white letters painted most likely with an index finger in a hurry, it read, SIGN THESE PETITIONS.

The man standing in front of his vehicle, wearing a straw cowboy hat with a veteran's poppy stuck on its brim, was struggling to keep the piles of paper from blowing off the hood of his truck by placing large sandstone rocks on top of them. The winds were picking up as the heat began to rise. It was the summer solstice. Even so, he had on a long-sleeve plaid cowboy shirt, Levi's, and boots.

Driving in my own truck, I picked up my mail, pulled over to the side, got out, and walked across the road to see what the petitions were about. He turned around and extended his hand. We shook hands and introduced ourselves. His name was Bo. He smelled of gasoline. He took care of a local campground in the town of Moab. He rewound his gray ponytail with a rubber band.

"So what are these petitions about?" I asked.

"Sign here if you want to repeal the USA Patriot Act," he said matter-of-factly, his voice registering a slight whistle due to a line of missing front teeth.

"These petitions are to get rid of the Patriot Act?" I asked.

"That's right, ma'am."

"Well, sir, I'm right there with you and I'm a liberal environmentalist."

"Doesn't surprise me a bit, ma'am. We've got to get our government back in the hands of the people."

He handed me a blue pen and I signed my name on both petitions, one for Grand County, Utah, and one for the United States of America.

"I couldn't agree with you more. Have you had many people in the valley stop and sign these?"

"Nope, 'fraid you're the first."

"Forgive me for interfering, but I think folks might be a bit put off by your truck. Perhaps if you had a sign saying something about the Patriot—"

He turned around and looked at his vehicle and then looked at me.

"What's wrong with my truck?"

"Nothing, sir, not a thing, I promise, it's just they might be getting the wrong idea."

"I painted this truck myself. It expresses who I am."

"Of course it does, which is why I'm here. Honestly, I've never seen anything like it—it's just you might want to put a sign up or sandwich board that says 'Sign a petition against the Patriot Act,' and I'll bet you'll get the whole town to drop by."

"I appreciate your suggestion," he said. "I'll paint one tonight."

We kept talking and I explained that Castle Valley with all its Mormons, aging hippies, environmentalists, climbers, artists, attorneys, river rats, and winemakers had been the first town in Utah to register its dissent against the Patriot Act.

"You know people in town call us 'The People's Republic of Castle Valley,' " I said.

He smiled. "I heard, that's why I'm here."

There was a long pause, then he handed me a magazine called *The New American*.

On the cover was a soldier in Iraq. The headline read, "Trading Freedom for Security." An article inside traced the symbolism of the peace sign, how it originated in ancient pagan rituals, a token not of peace but of evil.

"Ma'am, have you ever heard of the Trilateral Commission?" He handed me a flow chart complete with a genealogy of those in power with David Rockefeller in bold letters at the top of the chart as chairman of the Council of Foreign Relations and North American chairman of the Trilateral Commission. "A private organization formed in 1973," it read. Laterally, to the left of Rockefeller, were the names of Henry Kissinger, advisor, followed by R. S. McNamara, World Bank. On Rockefeller's right, W. B. Dale from the International Monetary Fund, with R. A. Dungan, Inter-American Development Bank, to the right of him.

Directly beneath David Rockefeller's boxed name was James Earl (Jimmy) Carter, "Charter member, Trilateral Commission." And I quote, "Selected in 1973 by the Trilateral Commission & Council on Foreign Relations to be THEIR PRESIDENT! Groomed and Trained by Brzezinski!"

With a quick scan, I realized I was looking at a map of the "New World Order."

The small print was the most interesting. "Notice that every State Dept. Bureau which has betrayed America's anti-Communist friends is headed up by Rockefeller's agents. After a country has been 'pushed' into our enemies hands, a move is made to shore up the Marxists regime with large amounts of American tax monies."

I noticed several of the men named on the chart were dead: Adlai Stevenson, Hubert Humphrey, Tip O'Neill, Daniel Moynihan and, most recently, David Brinkley. I also noticed the "information was compiled in 1980." At the bottom of the map, it said, "Please send $2.00 to F.R.E.E. P.O. Box 293339, Kerrville, Tx. 78029."

"Have you heard of them, ma'am?" he asked again.

"I have, Bo, but I've never seen this chart."

"What da ya think about it?"

"In my circle of friends, we call these men in power 'The Federalists.' " I noted Secretary of Defense Donald Rumsfeld's name would appear on both lists.

If loss of freedom and loss of wildlands translates to "A New World Order," Bo and I were comrades. I might as well paint my own truck with my tribe's mantras, "Save the Whales," "Save the Spotted Owl," "Wild Utah," and "Bush is an avowed eco-terrorist." I began to see an American flag and Edward Abbey's monkey wrench as part of the same brand of patriotism.

Bo handed me some more information, a sheet printed in red and blue ink with the heading, "The Unofficial Open Gathering of the Southeastern Utah Unorganized Militia." It went on to read, "as allowed pursuant to the Utah Constitution, Article XV, I, 'The militia shall consist of all able-bodied male inhabitants of the state, between 18 and 45 years of age, except those exempted by law.' "

"Did you know that Utah's one of the only states in the union that can lawfully and legally have a militia?" Bo said.

"Is that true?"

"Utah Code, 39-102." He then pointed and read from the Utah State Constitution, "Divided into National Guard and Unorganized Militia, 'The militia of this state shall be divided into two parts: the

National Guard. . . . The Unorganized Militia shall consist of all militia not members of the Guard."

"I had no idea."

"Most people don't, ma'am."

"But I have to say, it makes sense given Utah's history of the Mormon Battalion and 'the four strike policy' mentioned in the Mormon scriptures. Enemies of the Mormons could expect pacifism from the Mormons on the first, second, and third attacks. But on the fourth attack, Mormons could fight back with religious justification and God's blessing."

"Yes, ma'am. We meet the fifth of every month at the campground." I could tell what was coming next. "But I'm afraid women . . ."

"I know," I said. "We're in Utah." Utah is a state of extremes: extreme beliefs, extreme landscapes, extreme behavior. It is also a state of paradoxes. Where Bo and I met, geologically speaking, is called Paradox Basin. That a man married to the idea of militias in the name of freedom and a woman married to the idea of peace in the name of wilderness preservation could find meaningful conversation, even common ground, is at the heart of what defines Utah. We understand what it means to come together in times of crisis. It is written into our history.

When the Mormon pioneers arrived in the Salt Lake Valley in 1847 under the leadership of Brigham Young, having endured religious persecution and even the murder of their prophet, seer, and revelator Joseph Smith, they gave prayerful thanks for the isolation of the Great Basin they saw before them. Physical isolation meant spiritual sovereignty. "If there is a place on earth nobody wants, that is the place I am hunting for," said Brigham Young, their own American Moses. Here on the edge of the salt flats and the shimmering Great Salt Lake, these "latter-day saints" could worship what they wished, as they wished, and began their dream of building Zion.

Which the Mormons did. And in time, as Brother Brigham would prophesy, "The desert would bloom as a rose." Their epic journey across the Great Plains and through the Rocky Mountains over 1,300 miles of wild country, much of it in the deadly grip of winter and the searing heat of summer, only strengthened their resolve that this was the "right place" for the Saints to settle.

To understand contemporary Utah one has to understand Mormon history.

"No unhallowed hand can stop the work from progressing; persecution may rage, mobs may combine, armies may assemble, calumny may defame, but the truth of God will go forth boldly, nobly and independent, till it has penetrated every continent, visited every clime, swept every country, and sounded in every ear, till the purposes of God shall be accomplished, and the Great Jehovah shall say the work is done" (History of the Church, 4:540). People in the state of Utah are on a mission and the work is never done. Our symbol: a beehive. We are busy people whose loyalties are to the hive. The metaphor stops, however, at the queen bee. Within the Mormon religion, only men can hold the priesthood. Women's power is their reproductive power and their capacity to work behind the scenes. Large families are common in Utah. If you ever doubt who you are, all you have to do is go to a family reunion and see yourself mirrored in the eyes of a hundred relatives.

Which brings us to polygamy. Everyone is related in Utah, more or less. If Bo and I had pursued our genealogy, no doubt we would have found a common relative.

Mine can be traced to Mexico—Colonia Dublan, to be exact, somewhere in the arid desert of Chihuahua. My ancestors fled southern Utah in 1885 when the U.S. government was pressing down hard against plural marriage within the Deseret Territory. John Taylor, prophet of the Mormon Church, set up a "City of Refuge" in Mexico for those "latter-day saints" who were at risk of being arrested for practicing polygamy. Word traveled quickly among polygamist families and another migration ensued, one that would last decades and establish nine colonies in Mexico.

The Romneys, my mother's kin, were among those families that fled the United States to seek both religious and political cover across the border.

My grandmother, Lettie Romney Dixon, was born in Colonia Dublan on June 12, 1909, to Vilate Lee and Park Romney. One year later she would be part of the Mormon-Mexican Exodus, where 2,300 women and children were forced to leave their homes in the colonies under orders from General Salazar. Pancho Villa was leading the revolution. He wanted the Mormons "to go home." As they crossed the border of Mexico into America, they were corralled, literally, in El Paso, and given as Mormon refugees a one-way ticket to the town of their choice. My family returned to Utah.

Our identity is forged through stories, and we learn them in our youth. My great-grandmother Vilate recounted fleeing Mexico with my grandmother Lettie strapped behind her on their horse, in such a hurry that a cake was left in the oven. Translation: when the Church calls, you act accordingly. Uncle Junius Romney, leader of the Mormons in Mexico, had instructed them to move and they moved without question.

No wonder the paradox of obedience and revolution is inherent in our bones. We respect authority within our religious views yet deplore it when told what to do by our government. Little has changed more than 150 years later. The memory of persecution is still in our blood.

But this is speaking as a Mormon.

In the state of Utah, there is a diversity of peoples. Members of the Church of Jesus Christ of Latter-day Saints make up only half of the state's population. The myth is more dominant than the numbers. Healthy, influential communities of Jews, Greeks, Latinos, Polynesians, Asians, and African-Americans live alongside one another, especially along the Urban Terrace with Salt Lake City at its center, where the majority of Utah's residents live along the foothills and in the valleys of the Wasatch Mountains, north to Ogden and south to Provo. Population for the state of Utah at the turn of the second millennium: roughly 2.5 million, and growing. St. George, Utah, located in the bottom left-hand corner of the state (if you are looking at a map) is one of the fastest-growing cities in the United States. It is one hour from Zion National Park, two hours from Bryce Canyon, and in the other direction south, it's a two-hour drive to Las Vegas. Warm weather and spectacular scenery are the magnets drawing people down.

But Utah's deep history is held by the six Indian tribes: the Northwestern Shoshone; the Goshute; the Paiute; the Northern Utes; the White Mesa Utes; and the Navajos or Dine, all of which maintain strong, viable communities within Utah with their own tribal governments. Tribal sovereignty has a large voice when it comes to oil and gas development and the storage of nuclear waste in Utah, and to how natural resources are being used regarding the oil and gas fields found on Indian lands. Like all Indian peoples, their histories have not been without heartbreak, broken treaties, and abuses.

Forrest S. Cuch, raised on the Uintah and Ouray Ute Indian Reservation, writes, "All Utah tribes have experienced their moment of great suffering. For the Shoshone, it was the Bear River Massacre of 1863. For the Utah Utes, it was forced removal in 1865 from their beloved Utah Valley into the arid Uinta Basin. For the Goshutes, it was broken promises and removal from traditional sacred lands. For the Navajo and Paiute, it was countless skirmishes with Mormon settlers in southern Utah. The Paiute suffered again late in their history, when, during the 1950s, they were terminated from federal assistance and their reservation lands were taken from them" (*A History of Utah's American Indians*, Utah State Division of Indian Affairs, p. xvii). Herein lies the crux of Utah: the land. Regardless of who we are, what we believe, or where we have come from, we are here because of the land. Our identity is tied to the land. Clay figurines found in the bottom of caves near Great Salt Lake made by the Fremont people a thousand years ago; handprints left on slickrock walls above the Colorado River; ancient kivas still intact on

Cedar Mesa created by the Ancient Puebloans remind us that our humanity has evolved in place. And Utah's landscape is extraordinary in its variety of forms, from the searing light of the salt flats on the edge of Great Salt Lake, to the pine forests and alpine lakes in the Uinta Mountains, to the red-rock serpentine canyons of southern Utah.

When Professor Thomas Lyon and I were asked to compile a literary history of Utah for its centennial in 1996, *A Strange and Peculiar Beauty—A Utah Reader*, the bones of our book were based on the five physiographic regions of the state: Great Basin, Rocky Mountains, Urban Terrace, Colorado Plateau, and Dixie, a corner of the Mojave Desert in southwestern Utah. This became our organizing principle. What we found mirrored Aldo Leopold's notion that, in fact, landscape shapes culture.

Leopold writes: "The rich diversity of the world's cultures reflects a corresponding diversity in the wilds that gave them birth."

We realized the history of Utah is written on the landscape of Utah. The driving of the Golden Spike in 1869, which drew the nation together in one continuous rail, was done on the edge of Great Salt Lake, an inland sea, in the interior West. This was an arid landscape largely invisible to outsiders, yet it bound the country together.

We realized it was in the red-rock desert of southeastern Utah on the banks of the Colorado River, where uranium was mined and cured for the future of America's military might. And it was in the Mojave Desert near St. George, Utah, at the Nevada Test Site where the atomic test bombs were detonated. The winds blew and it was Utah residents who bore the burden of nuclear radioactive fallout and ultimately paid for it with their lives.

Our lives in this landscape are intrinsically bound together. This is our history. And our history has always been charged with an intensity more akin to religious fervor than political heat. This is also in our blood. Whether it is fleeing to Mexico to practice polygamy so Utah can gain statehood, or debating the fate of America's Redrock Wilderness, or whether or not Utah's militia should be organized or unorganized as the threat of the United Nations grows in the minds of some Utahns, we will always meet on the common ground of our own sovereign spirits. This is the irony of living in Utah, where the boundaries between church and state are often blurred, where the line between obedience and anarchy is often just a matter of intonation and inflection inside a slow, controlled drawl. What struck me about my encounter with Bo was this: when it came down to our core beliefs, we agreed more than we disagreed, even though on paper, we were on opposite sides of the political spectrum. This is quintessential Utah.

In truth, when I saw his vehicle parked across from the mailboxes in our little town of Castle Valley, I thought two things: either he was an escapee from the "Days of '47" parade in Salt Lake City (a celebration of when the Mormon pioneers entered the Salt Lake Valley in 1847), or that he was here to harass our local land trust, which had just received monies from the Utah Division of Wildlife Resources to secure five hundred acres of state lands for deer habitat instead of development. Rednecks versus environmentalists. Typical paranoia (also a Utah trait). Traditionally, this is not a friendly alliance. But when all Bo wanted was to gather signatures to petition and protest against the unlawful nature of the Patriot Act, I had to confront my own prejudices and look at what stops me from honest engagement with my neighbors.

What does this suggest?

It suggests to me that given our history as Utahns under the various tensions and oppressions we have experienced with the federal government through decades of trying to fight for our rights as westerners—be it water or land or religion—unexpected conversations and coalitions can be forged. Nothing is as it appears, especially here in "The Beehive State." That beyond our traditional labels, positions, and projections, there are real concerns about the just nature of a true democracy that we share, particularly now as we begin this new millennium in a world that is being defined by those in power as a war against terror.

Terror comes to a people in many forms and it registers in our memory as suspicion.

Something is terribly wrong, out of balance. This we know. This we feel as red-blooded Americans who believe in freedom in all its strange, peculiar, and wondrous configurations.

For those of us who choose to live in the outback of mainstream America—and surely those of us who live in Utah qualify—we choose to believe that voices on the margin have always exerted pressure on the center. Listening is required. Belief and hard work are seen as allies. Suddenly dialogues spring forth like water bubbling up in the desert. And a community rises to the call of its members. We did it during the floods of 1983 when the Great Salt Lake was rising and State Street turned into a river. We did it again when Elizabeth Smart was kidnapped from her own home and thousands of volunteers took to the hills in search of a missing child and never gave up hope. And we will do it again as the next situation of adversity reveals itself.

In Utah, there is a belief that this is not only a place, as Brigham Young professed, but a varied landscape with a people in a place, who speak from the hardscrabble truth of the land that inspires them.

Utahns live in a state of extreme views.

We can climb twelve-thousand feet to the summit of Lone Peak and look out over the Salt Lake Valley and witness a city of increasing sophistication.

We can wander across the salt flats of an inland sea, the size of Delaware and Rhode Island, and become disoriented by dazzling mirages in all directions, as we pray for water.

We can travel south to the Redrock Wilderness and stand in the sweep of a sandstone bowl looking out through Delicate Arch and believe in the erosion of all that is secure. Stone in converted to air by water and wind in time.

Extreme faith in an extreme state becomes just another point of view.

VERMONT

THE VIEW FROM VERMONT

Jay Parini

I never get back to Vermont without thanking the heavens that I live here. Driving in from the west, I love the sudden emergence of small farms, with their red-roofed barns, with hundreds of grazing cattle hunched in sloping fields, and the little sugar houses with their smokestacks huffing in spring. I know: this sounds like tourist-board propaganda. But unobstructed rural views are, indeed, comforting and rare in the Northeast. Vermont has more of these than any other state in New England, and more variety of landscape as well, with the Green Mountains snaking their way through the center of the state from north to south, with Lake Champlain shimmering along the western border of the state, with views of the White Mountains to the northeast, and the gentle landscape of the south, near the hill country of western Massachusetts. Were I Walt Whitman, I'd lengthen the catalogue of natural wonders.

Billboard advertising is banned in Vermont, which helps to preserve the views. There is fierce town planning in force that keeps many of the local hamlets intact. (You need five acres to build a house in my village, largely because of septic tank matters.) The chain stores—Wal-Mart, Best Buy, Costco, Staples, Circuit City, Home Depot, and so forth—have been banished to isolated preserves. I think of them as shopper reservations. These are thoughtfully tucked into areas where the general population doesn't usually have to see them on a daily basis.

Of course erosions occur. The closest major town, Middlebury, has a string of car dealerships and restaurants, including a McDonald's, to the south of the village green. This unsightly and unpleasant reminder of twenty-first-century reality stretches for about two or three miles, then stutters into countryside as one drives toward Rutland. I've noticed that you don't really notice these eyesores after a while. You take the McDonald's for granted, more or less; it only upsets you slightly. You even stop for a fish sandwich or a cup of coffee now and then.

This all sounds ridiculous, of course. America is, after all, a capitalist nation, where people make good money on commerce, and where the population seems to enjoy the fruits of their relatively free enterprise. I keep in touch with the country at large by visiting my eighty-six-year-old mother in Scranton, Pennsylvania, on regular occasions. I grew up there, amid the industrial ruins of anthracite mining. It always strikes me that the population of that region takes for granted the ruins around them, with abandoned breakers and culm dumps still dotting the landscape. The trees have all been cut down on the street where I once played beneath huge oaks and maples. When my old neighbor cut down the last tree on his property, I asked him why he would do such a thing. "They were attracting birds," he explained.

From what I can tell, Scrantonians love the malls, which are located about five miles from the city. They don't even seem to notice that the construction of these malls actually destroyed the city's once thriving commercial sections. When I was a child, the local Main Street in West Scranton was lined with businesses owned and run by people from West Scranton. There were shoe repair shops, small groceries, diners, stores that specialized in clothes for children, hardware stores, barbershops, and so forth. These are all gone. The buildings that once housed them are shockingly empty, with broken windows and crumbling facades. The only working businesses are gas stations and funeral parlors. For all intents and purposes, the place is dead.

The people either don't care or don't notice, and I confess that I don't understand their attitude, or lack of attitude. I leave Scranton with a sigh of relief every time I go there for my ritual visits, usually at the major holidays. I drive anxiously north, through the fairly deserted Poconos, through the congested city of Albany, up through the Adirondacks, crossing over the southwestern border of Vermont with a huge sense of coming home. I look forward to the sight of the Green Mountains in the middle distance, and the views of Lake Champlain. (I spend a lot of time on that lake in the summer, in my little boat, and it has become a kind of religion for me, a place where a lively spirit seems to have unrestrained access to my senses.)

These days, the relief of living in Vermont is also political. We have only one congressman, Bernie Sanders, who was the socialist mayor of Burlington before he ran as an independent progressive a decade or so ago, and became our representative in the lower house. Everyone knows Bernie: he is frequently seen on the street. I've been to his house for chats about public policy. He is responsive to telephone calls and e-mails. He thinks government should actually help, not hinder, working people—which makes him fairly isolated in the House, where he's surrounded by blow-dried Young Republicans who want mainly to get the government off the backs of the rich and onto the fronts of gays and lesbians. Our senators are Patrick Leahy and Jim Jeffords, two of the most sensible voices in the upper house, which also puts them at odds with their senatorial colleagues, who seem hell-bent on taking back America for the wealthiest 5 percent while occupying the Middle East with U.S. troops.

This is a progressive state, for the most part. We were the first state to ratify the notion of civil unions. We have a fairly humane (though still evolving) tax system in which money from wealthier towns is funneled to poorer towns for schools. Health care for children is guaranteed: one of the great achievements of our former governor, Howard Dean, now a leading presidential contender for the Democratic nomination. Our environmental laws are fairly rigorous. In so many ways,

Vermont ought to serve as a model for the rest of the country. Unfortunately, the rest of the country doesn't care, and regards this state as some sort of hippie throwback, a progressive ghetto.

There is, as might be expected, a vigorous opposition here, made up of conservative farmers and businessmen, who would like to see Vermont resemble other states and would like to relax the progressive measures that have been put into place. They resent interlopers like myself, part of the progressive migration of the late sixties and seventies, who have sometimes been at odds with the old Vermonters, who are by nature very conservative—in a real sense, which is to say they wish to preserve the land, the traditions, of their families and communities. Tensions between the "old" and "new" Vermont have, I think, lessened over the years. Nobody wants to see measures taken that would radically alter the social or physical environment. But one can never rest. In a country that seems only to turn right, then right again, I feel some apprehension that the Vermont I love may gradually dissolve before my very eyes.

With the Bush regime in control of weapons of mass destruction, I have more than ever become grateful for the company of Vermonters. There were peace vigils on the village green in Middlebury every Saturday for months before the U.S. invasion of Iraq. There have been regular and well-attended demonstrations against the Iraq war in most of the larger towns and cities. One commonly sees more peace stickers than American flags on the bumpers of Vermont cars. This is not the case in, say, Scranton—or other cities in the nation where antiwar activists feel isolated, aware of their minority status.

The view from Vermont toward the rest of the nation is an anxious one, at least in my case. The large corporations that run this country have managed to get almost total control of the mainstream media, which use their fearsome influence to promote policies detrimental to the public good. Thought control is rigorously upheld, and those who oppose the status quo are branded as anti-American. The war against Iraq is a case in point: it has been pursued with an almost unbelievable arrogance by Bush and his cronies, largely for the benefit of a small group of arms manufacturers and oil dealers. It has been waged, as Senator Jeffords recently told an audience at Middlebury College, to bolster a failing regime—that of George W. Bush. He needed the hype, the artificial patriotic boost, that comes with war. Without terrorism to combat on every front, real or imagined, the working people of America might notice that their pockets are being picked, that the economy is a shambles, that the laws are being tailored to benefit the corporate elite. They might realize that the environment is being threatened by the Environmental Protection Agency itself, and that the "education president," as Bush dubbed himself during his campaign, has indeed had his eyes firmly on the school systems of America, determined to undermine all efforts to educate the broadest segment of the population. The fact that our civil liberties have been challenged in ways not seen before has hardly registered with the larger public, most of whom don't realize that the suspension of habeas corpus is a very serious affair.

The issue of homeland security has not, I'm glad to say, reached Vermont in any significant way. We have not been hoarding duct tape for a bad day. We have not been overly worried about terrorists. Not having any concentrated urban centers, and without obvious targets that might interest Osama, we seem immune from attack. This may well be an illusion, and Tom Ridge, who heads the Department of Homeland Security, may be proved right when he tells the nation to prepare for further, devastating attacks by Islamic fundamentalists who "hate our freedom." But I personally think there is really nothing much we can do about terrorism except try to alleviate the conditions in the Islamic world that have made terrorism possible. Our best defense against terror is an alliance with the mainstream of Islam, which is moderate and sensible.

I live on an isolated hilltop some miles from Middlebury, with a view of the rolling hills, surrounded by pastureland, ponds, and maple woods. My clapboard farmhouse, built in 1850, is a wooden affair, badly insulated, with creaking floorboards and windows made of old-fashioned blown glass, which distorts the view outside. Perhaps my whole environment distorts my view outside of Vermont to the nation at large? Nevertheless, whenever I gaze at America from the Green Mountains, I see a country mired in its own spectacular greed, its anxious xenophobia, its dismal conformity, its foolish obeisance to a government that feeds its narcissistic fantasies in exchange for the power to skew laws and regulations in favor of the corporate interests who have made their political lives possible. It is not a pretty scene.

The scenery, in Vermont, however is—perhaps fatally—"pretty." If you dig below the surface, you will discover that small family farms have been losing ground for decades, their numbers dwindling. Our dairy farmers, in particular, are having a miserable time. Agribusiness has threatened their very existence, and many have slipped into bankruptcy in the past few years. I don't really know how long this state will be able to maintain its rural character, given the pressures from outside the state, largely economic. Even my beloved Lake Champlain—which is eight miles from my house—is, I'm sad to report, fairly polluted—a victim of acid rain and other environmental depredations. Vermont is not some fantasy island, unaffected by decisions made by the owners of factories in Ohio and New York. There are good reasons to worry about the future.

On the other hand, I'm still glad to live where I do. The alternatives, as I see it, are not pleasant, and there are things about this state—its progressive experiment—that may well provide a beacon of sorts for the rest of the country. If Howard Dean ever becomes president, who knows what might happen? Cows in the Rose Garden? Civil unions taking place in Texas? Schools with all the money they need to provide a decent education for even the poorest children? Armies asleep in their barracks, at home? Gun dealers on the run? More of our citizens in college than in prison? Corporations having to pay for the pollution they have caused? Third World countries chanting "God Bless America" instead of "Yankee Go Home"?

Hey, it's a crazy world. Anything can happen.

VIRGINIA

A COMPOSITION ON VIRGINIA

David Berman

I was born in Williamsburg, Virginia, in 1967, exactly 360 years after the first British colony in North America was founded, down the road, at Jamestown. In mathematics 360 degrees is regarded as a return to zero. A flipping of the odometer, as it were.

In 1967 my father was a waiter at the King's Arms Tavern in Colonial Williamsburg. The employees wore period dress. Because he was just getting off work when my mother finished labor, the nurses handed me over to a man wearing knee breeches, buckled shoes, and a tricorne hat.

I was an unwitting solipsist as a child. I believed that God had left clues embedded in the world for me to interpret and make use of.

Once I discovered the secret of the 360 years, I had to wonder what he was trying to tell me. That I would be a witness to (pardon the stupid name) America II? Or (as I secretly hoped) that I would be a leader, a general, a statesman, in that new era?

I couldn't know, but I could train. I read every founding father's biography I could get my hands on. I hardened the soles of my feet on long driveways spread with sharp gravel and ate whole lemons to test my fortitude. I wanted to be rough and ready.

In 1975 my father took a job with the Steak and Ale Corporation headquartered in Dallas. Steak and Ale's founding father was Norman Brinker, the man who popularized the pre–sneeze guard salad bar, created Bennigan's Tavern, and resuscitated Chili's from the wide graveyard of 1980s fern bars. He remains an industry legend.

Meanwhile my head was still in Virginia. I consumed presidential biographies. I was the kid who could tell you LBJ's favorite soda (Fresca) and George Washington's favorite song ("The Darby Ram"), that Franklin Pierce's secretary of war was Jefferson Davis, and that Zachary Taylor's son owned a plantation in Louisiana called "Fashion."

Around that time Steak and Ale was having a problem with Virginia. The state's liquor laws prohibited a business from having the word "Ale" (or any other intoxicant) in its name. For that reason the Steak and Ales in Virginia were known as The Jolly Ox.

As the company's attorney my father traveled to Richmond to lobby the state legislature into changing the law. Of course, Virginia would not budge (to my secret delight).

I had the feeling that Virginia had earned its arrogance fairly. It had gifted history with so many great men and ideas, been the cradle of representative government in North America, yielded eight presidents, and been the sacrificial site of more military battles than any other state.

William Faulkner pissed a lot of Virginians off when he said "I love Virginians because Virginians are snobs and I like snobs. A snob has to spend so much time being a snob that he has little time left to meddle with you." If this sounds like a put-down, consider that he was arranging to buy a farm outside of Charlottesville at the time of his death, and that his daughter and grandsons continue to live in central Virginia.

When I refer to "Virginia" I primarily mean that part of the state that lies south of the Rappahannock River, the area north of that having been co-opted by the District of Columbia.

Texan arrogance is taxonomically different from Virginian arrogance. Texans loudly revel in their Texanhood. Virginians, assured in their deportment, must be drawn out, but the state seal warns all who might do so. On it the sworded goddess Virtue stands over a fallen challenger with the words *Sic semper tyrannis*, "Thus always to tyrants," written below.

The far western part of the state split off during the Civil War to remain with the Union. It had few slaves working its rocky hills where farmers were said to "fall out of their fields." At the convention for statehood many names were offered up for the new state, the most popular of which was "Kanawha," but "West Virginia" at the last minute won the most votes. It seems queer and defeatist. The Carolinas and Dakotas share a name, but West Virginia signaled its subjugation to the mother state with its choice. Somewhere in here lies the quiet power of Virginia.

Anyhow, to the degree that Virginians are snobs I imagine they were glad to be rid of all those unwashed mountaineers. Few could dance the quadrille in Wheeling.

When I turned seventeen I applied to and was accepted at two schools, the University of Texas and the University of Virginia.

One evening as I dug into my Henry the VIII Filet at a Dallas-area Steak and Ale my father proposed a deal. He wanted me to choose Austin over Charlottesville, so I'd be closer to home. If I would do so, he offered to give me the difference in tuition between the two schools. In cash. It would mean I wouldn't have to work a job to pay for living expenses, as in-state tuition in Texas was very cheap at the time. Something like $350 a semester.

I chewed my steak thoughtfully before turning his offer down. I chose the Old Dominion, the mother of states and statesmen, where liberty and independence were born. The waitress came and took my salad plate away.

(At this juncture I would like to note that the decor and menu of Steak and Ale were inspired by the movie version of the novel *Tom Jones*, while the manners and lifestyle of antebellum Virginians were largely inspired by the novels of Sir Walter Scott.)

The student employment office at the university placed me at the local hospital. I worked as an orderly, lifting incredibly large Virginians onto gurneys and periodically transferring deceased patients to the morgue. I am not proud to admit that my co-workers and I frequently got stoned in the morgue and made the corpses wave at each other and do other silly things.

On my walk to work I liked to stop in at an ancient drugstore where they sold the products of the Caswell-Massey company. George Washington and Thomas Jefferson wore their men's cologne and I loved to sniff a bottle with my eyes closed and pretend I had quietly snuck up behind Jefferson at Monticello, sleeping head-down at his roll-top desk, and inhaled the odor coming off his neck.

Amazing! One could actually smell the founding fathers! Approximate their presence! Perhaps this is why inventors had created the camera and the tape recorder but never a device to capture smells.

In my sophomore year the $2 bill came out. All of Charlottesville was abuzz. It was very Virginian and not just because of the artwork. It was born obsolete, but still has the power to amuse customers and cashiers alike.

I seemed to meet the offspring of Virginia's old families wherever I went on campus. The Randolphs, Harrisons, Byrds, and Lees were all represented around the keg at most any party. Sometimes I knew their family histories better than they.

I remember arguing with a descendent of Stonewall Jackson. At issue was the general's dying words. I knew them by heart: "Let us cross the river and rest in the shade of the trees." My opponent insisted that Jackson's words were "Let us cross the river and rest in the tall grass." This infuriated me. "Why," I asked, "would a dying man want to rest under the direct sunlight in tall grass filled with insects, prickers, and burrs?"

Thomas Jefferson wrote his own epitaph. It reads as follows:

> Here was buried Thomas Jefferson
> Author of the Declaration of American Independence
> Of the Statute of Virginia for Religious Freedom
> And Father of the University of Virginia

Jefferson was terribly proud of the short three-clause statute for religious freedom, but the signers of the Declaration of Independence were not willing to subscribe to such a radical bill, so it sat in the Virginia legislature until the 1780s when it was finally passed, to his great joy.

To this day the state is rife with all sorts of low-profile communes, temples, cults, and schools of secret knowledge.

In 1988 I was a dishwasher in an upscale Charlottesville restaurant whose head bartender underwent a kind of molting process. He began to glow and speak of visions he had received in his off-hours. Eventually he declared himself a prophet and moved to a farm with three of our best waitresses. He got each of them pregnant and then promptly hung himself.

I have always enjoyed getting drunk, but Virginia's liquor laws make it tough. There are no proper bars in the state. Liquor licenses go only to establishments that sell a higher percentage of food than alcohol, so a Virginian must drink at home or in a restaurant. There are no old-man bars, roadhouses, or dramshops.

For that reason I have always considered Virginia the least "rock and roll" of all the states I've lived in. Virginia may be for lovers, but it is not for hell-raisers.

Football games at the university are mostly wine and cheese affairs, lacking the brutal crowd participation enjoyed by the teams in Knoxville, Athens, and Ann Arbor.

Even the state's great contributions to popular music, the Carter Family and Patsy Cline, came from counties at the very edge of the state.

Liquor is sold through state-run ABC stores. ABC stores sell only wines made in Virginia. Virginia takes care of Virginia.

To visit one of these is to get a feeling for what it must be like to shop in a Communist country. There is no flash, no advertising, just bottles on shelves monitored by state employees.

Much like the four-way-stop intersection is a citizen's only opportunity to experience anarchy as a political system. No one monitors the order in which four autos coming from four different directions may proceed. The government knows we must manage these tiny conflicts on our own.

I have been told that in the days of train travel the bar car would open and close according to which county they were passing through. It might be open for ten minutes and then shut down for twenty as they passed through a dry county. On and off through the black Virginia night.

After graduation I left Virginia, no longer believing in the secret of the 360 years.

It was soon after, on a Christmas visit to my mother's home in central Ohio, that I discovered how I was nearly never born. I was rifling through her personal files while she was at the mall when I discovered a letter from the public relations department of a spermicidal-jelly company, addressed to my mother and dated four months before I was born. They had received her complaint letter and were sorry that the product had not protected her from impregnation. Finally they reminded her that no contraceptive was 100 percent effective and hoped that she would continue to use their jelly in the future.

Needless to say, this blew my mind.

Over the past fourteen years I have returned to Virginia to live five times and left five times in turn. I've always been fond of Emerson's quote, "The man must be so much that he makes all circumstances indifferent." Yet circumstances encroach from all sides, and I have always been swayed by them.

The times I have left Virginia have been informed by the sense that nothing was happening there. To a large degree Virginia is finished. It has become what it is and only seeks to preserve its condition. Stores in Virginia have gone from being shoppes to shops to shoppes again. One is not in Virginia. One is on Virginia. It has been glassed in as a heritage showcase and neither needs nor seeks any adjustment.

Yet I am always drawn back. The sheer physical beauty of the land pulls on my heart. As a writer, I am unskilled at describing landscapes. I never learned the names of the trees or flowers so I won't try to describe those blue-green valleys and lush foothills here. I know that when circumstances in my life drive me to seek a place to be alone, where the wild plums grow, I will always return to the stillness and solitude of the Old Dominion.

I live in Nashville now and wake in the morning to the sound of buzz saws and roofers' hammers. The city is growing, taking its place as a player in the New South. It's an exciting place to live, with honky-tonks, strip bars, a great NFL team, and plenty of rule-breakers and hell-raisers to pal around with.

When I am weary of all this it's likely that I'll settle in Virginia again. In fact, I can imagine moving to the state and then moving away, over and over again for the rest of my life, until I am very, very old and finally ready to cross the river and rest in the shade of the trees.

WASHINGTON

COYOTE'S UNAUTHORIZED GUIDE TO WASHINGTON STATE

Sherman Alexie

Native Americans were the first people to live here in "The Evergreen State" of Washington, though this land was not yet the United States of America (and, of course, was not yet a state named after a slave-owning political and military genius), so it was Indians who first lived here, but the Indians weren't Indians at all, despite Christopher Columbus's geographical confusion, so linguistically speaking, it was the indigenous who first lived here (and I like to goofily claim that "Indian" is short for "indigenous"), and yet, anthropologically speaking, the indigenous might not be so indigenous after all, because our ancestors could well have been adventurous Asians who traversed the Bering Strait Land Bridge (which, despite popular myth, remains only a muddy theory, best guess, and incomplete estimate) and trekked south all the way from what is now called Alaska to what is now called Cape Horn in South America, though only a few of those ancient and hypothetical Asians were adventurous enough to make the entire journey, while far more of them simply stopped walking at various points along the way and, over the course of a few thousand years, created a vast network of tribes and communities that eventually filled up two continents (one of which will be our focus) before a colonial force of Europeans, Africans, and yes, more Asians, showed up a five-centuries ago and, well, kicked the holy-moly out of the Indians, completely wiping out dozens of tribes while subjugating the rest, and created the highly imperfect, woefully violent, and utterly magical place known as the USA, of which the state of Washington is a very small, imperfect, violent, and magical part.

As of July 2003, there are twenty-nine federally recognized Indian tribes and a few unrecognized tribes, indigenous to Washington, and approximately 107,000 Native Americans, who are still surviving and thriving, and many of those tribes have absorbed the bloodlines and cultural heritage of other tribes that have ceased to exist as separate entities. And heck, the tribes own and operate dozens of new-money casinos that are wildly successful, and benefit from the old-fashioned American exploitation of vice, so it would seem that the Natives of Washington have completely assimilated into a capitalistic culture and country. But the journey, for lack of a more detailed and bloody analysis, has been difficult.

In 1492, the entire Native American population was, according to estimates that vary widely because of political, scientific, and poetic conflicts, somewhere between 5 and 15 million. By 1900, the population was down to 250,000. *O genocide, by what other name should we call thee?* So how many Indians were living in the area that would come to be called Washington when Columbus first landed on the other side of the country? By using highly amateurish math, we can unsafely assume there were, well, a lot more than 107,000 Washington Indians pursuing their aboriginal version of life, liberty, and happiness. And, according to tribal myth-science, how exactly did these hundreds of thousands of Washington Indians come to exist here? Of course, the creation stories vary from tribe to tribe, and they are as outlandish and metaphorical as the Judeo-Christian story of building women out of men's ribs in the warm shadows of a perfect garden. Some

Washington Indian tribes emerged from lightning-struck logs and others were built of stone, water, and mud; a few seemed to have been dropped from alien spacecrafts; and one or two were left behind after a Great Flood (a geological disaster long since confirmed by white scientists, which almost proves that myth and science are first cousins who strongly resemble each other and passionately hate the resemblance).

There are also plenty of ancient stories that detail the pre-Columbian visits of strange visitors (like pale men with horns in their heads and tiny brown men who almost looked Indian except for their narrow eyes and gigantic black men who touched the clouds with the tops of their heads) who arrived in huge canoes and traded various goods and more stories before they hopped back into their luxurious canoes and sailed away.

A few years ago, construction workers unearthed an ancient set of human remains in Eastern Washington. Dubbed the Kennewick Man (because the remains were discovered near the radioactive town of Kennewick), these bones and rags were given a face and body by forensic scientist-poets. Of course, we were all shocked and amused to see that Kennewick Man strongly resembled the actor Patrick Stewart. According to more than a few anthropologists, this resemblance proves that white guys were the first Americans (a belief shared by Mormons, those other rigorous anthropologists), but since this Star Trek caveman died with an arrowhead lodged in his hipbone, I would guess he was yet another very lost European explorer who was shot in the ass while fleeing hostile Indians. Of course, that's just my version of an ancient story. Nobody believes that any of these ancient Indian stories are anything other than tribal lies that have, through the passage of time, become myth, unlike those other more important tribal lies, like *The Odyssey* and *The Iliad*, that have, through the passage of time, become truth.

In 1805, Meriwether Lewis and William Clark were among the first federally recognized white men to travel among the Washington Indians, and those brave and crazy paleface explorers survived renegade warriors, revolts, desertions, disease, food poisoning, hungry bears, vene-real disease, and more renegade warriors before they reached the mouth of the Columbia River and the Pacific Ocean on the Washington coast. "Great joy in camp," Clark wrote in his journal that day, "we are in View of the Ocian, this great Pacific Ocian which we been So long anxious to See." It wouldn't be the last time a white man expressed, with such arbi-trary spelling and grammar, happiness at being free of Washington State Indians. After that first amazing journey, Lewis and Clark settled down to lives of relative obscurity, bureaucratic numbness, broken dreams, mental illness, probable suicide, and absolute canonization two centuries after the fact, but there was a nineteenth-century explorer who spent far more time and energy in Washington.

From September 27 through October 6, 1809, Canadian explorer David Thompson, a fellow traveler named Beaulieu, and an anonymous Indian boy (the Indians on such adventures are usually anonymous and are always the ones who know exactly where they are going) followed the Pend Oreille River from Lake Pend Oreille in northern Idaho into Washington. Thompson hoped the river would provide a route to the Columbia River that would in turn provide a route to the Pacific Ocean. Along the way, Thompson and his com-panions met a party of Kalispel Indians "who had so little contact with white society that they had no iron tools." The Kalispels (who now enjoy highly profitable contact with white society by operating a casino located just a few miles from Fairchild Air Force Base in eastern Washington) presented Thompson and his posse with bread, roots, and salmon, and received tobacco, flint, and steel in return.

"Smelly white man, we give you our most sacred food, the salmon, who always returns to us, and we will accept your tobacco, and the many generations of tumors that will come with it."

It would be the first of many such inequitable trades that Indians would make with David Thompson, and many other white folks. But Mr. Thompson was nothing if not persistent. After many failed explorations, Thompson finally found the route to the Pacific in 1910, and over the course of the next few years, managed to map all of it in great detail, enabling other explorers and traders to safely colonize the area; and yet, despite the Columbian and Lewis-and-Clarkian scope of his accomplishments, David Thompson has yet to have one Washington State high school named after him, though I gather that he is still really popular in Canada, ay?

Now if I were a history and current-affairs teacher at the mythical David Thompson High School in Spokane, Washington, what would I teach my students about the past and present of their state? I'd want to teach them about myth and myth-making, and lies, bold lies, and statistics.

"OK, students," I'd say. "I once read somewhere, and I can't remember the source, and I couldn't find the source during my highly passionate and incredibly limited Google Internet search, but I'm still positive I am speaking the truth when I tell you that Washington State has the lowest percentage of churchgoers in the entire country. Yes, we are, demographically speaking, the most secular state in our union. And what's more, I once heard a guest lecturer give a talk on regional linguistics, during an address he gave at either Gonzaga University or Washington State University, the two schools I attended, and during the course of this lecture, he said, and I'm paraphrasing here, that 'the English speakers of Washington have the least accented speech in the country.'"

"But Professor Alexie, what do those two things mean when you talk about them together?"

"Well, it means we're a bunch of heathens who will be screaming with great clarity as we descend into the pits of hell, or it means we're a very libertarian and homogeneous state, or it means nothing at all."

Of course, I'm not a teacher, and I'm not much of a researcher either, but I am a lifelong resident of Washington and can give you a few personal observations and banal trivia bits that may or may not be accurate or important.

Washington is divided into two political, social, economic, and cultural regions: Seattle and Everywhere Else. The residents of Everywhere Else lovingly refer to Seattle as "The People's Republic of Seattle," because Seattle residents often vote for Democrats. Conversely, the commuting communists of Seattle gently refer to the residents of Everywhere Else as trailer-park Nazis because they often vote for Republicans.

Seattle is the birthplace of Jimi Hendrix, Carol Channing, Kurt Cobain, and Judy Collins.

Everywhere Else is the birthplace of Bing Crosby and Chuck Jones.

Bruce and Brandon Lee are buried in Seattle.

Chief Joseph of the Nez Perce is buried in Everywhere Else.

Alex Haley and Carl Sagan died in Seattle.

Many famous folks have both lived and died in Seattle. I couldn't find one famous person who both lived and died in Everywhere Else, except for the Indian chiefs.

So what does that say about Washington?

Do the gifted and talented artists, those amazingly passionate and often self-destructive folks, flee Everywhere Else as soon as they can and never return? Yes, they do, just like those same folks flee small towns in every other part of the world and live and suffer in the big city forever.

But many of the future accountants and middle managers of Everywhere Else also flee their small towns and head for Seattle, the Big City of Washington. When you grow up in the small Washington towns of Brewster, Wenatchee, Reardan, Selkirk, Dayton, Toutle Lake, and Neah Bay, a city like Seattle might as well be New York, Los Angeles, and Chicago combined. Never mind that Seattle is only a generation removed from the barbarous seaport of drunken sailors, drunker Indians, and homicidal loggers it used to be, and don't you bother to note that it has only recently become the dream city of all things computerized and Caucasian.

When a young citizen of Everywhere Else drives at night into Seattle for the first time and is mesmerized by the occasional neon and the medium-sized skyscrapers, then this small town disguised as a big city really does become the Emerald City, and everybody from Everywhere Else does feel a little bit like Dorothy or Toto, and hell, maybe one can find home, heart, brain, and courage in Seattle, even if all those damn liberals keep getting in the way.

But then again, Everywhere Else is also the destination point for a host of other travelers and wanderers. A few hundred ex–Los Angeles cops live in eastern Washington and northern Idaho, two areas so similar in politics and culture that they should secede from the United States and form a state of their own called David Thompson. Why do so many ex–LA cops move to the state of David Thompson? Well, the fifty-first state is about 98 percent white and most of the remaining 2 percent are Indians, Mexicans, and Asians, who are plenty dark but not quite as dark as those African-Americans. David Thompson State is also home to countless white separatists, revolutionary militias, religious fundamentalists and fanatics, apocalyptic cults, organic farmers, Vietnam draft dodgers addicted to the dodge, and methadone kingpins.

Most of David Thompson remains mostly unexplored. A person can still disappear in David Thompson. Plenty of folks do disappear in David Thompson. It's no accident that Washington is home to so many serial killers. Our homegrown sociopaths enjoy easy access to the defenseless prostitutes and homeless women of Seattle and equally easy access to the impenetrable wilds of David Thompson and Everywhere Else.

Ted Bundy killed women in Seattle during sunny mornings, drove their bodies deep into the ponderosa pine wilderness, buried them, and then drove back to Seattle in time for dinner.

The disturbed director David Lynch spent long stretches of his childhood in Everywhere Else. *Blue Velvet*, his strangest and most violent film, was set in a fictional town called Lumberton, but I believe it was based on the city of Spokane, an idyllic blue-collar town that hides deep and shameful secrets.

If you've never been to a karaoke bar in Spokane, Washington, then you have never truly experienced existential dread.

There's a story—equally apocryphal and truthful—of a Spokane man who committed suicide only after he hanged all ninety-nine of his cats from the branches of the tree in his backyard.

I love to espouse the theory that the U.S. government hides many of its Secret Witness Relocation Program witnesses in Everywhere Else and David Thompson. It would help explain why there are good pasta places in small towns like Colville, Washington.

But, hey, before I get too carried away with the macabre, let us remember that the farmers of Everywhere Else and David Thompson also plant and harvest nearly as much wheat, corn, peas, and lentils as Iowa.

And let us also remember that the right-wing Republican citizens of Spokane and eastern Washington kept the semiliberal Democrat Tom Foley in the U.S. House of Representatives for thirty years before they kicked him out in 1994 in favor of George Nethercutt, a conservative Republican who used to believe in term limits. And yes, as civic American citizens, we shall have to forgive that healthy percentage of eastern Washington voters who naively believed that Nethercutt, once elected, would replace Foley as speaker of the house.

Let us celebrate the fact that Washington's current United States senators are both women. Hail to Patty Murray and Maria Cantwell! Hail to the Evergreen Matriarchy! Hail to the old Boeing and new Microsoft money that keeps them in office!

And lastly, let us celebrate Dixie Lee Ray, who on November 2, 1976, became the first and only woman to be governor of Washington. Combative, gregarious, angry, ridiculously smart and impulsive, homely, eccentric, and generous, and knee-socked, Ray contained multitudes. Dixie Lee wasn't even her real name. She was a pseudonymous governor. As a little girl, she was "full of the dickens," and was a precocious admirer of the Confederate general Robert E. Lee, so she christened herself Dixie Lee, and won election as a conservative Democrat in her first political campaign.

She climbed Mount Rainier at age twelve, hosted a PBS science show for children, taught zoology at the University of Washington for three decades, served as head of Richard Nixon's Atomic Energy Commission while living in Washington, D.C., in a mobile home along with seven or eight dogs, spent less than $100,000 in winning the governorship, and lost reelection largely because she told the truth when a prominent Republican legislator asked a question on behalf of a constituent.

"You can tell your constituent to go to hell," Ray said, and promptly lost the primary election to a fellow Democrat, after which she founded Democrats for Reagan, and spent the rest of her life rallying against environmental extremists and liberal crybabies ("You receive more radiation watching television than you do from a nuclear waste dumpsite"), while living on tiny little Fox Island in the Puget Sound. There she wrote books and carved wood in the style of the Coastal Salish Indians and became such an accomplished and successful carver that the chiefs of the Kwakiutl Nation conferred upon Ray the Indian name of Umah, "respected lady of nobility."

This respected lady (whose governorship, by the way, is generally believed to have been a complete failure) died of a bronchial condition on January 2, 1994, in her cabin on Fox Island. Hundreds of people attended her funeral, including her most bitter political rivals and a few members of the press whom Ray had named her pigs after and then butchered and served at a media lunch.

During her funeral, Lou Guzzo, her longtime friend and ally, said, "She was the most courageous person I have ever known, unconquerable, a remarkable woman."

Of course, I wish Guzzo had been more truthful and poetic and ridiculous in his assessments of Ray, though I feel perverse at offering constructive criticism of a eulogy. I wish Guzzo had said something like this:

"Dixie Lee Ray was magical and violent. She was epic and unknowable. She was loving and small-minded. Like almost all of us, she tried very hard to be a decent human being and did OK. Dixie was a contrarian, a trickster, like the Native American mythical figure of Coyote. Now, I don't know how many of you know this, but Coyote, who is God

and not God, created Washington State. More specifically, Coyote created salmon and all the salmon falls and all the rivers in this state. You
see, Coyote woke up one morning and felt lonely and horny. So he traveled to every Indian tribe in the state and asked for a wife. Coyote was
vain and ambitious. He desired only the youngest and most beautiful
women, but those women wanted nothing to do with Coyote. And the
tribes refused to give Coyote any woman, let alone the very best women,
so Coyote become angry and started smashing the ground with his fists.
He ran all over the state, punching holes in the ground with his fists and
feet and claws. In rage, he dug holes and channels and tunnels, and he
wept copious tears, the Great Flood of Tears, that filled these holes
and channels and tunnels with water. And yes, these tear-filled holes and
channels and tunnels become our lakes and streams and ponds
and rivers. And Coyote's heart broke into a million pieces and turned
into the salmon that now swim these lakes and streams and ponds and
rivers. So, you see that Coyote formed our wonderful state out of his
pain and loss. And maybe, when you think of Dixie Lee, you can understand that she created her wonderful life out of her pain and loss. You
see, Coyote is a contradiction. He makes no sense. And, frankly speaking,
Dixie made little sense, either. Who could have predicted her election,
her fame and fortune? As the Indians say, we live in the Great Mystery,
and as the scientists say, we live on scant knowledge, and as Coyote says,
we're always hungry for more. Well, Dixie is out there, a scientist moving
deeper into the Great Mystery, and I hunger to know what she knows."

Yes, this is my hungry and angry state, home to my people for at least
ten thousand years, granted U.S. statehood in 1889, but granted grace
when my probable Asian ancestors first walked through the rain forest
or climbed a mountain or traversed a desert or swam the great river. I
have lived here since the first Washington State citizen discovered fire
and since another Washington State citizen wrote "Louie, Louie" in his
basement. I buried my father in this state's secular soil and my sons will
someday bury me next to him. Amen. Amen.

Washington, D.C.

The Last Colony

William Greider

Three questions are commonly asked of those who happen to live in the peculiar nonstate called the District of Columbia, better known as Washington. "Is it really a place?" People from afar often suppose that the nation's capital is a series of monumental buildings, framed by lovely lines of trees and flower beds, where the federal government does its business. It is the place where TV correspondents stand on the White House lawn or the senators sit at antique desks, listening to colleagues. Or the admission-free theme park based loosely on national history, with many bronzed generals on horseback and gleaming memorials to Lincoln, Jefferson, and our country's noblest ideals. But do people actually live there?

Yes, we answer smugly. D.C. is a real place of ordinary life, too, a charming city actually, with commerce, schools and universities, churches, parks, and neighborhoods. It is a company town, of course, not unlike Detroit or Los Angeles, only the industry is government and politics. The district has 572,000 inhabitants by the 2000 census, and is growing again slightly after thirty years of decline, though the real estate prices seem to move perpetually upward because, like

Manhattan, the district is forever a confined space. It was created by the founders in 1791 as a neutral seat of government, a boxlike territory roughly ten miles on each side, formed from land ceded by Maryland and Virginia on both sides of the Potomac River. Virginia "retroceded" its share in 1841, leaving a jagged southern border and roughly sixty-eight square miles.

Most of us came from somewhere else in the country to engage, one way or another, in the governing affairs of the republic and, oddly enough, this made us into citizens of nowhere. Unlike the capital cities of every other democracy in the world, D.C. residents are not allowed representation in the national legislature, though we pay federal income taxes and our young people are subject to military draft. We may vote for president (a relatively recent reform adopted by constitutional amendment in 1961) but our elected delegate to Congress is not permitted to vote on anything, just like delegates from the territories. Our political rights are thus inferior to those of American Samoans, since they are exempt from federal taxation and the draft. This anomaly in our democracy does not much disturb other Americans, even if they understand it.

"But do you actually live in Washington?" When a distant cousin asks this, he is obliquely hinting at the city's unfavorable reputation. If you are white and say you are from Washington, people assume you really mean the suburbs of northern Virginia or Maryland. The district briefly held the title of "murder capital" a few years back, when youthful drug lords were killing one another with great frequency. The city was a fiscal mess that Congress had to take into receivership, while the mayor went to prison for smoking crack. And the city is regularly the scene of monster demonstrations that clog the downtown streets and (if you believe the television) seem to threaten civil order. Not to mention all those politicians. How could anyone want to live here?

It is our shared secret. Whatever you may have read or heard,

Washington is surely one of the most livable cities in the country, designed to human scale and splendidly appointed on the whole. The broad avenues and stunning vistas have a flavor of European grace and formality, not by accident, since Pierre L'Enfant laid out the city plan with Versailles in mind. A ribbon of forest, Rock Creek Park, runs southward through the city to the river and makes possible an easy commute downtown (Rock Creek was consecrated as a national park by the great conservationist Teddy Roosevelt, who used to ride horseback through these woods). The subway system is first-class and so are the restaurants. To insure that commercial interests would never overwhelm the dignity of government, office buildings are restricted to twelve stories in height, a nice size that still allows touches of grandeur. Most residents (we will not speak for the poor—who are numerous) enjoy these amenities. They are grateful to U.S. taxpayers for the Park Service's ever-changing flowerbeds.

But there is something more we do not usually disclose about ourselves. Living in Washington imparts a warm air of privilege, a sense of self-importance that is unearned, since one absorbs it simply by being near so much power and living among the everyday fragments of American history. This feeling of connectedness, I suspect, applies even to people of pedestrian status. The Nigerian cab driver will talk of politics with knowing savvy, sharing what he heard the senator or lobbyist say. My next-door neighbor, who is 100 years old, recalls growing up in Georgetown (before that neighborhood became rich and fashionable) and the time she and a girlfriend were in the middle of the road blocking Woodrow Wilson's open-air touring car (Wilson waved good-naturedly as they stepped aside). At Christmas, years ago when the children were small, we went sledding on Capitol Hill, gliding down the snow-covered lawn with the vast expanse of shining democratic temples spread before us on the Mall. It felt grand and slightly impertinent, but it was our secret entitlement as D.C. residents (in the new age of high security, we would be shooed away, maybe detained).

Great moments from the past do begin to feel like personal memories. The woods in Rock Creek Park next to our neighborhood contain shadowy remnants of Civil War entrenchments from when D.C. was under attack. At nearby Fort Stevens, Lincoln went out to watch the war from the ramparts (where someone shouted, "Tell that damn fool to get his head down!"). When the president's limousine races up Connecticut Avenue, accompanied by the armada of flashing motorcycles and dark vans, tourists gawk and some even wave meekly at the car's darkened windows, not sure anyone is inside. We hardly notice. D.C. remembers the afternoon when Gorbachev stopped his limo at the intersection of Connecticut and L streets, jumped out and waded into the startled throng of office workers returning from lunch. That was memorable.

A pretense of knowingness is more or less expected of us by family and friends. When we first moved to the capital some thirty-five years ago, I noticed that long-distance conversations with relatives communicated our new authority as insiders. My father would bring up various public issues and ask: What does Johnson think? Well, how is Nixon going to handle that? My response was, how should I know? After a time, as I saw that this always disappointed, I began to give him answers. Harmless bits of gossip at first, then deeper analysis and elaborate predictions.

My insiderness felt satisfying to both of us and my answers were probably no worse than what Dad might read in the newspapers. Perhaps, as often happens to Washingtonians, I began to believe in it myself. The radiant charm of living in the same town with important leaders and powerful events wears thin eventually, though it is harder to let go of the pretensions.

Pleasant privileges aside, D.C. is an anomaly for more substantial and disturbing reasons. Its subtext of social realities does not conform to the noble ideals chiseled on the marble temples. This is reflected in a third question often asked of the people who live here. "But where do your children go to school?" The answer, if you are white and middle-class, is nearly always a private school, often followed by defensive explanations about the awful quality of the city's public education. The district's population is 60 percent African-American, 30 percent white, 8 percent Hispanic and the remainder Asian. But, except for a hearty few, whites abandoned the public schools thirty years ago and white children make up less than 5 percent of the system's enrollment. There is nothing unique about this pattern of urban White Flight except, because this is the nation's capital, it acquires special burdens of hypocrisy.

In their day jobs, many lawyers, lawmakers, and policy specialists are actively engaged, one way or another, in advancing integration, as liberal advocates of racial equality. Home at night, they tell themselves that their children are simply too tender for such a real-world experience. Conservatives have lately taken up their own version of racial hypocrisy, expressing bleeding-heart laments for the poor, inner-city black kids allegedly trapped in D.C.'s public schools. These children are being used as a foil in the conservatives' long-term campaign to win school vouchers, a mechanism for transferring public money to private schools (many of which would never let these black kids through the door). Right-wingers seemed more honest to me in the days when they were frankly antiblack. Washington's public schools, it is true, have all the afflictions and frustrations of a large urban system in which a third or more of the students are poor. But, on the whole, the D.C. schools are OK, at least far better than their reputation. Those of us whose children attended them know this to be true. We gave up, long ago, trying to convince friends and neighbors that perhaps their fears are grounded in race, not quality education.

Despite the progressive sensibilities of its citizens, white and black, the capital city remains profoundly segregated by race and, as everyone knows, Creek Park serves as the marker. West of the park, the neighborhoods running out along Connecticut and Massachusetts avenues are overwhelmingly white and become progressively more affluent, blending naturally into still greater affluence next door in Chevy Chase and Bethesda, Maryland. East of the park is mainly black (also Latino now) and usually less well off, if not poor. The grand old homes along upper Sixteenth Street, however, remain the "Gold Coast" of the black bourgeoisie, the patrician families and upper-income professionals, those who haven't moved to Georgetown or affluent outer suburbs. For a wonderfully intimate portrait, read Stephen L. Carter's *The Emperor of Ocean Park.* The city's northeast quadrant belongs to the black working class—civil servants, teachers, and other solid citizens. The precincts of the poor and near-poor all lie east of Rock Creek, from the bleakness of public-housing projects near Howard University to the underdeveloped hillsides of Anacostia in the far southeast, where the abolitionist Frederick Douglass lived in Lincoln's time. The D.C. school system was the defendant in one of the companion cases that produced the Supreme Court's *Brown v. Board of Education* decision in 1954, dismantling lawful segregation by race.

The civil rights era vastly improved the social landscape, certainly. It liberated personal aspirations, integrated most workplaces, and opened municipal political power to the black majority. Yet these advances seem less exceptional in historical context, because D.C. has always been a special place in the black experience and mostly of their own making. At the founding, the Capitol and other original government structures, roads, and bridges were, indeed, built by slave laborers. These men were "rented" by their owners in Virginia and Maryland and worked side by side with Irish immigrant laborers who were typically paid the same wage but got to keep the money. From the beginning, D.C. became an attractive redoubt for runaways who could blend into city life and escape the identity of chattel property. The Civil War and its aftermath of Reconstruction greatly accelerated the rise of a substantial black middle class, professionals, intellectuals, and artists. By 1900, before it was eclipsed by Harlem, Washington had the largest African-American community in the nation and was the social and cultural capital of black America—thriving and self-sustaining despite the enforced isolation of segregation. When native son Duke Ellington moved north to play Harlem, he called his first band "The Washingtonians." When D.C. elected its first black mayor in the 1970s, black folks joked among themselves about the "chocolate city."

This strand of history, mostly unknown to white Americans, suggests to me a terrible incompleteness in the city's story (and the nation's), like the half-built Capitol and Washington monument which stood unfinished through much of the nineteenth century. The government ran out of money or energy. In the same sense, this country lost its resolution to complete the great social imperatives that black people and others launched half a century ago. Naturally, like many other D.C. residents, I tend to focus on the meaningful progress all around—the slow, steady integration of many neighborhoods, the subsidence of fierce racial hostilities—rather than the enduring divisions. Yet, whenever I encounter a first-time visitor from abroad, the conversation pulls me back forcibly to the unfinished reality. Foreign visitors see racial apartheid, plainly enough, as well as the stark divisions of class and income (never mind that these consequences are now ostensibly voluntary, instead of legally enforced). They are rightly aghast (or cynically amused) to discover that these American contradictions live on so starkly in the capital of democracy. Many years ago, when racial inequality was still the subject of earnest public discussion, I imagined that the country might eventually be shamed by Washington's embarrassing example and moved to do something more substantial about it. Now, less naïvely, I think of D.C. simply as a peculiar public marker of social progress, the living tableau of unrealized democratic values.

Americans at large might also find the capital city relevant as a perverse indicator of another kind of inequality, the growing extremes in incomes and wealth. I say perverse because, in fact, Washington and environs have prospered fabulously in the past generation, even though this was a conservative era in which the powers of government atrophied, the market orthodoxy gained hegemony in politics, and faith in Washington as the source of social progress lost its popular following. It seems that the more Washington came under attack, the richer it became. In 1960, when John F. Kennedy described D.C. as a city that combines Southern efficiency with Northern charm, the joke was dead-on. The city was slow-moving and underdeveloped, content with its seediness and second-class restaurants. Then the money arrived. And the crumbling old row houses along K Street were replaced by supersmart glass office buildings with first-class air-conditioning and ferns in the lobby. Social and cultural affairs escalated to a higher order of refinement (though not nearly as hip as the doyens imagine). Men started wearing very expensive suits, getting executive-class haircuts.

The paradox of Washington gaining its new affluence from the conservative assault is easily explained: business came to the company town and captured it with money—lots and lots of money. The corporate counterreformation began in the mid-1970s as a calculated response to liberalism's successes and excesses, the expanded reach of government regulation (clean air and all that), and the proliferation of effective public-interest nettles like Ralph Nader. The Business Roundtable and other corporate institutions were reasonably upfront about their intentions. They set out to reclaim the high ground and put up the money to deploy an entirely new infrastructure of political action that would speak for business and finance, applying leverage on many fronts. For D.C., this was the equivalent of a high-end jobs program, plus the complete makeover of the once-sleepy downtown. The new office buildings house the exploding army of lobbyists and prestige law firms, plus the hundreds of flanking organizations to drive the public agenda—think tanks, public-relations firms, political consultants, the money guys who distribute the cash to politicians in both parties, even those quaint boiler-room operations that dial around America, recruiting authentic "grassroots" citizens to endorse what the big mules are pushing in Congress. It also helped that the defense budget was nearly doubled in the Reagan years.

Washington itself became a much tonier place, but naturally, most of the high-priced lawyers and lobbyists choose to live in safe, suburban splendor. They buy those mini-mansions that sprouted in the cornfields of McLean, Virginia, or Montgomery County, Maryland (as a rule, Republicans tend to favor the southern side of the river; Democrats of very high incomes gravitate to places like Potomac, Maryland). The new wealth is breathtaking and mostly lovely, but has also created its own urban nightmare of traffic congestion and lost landscapes.

What would Americans make of the fact that the national capital and environs now collectively constitute the highest-income metropolitan region in the country? Four of the suburban jurisdictions surrounding D.C. rank in the nation's top ten for median incomes (led by Fairfax County, Virginia, No. 2 with $81,050) and a fifth suburban county (Montgomery County) ranks thirteenth. New wealth poured over the city, too, though with the usual disparities of class and race. Washington, with a median income of $40,127, ranks fifth in the nation among the jurisdictions with majority-black populations. Several decades ago, D.C. ranked first, but that distinction now belongs to Prince Georges County, Maryland, on the district's eastern border, where D.C.'s black middle class makes its "black flight" from the city. These social realities are unlikely to change very much or very soon, since they reflect the deeper economics now running the country, the same forces that led to the general rise of inequalities in wealth and income.

Citizens of D.C., meanwhile, persist in bringing up that other matter of inequality—their own lack of political rights. D.C. license plates now carry the slogan, TAXATION WITHOUT REPRESENTATION, to remind politicians and tourists of how Washingtonians are uniquely deprived. While they pay federal income taxes like other Americans, they are allowed to elect only a nonvoting delegate to Congress, just like the offshore territories. In fact, members of Congress, especially Republicans with a right-wing cause, enjoy dabbling in city affairs, vetoing ordinances passed by the City Council or instructing the mayor on street signs and how the municipal taxes may be spent. D.C., like a number of western states, held a voter referendum on legalizing marijuana for medical uses. No one doubts that the issue won an overwhelming majority, but thanks to a last-minute rider by a tin-pot overseer from Georgia, the votes were never counted. Congress forbade it.

"A pathetic paradox," says D.C. delegate Eleanor Holmes Norton. She and others keep pointing out that the city suffered more casualties in Vietnam than ten states. And that D.C. has 85,000 more inhabitants than the state of Wyoming and only 35,000 fewer than Vermont. Yet each of those states has a voting representative in the House and two senators. Unfortunately, these facts may not help the cause, since they merely remind the many states with smaller populations of their own peculiar power advantage—the anomaly in representation created by the Constitution itself and one they are most unlikely to give up in the name of improving democracy.

D.C.'s predicament is a classic case of injustice, in which the injured people have no power whatever to change things, while others have potent self-interested reasons to preserve the status quo. A simple remedy, for instance, would be to "retrocede" the district back to the state of Maryland and thus allow Washington citizens to vote for a U.S. representative (as well as for Maryland state officials) in a new congressional district. D.C. politicians are generally unenthused, but Maryland's are downright hostile. By order of Congress, D.C. is prohibited from collecting a city income tax on suburban commuters, though that fiscal measure is standard in every other major city. Thus, if DC were to join Maryland, the lawyers and lobbyists who live in Chevy Chase or Potomac or northern Virginia (along with the many other commuters of more modest means) would doubtless start paying DC income taxes. Furthermore, adding D.C.'s African-American majority to the black populaces of Baltimore and Prince Georges County would tip the balance of power in Maryland politics in favor of the racial minority. These seem reasons enough to let the injustice linger on.

The District of Columbia may not be a real place in the way that other states are, but I suggest that it is more representative of the country than we perhaps wish to acknowledge. It is the garden in which we celebrate the national ideals and the place where the laws are made. It is also a fair portrait of what we have become as a nation and what we have not yet been able to become.

WEST VIRGINIA

THE SOUTH CREEPS NORTH

Michael Tomasky

When I was growing up in Morgantown, West Virginia, we had a tattered Rand McNally world atlas that was published in 1960, the year I was born. The atlas covered the United States by grouping the states into a handful of regions. A case could be made for putting West Virginia in any of two or three different regions. But in 1960, at least, Rand McNally's cartographers decided the state belonged to the North Atlantic region, with Pennsylvania, New York, and every other Yankee jurisdiction right up to Maine.

This will surprise the northern reader, I suppose; but to me, it made perfect sense back then. West Virginia was not a southern state. Indeed it exists only because it broke off from the Confederacy in June 1863, and it joined the Union for the duration of the Civil War. As a result, the state's traditions were not southern. It didn't have a large black population, so, while there was some segregation in the state, it was hardly Mississippi, and for the most part the state integrated comparatively smoothly after the *Brown v. Board of Education* decision in 1954. West Virginia University's football team—and football teams are important psychic markers in states like West Virginia—started taking black players in the early 1960s, almost a full decade before Alabama or Arkansas or Texas or any of the major southern schools did. As a coal-mining state first and foremost, it was heavily unionized, which also separated it from the South. It had an unusually progressive state supreme court back then, and a liberal state legislature. While even Massachusetts didn't get around to abolishing capital punishment until 1984, West Virginia banned the death penalty back in 1965 (the ban holds, and West Virginia remains one of just twelve states without capital punishment). It had—and still has—an unusually liberal flagship newspaper, the *Charleston Gazette*. So the West Virginia I grew up in, at least in my neck of the woods, seemed a northern state.

But West Virginia sits right on the geographical fault line— between North and South, between the Atlantic seaboard and the eastern edge of the plains—and therefore its chief regional identity has always tended toward a kind of sui generis insularity. Because finally, it belongs to no region.

It was northern in the ways I described above. But it was also southern. The whole state, except for one little finger that includes the steel-producing towns of Wheeling and Weirton, sits below the Mason-Dixon line. And when you get down into the southern part of the state—Huntington, Beckley, Bluefield—it really feels southern. The accent is different; my cousins who grew up in Huntington possessed a more richly and straightforwardly southern accent than the gentle hill twang that predominates around Morgantown and other cities in the northern part of the state. So maybe being up there gave me a skewed perspective. I used to go to a basketball camp some summers that boys from around the state attended. They regarded us Morgantown kids as sort of effete, not really West Virginians. I got the sense this had mostly to do with the fact that the state university is in Morgantown, which I suppose in their eyes (or their parents') rendered us pretentious, a little sissified, and uniquely susceptible to the kinds of diseases that were spreading across college campuses at the time[1]—Morgantown was the place where nice small-town kids went and got their heads filled with strange ideas, or, in other cases, with the aftereffects of the various intoxicants readily available on any college campus.

At any rate, so West Virginia sits, several places all at once, and of no larger place in particular. And among the different parts of the state—before the interstate highways were built in the 1970s, it could take eight hours to drive the three hundred or so miles from Bluefield to Wheeling—there were, and are, rivalries, resentments, suspicions. Those southern coal towns that typify the state in the national mind—the kind described by Presidents Kennedy and Johnson, probed in CBS documentaries of that era, and later made famous in John Sayles's *Matewan* and Joe Johnston's *October Sky*—were as remote to me growing up as they were to most Americans.

Now, when I go back for visits, which are frequent, I notice something.

Culturally, West Virginia is much more of a southern state today. Does it just look this way to me because I've lived in New York City for nearly two decades? Perhaps. But I know the place, and I know what I see.

There are many reasons for the change. But on the gut level, it can be summarized in two sentences:

1. In 1960, there were 48,696 coal-mining employees in the state, and 75 percent of those were members of the United Mine Workers of America.

2. In 2002, there were just 15,377 such workers, and only 38 percent of those were UMW members.

---

[1]Yes, even in West Virginia: in 1972, the WVU student body elected as its president one Ben Borsay, the standard-bearer of a leftish tendency called Mountaineer Freedom Party. I knew Ben, through my older sister. He had a poster of Ho Chi Minh above his bed. Last I heard, he's a fundamentalist minister now.

That about sums it up, really. The decline in the number of mining-related jobs,[2] alongside the dip in union penetration into the workforce, has altered the state's political and cultural temperature in profound ways. So while the state is still heavily Democratic in voter-enrollment terms (641,000 to 309,000, with just 99,000 nonpartisans, in 2002), it is no longer necessarily "Democratic" with all the social implications that word carried back when I was growing up—support for government regulations and programs, for a redistributionist fiscal policy, and so on. When those beliefs go by the wayside, a place finds itself transformed—at first slowly, until finally a moment arrives when something big happens to offer irrefutable evidence that the change has occurred.

And we know what that something big was. Since the New Deal, West Virginia has occasionally supported the Republican presidential candidate, but only when he was already the incumbent, and only when he faced a fairly marginal Democrat. Dwight Eisenhower, Richard Nixon, and Ronald Reagan carried the state in their reelection campaigns, but only in their reelection campaigns. West Virginia had not backed a nonincumbent Republican presidential candidate since Herbert Hoover in 1928, until George W. Bush won in 2000.

My friends down there speak of the "unholy trinity" of surface mining, guns, and abortion as the three reasons Bush carried West Virginia by a comfortable six-point margin, collecting the state's five electoral votes and thus eking his dubious way into the White

---

[2] I should note that there is a caveat to those numbers. In 1960, all sorts of ancillary, nonmining tasks—maintenance, hauling, on-site construction, and painting—were performed by coal-company employees. Now those tasks are performed largely by independent contractors. There are around 26,000 of those, which brings today's actual total to roughly 41,000. That's not so different from 48,696; however, relatively few of those 26,000 are unionized, and many work intermittently (even those who work only one day a year are counted in this category). So the overall point, about today's comparative lack of union penetration in the industry and the resulting lack of a collective consciousness among the workforce, still holds.

House. I don't mean to minimize the last two, more on which later. But undoubtedly, it was Bush's support for mountaintop-removal mining, and the widespread perception of Al Gore as a tree-hugging scold who would have killed off the mining industry (and therefore the state's basic raison d'etre), that was most important.

In the good, or perhaps bad, old days, all mining was done underground. It was, of course, difficult, dirty, dangerous work. Back in 1940, there were 130,457 mine employees. There were also 376 fatalities that year.[3] By 1960, the aforementioned 48,696 miners suffered 115 fatalities. Such were the hazards. I remember a large accident myself, at Farmington No. 9, which took a ghastly toll of seventy-eight men in an explosion in 1968.

But in more recent years, technological advances have changed the equation. Now, a lot of coal is extracted by huge machines tearing into whole mountains, slicing off their peaks, flattening them as a child would a pile of mashed potatoes with a spoon. What a godsend to the operators! It's faster, it's cheaper, it's much less dangerous (just six mining fatalities in 2002)—and best of all, it delivers just as much product, or more. Those 130,000 miners in 1940 extracted 127 million tons of coal, while 2002's 15,000 miners extracted 164 million tons. And, in case you're wondering, there's plenty enough coal in them thar hills for mining to continue for a century or more.

But there is a lingering inconvenience—namely, that all that dirt has to go somewhere. It is ladled into the surrounding valleys. Through the summer of 2003, more than 1,000 miles of streams in the state had been covered over with fill. Water tables, and water quality, are dramatically affected, and the process of dumping all that "fill" isn't much good for the air either. It's an environmental nightmare, but one most West Virginians accept, or choose not to dwell on, in the name of jobs. Even so, people have known since

[3] The State Office of Miners' Health, Safety, and Training records roughly 21,000 fatalities since records were first kept in 1883.

mountaintop removal began in earnest in the 1970s that push would someday come to shove.

Enter Charles H. Haden II, chief judge of the U.S. District Court in the capital city of Charleston, the central figure in the most critical drama in the state's recent history, even counting the homecoming of Private Jessica Lynch.

In July 1998, the West Virginia Highlands Conservancy gathered ten coalfield residents and filed a lawsuit against the state Department of Environmental Protection and the U.S. Army Corps of Engineers, charging that the agencies had been derelict in their enforcement of state and federal environmental regulations (they chose this strategy over one of suing the coal operators, which is rather difficult to do in the state with success). The defendants' counsel was pleased at first when the case, captioned *Bragg v. Robertson*, was given to Haden. He is a Republican and had been a state legislator who was active in party politics.[4]

What did Haden do? Well, as the journalist Rudy Abramson wrote, "Not since the late U.S. district judge Frank Johnson desegregated Alabama buses and schools and opened state voting booths to African-Americans in the 1950s and '60s has a federal judge confronted the political and economic powers of his native state more conspicuously." In October 1999, Haden ruled for the plaintiffs, saying that the practice of mountaintop removal violated federal and state environmental laws. A three-thousand-acre mountaintop-removal project near the town of Blair, which would have buried about four miles of streams, was halted. One coal company, citing the chilling effect of the ruling, immediately shut two strip mines

---

[4] I have known Chuck Haden since I was a little boy. Despite their political differences, he and my father—one of the state's leading trial attorneys in his day—were great friends, and when my father died in late 1997, Chuck delivered one of the eulogies at his funeral. I hold him in awfully high esteem.

that employed 148 people. Then-governor Cecil Underwood, a Republican, said that Haden had sounded the industry's death knell and went so far as to freeze all state spending for a time. In Congress, Democratic senator Robert Byrd also railed against Haden's decision and tried to undo it legislatively. In less decorous circles than the halls of government, Haden was denounced, harassed, threatened.

Ultimately, in April 2001, Haden was overturned by Richmond's fourth federal circuit, the country's most conservative federal district court. Later, the U.S. Supreme Court, without comment, declined to review the case, and the fourth circuit's decision stood. But the fire had been set. After Haden's ruling, an atmosphere of panic gripped the state—politicians, operators, union reps, and workers alike. All this is not to say that there isn't an active environmental movement in the state. There is, and it consists not just of college-pudding do-gooders, but of a growing number of ordinary citizens like the plaintiffs in Bragg. The number of people so inclined may grow as more and more regular folks are forced to, say, go out and buy potable water by the gallon as their wells are befouled. But green-ism is still very much the minority view. The passion of the majority is to do anything and everything to save the industry. And it didn't take terribly clever footwork—especially against Mr. "Earth in the Balance," Gore—for Bush to exploit that sentiment. The state supported Bush, and, in the spring of 2002, he paid the state back when his administration ruled that dumping tons of rock and dirt into streams was just fine under the terms of the federal Clean Water Act.

So the main story line in the southernization of West Virginia is economic. But there is a cultural subtext as well.

Put simply, religious fundamentalism has marched to the fore. This impulse has long existed in West Virginia. In 1984–85, I worked on Capitol Hill for then Representative Harley O. Staggers, Jr. A liberal—

even a flaming liberal—on many issues (he opposed contra aid, the MX missile, and virtually everything Ronald Reagan wanted to do), he was pro-life and pro–Second Amendment. It would have been very tough for him to be otherwise. But even so, the religious-conservative tendency was mostly latent in my day. I recall a fair amount of talk about limiting abortion or bringing back the death penalty, but precious little action.

This, too, is changing. There is now a Christian high school in my hometown. Such a concept when I was at Morgantown High in the late 1970s would have been unthinkable. Home schooling is on the rise. And the Southern Baptist Convention has made ample inroads in the state in recent years. My friend Susan Williams, once my freshman English professor (we bonded when I visited her during office hours and noticed the *White Album* photo of George Harrison tacked up in her cubicle) and now a reporter for the *Gazette*, was raised American Baptist in Oak Hill, in the southern part of the state. "When I was growing up, I wasn't aware that there were any Southern Baptist churches around," she says. "But in the last few years, they've established a huge presence." The distinction is crucial. The American Baptist Convention, based in Valley Forge, Pennsylvania, is basically a liberal faith. The Southern Baptists, I suppose you know about.

And yet . . . the state has moved in the other direction in certain respects, too. Today, the eastern panhandle is a lively exurb of Washington, basically. In Shepherdstown and Berkeley Springs, there is a new yuppie-ish class of professionals, along with the eateries and art galleries that are the inevitable by-product of such a class; Shepherdstown's summer theater festival has started to attract New York attention. West Virginia University is constantly expanding; a good friend of mine is overseeing the founding of an eastern-panhandle branch of the medical school at a time when I doubt many land-grant institutions in poor states are in growth mode (thank you, Senator Byrd). Morgantown retains its bohemian pockets; thanks to the university's presence, and growth, it seems to me to have turned a corner toward becoming a genuine regional destination, a place where people from outside come to make a life (not many towns in West Virginia can say that). In Charleston, the weekly music show "Mountain Stage" brings in major performers—Elvis Costello, R.E.M., k.d. lang, Randy Newman—and has done more for the state's national reputation (at least among a certain demographic subset) than anything since Jerry West. These are all things that wouldn't have been possible in the West Virginia I grew up in. They are happening for several reasons, but a chief one is that some people in the state are acting on an idea about its progress and potential that aims to do battle with the place's age-old insularity and (often justifiable) suspicion of the world beyond its borders, and that amounts to a cultural counterargument to the trends that have dominated in recent times.

Another reason that interesting things still happen is that good, creative people are drawn to the place by simple virtue of its beauty. The mountains roam and wander, endlessly one after the other; here, sloping and gentle, there, sinewy and buff; sunlight plays off their ridges and folds, suggesting something deep, ancient, and unknowable. Autumn is stunningly gorgeous. It is all accessible (the state maintains a very good public park and forest system), and the people are generous and wise enough to cherish it.

But it is the state's paradoxical curse: the beauty depicted by the profile of those mountains cannot exist in peace with the urge to dig out the minerals within them. The state has two real commodities: its beauty and its coal. Perforce, especially in the age of surface mining, one wins at the expense of the other.

So: nature or coal? North or South? These, owing to the state's intensely fateful geology and geography, are the cleavages. And from them results a psychic duality that is probably natural to a place that, because wealth is scarce and opportunities are limited, was bound to be constantly torn in warring directions. There may never be a clear victor. There will only be trends in one direction or the other, with an occasionally robust opposing tendency counterposed here and there. And I wouldn't look for the current trend to change anytime soon.

WISCONSIN

A STATE OF CONTINUAL AND FEARLESS
SIFTING AND WINNOWING

John Nichols

S eptember 11, 2001, was supposed to be the day when everything changed in America. The peddlers of this nugget of conventional wisdom will gladly identify a thousand
examples—political, economic, social, and cultural—to shore up
their "nothing will ever be the same" line. I don't begrudge them their
spin. But I am delighted to report that they are wrong. Their America
may have changed; my America did not.

My America is Wisconsin, the state my family has called home for
180 years. No matter where I have lived, no matter where I have traveled, I have remained a Wisconsinite first, an American second. This
is by no means an insult to the United States, but rather an honest
expression of a rather broadly felt sentiment among Wisconsinites,
which holds that our state is more than just one piece of the national
puzzle. We Wisconsinites have, for a very long time, tended to think
of ourselves as the odd state out. And, of this, we have always been
inordinately proud.

But in the difficult late summer and early fall days of 2001, my
own rather well-developed sense of regional identity was reinforced
by the experience of being in and out of Wisconsin during a time

when my state and my nation were deciding what they would do with the rest of their lives.

When the planes struck the World Trade Center and then the Pentagon, I was in Washington, D.C., where I travel often to keep tabs on what Mark Twain—a frequent visitor to Wisconsin's Mississippi River towns—referred to as the nation's "distinctly native criminal class": Congress. I first heard about the attacks not from television or radio broadcasts, and not from the members of Congress who were every bit as confused as the rest of us, but in a call from a Wisconsin friend who wanted to know if I was OK. When she was satisfied that I was, she closed the conversation by saying, "Better get back to Wisconsin before everyone out there goes crazy."

Her point was well taken. Within hours, the reconstruction of America had begun. With jarring speed, a land that against all odds had clung to a youthful sense of eventual perfectability was being transformed by politicians and pundits into a very old, very angry, paranoid, security-obsessed, vengeance-driven country that seemed incapable of reflection or education. A political class that no longer sought to lead settled with a media class that no longer sought to learn into a sickbed of impassioned ignorance, refusing the medicine of nuance and insight. Official explanations were gospel, skepticism was sin. Don't joke about the president, Ari Fleischer told us. Don't debate. Don't ask questions. Don't search for cause and effect, this was about evil—pure and simple. America was putting on a broad-brimmed hat, loading its six-gun, and riding out at dawn to hunt up some bad guys or whoever else might get in the way. If you were not with us, you were against us. And if you were against us, our cowboy president wanted you "dead or alive."

Over the next few days, in Washington and New York, I saw scenes of great humanity and nobility. At impromptu memorial services, exploring the wreckage around the Pentagon, riding an Amtrak train into New York City and watching for the eerily transformed skyline, sitting with rescue crews near Ground Zero, I was reminded often of the decency, dignity, and strength of the people who live in those cities. Over the next few weeks and months, as lecture and book tours took me to more than a dozen other major cities around the United States, I saw more decency, more dignity, and more strength.

But, in the days and weeks that followed September 11, I found myself increasingly unsatisfied with the nature of the national discourse, especially as it unfolded on television screens and in the halls of Congress.

The response to this tragedy was not the one I was familiar with, not the one that I had known growing up in Wisconsin as we dealt with the news of wars, assassinations, and impeachments. All the wild ranting and raving about avenging wrongs and hunting down evildoers seemed to miss the point. In Wisconsin, where the state constitution explicitly spells out the separation between church and state, we were never particularly satisfied with explanations that began and ended with talk of evil. And, in a state where capital punishment has been outlawed since 1851, we had always been very big on getting our emotions in check and getting down to the serious business of addressing the root causes of why bad things happen. To that end, at the turn of the last century, the state's elected leaders got together with professors at the University of Wisconsin and hit upon "The Wisconsin Idea," which argued that it was possible to solve problems—even problems as serious as economic inequality, corporate irresponsibility, and environmental devastation. All that was needed, so The Wisconsin Idea told us, was to get the best academics to study the underlying causes and identify a "scientific" course of action, which would then be submitted to the legislature for fine-tuning, allocation of proper funding, and implementation of the program. In the year 1911 alone, a coalition of rural Republicans and Milwaukee socialists planted their Scandinavian and German 1848er roots in the capital for a wild, six-month-long legislative session that saw them establish the first successful progressive income tax in the nation; institute a state life-insurance plan; impose maximum work hours for women and children; create an industrial commission to protect workers; write a pioneering worker's compensation plan; regulate railroads; reform the insurance industry; develop a new plan for taxing utilities; set up programs to aid farm cooperatives; put in place systems for technical and vocational education; design plans to conserve water and forests; and pass the Corrupt Practices Act, to clean up politics. They also enacted a law that identified schools across the state as "social centers," where citizens were encouraged to gather to discuss the great issues of the day—and to formulate responses to them. It was no wonder that Louis Brandeis would refer to the Wisconsin of those days as "the hope of democracy." And it was no wonder that talk like that gave rise to the sociopolitical phenomenon known as "Wisconsin exceptionalism," which refers to the absolute certainty of a good many Wisconsinites that every bit of progress America has made over the past 150 or so years can somehow be traced to Wisconsin's willingness to take the lead. It is the prevalence of this belief that allowed former U.S. senator Gaylord Nelson to note, as he was crusading to end the Vietnam War and start the modern environmental movement, that America would be a sorry land indeed were it not for Wisconsin. Wisconsin crowds still tend to respond with nods of thoughtful affirmation to such statements.

When I was growing up in rural southeastern Wisconsin, my teachers taught me that The Wisconsin Idea was not a historical footnote, but rather a constant. Reverence for the "continual and fearless sifting and winnowing by which alone the truth can be found"—to quote a plaque referring to a long-ago free-speech fight on the University of Wisconsin campus—was very much the order of the day in Mrs. Caroline's fourth-grade class at the red-brick Union Grove Grade

School. We were taught to share the assessment of Adlai Stevenson, a properly respectful Illinoisan, who observed that "the Wisconsin tradition meant more than a simple belief in the people. It also meant a faith in the application of intelligence and reason to the problems of society. It meant a deep conviction that the role of government was not to stumble along like a drunkard in the dark, but to light its way by the best torches of knowledge and understanding it could find." It was a belief in The Wisconsin Idea that guided me, with a little push from Carl Bernstein and Bob Woodward, into a career in journalism. And that belief imbued me with a sense of optimism that the United States might yet be guided toward the truths that would indeed free it from the folly of war, racism, and social and economic injustice.

But in September 2001, when my television and my Congress told me that America was determined to avoid hard truths and the even harder task of asking whether it really made sense to make "an eye for an eye" a guiding principle of our country's foreign policy, that optimism wavered long enough for me to wonder whether there was much room left for hard questions and harder answers, for sifting and winnowing, and for what remained of the spirit that had made my cold corner of the upper Midwest "the hope of democracy." After all, Wisconsin had its Wal-Marts, its McDonald's, its urban sprawl eating up dairy farms, its Republicans ranting about the need for welfare reform and school vouchers, and its radio stations broadcasting Rush Limbaugh and Sean Hannity's quivering commentaire on the "need" for America to respond to a big, scary world by being bigger and scarier. Was it really reasonable to imagine that the Progressive movement of another century had planted deep enough roots to withstand the winds of change and the windbags of contemporary conservatism? Perhaps all of America had changed. Perhaps, I feared, Wisconsin would join the rest of the country in stumbling along like a drunkard in the darkness of fear and ignorance that followed upon our grief.

I shouldn't have worried.

Less than two weeks after September 11, I found the antidote to my uncertainty at Annie Randall's Village Booksmith shop on the courthouse square in the south-central Wisconsin city of Baraboo. Baraboo is probably as typical a Wisconsin community as you will find, although we Wisconsinites don't really appreciate that there is such a thing. The state statutes identify Baraboo as a "fourth-class city," which means it is home to fewer than ten thousand people. But locals will tell you that there is nothing fourth-class about the city's Circus World Museum or the surrounding countryside, which inspired naturalist Aldo Leopold's *Sand County Almanac*. With its tree-lined streets, bungalows, and historic downtown, Baraboo looks a little conservative. But this is not part of "the red country" that you saw on those post-2000 election maps that seemed to suggest that everyone who lived in America's rural heartland backed George W. Bush. Al Gore actually carried Wisconsin by winning small towns and cities like Baraboo, where a lingering Progressive tradition and concern about declining dairy prices and deindustrialization makes voters wary as to whether compassionate conservatism is going to solve their problems.

My friends Jack Holzhueter, Curt Meine, and Gail Lamberty had arranged, months before September 11, for me to join their gathering at Annie's to celebrate the 100th anniversary of the progressive movement's arrival as a political force in America. We were to mark the occasion with coffee, cake, and readings from the speeches of U.S. senator Robert M. La Follette, his wife and comrade, Belle Case La Follette, author Zona Gale, and the other Wisconsin Progressives whose radical movement gave its name to what would eventually become an era of reform. Baraboo and the surrounding Sauk County was a Progressive stronghold in La Follette's day and after—it was in nearby Sauk City that the "Joe Must Go" movement was organized to displace the worst representative Wisconsin ever sent to Washington,

"Tailgunner Joe" McCarthy—so we figured this was a perfect place to toast the tradition. Besides, Jack and Curt and Gail lived nearby.

While I had wondered from afar whether folks in Baraboo would tear themselves away from the round-the-clock cable television coverage of presidential pronouncements, congressional cowering, and saber rattling, the folks in Baraboo assured me that, as we Wisconsinites say with our usual dose of double precision: "Everyone's all excited." They were right. When I got to Annie's place, it was packed with a crowd that numbered more than 100.

So there we were, Wisconsinites gathered in Baraboo on the night after Congress—with nary a complaint from the nation's so-called opposition party—allocated $15 billion to airline corporations that were paying their executives multimillion-dollar bonuses while laying off flight attendants.

Someone in the crowd asked me how Robert M. La Follette, who is well remembered in Wisconsin for his passionate opposition to World War I and his crusades against profiteering by the munitions merchants of that earlier day, would have reacted to the airline bailout bill. Having just flown in from Washington, and thus not being fully reacclimated to Wisconsin, I ventured a cautious response. "Well," I suggested, "I kind of think that he might have been uncomfortable with the idea that September 11 would be used as an excuse to bail out some very badly run companies. I think that even though we are not yet at war with anyone in particular," and here I do recall taking a deep breath, "La Follette would have called it war profiteering."

The crowd burst into applause. I knew I was home.

As the night progressed, there was much talk of the eerie similarities between the early days of the twentieth century and the early days of the twenty-first. It was striking to note how many of the readings from Wisconsin Progressive thinkers and leaders had to do with concerns about militarism, wartime profiteering by monopolies, and the need to protect the rights of immigrants. Roughly a dozen readers rose to offer lines from Wisconsin's Progressive past and, after each finished, a rumble would go through the crowd: "Things really haven't changed." "Same problems as now." "She could have written those words today."

In 1917, following attacks on U.S. ships by German submarines, the country degenerated into a frenzied fervor for war. But in Wisconsin, and especially in the regions of the state with strong Progressive traditions, there was a great debate about how best to respond to horrifying attacks on American civilians. Wisconsin developed its identity as an antiwar state in those days. But even then, the state was not so much pacifist as it was distrustful of Washington.

Wisconsin has never been a "my country right or wrong" state. It's a place where people like to decide for themselves when it comes to warmaking. A civil war to end slavery? You bet. Take on Hitler? Sure. But don't expect much enthusiasm for a fight between the kaiser and the king of England, or between the Bush family and Saddam Hussein. And don't ever ask us to surrender our faith in democracy, or our belief that this democratic experiment functions best when debate and dissent push leaders to consider their actions. Nothing so distinguishes the Wisconsin Progressive tradition as its adherence to the view that, while big corporations are certainly dangerous, big government can be just as dangerous. Or that, when big corporations and big government get together to promote a big war, big trouble is sure to follow.

In Baraboo, on that Friday night, the voice of that Wisconsin Progressive tradition was speaking, especially during a long discussion about the complex questions that arise in wartime.

At a point when the politicians and the pundits in Washington were telling us that Americans were too traumatized to think straight, the good people of Baraboo were more than ready to weigh the wisdom of doing as their president—or anyone else in Washington—told them. No one was expressing sympathy for Osama bin Laden or Afghanistan's Taliban leaders, but there was plenty of concern for the Afghan people—and genuine worry that they might be the innocent victims of a war that they did not ask to be a part of. Armchair military strategists had some ideas about Special Forces strikes, which were definitely preferred to prolonged ground or air wars. Armchair diplomats proposed dramatic shifts in U.S. relations with Israel and the ruling families of various Arab oil states. No one liked the idea—that had been floated to create an Office of Homeland Security—"sounds like the Soviet Union," one fellow told me. And everyone in the room said that the jokers in Washington had better not use September 11 to tamper with our constitutional rights.

A few weeks later, when Congress voted on the Bush administration's USA Patriot Act, with its draconian assaults on civil liberties, a single senator stood in opposition: Russ Feingold. The son of a La Follette Progressive, Feingold got his start in politics as a state legislator representing the Baraboo area. In Washington, they call Feingold a "maverick" because he so frequently casts lonely—one might even say "exceptional"—votes against the dictates not merely of a Republican White House but of his own Democratic party. In Washington these days, Feingold is an outsider. His fellow senators joke about him, just as some of my Washington friends laugh at me when I tell them there really are small towns in America where folks buy "Not In Our Name" antiwar ads in their weekly newspapers, where farmers drive pickup trucks with bumper stickers reading MEAN CORPORATIONS SUCK and where good citizens will come out on a Friday night to discuss the perils of imperialism.

It may not be wise to speak in broad terms about a particular state. There are exceptions to the rule of any place. Even Texas has an Austin. And it must be said that Wisconsin has always had its share of homegrown conservatives, most of whom now cluster in the suburbs, which send a reasonably lamentable class of Republicans to Congress.

But the United States is still an island nation. For all of the cultural and political homogenization that has been forced upon us by marketing executives and political spin doctors, we live in states that are separated from one another by distances that require more than the tools of cartography to measure. I know that it is getting harder to see the distinctions. But I know, as well, what I saw and heard in the fall of 2001, and in the months that followed as I traveled to Ashland and Viroqua and Eau Claire and Fond du Lac and a dozen other Wisconsin towns to join in conversations about the perilous course our leaders have charted for these United States. Long before anyone on television dared suggest that Americans might not be marching in lockstep to war with Iraq, I heard Wisconsinites who lived far from college towns and the hip urban neighborhoods asking again and again, "Why?" And I heard them rejecting, more and more loudly, the claim that fear or some spin-doctored version of patriotism ought to guide their country's relations with the rest of the world. I was back in Baraboo to speak on the eve of George W. Bush's war with Iraq. The crowd was so large that we had to use the old meeting hall above Annie Randall's bookshop. We were not all of one mind. But we were all determined, even at that late date, to carry on with that continual and fearless sifting and winnowing by which alone the truth can be found. And we all knew that this, more than any line on a map, was what made us Wisconsinites.

WYOMING

THE COWBOY STATE

Annie Proulx

Wyoming still calls itself "The Cowboy State," a name more representative of the nineteenth century day of the cattlemen than contemporary reality, for traditional ranching in a time of corporate agribiz and feedlots is a hard way to make a living. Still, the license plate with its bucking bronco and rider serves to identify not only the vehicle but the free and independent cowboy-driver, feeding the illusion that the tough people of the pioneer days are still here. Isolation is easy to mistake for independence. The state and its tourist industry depend heavily on the cowboy myth for character. And it is allegiance to the cowboy code that solaces families who lose a relative in a rodeo accident— "He died doing what he loved" is not an uncommon statement.

Wyoming also thinks of itself as "The Equality State," largely because, in 1869, when it was still a territory, it passed a law giving women the right to vote and hold office and, in 1890, became the first state with women's suffrage. (Sly politics to lure scarce women within the reach of the predominantly male population? In 1870 there were six men to every woman.) Today sex discrimination and wage inequities put Wyoming near the bottom of the national scale.

Women earn about sixty-five cents for every dollar a man earns, and ranch women, who are expected to raise children and orphaned stock, participate in community life and help with heavy ranch work, rarely have a say in ranch management decisions, and have little money of their own. "Equality State" is as shallow a reflection of the real Wyoming as "Cowboy State." One cannot help but wonder if the low wages paid women are linked to the not-infrequent newspaper accounts of female-employee embezzlements.

Yet in 2002 the state was rated Number One in friendliness to the wealthy by *Bloomberg Personal Finance* magazine. There is no income tax in Wyoming, and retired multi-millionaires with a yen to play rancher find the state seductively attractive, especially in the Jackson area which combines world-class scenery and with luxury dining and shops.

Wyoming is made up of diverse landscapes, from rolling plains of sagebrush grasslands to jagged mountains and lodgepole forests. Several weighty geographical and climatological features define the state. Yellowstone National Park occupies the northwest corner (the edges overlap into Montana and Idaho). It is the oldest national park in the world, an extraordinary place of geysers and wildlife so diverse that naturalists call it "the Serengeti of North America." Some have called the creation of the park in 1872 the American government's single most intelligent act. Today the park and surrounding national forest form what some believe is the largest intact ecosystem on earth.

The natural attributes that determine Wyoming's overall high-plains character are its altitude and aridity. It has the lowest population of any state, with only 493,782 people scattered about its 97,914 square miles (an increase of 8.9 percent since the 1990 census), but to many who live here the scanty population is a positive value that puts life in Wyoming—embedded in a world that exalts the megalopolis—on a human scale. The federal government owns 49 percent of Wyoming's surface land and that gives government agencies—the Bureau of Land Management (BLM), the Forest Service (USFS), the

National Park Service, and the Bureau of Indian Affairs a large presence. The mean altitude is 6,700 feet, making it the second highest state. Anyone flying over Wyoming can look out the window onto the dry bones below and recognize a land of little rain. It is semi-arid country with large swatches of desert. The state's annual average rainfall is fourteen inches, with many areas getting much less, the low humidity and strong winds quickly sucking up what scanty moisture falls. In the last three years the region suffered severe drought and fear of wildfires; ranchers hoped for federal disaster aid to see them through tough times. (Some wonder that these self-declared free and independent spirits who so hate the federal government can bring themselves to accept that government's largesse.) Although good spring snow and rain in 2003 seems to be easing the drought, the ruling fact of nature is that the American West is subject to climate patterns of the kind that made the dust storms of the dirty thirties and fifties. All that kept Wyoming from blowing away then was its grass and sagebrush cover—less than 8 percent of the state's land has ever been put to the plow.

The Rocky Mountains cut diagonally through the state in fabled ranges—the Tetons, Wind Rivers, Absarokas, Bighorns, Medicine Bows. It is a grand place for geologists, archeologists, and paleontologists, the uplifted rock strata illustrating most stages of the earth's history. There are geological oddities such as the wandering Killpecker Dunes and the colonnaded monolith called Devils Tower. Underground lies the state's wealth—uranium deposits, and great coal and gas beds left by the Cretaceous swamps that covered the state fifty million years ago. The rich fossil beds yield the preserved skeletons of sea creatures, dinosaurs, and tropical plants.

Tepee rings and stone tools of ancient people, rock paintings, and petroglyphs speak of the Native American past. Wyoming has been occupied for about twelve-thousand years, the old inhabitants' flint tools found with the bones of slain mammoths and *bison antiquus*. By the nineteenth century Crows, Sioux, Cheyenne, Arapaho, and Shoshone lived in and hunted the region. Today most of the state's Native Americans live on the Wind River Reservation, the home territory of Chief Washakie, who never went to war against the United States and so, at the end of the Indian Wars, was allowed to remain on ancestral ground.

The first white men in Wyoming were French-Canadian, the La Vérendrye brothers in 1743, followed by trappers and mountain men in the late eighteenth and early nineteenth centuries. Many French place names persist. Then came traders, missionaries, geologists, and emigrants heading west. The pioneer routes to Oregon, California, and Salt Lake City cut through Wyoming Territory, tracing up the North Platte and the Sweetwater rivers as the Overland and Oregon trails, which then broke into a complex network of subsidiary short cuts and divergences. A major stopping place for all travelers was Fort Laramie on the Laramie River in eastern Wyoming, today handsomely restored as a national park. Most emigrants traveled on, glad to leave Wyoming's treeless emptiness behind; only wheel ruts on the prairie and a few names chiseled on rocks now show their passage. Today three interstate highways as well as major railroad freight lines cut the state, part of the proposed corridor for transporting the nation's nuclear waste to Yucca Mountain in Nevada.

The events of the nineteenth century shaped the state's character. The first great treaty council between the U.S. government and the western tribes took place in 1851 at Fort Laramie in southeast Wyoming. As many as 10,000 Indians came to the council. That number seems large, but the year before, 65,000 emigrants had made the overland crossing on their way to California gold and new lives. The Plains Indians tried to defend their territory against the tidal wave of whites, but the discovery of gold in the Black Hills of northeast Wyoming and the nutritious grass of the Powder River basin, coveted by ranchers who wished to replace bison with cows, led to the decision by Ulysses S. Grant and his cabinet to seize the Black Hills and the Powder River country from the Indians—particularly from the Sioux whose territory it was—despite earlier treaties poetically flavored with the rhetoric of "as long as the rivers run."

The massacres and last-stands of the Indian Wars soaked the prairie in blood. The Battle of Greasy Grass, where Custer fell in 1876, just over the Montana line, was preceded by a hunt through the Powder River basin in northeast Wyoming where Generals Crook and Terry were trying to force "the hostiles" to reservations. Concurrently buffalo hunters and diseases introduced by Texas cattle drivers decimated the herds. Immediately after the Indians were driven out of the Powder River country, ranchers rushed in with their cows. In just a few years the range was overcrowded and overgrazed in the hunger for profit.

In the 1880s Wyoming really was the cowboy state, part of the famed Wyoming–Montana open summer range, where Texas cows driven up the trail fattened, and where absentee British and Scottish investors owned or backed big spreads. From the beginning there was friction between big ranchers and homesteaders fueled by absentee ranch ownership, the notorious 1884 Maverick Law, cattle rustling, monopoly of water resources, and barbwire fences. (The Maverick Law gave full control of roundups and the right to decide maverick ownership to the Wyoming Stock Growers Association, the powerful organization of big cattlemen who owned four-fifths of the cattle.) It is estimated that roughly 900,000 cattle were on the Wyoming range in the fall of 1886. The frightful winter of 1886–87, still spoken of today as "the big die-up," decimated the herds. By 1894 their numbers had been reduced by two-thirds, an early entry in the long cycle of boom and bust economic ventures that still afflict the state.

The state's horseback character faded, according to Wyoming historian T. A. Larson, after World War II. Today's rancher antipathy toward the federal government some see as rooted in the 1934 Taylor Grazing Act, which ended homesteading, divided public lands into grazing districts, and, for the payment of a modest fee per animal unit, leased the land for grazing. The smallness of the fee and the generous use ranchers make of the leased land has incited opponents to coin the derogatory phrase "welfare ranchers." Ranchers see these fees as onerous and have a tendency to regard leased public land as their private property, fencing, ditching, and chasing away any member of the public who dares tread on it with shouts and sometimes bullets. When private land is sold, any public-land leases the previous owner enjoyed are passed on to the new owner, fostering the sense of ownership. Others name the 1979 law directing the BLM to hold federal land "in perpetuity" (instead of allowing it to come into the hands of the states) as the catalyst for a mostly paper uprising, the so-called Sagebrush Rebellion, which held that local people, not urban bureaucrats in the east, should make the decisions on the use of western public rangeland.

As the nineteenth century eased into the twentieth many of the giant ranches broke up. Settlers and European immigrants came in, hoping to make a go of it. Some tried to prove up on government-grant homesteads of 160 acres in a region where one cow needs 30 acres of grazing space. Today those smaller ranches are fracturing into 35-acre house lots, and many of the last generation of ranch-born children are living out-of-state lives. Developers are here to front for new homesteaders, often retirees.

From the beginning of the cattle days, ranchers, through the Wyoming Stock Growers Association, had a stranglehold on the legislature, a domination that continues today despite the glaring fact that ranching and farming together provide only 2 percent of the state's income. But ranching is important beyond economics—big spreads maintain the state's open, wild appearance, a hedge against housing developments. Every time a ranch goes to the developers, and inheritance taxes make that increasingly likely, the open country shrinks.

Captain Howard Stansbury of the Corps of Topographical Engineers surveyed and mapped Wyoming in his 1849–51 expedition to Great Salt Lake. He (as did many emigrants) noticed coal outcroppings near what is now Rock Springs, and near present-day Cheyenne discovered "the ramp," a comparatively moderate incline into the Rockies. This gradual slope became the Union Pacific's way through the mountains in 1867–69, a link in the transcontinental railroad and the source of roistering, hellish shack-towns that accompanied the construction crews. The UP ran its trains on the Rock Springs coal through the services of a Missouri mine owner, but when, in 1874, Jay Gould took over the railroad, he seized the mines. Wage cuts and labor troubles in the form of imported Chinese workers erupted in 1885—the infamous Rock Springs Massacre—when striking white miners killed the Chinese and drove them into the surrounding desert, burning their houses. Violence against Chinese in other Wyoming mining and railroad communities followed.

Mistreatment of minorities in the "Equality State" is not a new story. During World Wars I and II the state was rabidly anti-German. Japanese-Americans were interned at Heart Mountain Relocation Center in World War II. During the forties, Rawlins residents rose up against Jehovah's Witnesses. In the fifties the University of Wyoming was infected by a fever to seek out faculty members suspected of "un-American activities." In the sixties fourteen football players at the university, in protest against the regional Mormon Church's negative attitude toward blacks, were kicked off the team. Matthew Shepherd's murder in 1998 has come to represent the state's homophobia.

The last decades of Wyoming's nineteenth century were violent and murderous. Train robberies, stage holdups, Butch Cassidy and the Sundance Kid, Big Nose George were all part of the outlaw color that painted the state in those days. In 1889 a band of horsemen hanged James Averell and Ella Watson (erroneously nicknamed "Cattle Kate" by a Chicago news reporter) for cattle rustling. The perpetrators were neither publicly identified nor punished. Two years later a group of ranchers who belonged to the Wyoming Stock Growers Association felt that rustling was out of hand (although the county court records show very few cattle-stealing cases in the period, which may mean that rustling was not the real problem, or else that vigilante action was the preferred mode of law enforcement), and made a plan to import Texas gunmen and permanently wipe out the troublemaking rustler homesteaders, most of them ex-cowboys with small outfits, who were blamed for the rustling. The gunfight at the T.A. ranch near Kaycee that followed was the major battle of the Johnson County war, said to be the subject of more Hollywood Westerns than any other incident in the Old West, pitting, as it did, big ranchers against small homesteaders. Hard feelings and local flare-ups continued. In 1892 the government, which frequently used black troops in the west to settle civil strife, sent in the all-black Ninth U.S. Cavalry to keep the peace, and perhaps to divert public animosity away from the big ranchers to the color of the troops, for white supremacist sentiments characterized the local populace. (Wyoming is still a white state, only around 8 percent of the population listed as Native American, African-American, Asian, and Hispanic.) In the end the attacking ranchers and their hired gunmen were arrested and brought down to Cheyenne, but all went free when the county said it could not bear the expense of a trial.

The United States attracts the brainy and talented from other countries, and the East Coast absorbs most of them as well as the brightest from its own hinterlands. Wyoming is not cut from this cloth. The constricted nature of the state's economy means that a large proportion of its young people leave. Estimates say that 50 percent of the university's graduating classes leave Wyoming to find jobs. No matter how much a Wyoming person loves the home state, unless mining, oil and gas work, logging, ranching, service occupations, administrative support, repairs, retail sales, or teaching appeal as a way to make a living, or unless you have outside sources of income, it's over the horizon and away. Retirees and people who can afford second homes have discovered the beauty and laconic character of Wyoming, but they are attracted to mountain scenery, not the sagebrush flats, so relatively crowded pockets of luxury punctuate hardscrabble open land.

The University of Wyoming, in Laramie, serves the entire state. Half a dozen community colleges supported by the state are also scattered through the larger towns. The university, in its early years, received less money than the state paid out in wolf bounties. It is still on a starvation diet. The university suffers from something one faculty member calls "a silo mentality," meaning that ideas and projects go up and down within instead of across departments; cross-departmental cooperation is rare. The university's geology department is famous, in part because of John McPhee's profile of David Love in his 1980 book *Basin and Range*.

Health care in much of Wyoming is of the frontier type—a long drive to the nearest town that has a doctor or hospital. Except in dire necessity people tend to let nature take its course, hoping for the best.

Laramie, which thinks of itself as the state's most liberal and educated town because of the university's presence, still smarts over the national media's tarring of its character as a homophobic, bigoted hick hamlet during the coverage of the 1998 murder of gay student Matthew Shepherd. The media uproar and the Moisés Kaufman play and film, *The Laramie Project*, certainly made local people think about hate crimes, but outside Laramie the old homophobic standard still holds. Though most people are cheerful and kind-hearted, Wyoming can be a mean place.

Wyoming is full of contradictions and anomalies. The state thinks small and likes its elbow room. There are towns with a population of three people, there are temporary boom towns that are little more than a cluster of ratty trailers and junk—and then there is Jackson, rich and stunningly beautiful. Here, adjacent to Grand Teton National Park and Yellowstone, is a sprawl of trophy mansions, some exceeding fifteen-thousand square feet despite the county's ten-thousand square-foot size limit. Most of the rancho-deluxe builders are wealthy people from out of state attracted by the absence of income taxes, the spectacular scenery, and the upscale cowboy ambience. A big log house, a pair of lizard-skin boots, a few cows, and a wine cellar, and you have an instant contemporary rancher who likely spends a few weeks a year on the spread. Residents call them "suitcase ranchers," and such outfits are displacing the homegrown variety; if he or she is lucky, the native-born ex-owner gets a job as foreman on the old place. Three new ski resorts are currently under construction in the Jackson area. The explosion of tourism and multimillion-dollar houses here breaks away from the boom-and-bust cycle but the catch is that Teton County residents in the service industries that support tourism are inexorably squeezed out of the local housing market, many forced to live in Idaho and commute long distances.

There are wild animals in Wyoming—the largest herds of antelope and elk in the world, grizzlies and mountain lions, bighorn sheep, wolves and mule deer, prairie dogs, eagles, and large trout. Several thousand so-called wild horses run in the state's southwest Red Desert and the Pryor Mountain Wild Horse Range, descendants of the mounts of the Spanish conquistadores and the horses of Indians, explorers, traders, settlers, and the military. Local residents sometimes turn their mares loose to run with the wild ones for a while hoping for colts with beauty and stamina. Although many people see the horses as symbols of the untamed wild, some ranchers dislike them, claiming they are nothing but feral horses that compete with cattle and sheep for grass and forage, and shoot them. The vast sagebrush ocean, which looks endless to the driver, supports the diverse wildlife. Unfortunately the sagebrush is in trouble, affected by drought and overgrazing.

Until very recently you could drive up to a curbside bar, order a Scotch on the rocks, and drive away sipping it. Wyoming was one of the last holdouts that allowed drinking and driving, and if you had to travel on Friday or Saturday night, you took your life in your hands. A horrendous drunk-driving accident that killed eight University of Wyoming students in 2001 changed legislative and public opinion and, coupled with the federal regulation that could deny Wyoming highway funds unless it complied with the national standard, the legislature voted for the new alcohol limit of .08. Still, there are annoyed Wyomingites who accuse the legislature of being weak-kneed while the federal government tramples the state's rights.

There is virtually no public transportation in the cowboy state: Amtrak pulled out several years ago and though a few buses traverse the state between major cities, there are almost no local bus lines. Air travel is important here because of the huge distances, but following September 11, 2001, commercial aviation declined 6 percent in Wyoming. It is hard to get around.

The state penitentiary at Rawlins is overcrowded and, even with a new facility, prisoners are double-celled, 591 housed out of state. Wyoming's excellent[1] newspaper, the *Casper Star-Tribune,* frequently carries letters from inmates complaining of structural problems and overcrowding in the prison.

In its politics Wyoming is belligerently Republican, conservative— even reactionary—and fulminates against the heavy federal hand, people from somewhere else, taxes, environmentalists. Yet in 2002 the state elected a Democratic governor. (Although Wyoming has no income tax, the subject of introducing one comes up for legislative

---

1. *The Casper Star-Tribune* was sold to Lee Newspapers in 2002. It remains to be seen if the new management will affect the outstanding coverage.

discussion every year, and it does have a sales tax.) Increasingly there are liberal voices and enlightened thinkers all over the state, and some of them are fourth-generation ranchers. Even tiny communities have a few quirky, free-thinking, smart, and influential people with amazingly diverse interests, from aeronautic design to old books to international politics. Wyoming does not pride itself on the individuals right to an independent opinion.

The big corporate names in Wyoming are Exxon, Sun, Texaco, Shell, Continental, Mobil, Standard Oil of California, Pacific Power and Light, Union Pacific. The longtime control of the state's resources by outside corporations makes Wyoming a classic economic colony. Energy resources are its lifeblood. Vast beds of high-grade, low-sulfur coal continue to be important. There are enormous open pit mines near Gillette and coal trains rumble non-stop through the state.

Mineral-extraction economics are familiar to Wyoming people: copper, silver, gold, iron, trona (soda ash), and uranium, as well as oil, have taken the state on the apparently inescapable roller-coaster ride of boom and bust with out-of-state workers rushing in and setting up trailer cities surrounded by vice and sin businesses, then abruptly departing for some other discovery town. The current boon is in methane gas, with new roads and wells speckling the state, especially the Powder River basin and the Red Desert.

Even overland emigrants on their way to California gold fields noticed the oil seeps. In 1883 the first flowing well was brought in near Lander but the big oil was in the Salt Creek field north of Casper and eventually yielded 400 million barrels of crude. The boom roared through the 1970s and early 1980s, then took a cliff-dive in 1986. The oil fields are fading away now. Though there are massive amounts of oil shale, the extraction process remains too expensive to make it worthwhile—so far. All over the state abandoned machinery and derrick parts lie rusting in the sagebrush. The oil, gas, and mining business is a complex tangle of land ownership, leases, and permitted uses. Mineral rights below the surface of 72 percent of Wyoming's land belong to the federal government. Much of the state's income is from royalties paid for mineral extraction by the federal government. The state is often faulted because its economy is tied to the same base as a hundred years ago—mining, ranching, tourism, retail sales, and the federal government. Wyoming seems incapable of escaping this limited set of choices in ways to make a living. And in the state's mountains (as in all the world's mountain ranges) tourism is showing its true self as destructive to habitat and fragile ecosystems.

While legislative opinion, which rarely sees beyond raw job numbers, along with historians and others studying the social and political climate of Wyoming, have seen boom years as economically healthy and bust years as the regrettable downside of raw-material exploitation by colonialist powers, there is a growing feeling that little-studied bust years have a positive side. If tourism continues to be an increasing part of Wyoming's economic future, the environmental quality and preservation of the state's scenic landscape, both of which flourish in bust years, are important. The current exemplar is the incursion of methane gas extraction in the unique red desert. To recognize that the state's natural beauty may be its most precious asset will take some serious revisionist thinking. Since the abolishment of the state's Board of Immigration in the 1920s, Wyoming has preferred tourists to settlers. Escaping the old economic and cultural straitjackets may depend on encouraging new settlement and the fresh ideas and vigorous entrepreneurship that come with immigration. Yet, as Emory University philosopher Donald Livingston says, ". . . economic exchange is always embedded in a cultural landscape of noneconomic values, which impose restraints." The myth that ranching is the defining occupation in Wyoming continues to have the strength to defeat diversification. The Wyomingite has only to look at the latte parlors of Montana and the despoiled Front Range of Colorado to see the trade-off.

Perhaps that is how it should be. Maybe Wyoming is the country's empty quarter, a place of harsh and striking beauty and not much else, a rare territory that retains the ancient sense of space. Not a Buffalo Common, not an enlarged Yellowstone, not a miner's bonanza nor a tourist mecca nor a rancher's paradise, but an original place whose few residents understand the terrain and live quiet lives within it without coffee bars and arugula.

ABOUT THE
CONTRIBUTORS

Alexie, Sherman
Washington
Sherman Alexie lives with his family in Seattle. He is the author most recently of *Ten Little Indians*, and his latest film, *The Business of Fancydancing*, has just been released on DVD.

Allen, Dwight
Kentucky
Dwight Allen was born and raised in Louisville, Kentucky. He is the author of two books of fiction, *The Green Suit* and *Judge*. He lives in Madison, Wisconsin, with his wife and son.

Allman, T. D.
Florida
A veteran war correspondent, T. D. Allman wrote the classic *Miami: City of the Future*. He paints a portrait of the entire state in his forthcoming *Finding Florida*.

Barthelme, Steven
Mississippi

Steven Barthelme has published a short story collection and the memoir *Double Down*, co-authored with his brother Frederick. Recent stories are in *McSweeney's*, *The Atlantic*, and *Yale Review*. He has lived in Mississippi for seventeen years.

Benedict, Elizabeth
Massachusetts

Elizabeth Benedict is the author of four novels, including *Almost*, set on an island off the coast of Massachusetts; *Slow Dancing* and *The Beginner's Book of Dreams*, as well as *The Joy of Writing Sex: A Guide for Fiction Writers*. She writes fiction and nonfiction for many publications and has taught writing at Princeton, the Iowa Writers' Workshop, Harvard Extension School, and MIT. She divides her time between Somerville, Massachussetts, and New York City.

Berman, David
Virginia

David Berman is the author of *Actual Air*.

Berman, Marshall
New York City

Marshall Berman, Distinguished Professor at CCNY/Council, is working on *One Hundred Years of Spectacle: Metamorphoses of Times Square*.

Bowden, Charles
Arizona

Charles Bowden has lived in Arizona almost all of his life and has been condemned to survive by his limited wits. He sells things to magazines in New York in order to finance his foolish passion for scribbling books, most recently *Down by the River: Drugs, Money, Murder, and Family*. He prefers noon on a June day in the Sonoran Desert to any drug, legal or illegal, that he has yet encountered.

Burke, James Lee
Louisiana
James Lee Burkeis a novelist who lives in Louisiana and Montana.

Castillo, Ana
Illinois
Ana Castillo is a poet, novelist, short-story writer, essayist, playwright, editor, and author of children's books. Her novels include *The Mixquiahuala Letters, Sapogonia, So Far from God*; short stories, *Loverboys*; essays, *Massacre of the Dreamers*; poetry, *My Father Was a Toltec*, to be published in a revised edition in spring 2004, and *I Ask the Impossible*. Ana lives in Chicago where she is currently working on a novel, her plays, and her poetry.

Conroy, Frank
Iowa
Frank Conroy is the former director of the literature program at the National Endowment for the Arts and became the fifth director of the Iowa Writers' Workshop in 1987. He is the author of three books: *Stop-Time*, nominated for the National Book Award; *Midair*; and *Body & Soul*. He lives in Iowa City, Iowa.

Cooper, Marc
Nevada
Journalist and author Marc Cooper lives 282 miles from Las Vegas. He is author of *Pinochet and Me* and *The Last Honest Place in America: Paradise and Perdition in the New Las Vegas*, forthcoming from Nation Books.

Davis, Kathryn
Pennsylvania

Kathryn Davis was born in Philadelphia in 1946. She is the author of five novels: *Labrador*, *The Girl Who Trod on a Loaf*, *Hell*, *The Walking Tour*, and *Versailles*. She lives in Vermont.

Davis, Mike
California (South)

Mike Davis is a San Diego–based writer and historian.

DeLancey, Kiki
Ohio

Kiki DeLancey is the author of the story collection *Coal Miner's Holiday*. She is a lifelong resident of Ohio.

Early, Gerald
Missouri

Gerald Early teaches at Washington University in St. Louis, Missouri, where he is the Merle Kling Professor of Modern Letters and Director of the African and Afro-American Studies Program. He has won a number of awards, including the National Book Critics Circle Award for Criticism for *The Culture of Bruising*. His latest book is *This is Where I Came In: Black America in the 1960s*, published by University of Nebraska Press.

Ferré, Rosario
Puerto Rico

Rosario Ferré has published novels, short stories, poetry, and essays, written and/or translated by her both into Spanish and into English. Some of her books in the two languages include *The House on the Lagoon*, *Eccentric Neighborhoods*, *Flight of the Swan*, and *Language Duel* (poems). She is currently at work on a book of essays, "Gates of Pleasure," and a series of novellas, "Battle of the Virgins and Other Stories." She lives in San Juan, Puerto Rico, and New York City.

Freeman, Judith
Idaho
Judith Freeman is a novelist and critic and the recipient of a Guggenheim Fellowship in fiction. Her novels include *The Chinchilla Farm* and most recently *Red Water*, published by Pantheon in 2002.

Giovanni, Nikki
Tennessee
Nikki Giovanni is the author of *Racism 101*, and more than fourteen volumes of poetry, including *Black Feeling Black Talk/Black Judgement*, *My House*, and most recently, *The Selected Poems of Nikki Giovanni*.

Gogola, Tom
Long Island
Tom Gogola "floats the measureless float" between Montauk and New York City.

Greider, William
Washington, D.C.
William Greider is national affairs correspondent for *The Nation*.

Grimsley, Jim
Georgia
Jim Grimsley is the author of six novels, a book of plays, and various stories. He teaches writing at Emory University. His most recent novel, *Boulevard*, was published in 2002 by Algonquin Books.

Hall, Donald
New Hampshire

Donald Hall continues to inhabit his family's old farm-house in Wilmot, New Hampshire. He has published fifteen books of poems and won the National Book Critics Circle Award, and the *Los Angeles Times* Book Award. In 2003 he published a collection of short stories, *Willow Tempo*. Donald Hall was the poet laureate of New Hampshire from 1984–1989, and from 1995–1999.

Hansen, Ron
Nebraska
Ron Hansen's most recent books are *A Stay Against Confusion: Essays on Faith and Fiction* and *Isn't It Romantic?: An Entertainment*.

Harrison, Jim
Michigan
Jim Harrison was born in Grayling, Michigan. He is the author of many novellas including *Legends of the Fall*, seven novels, seven collections of poetry and a collection of nonfiction. His most recent book is *Off to the Side: A Memoir*. He has recently moved to Montana.

Hillerman, Tony
New Mexico
Tony Hillerman is the author of *The Sinister Pig*, *The Wailing Wind*, *Hunting Badger*, *The First Eagle*, and *A Thief of Time*. His honors include a Center for the American Indian's Ambassador Award, the Navajo Tribe's Special Friend Award, and the Public Service Award from the U.S. Department of the Interior. He was voted a Grandmaster of the Mystery Writers of America and is a former editor of the *New Mexican*. He lives with his wife in Albuquerque, New Mexico.

Howard, Maureen
Connecticut
Maureen Howard is a novelist and writer who lives in exile in New York City.

Ivins, Molly

Texas

Molly Ivins, a syndicated newspaper columnist, is co-author of *Shrub: The Short but Happy Political Life of George W. Bush.*

Karlin, Wayne

Maryland

Wayne Karlin is the author of a memoir and six novels. He lives in St. Mary's County, Maryland.

Kirn, Walter

Montana

Walter Kirn is the author of four works of fiction, *My Hard Bargain: Stories*, *She Needed Me*, *Thumbsucker*, and *Up in the Air*. His work has appeared in the *New York Times Magazine*, the *New York Times Book Review*, *GQ*, *Vogue*, *New York*, and *Esquire*. He lives in Livingston, Montana.

Lingeman, Richard

Indiana

Richard Lingeman is the author of *Don't You Know There's a War On?* and biographies of Theodore Dreiser and Sinclair Lewis.

Gene Lyons

Arkansas

Gene Lyons is a Little Rock author whose most recent book (with Joe Conason) is *The Hunting of the President*. He writes a syndicated column for the *Arkansas Democrat-Gazette*.

MacKay, Scott

Rhode Island

Scott MacKay is a reporter at the *Providence Journal* and was born in Providence.

McCorkle, Jill

North Carolina

Jill McCorkle is the author of five novels and three collections of stories. She is on the faculty at the Bennington College M.F.A. Program.

McWhorter, Diane

Alabama

Diane McWhorter's book about her native Birmingham, *Carry Me Home*, won the 2002 Pulitzer Prize for General Nonfiction.

Moore, MariJo

South Carolina

MariJo Moore (Cherokee/Irish/Dutch) is the author of *The Diamond Doorknob*, *Spirit Voices of Bones*, *Red Woman With Backward Eyes and Other Stories*, and editor of *Genocide of the Mind: New Native American Writing*.

Joanne B. Mulcahy

Oregon

Joanne B. Mulcahy directs the Writing Culture Program and teaches at the Northwest Writing Institute of Lewis and Clark College in Portland, Oregon. She is the author of *Birth and Rebirth on an Alaskan Island*.

Mura, David

Minnesota

David Mura is the author of *Turning Japanese* and *Where the Body Meets Memory*.

Nelson, Antonya

Kansas

Antonya Nelson grew up in Kansas, and now lives in Houston. She is the author, most recently, of *Female Trouble*, a collection of stories.

Nichols, John
Wisconsin

John Nichols is a native Wisconsinite, who has covered Progressive politics and activism in the United States and abroad for more than a decade. He is now editorial page editor for the *Capital Times* in Madison, Wisconsin. Nichols is the author of two books: *It's the Media, Stupid* and *Jews for Buchanan*.

Noel, Thomas J.
Colorado

Thomas J. Noel is a Professor of History at the University of Colorado, Denver, where he directs Colorado Studies and writes the "Dr. Colorado" column for the Saturday joint issue of the *Denver Post /Rocky Mountain News*. He conducts tours of his favorite state and has written numerous books, including *Colorado: The Highest State, Colorado: A Liquid History & Tavern Guide, Historical Atlas of Colorado*, and *Buildings of Colorado*.

Norris, Kathleen
South Dakota

Kathleen Norris is the award-winning poet and author of *The Cloister Walk, Dakota: A Spiritual Geography, Amazing Grace: A Vocabulary of Faith*, and *The Virgin of Bennington*. Since 1974 she has lived for over thirty years in her grandparents' home in Lemmon, South Dakota.

Parini, Jay
Vermont

Jay Parini, a poet and novelist, teaches at Middlebury College. His books include *The Last Station, Benjamin's Crossing, House of Days, Robert Frost: A Life*, and *The Apprentice Lover.*

Proulx, Annie
Wyoming
Annie Proulx lives in Centennial, Wyoming. She is the author of *That Old Ace in the Hole, Shipping News, Close Range* and *Accordian Crimes.*

Sante, Luc
New Jersey
Luc Sante immigrated to New Jersey from Belgium as a child. His books include *Low Life, The Factory of Facts,* and *Evidence.* He lives in Ulster County, New York.

Seay, Elizabeth
Oklahoma
Elizabeth Seay's stories have appeared in the *Wall Street Journal* and the anthologies *Before & After: Stories from New York* and *Floating Off the Page: The Best Stories from the* Wall Street Journal*'s Middle Column.* Her book about endangered Native American languages, *Searching for Lost City,* will be published by Lyons Press in November, 2003.

Siegel, Lee
Hawaii
Lee Siegel is the author of the novels *Love in a Dead Language: A Romance,* and *Love and Other Games of Chance: A Novelty.* He lives in Hawaii.

Solnit, Rebecca
California (North)
Rebecca Solnit has been a resident of San Francisco for twenty years, and is the author of seven previous books including *Hollow*

City, As Eve Said to the Serpent, Secret Exhibitions: Six California Artists of the Cold War Era, A Book of Migrations, Savage Dreams, and *Wanderlust: A History of Walking.* An environmental activist and former art critic, she writes about place, environment, politics, and culture.

Straley, John
Alaska
John Straley is the author of six novels featuring Private Investigator Cecil Younger. He lives in Sitka, Alaska.

Tomasky, Michael
West Virginia
Michael Tomasky is the co-editor of *The American Prospect.*

van de Wetering, Janwillem
Maine
Janwillem van de Wetering is the author of a series of police procedurals, set in Amsterdam and books on Zen.

Watson, Larry
North Dakota
Larry Watson was born and raised in North Dakota and educated in its public schools. His books include *Montana 1948, Justice, White Crosses, Laura,* and most recently, *Orchard.* Watson is a visiting professor at Marquette University in Milwaukee, where he lives with his wife, Susan.

Williams, Terry Tempest
Utah
Terry Tempest Williams is a writer of creative nonfiction whose work focuses on landscape and culture. Her books include *Refuge: An Unnatural History of Family and Place, An Unspoken Hunger, Leap,* and

most recently, *Red: Passion and Patience in the Desert*. A recipient of a Guggenheim and Lannan Literary Fellowship, she lives in Castle Valley, Utah.

Wypijewski, JoAnn
Upstate New York
JoAnn Wypijewski was born in Buffalo, attended college in Syracuse, and is a writer living in New York City.

Zencey, Eric
Delaware
Eric Zencey is the author of a novel, *Panama*, and a collection of essays on nature, *Virgin Forest*. He is at work on a second novel and a second collection of essays. He lives and works in central Vermont.

ACKNOWLEDGMENTS

This book would have been impossible, even unimaginable, without the editorial wisdom and resourcefulness of Ruth Baldwin and Carl Bromley, who made the instruments into an orchestra.

PERMISSIONS